AN INTRODUCTION
TO PSYCHOLOGY OF RELIGION

AN INTRODUCTION TO PSYCHOLOGY OF RELIGION

" . . . our science [knowledge] is a drop,
our ignorance a sea."
—*William James*

by
Robert W. Crapps

MERCER

ISBN 0-86554-194-9 (cloth)
ISBN 0-86554-195-7 (paper)

Scripture quotations are from the
Good News Bible: The Bible in Today's English Version.
Copyright © 1966, 1971, 1976, by the American Bible Society.

The paper used in this publication meets
the minimum requirements of American National Standard
for Information Sciences—Permanence of Paper
for Printed Library Materials, ANSI Z39.48-1984.

Library of Congress Cataloging-in-Publication Data
Crapps, Robert W., 1925–
    An introduction to psychology of religion.
    Bibliography: p. 371
    Inlcudes index.
    1. Psychology, Religious. I. Title.
    BL53.C73   1986   200'.1'9   86-8586
    ISBN 0-86554-194-9 (alk. paper)
    ISBN 0-86554-195-7 (pbk. : alk. paper)

Contents

PART III
Psychosocial Development
and Religious Growth   161

To Dovie . . .

PREFACE

Over most of the last century the fields of scientific psychology and religion have been in touch with each other. At times the meeting has been cordial, but at other times psychology's interpretation of religion has been perceived as the incursion of a hostile enemy. Psychology has sometimes patronized religion as the mark of immaturity, and religion has sometimes feared psychology as a "nasty little science" working with narrow vision. But usually the relationship has been cooperative, and out of the interchange, friendly or unfriendly, has come a wealth of welcomed information regarding those systems by which a person's religious belief and behavior serve or deter the humane functions of personhood.

This volume intends an orderly approach to the body of data derived from serious inquiry into exchanges between psychology and religion since the turn of the twentieth century. The boundaries of psychology of religion are not always clear, and the discipline's self-identity remains frustratingly vague, but data coming from careful psychological study and disciplined theological reflection are nonetheless essential to a comprehensive and cohesive interpretation of religious belief and practice. The book has grown out of the classroom and in both approach and format is designed for use with students as an introduction to the psychological study of religion. The beginning student may have some difficulty with technical words and phrases, but as far as possible complex professional vocabularies of both theology and psychology have been avoided and care is taken to explain those professional terms that are used. The footnotes, bibliography, and suggested readings will direct serious students who care to pursue more extensively items of their own interest.

The book makes its point not only in the materials that are selected for discussion but also in the way in which they are arranged. No attempt is made to incorporate all the bits of psychological research on religion, but the aim is to develop a general framework within which the questions that have dominated the psychological study of religion over most of the last century may be given attention. Further, such an overview should suggest areas in which major research remains to be done. Even if all the details of the big picture may not yet be filled in, the comprehensive model will serve as an outline to which the details may be added as research makes the picture more complete.

The discussion is divided into four parts. Two chapters in Part I suggest the problems and possibilities for the psychological study of religion in light of the nature of religion and the scientific method. The questions here are basically methodological: What does psychology of religion study? And how does it go about its task? Part II sketches the contributions of three intellectual currents in contemporary psychology to the study of religion: psychoanalysis, classical and modern, with its examination of the depth functions of persons; behaviorism in its attempt to replace concepts of mind and consciousness with rigorous measurement and control of behavior; and humanistic psychology with its optimistic affirmations of human potential. In Part III the interconnections between psychological development and religious growth are explored from the viewpoint of understanding religious thinking, feeling, and acting in terms of the development of cognition, affection, and volition. Finally, Part IV directs attention to religious life styles by which differentiated parts of human experiences are woven into a cohesive whole. Three unifying belief-behavior systems that organize the religious life around obedience to external forms, the affirmation of personal and corporate history, or subjective apprehension of the Holy are described.

The treatment here is obviously weighted toward the Western Judeo-Christian tradition. Throughout my life I have been affili-

ated with American Protestantism and by personal exposure and
academic preparation know the Western religious tradition best.
Most of my students share this background. But more importantly,
the history of psychology of religion itself gives it a decidedly Western Judeo-Christian flavor. The discipline belongs largely to the
Western academy, and the subject matter has usually been the
Christianity that informs Western culture. Nevertheless, neither my
and my students' cultural and religious heritage nor the historical
development of the discipline necessarily precludes the examination of phenomena with reasonable objectivity or the application of
the same psychological principles to religion in non-Western and
non-Judeo-Christian contexts.

No book is the product of a lone individual, and numerous persons have contributed directly and indirectly to the preparation of
this manuscript. I am especially indebted to scholars whose research and interpretation have extended the horizons of the psychological understanding of religion and who through instruction
and the printed page have become my teachers; to faculty colleagues at Furman University, particularly in the Religion Department, whose cordiality, candor, and openness over many years have
kept alive the discussion of these issues; to Furman administration
for time and encouragement to do the research; to Mrs. Barbara
Price, Mrs. Rebecca Miller, and Mrs. Sherry Abernathy, who have
typed and retyped the manuscript; and to my family, whose time
and interest are also invested here. To all these I acknowledge my
debt and gratitude.

Robert W. Crapps
Greenville, South Carolina

Part I

THE PSYCHOLOGICAL STUDY OF RELIGION: PROBLEMS AND POSSIBILITIES

CHAPTER ONE

THE PSYCHOLOGICAL DEFINITION OF RELIGION

The concerns of the psychological study of religion are as old as the human race itself. Ancients, as well as moderns, have pondered fundamental questions regarding "the life of the soul." Since the dawn of human consciousness, persons have reflected upon the meaning of existence, why people behave the way they do, and how both meaning and behavior relate to divinity. But only in recent years have these concerns been subjected to the scrutiny of scientific examinations. The psychology of religion as a scientific discipline belongs largely to the Western world and to shifting emphasis during the nineteenth and twentieth centuries. It came as a spin-off from the development of the social sciences in general and particularly scientific psychology.

By mid-nineteenth century a modern mentality with roots deep in the previous two hundred and fifty years was ready to come into full flower. The medieval world was marked by order and arrangement with humanity enjoying a central place in the cosmos. The earth was the focus of the universe, and all things on earth were understood to be for the benefit of God's crowning creation. But the heliocentric theories of Copernicus and the telescope of Galileo, to say nothing of the erosive influence of Descartes and Newton, set in motion new forces that by the nineteenth century were beginning to change the perception of the role of human beings. No longer were the heavens and the earth understood to serve human ends; persons came more and more to be interpreted as belonging to the order of things. The natural sciences began to come of age, and increasingly their searchlights were turned, not only on the surrounding environment, but also upon persons themselves. The publication in 1859 of Charles Darwin's *Origin of Species* may be understood as a kind of symbolic act, reflecting a willingness to submit human life itself to scrupulous observation and reasoned hypothesis-making. Gone forever was the mentality that made people the center of, or superior to, other items in nature; human animals were increasingly considered as being among those items to be understood through rigorous, reasoned examinations.[1]

Scientific psychology was born out of this intellectual milieu. Two decades after Darwin's publication Professor Wilhelm Wundt established at the University of Leipzig, Germany, a laboratory to design and utilize experimental methods suited to the study of human behavior. The year was 1879, the usual reference point for dating the beginning of modern scientific psychology. Soon after Wundt's experiment numerous laboratories were established, and by the end of the century scientific psychology was well on its way.

During the formative decades of scientific psychology, religion did not occupy a significant place in the concern of researchers. Religion was often considered beyond the scope of pioneering techniques or, more seriously, it was regarded as a sacred precinct. Often theologian and psychologist alike judged the psychological study of religion to be an invasion of holy places by secular methods; religious explanation had better be left to the supernatural. Further, vigorous and vocal anti-science reactions appeared in American Fundamentalism in the 1880s and 1890s, challenging accommo-

---

[1]A helpful summary of these shifts may be found in John B. Magee, *Religion and Modern Man: A Study of the Religious Meaning of Being Human* (New York: Harper, 1967) 175-99.

dation between science and religion in any form.[2] Consequently, psychology of religion was almost nonexistent during the last half of the nineteenth century. When it did enter the discussion, the result was often loud and vigorous protest. The appearance of two books around the turn of the century contributed significantly to bridging the gap between psychology and religion and overcoming much of the hostility. Edwin D. Starbuck's book, *The Psychology of Religion,* was published in 1899 and William James's *The Varieties of Religious Experience* in 1902. By contemporary standards both books lack methodological sophistication and focus upon extreme forms of religious experience at the expense of more "normal" kinds of religion. Nonetheless, these works are monumentally important in pioneering the psychological examination of religious phenomena and in creating a positive attitude toward the possibilities of such studies. In the early decades of this century such stalwarts as Leuba, Coe, and Hall built upon the pioneering work of Starbuck and James, giving identity to the phrase "psychology of religion."

By the 1930s, however, little had been done to advance the work of the pioneers and refine their methods. Some historians trace the decline of "psychology of religion" to this time.[3] Indeed, at least one psychologist describes the decline as a quick and total demise.[4] History of the last several decades lends some support to these judgments. In spite of the high hopes implicit in the work of the pioneers, little progress has been made in the development of a discipline with a clear identity. Almost a century has failed to produce more than a limited number of professionals who devote most of their research to the psychological study of religion. Professional indifference characterizes large areas of the two fields. Theologians and psychologists "join hands to say that there can be no psychology of religion, at least as far as they are concerned, short of

---

[2]See below, 301-307.

[3]See for example, Orlo Strunk, Jr., "The Present Status of the Psychology of Religion," *The Journal of Bible and Religion* 25 (1957): 287-92.

[4]Benjamin Beit-Hallahmi, "Psychology of Religion, 1800-1930: The Rise and Fall of a Psychological Movement," *The Journal of the History of the Behavioral Sciences* 10 (1974): 84-90.

contaminating principles basic to their respective disciplines."[5] Although religion has largely lost its protection as a sacred precinct, many psychologists still tend to be cautious where appeal may be made to esoteric or transcendent authentication. And although the development of multiple and sophisticated methods has made it possible for psychology to examine religion more precisely, many theologians remain convinced that psychological studies of religion do not get to the "real" data. Thus since the 1930s psychology of religion has fallen on hard times, and thorough, systematic studies continue to be in short supply.

The decline of psychology of religion has been abetted by two additional factors. Psychology itself over the last several decades has become increasingly positivistic and behavioristic, leaving less room for evaluating religion along other than strictly empirical lines. And religion has translated its interest in psychology into "pastoral psychology,"[6] a turn to "the power of dynamic psychology to purify and clarify distortions of faith in the parishioner's existence."[7] Thus psychology and religion have run the risk of each desecrating the other: psychology by too narrowly constricting its study, thereby underplaying the dynamic role of religion; and religion by focusing its interest in the utilitarian understanding of developmental and socializing processes, thereby relegating psychology to second-class citizenship. In short, neither discipline seems to have taken the other seriously enough.

Yet, in spite of its prolonged illness, psychology of religion refuses to go away or to die. The terms "religion" and "psychology" continue to be used in relation to each other, and efforts to treat their relationship systematically are beginning to appear.[8] Evi-

---

[5]Peter Homans, "Toward a Psychology of Religion," in Peter Homans, ed., *The Dialogue between Theology and Psychology.* Essays in Divinity series, Gerald C. Brauer, ed. (Chicago: University of Chicago Press, 1968) 53.

[6]This is the major thrust of the work of men such as Carroll Wise, Seward Hiltner, Wayne Oates, and Paul Johnson.

[7]Homans, "Toward a Psychology of Religion," 62.

[8]For example, Paul W. Pruyser, *A Dynamic Psychology of Religion* (New York: Harper, 1968); Wayne E. Oates, *The Psychology of Religion* (Waco TX: Word Books,

dently the serious psychologist cannot in good conscience avoid religion because it occupies such a significant place in human behavior. Nor can the serious theologian afford to sidestep "scientific man" if he attempts to develop an anthropology of the whole person. Psychology of religion then is about the business of reconciling these two disciplines in ways that take seriously both areas.

THE PSYCHOLOGICAL APPROACH TO DEFINITION

Reconciliation between psychology and religion cannot proceed without some common answer to a simple question: What is to be studied when religion is examined? Hardly any word is more ambiguously or diversely understood than "religion." For some, religion indicates going to church, synagogue, or temple; for others it designates a general sense that life is in order. Some expect their religion to guide daily routines; others see it as a vehicle for escaping the trials and tribulations of this present age. Religion is faith and feeling, organism and organization, doing and being.

Over many years philosophers and theologians have attempted to penetrate the core of religion's manifold expressions and formulate a concise and coherent statement that would label the common ground in diverse experience. The result has been an interminable list almost as varied as the experiences that were being brought together. Nineteenth century Deists were impressed with the order of the universe and concluded that God had set in motion a giant machine to operate according to implanted and immutable laws, but Friedrich Schleiermacher, arguing against their rationalism, insisted that religion in essence is the immediate conscious-

1973); Geoffrey E. W. Scobie, *Psychology of Religion* (New York: Wiley, 1975); and Heije Faber, *Psychology of Religion* (Philadelphia: Westminster, 1975). An article by Bernard Spilka, "The Current State of the Psychology of Religion," *Bulletin of the Council on the Study of Religion* 9 (October 1978): 96-99, suggests the need and possibility of psychology of religion now moving from particular research to theoretical formulation. The 1980s have produced several general treatments that are significant, including Joseph Byrne, *The Psychology of Religion* (New York: Free Press, 1984); Mary Jo Meadow and Richard D. Kahoe, *Psychology of Religion: Religion in Individual Lives* (New York: Harper & Row, 1984); Raymond F. Paloutzian, *Invitation to the Psychology of Religion* (Glenview IL: Scott, Foresman, 1983); and Bernard Spilka, Ralph W. Hood, Jr., and Richard L. Gorsuch, *The Psychology of Religion: An Empirical Approach* (Englewood Cliffs NJ: Prentice-Hall, 1985).

ness of being absolutely dependent upon God.[9] The brilliant philosopher Alfred North Whitehead saw religion as what persons do with their solitariness.[10] The equally brilliant Nicholas Berdyaev argued that it is "an attempt to overcome solitude, to release Ego from its seclusion, to achieve community and ultimacy."[11] The renowned William James understood religion as "the feelings, acts, and experiences of individual men in their solitude."[12] The theologian Paul Tillich identified religion as "ultimate concern."[13] The psychoanalyst Erich Fromm has spoken vaguely of "any system of thought and action shared by a group which gives the individual a frame of orientation and an object of devotion."[14] These and numerous other statements illustrate the tendency of definition to isolate an impressive feature of religion, but they typically omit as much as they include.

The wide range of definitions and the attempts to catalog them have shed important light on various facets of religion, but they have not been too fruitful in producing normative statements that satisfy everyone. Regularly, the final products have been either too particularized to the intent of the definer to be comprehensive or too vague to be useful. The prospect for coming to a definitive statement that might be agreed upon by all adherents and researchers, that includes the varieties and the nuances of complex experiences, and that maintains neutrality toward each individual form of religion[15] seems no brighter now than it has been through the years.

---

[9]Friedrich Schleiermacher, *On Religion: Speeches to Its Cultured Despisers,* John Oman, trans. (New York: Harper, 1958).

[10]Alfred North Whitehead, *Religion in the Making* (New York: Macmillan, 1926) 16.

[11]Nicholas Berdyaev, *Solitude and Society* (London: Centenary, 1938) 68-69.

[12]William James, *The Varieties of Religious Experience* (New York: Modern Library, 1902) 31-32.

[13]Paul Tillich, *Systematic Theology,* vol. 1 (Chicago: University of Chicago Press, 1951) 11-14.

[14]Erich Fromm, *Psychoanalysis and Religion* (New Haven: Yale University Press, 1950) 21.

[15]See Frederick Ferrè, "The Definition of Religion," *Journal of the American Academy of Religion* 38 (1970): 3-16.

In short, psychology and religion are not likely to be reconciled by agreement on a precise, normative definition of religion. The list is already too long, and the psychology of religion possesses neither distinctive insight nor unique method that simplifies theological complexity. Nor does it have a special inherent dispensation to stand against all the definitions that have been offered and decide which is best *on normative grounds*. Nonetheless, the issue of definition is one of the unavoidable questions. What is to be studied by psychology of religion? What are the materials that it attempts to understand? What do people do when they "do" religion? Psychology of religion, as any other discipline would be, is immobilized until some decision has been made about the data with which it works.

How then may the dilemma be resolved? If psychology brings to the ambiguity of normative definition no magic wand but nonetheless must proceed with some understanding of its subject matter, how shall it get on with its tasks? Certainly some progress may be made by reframing the definition issue for purposes of psychological study.[16] The normative question may be translated into the phenomenological question. For psychology of religion the question is not, "What *is* religion?" or "What *ought* religion be?" Rather, the question is, "What do persons identify as their religion?" or "What functions as religion for persons?" Through what channels do persons discover their supreme loyalty and make sense of their existence? What motivates them as if it is the "voice of God?"[17] These are not normative statements, defining ultimate value and meaning, but phenomenological statements grounded in the present ex-

---

[16]J. Milton Yinger delineates three kinds of definition: (1) those that are evaluative, stating what religion ought to be; (2) descriptive or substantive definitions, designating belief and practices; and (3) functional definitions, emphasizing the full range of uses a religion has in larger personal and social systems. See his *Sociology Looks at Religion* (New York: Macmillan, 1963) 17-34; cf. also his *Religion, Society, and the Individual: An Introduction to the Sociology of Religion* (New York: Macmillan, 1957) 252-57.

[17]Oates, *The Psychology of Religion,* 22-28, sees five themes consistently present in philosophical and psychological definitions of religion: central importance of a supreme loyalty or value, the uniqueness of individuality, the need for human relationship, the interpretation of duties as divine commands, and purposiveness.

perience of human beings. One kind of statement is not necessarily more important than the other; each represents a perspective. Theology focuses upon what religion ought to be; psychology of religion centers upon the role of religion in the maintenance of personhood. The latter proceeds with the understanding that its task is to study all those varieties of activity to which persons give religious labels and to raise seriously the question of their function in personal survival. The discipline tends to focus its concerns at three points: (1) the institutional forms taken by religion, (2) the personal meanings that persons attach to those forms, and (3) the relationship of the religious factor to total personality structure.

THE INSTITUTIONAL FACES OF RELIGION

Most typically, religion for the social scientist designates institutional forms, all those observable structures and practices that in a given society have come to be associated with religious traditions. Church and synagogue, priest and shaman, creed and commandment, reredos and altar, prayer and worship, God and Om are so many words that persons use to label their religion. These, along with many others, are items that by popular consensus are understood to be religious; they are the concrete forms that readily come to mind when persons in the street are called upon to define their religion. Religious systems may be partially understood as the selection and organization of these forms into some type of cohesive pattern. Three main types of institutional religion can be distinguished.[18]

The first type appears in classical forms. These include those mainline, established institutions that have served their constituents over many years, usually centuries, as the embodiment of cherished values and meanings. This category covers not only the long dead religions of ancient cultures such as those of Mesopotamia, Egypt, Greece, and Rome; but, more particularly, it encompasses the contemporary living religions of the world, Eastern and Western. This face of religion is modified by such adjectives as

---

[18]The classification here is similar to that found in Ernst Troeltsch, *The Social Teaching of Christian Churches,* vol. 2, Olive Wyon, trans. (New York: Harper, 1960) 993f.

Hindu, Jewish, Christian, Moslem, Zoroastrian. The general profile is sometimes fuzzy because each of these larger bodies has become fragmented into a multitude of splinter groups—some with established history and traditions (denominations) and others more fleeting and nondescript (sects).[19] Persons tend to identify themselves more in terms of the specific than the general group to which they belong. They are Orthodox Jew or Zen Buddhist or Lutheran or Southern Baptist. In spite of inordinate proliferation into denomination and sectarian groups, mainline establishment affords persons a significant option for defining their religion phenomenologically.

A second institutional face of religion consists of those expressions that have their own internal organization but operate independently of the historical mainstream of religion. This type is generously represented in the contemporary religious scene in the United States and includes such theologically divergent groups as mystical and charismatic cults drawing heavily upon the spirituality of the East (as for example Theosophy, Eckankar, and Transcendent Meditation);[20] highly organized revival movements (such as the Billy Graham Evangelistic Crusade); nondenominational and interdenominational special interests organizations (such as World Discipleship Association and Fellowship of Christian Athletes); or independent "preacher" movements (such as Rev. Ike, Oral Roberts, and Jerry Falwell). These, like mainline denominationalism and established sectarianism, have their own identifiable structures including doctrinal stance, preferred cultus, extensive budgets, and elaborate organization. They count among their adherents those who also belong to the religious establishment. Religious commitments and energies that sustain these groups may in fact derive their vitality largely from mainline affiliation. However, the institutional face in this instance is different from mainline religion because identity is maintained through separate religious structures. Often

---

[19]Frank S. Mead, *Handbook of Denominations in the United States,* 6th ed. (Nashville: Abingdon, 1975) lists over two hundred and thirty major denominational groups in the United States.

[20]A useful discussion of such groups is Robert S. Ellwood, Jr., *Religious and Spiritual Groups in Modern America* (Englewood Cliffs NJ: Prentice-Hall, 1973).

an aggressive, hostile, or even paranoid attitude toward the establishment is promoted as a way of self-authentication.

A third face of institutional religion is more obscure because it depends upon nonreligious social structures for its social expression. A telling statement by the sociologist Will Herberg testifies to its presence in American religion.

> The fact that more than half the people openly admit that their religious beliefs have no effect on their ideas of politics and business would seem to indicate very strongly that, over and above conventional religion, there is to be found among Americans some sort of faith or belief or set of convictions, not generally designated as religion but definitely operative as such in their lives in the sense of providing them with some fundamental context of normativity and meaning.[21]

Herberg is suggesting a "religion above religion" in which those values and meanings usually associated with church and synagogue function separately from them. But Herberg needs to go a step further. In this religious expression not only have the values been separated from their traditional mooring; they have also come to be attached to existing nonreligious structures, riding piggyback upon the available political and economic order. Structurally, this face of religion borrows by using the available forms and contributes by providing value and vitality.

The intimate connections between religious vitality and political form have been extensively discussed in recent years under the general label of "civil religion." In 1967 Robert Bellah called attention to "an elaborate and well-institutionalized civil religion in America" that exists alongside of, but is rather clearly differentiated from the churches.[22] According to Bellah, the American ex-

---

[21]Will Herberg, *Protestant-Catholic-Jew* (Garden City NY: Doubleday, 1960) 74.

[22]Robert N. Bellah, "Civil Religion in America," *Daedalus* 96 (1967): 1-21. The presence of an "American" religion had been noted earlier in such works as William J. Wolf, *The Almost Chosen People: A Study of the Religion of Abraham Lincoln* (Garden City NY: Doubleday, 1959). The Bellah article, however, stimulated discussion of the subject, and subsequently an extensive bibliography on civil religion has been produced. A helpful series of summary articles appears in Russell E. Richey and Donald G. Jones, eds., *American Civil Religion* (New York: Harper, 1974).

perience has been replete with "its own prophets and its own martyrs, its own sacred events and sacred places, its own solemn rituals and symbols" that serve as thinly veiled cloaks for national interests and passions.[23] It is the religion of the American Way of Life with possibility for either "a genuine apprehension of universal and transcendent religious" reality or "various deformations and demonic distortions."[24] Civil religion provides content for ceremonial occasions such as the inauguration of the President and furnishes symbols (such as exodus, chosen people, and promised land) for the interpretation of the life and destiny of the nation. In civil religion the heaven of evangelical Western Christendom and the Utopian hope of the American dream have been wedded to the extent that one is hardly distinguishable from the other.[25]

The piggyback model may also be applied beyond the political realm. American economics and entertainment bear the imprint of American religion. Many years ago Max Weber suggested ways in which the Protestant ethical emphasis upon the virtues of work and personal achievement aided the competitive spirit of capitalism.[26] Gospel singing, an intimate expression of early American frontier religion and continuing into the present century as a facet of the religion of just plain folks, has in the last several decades fallen into the hands of commercial entrepreneurs and presently thrives as an economic enterprise.[27] The three-decade metamorphosis of Oral Roberts from free-lance revivalist to master of ceremonies for a television spectacular is little short of incredible. Games from football to ice hockey with some regularity are begun with prayers adorned with sporting lingo, many teams have official and unofficial chaplains, and the contests themselves bear remarkable re-

---

[23]Bellah, "Civil Religion in America," 18-19.

[24]Ibid., 12.

[25]William A. Clebsch, *From Sacred to Profane America: The Role of Religion in American History* (New York: Harper, 1968) 3.

[26]Max Weber, *The Protestant Ethic and The Spirit of Capitalism*, Talcott Parsons, trans. (New York: Scribner's, 1958).

[27]Tony Heilbut, *The Gospel Sound: Good News and Bad Times* (Garden City NY: Doubleday, 1975).

semblances to enthusiastic cult practices.[28] And in many circles the religious pronouncements of movie people are accepted as authentic by virtue of their having been made by stars. All of these phenomena illustrate piggyback institutional religion whereby secular structures serve as vehicles for expressing and preserving religious values and meanings.

Phenomenologically, then, religion is most easily identified in one of its three institutional forms: (1) as mainline denominationalism and established sectarianism, (2) as groups independent from traditional religion but nonetheless clearly labeled religious, and (3) as piggyback values attached to structures that in themselves are not ordinarily identified as religious. The researcher is most likely to encounter religion in one of these institutional forms. The structures represent social consensus as to what religion is, and consequently examination may proceed on this level with the least possibility of misunderstanding or distortion because of misidentification of the subject matter. Both the researcher and his subjects quickly find common ground in the immediate and concrete experience of religion as institutional structure.

RELIGION AS PERSONAL EXPERIENCE

Although psychology of religion is concerned with institutional religion on all these levels, the discipline also aims to get at the relationship of these structures to personal experience. Religious forms are likely to be time- and culture-bound, and psychological studies that limit themselves to examination of the institutional faces of religion are likely to suffer from the same limitation. Martin Marty, a distinguished student of American religion, remarks that "the Westerner once upon a time could have defined religion as that which relates to an otherworldly reference or object. But in the twentieth century large portions of Western religion have dropped the otherworldly reference without dropping everything else that has historically belonged to religion: they still form churches or attend synagogues, are ordained, wear religious garb, evoke theolog-

---

[28]Three popular but insightful articles by Frank DeFord on "Religion in Sport," *Sports Illustrated* 44 (19, 26 April, 3 May 1976) indicate interconnections.

ical symbols."[29] Psychological studies are compelled to acknowledge such changes and their interconnections with specific historical and cultural circumstances. Psychology of religion attempts to offer insights into the function of religion across time and cultures by examining religion beyond its institutional expression, concentrating upon meanings that those forms have for particular persons.

Psychological studies of conversion illustrate the point. Pioneer psychology at the turn of the century gave considerable attention to conversion.[30] At that time American religion still bore the marks of several Great Awakenings and frontier revivalism. "Conversion" meant observable forms—a revival meeting, "coming forward," mourner's bench, emotional disruption. Behavior patterns both commonly agreed upon and easily isolated were associated with the word. When subjects were asked about their conversion, they did not need clarifying explanation, but readily identified emotional crisis and upheaval usually associated with a specific time and place. They could tell the researcher when they had "been to the mourner's bench" and recount in detail a vivid episode. Neither investigator nor subject was ambiguous about the institutional form of conversion.

However, a half century later Gordon Allport encountered a quite different circumstance when he attempted to study the same phenomenon. Conversion was no longer so directly associated with specific forms. The college students who were his subjects were not so clear on what conversion meant.[31] Is conversion definite crisis of upheaval and reorganization precipitated by some traumatic or semi-traumatic event? Or is it a gradual awakening with no specific occasion being decisive? Or something between the two? Allport concludes that our grandparents attended revival meetings and re-

---

[29]Martin E. Marty, "Religious Development in Historical, Social, and Cultural Context," in Merton P. Strommen, ed., *Research on Religious Development* (New York: Hawthorn, 1971) 53.

[30]Edwin D. Starbuck, *The Psychology of Religion* (New York: Scribner's, 1899), and Elmer T. Clark, *The Psychology of Religious Awakening* (New York: Macmillan, 1929).

[31]Gordon W. Allport, *The Individual and His Religion* (New York: Macmillan, 1950) 33-34.

turned home with adolescents "formally converted," but the college student of the 1950s leaned more (71 percent of his sample) toward a gradual, less dramatic experience of conversion. For the contemporary student, now more than a quarter century after Allport, the vivid, traumatic, emotional upheaval conversion seems even further removed from personal religion. Frontier revival form has largely passed from religious culture and, except in pockets of American religion where it may be nostalgically preserved, is unavailable to the contemporary communicant as an institutional form.[32]

The Religious Appeal for Secularity

The subjective, personalized, internalized levels of religious meaning have been substantially interesting to theologian and psychologist alike. Often creeds, rituals, and organizations have been devalued on grounds that they were detrimental to personal and private values. Protesting students of the 1960s sometimes argued that radical rejection of religion in its traditional forms was essential to the discovery of a vital personal religion. For them traditional forms of Christianity had become so entrenched in Western decadent culture that both had to be rejected in the interest of becoming genuinely religious on a personal level. The 1960s rebels were compatriots with a host of protesters against the religious establishment who by their protest hoped to recover valid faith. In short, these iconoclasts, ancient and modern, have appealed for focused attention on personal religion, the place where traditional forms assume their personal meaning. Two theologians in this tradition illustrate the point.

Religionless Christianity. Søren Kierkegaard was a Danish theologian who died in 1855, but whose thought remained undiscovered until his writings were translated into English around the mid-

---

[32]The influential analysis by Gerhard Lenski also illustrates the idea. In a detailed study of religion's impact on politics, economics, and family life in Detroit Lenski carefully distinguishes between consensus structures (institution) and personal commitments that are attached to but not altogether revealed in the consensus forms (personal experience). See his *The Religious Factor: A Sociological Study of Religion's Impact on Politics, Economics, and Family Life* (Garden City NY: Doubleday, 1961).

twentieth century. Kierkegaard vigorously protested the assumption that Christianity was identical with "Christendom," that is, "Christianity in the Land," the cultural form assumed by genuine faith.[33] In Kierkegaard's Denmark the New Testament foundations of Christianity had become so entwined with contemporary cultural ideals that their compatibility was blandly assumed, even by the religious leaders. Christians in that context were blinded to any Christianity other than their own. For them "real" Christianity had become the acculturated Christianity that they knew—overlaid with contemporary practices to the extent that reflection was impossible.

For Kierkegaard such identification of Christianity and culture was intolerable. When Christian faith is enmeshed in Christendom, the former is always the loser. The essence of Christianity is sacrificed to cultural gods of value and power implicit in the culture itself and is made no more than a bondslave to a tyrannical master. According to Kierkegaard, this is sufficient reason for concluding that no culture can become Christian to the extent that persons may become devotees merely by growing up in Christendom.[34] To presuppose that Christendom can carry forward Christianity is to be compared to a person eating nuts who likes the shells but casts away the kernels.

Søren Kierkegaard appealed for radical action to recover the heart of faith. Resolution could never be found in the easy compromise that the Danish church had made with the ethos of the nineteenth century, but it lay beyond radical departure from official Christendom. Hence the path to recovery was by way of "religionless Christianity," a rejection of Christendom as religion in the interest of the discovery of Christianity as faith. Thus Kierkegaard

---

[33]This idea permeates most of Kierkegaard's writings; consult Robert Bretall, ed., *A Kierkegaard Anthology* (Princeton: Princeton University Press, 1951).

[34]An interesting contrast might be made between Kierkegaard on this point and the American Horace Bushnell. Bushnell's famous *Christian Nurture*, rev. ed. (New Haven: Yale University Press, 1916) was published shortly before the death of Kierkegaard. Bushnell, reacting to the excesses of revivalism in his day, proposed "that the child is to grow up a Christian, and never know himself as being otherwise." Kierkegaard would have considered Bushnell's view an impossible vision.

insists upon understanding religion beyond institutions, particularly those forms that derive their force from time and culture-bound values. Accordingly, the primary questions are those having to do with personal religion. The genuinely religious are not those who are neutral, uncommitted spectators or idle drifters within institutional structures. At the heart of genuine faith are thinking, choosing, and acting in the present moment filled with significance because in it converge past and present relations with self, with others, and with God. Theology in this tradition stresses the importance of the present over the past and future, and the superiority of persons over forms. Religion is being, not institution; faith is a verb, not a noun.

Religion as Unbelief. The Swiss theologian Karl Barth, like Kierkegaard, argues for the priority of personal religion. Writing a century later than Kierkegaard, Barth attempted to redirect theological inquiry away from concern with the human discovery of God toward the centrality of God's Word to humanity.[35] For Barth, being a Christian meant continual openness to God's revelation, an active Word to man. Barth believed that "religion" in all its varied organizational and creedal forms represented the historical accumulation of human endeavors to hear and know the divine. As such it assumes more authority than it deserves and easily becomes the enemy of revelation. Thus religion is its own worst enemy. Although unavoidable as the striving of human spirituality, religion becomes conventional, formal, and often rigid, deterring the work of the living Word insofar as adherents become more concerned to protect their forms than to be open to revelation. The fundamental Christian task is to overcome the conventionality of being religious. Cryptically, Barth appealed for the abolition of religion and the acceptance of religion as unbelief.[36] Only the loss of faith in the ac-

---

[35]This central thrust of Barth's thought emphasizing the crucial role of revelation as an act of God, who stands over against man, and the place of the Bible in that revelation has been understood as a return to "orthodox" positions. He therefore has been often designated as a key figure in "Neo-Orthodoxy."

[36]Karl Barth, *Church Dogmatics*, vol. 1, G. T. Thompson and Harold Knight, trans. (New York: Scribner's, 1956) 297-325. An introduction to Barth's thought appears in his *Evangelical Theology: An Introduction*, Grover Foley, trans. (New York: Holt, Rinehart and Winston, 1963).

cumulated efforts of persons to know God could pave the way for the Deity's revelation. No creeds, confessions, or other structures are true as objects of faith; they can become true only as vehicles of God's revealing Word. The "religious task is one of clearing out and tidying up in preparation for the expected fullness of the self-enclosed and self-sounding religious reality which will follow our emancipation from all representations."[37]

Kierkegaard and Barth have their counterparts in other religious traditions (Mahatma Gandhi, for example) who attack the tendency to define religion merely in its institutional forms. Their denunciations are often vigorous reactions to make a point in situations where religion as organization has lost its soul. Faith cannot long survive without institutional forms, and neither Søren Kierkegaard nor Karl Barth advocates forsaking organization in favor of pure subjectivism or esoteric mysticism. Their harsh pronouncements, however, serve as appropriate theological reminders that definitions of religion must include not only the external, consensus phenomena but also matters of the heart and that psychological studies of religion are to be concerned with experiential meanings as well as with overt forms.

The Psychological Attack upon Christendom

Psychology of religion, like theology, has underscored the importance of the personal dimension of faith. The pioneer psychologist William James in his classic *The Varieties of Religious Experience* distinguished between those for whom religion is dull habit and those for whom it is acute fever.[38] The former are stoically resigned, cool, phlegmatic; the latter are passionate and intense. Further, James contrasted two basic religious attitudes that he labeled "healthy-mindedness" and "the sick soul." The healthy-minded are positive, optimistic, happy, and unreflective. Repentance and remorse have little part in their personality. Sick souls, on the other hand, suffer. For them religion is attained through struggle and melancholy. Burdened with the consciousness of evil, the sick soul

---

[37]Barth, *Church Dogmatics,* 1: 318.

[38]James, *The Varieties of Religious Experience,* 41-45.

lives on the dark side of the misery line and maintains faith on the edge of despair. Nevertheless, their painful sensitivity to human helplessness opens them to more profound and meaningful religious experience.[39]

The James distinctions established a trend preserved in contemporary psychology to interpret religion beyond its institutional manifestations. Distinctions are regularly drawn between believers whose participation is formalized and habitual and those for whom faith is a matter of reflective commitment, recognizing that persons "holding the same beliefs and carrying out the same religious practices can differ radically in how religion affects their lives."[40] Consistently, conclusions drawn from research depend upon the recognition of the degree of personal involvement of the devotees.

Religion and Authoritarianism. The need to move beyond institutional to personal levels of commitment to properly understand religious phenomena is explicitly demonstrated in a definitive study of the authoritarian personality done in 1950 by a distinguished group of California scholars.[41] Among the numerous items considered by these researchers was the relationship between religion and prejudice. Does religion support or undermine prejudice?

In attempting to determine this relationship the investigators asked their subjects the open-ended question, "How important in your opinion are religion and the church?" Their answers were subsequently compared to their scores on an anti-Semitism scale. The findings are summarized as follows:

> Subjects who considered both religion and the church important were very considerably more anti-Semitic than were subjects who considered neither important or emphasized the ethical aspects of religion or differentiated between the church and "real" religion and, while rejecting the former, stress the more personal and more rational aspects of the latter.[42]

---

[39]Ibid., 132-33.

[40]James E. Dittes, "Two Issues in Measuring Religion," in Merton P. Strommen, ed., *Research on Religious Development* (New York: Hawthorn, 1971) 78.

[41]T. W. Adorno, Else Frenkel-Brunswick, Daniel J. Levinson, and R. Nevitt Sanford, *The Authoritarian Personality* (New York: Harper, 1950).

[42]Ibid., 221.

Particularly interesting are those who distinguished between the organized church and the personal, more rational aspects of "real" religion. These were less prejudiced than those who did not make the differentiation and considered both religion and church important. Are then religious people more prejudiced than nonreligious people? This research suggests that the answer may be quite different in terms of the institutional and personal definitions of religion. The researchers conclude that the acceptance or rejection of religion seems not so important as the way in which it is accepted or rejected. Prejudiced persons "seem to make use of religious ideas in order to gain some immediate practical advantage or to aid in the manipulation of other people."[43] Their association with institutional religion might thus be used to foster their prejudice. On the other hand, the religion of those more personally committed did not serve the same supportive function.

Intrinsic-Extrinsic Religion. Gordon W. Allport has also given extensive attention to the issue of the relationship between religion and prejudice and, like Adorno and his associates, concludes that interconnections between the two phenomena are conditioned by the intensity of personal commitment to religion.[44] Allport's study brought him face to face with the bothersome paradox that religious people seemed to be more prejudiced than nonreligious people, while at the same time most champions for human equality have been religiously motivated. His analysis led him to conclude that the resolution of the paradox was to be discovered in differences in persons' religious attitudes. Whereas prejudiced religious people were *extrinsic,* nonprejudiced believers were *intrinsic* in their religious orientation.

By extrinsic religion Allport means one that "serves and rationalizes assorted forms of self-interest."[45] It does not serve as master

---

[43]Ibid., 733.

[44]Allport has published extensively on the subject. *The Nature of Prejudice* (Reading MA: Addison-Wesley, 1954) is his most comprehensive statement. The issue under consideration here is discussed in an article written with J. M. Ross, "Personal Religious Orientation and Prejudice," *Journal of Personality and Social Psychology* 5 (1967): 432-43.

[45]Gordon W. Allport, *Personality and Social Encounter* (Boston: Beacon Press, 1960) 264.

motive in life, but plays an instrumental role only. In this orientation religion is subordinated to interests, desires, and needs that are independent from values inherent in faith itself. The extrinsic devotee does not serve his religion, but uses it to justify and support his life-style. Conversely, intrinsic religion "floods the whole life with motivation and meaning."[46] Here religion has its own power and in some measure gives direction to life. Whereas the extrinsic person *uses* religion, the intrinsic person *lives* religion. In the latter case personal interests are subordinated to the inherent values of religion itself.

Committed-Consensual Religion. Similar distinctions in the levels of religious experience have been made by Robert O. Allen and Bernard Spilka, using the labels "committed" and "consensual."[47] The distinctions made by Allen and Spilka are evident from their choice of labels: consensual religion refers to socially accepted institutional forms; committed religion suggests internal, somewhat inarticulate values and attitudes. Conversion, for example, may be either consensual or committed. Consensual conversion refers to nothing more than an alteration in institutional affiliation as a converted Catholic, a converted Protestant, or a converted Jew. Conversion in committed religion, on the other hand, designates more subjective and sometimes subtle shifts in values and orientation. The research of these men confirms the earlier findings that religion either supports or erodes prejudice according to the level upon which subjects are religious.

Kierkegaard and Allport, Barth and Adorno, in their critiques of practical religion reenforce the need to broaden the base of religious definition to include personal as well as institutional levels of experience. James drew a fixed line between institutional and personal religion, and consciously chose to concentrate upon the latter. Yet the two facets are so intimately interconnected that such separation seems arbitrary and unnecessary. Personal, subjective meaning inevitably takes on form; it becomes institutionalized.

---

[46]Ibid., 265.

[47]Robert O. Allen and Bernard Spilka, "Committed and Consensual Religion: A Specification of Religion-Prejudice Relationships," *Journal for the Scientific Study of Religion* 6 (1967): 191-206.

Further, established organizations may not only preserve consensus values but generate new meaning for those who participate in them. Thus the separation made by James and the division of the discussion in this chapter are more academic than real. An adequate understanding of religion takes seriously both dimensions of religious experience, incorporating the concrete institutional faces of religion and the deeper, personal meanings that lie behind the traditional or nontraditional structures. Psychology and theology have both demonstrated a willingness to move beyond consensus forms to examine private representations of God and elaborations that occur "in the secret chambers of the human heart."[48]

RELIGION AND THE WHOLE PERSON

A third issue in defining religion in phenomenological terms has to do with the relationship of religion to personality structures. Does religion belong to a peculiar category and arise out of the function of special parts of the personality? Or is is more properly understood as ways in which whole persons respond to their existence in the world?

Faculty, Instinct, Trait

A popular approach to personality during the earlier decades of scientific psychology was "faculty" psychology, an approach that in one way or another compartmentalized the self and explained human behavior by the independent action of the separated parts. William McDougall, a patron saint of faculty psychology, described a long list of instincts: those certain inherent agencies or dispositions, deeply rooted in biological makeup, that initiate and sustain all human activity.[49] One instinct accounts for aggression, another for flight from danger, another for tenderness, another for acquisitiveness, and so on. Personhood was thus understood as the end of instinctual function. The key questions were those having to do with

---

[48]Ana-Maria Rizzuto, *The Birth of the Living God: A Psychoanalytic Study* (Chicago: University of Chicago Press, 1979) 3.

[49]See William McDougall, *An Introduction to Social Psychology,* 16th ed. (Boston: J. W. Luce, 1923) originally published in 1908, and the later *Outline of Abnormal Psychology* (New York: Scribner's, 1926) for a discussion of his theories.

how many instincts there are and how they function in relationship to each other. McDougall, for example, thought that religion came not from a single instinct but from the combined operation of several instincts.

McDougall and his intellectual kinsmen who discussed temperaments or urges or the mind as an immaterial entity were describing little more than similar behavior patterns. But their descriptions were easily transformed into a topography of personality that clearly separated mountains from valleys. The perspective encouraged seeing persons as complex machines to be understood by breaking the larger unit into its component parts.

For a brief period faculty psychology served the discipline well as a model for analyzing personality, but it is now archaic in psychological circles. Textbooks rarely mention it, even when reviewing the history of psychology! The approach is judged to belong to that period when methodology was unrefined and speculative deduction played too large a role in attempts to isolate dynamic causes of behavior. More sophisticated procedures have made it quite unfashionable to discuss faculties or instincts or temperaments. Some psychologists are even suspicious of such categories as mind or consciousness because they appear to be more abstractions for theory building than phenomena for observation and analysis.

Yet considerable professional thinking about personality and religion contains residue that strongly resembles the faculty tradition, and the dominant model by which the man-in-the-street thinks of personality is a faculty paradigm. Ask him to describe a person, and he most typically will discuss body, mind, soul, and spirit in various combinations. Although faculty psychology has been declared professionally dead, it is popularly very much alive.

In the West the remarkable staying power of faculty approaches to personality derives in large measure from the patterns by which early Judeo-Christian ideas were reconciled with Western thought forms. Primitive Judeo-Christian religious traditions were rooted in the Eastern world, but the passage of Christianity from Asia into Europe introduced the infant faith to a new and different culture, and its survival depended upon accommodation to the new setting. The West had already been born and was being nurtured in those areas into which the primitive faith was moving.

Critical in the encounter of early Judeo-Christian faith and budding Western culture were the dualistic thought forms that typified the latter. Accordingly, the entire order of "things" consists of two parts: one seen and changing, the other unseen and unchanging.[50] Persons belong to both orders: in body they are seen, material, and transitory; in soul they are unseen, immaterial, and immortal. Ideal truth and value belong to the second category, and physical existence with its falsifications of sensory experience must be overcome to appropriate the higher value. The further persons get from the body, the closer they are likely to come to the truth.

In this fashion Greek philosophy before the arrival of Christianity ascribed a peculiarly important place to soul. In Homer soul had a relatively inconsequential role. It was associated with the afterlife as a kind of shadowy presence departing the body at death. But with the appearance of the Orphic mysteries in the sixth century B.C.E., a specific interpretation that assigned soul religious meaning and significance appeared. It became "a divine, immortal creation which had greater liberty outside the body than within it."[51] This theological doctrine of soul characterized the views of many Greek philosophers, including Plato, and was a significant part of the thought world in which early Christianity took root and flourished.

The dualism of the Aegean world was easily adaptable to early Christian thought and runs like a dominant thread through the fabric of subsequent Western religious development. Out of deference to scientific man, contemporary persons may add a third category and discuss personality as some combination of body, soul, and mind. Additionally, moral connotations have often been added to the formula, making the material world evil and the immaterial world good. The most typical expression of moralistic dualism

---

[50]The statement is from Plato's *Phaedo*. See J. D. Kaplan, ed., *The Dialogues of Plato* (New York: Washington Square Press, 1951) 101. In *Phaedo* Plato argues for immortality on grounds of psychological dualism.

[51]W. David Stacey, *The Pauline View of Man* (New York: Macmillan, 1956) 62.

identifies good with soul and assigns secondary or evil status to body and sometimes mind.[52]

Vestiges of the faculty tradition also remain in some psychological discussions of personality. Terms such as traits, attitudes, factors, sentiments, and tendencies are sometimes used to set off behavior patterns as if they were distinct, constituent parts of personality. Over several decades Gordon Allport argued for trait as a useful category for understanding persons.[53] These units, or traits, have their own dynamic power and determine human behavior. Thus traits are those enduring, persistent characteristics that distinguish one person from another and give to personality a consistent appearance.

Although it was not the intention of Allport, traits are easily made into things, as his early critics pointed out.[54] "John behaves aggressively" becomes "John has an aggressive disposition" becomes "John has a trait of aggression." In this sequence an observed pattern of behavior is transformed into a component part of personality, and faculty definitions are preserved. The same risk is implicit in factor analysis, those attempts to extract smaller units in personality and gather items that appear at the same time into clusters to be examined according to their correlation with other clusters.[55] For example, a selected population group might be typified by a cluster of behavior (a factor) labeled "prejudice." Definition and correlation of the factors is the business of factor analysis. Neither traits nor factors properly fall under faculty psychology, but they easily lend themselves to over-interpretation. The descriptive

---

[52]LeRoy Moore, Jr. offers the thesis that mind is coming into its own in American culture with educational institutions serving as the new church. See his article, "From Profane to Sacred America," *Journal of the American Academy of Religion* 39 (1971): 321-38.

[53]See Gordon W. Allport, "What Is a Trait of Personality?" *Journal of Abnormal and Social Psychology* 25 (1931): 368-72; and the later essay, "Traits Revisited," in *The Person in Psychology: Selected Essays* (Boston: Beacon Press, 1968) 43-66.

[54]See H. A. Carr and F. A. Kingsbury, "The Concept of Trait," *Psychological Review* 45 (1938): 497-524.

[55]The techniques for doing this vary considerably but in common depend upon highly sophisticated statistical and mathematical procedures. See Harry H. Harman, *Modern Factor Analysis*, 2d ed. (Chicago: University of Chicago Press, 1960).

categories, similar to what has happened to soul in religious circles, become independent units of personality. "Having a soul" accordingly makes one religious; "being conservative" makes one prejudiced. The fundamental wholeness of personality in which constituent parts are meaningful only in context is blurred by an intemperate emphasis upon the independence of the parts.

Holiness Is Wholeness.[56]

Recent theology and psychology incorporate an emphasis upon the wholeness of persons that should be taken as a necessary correction of the fragmentation of personality through analysis of part-processes. James insists that the route to personal health is by way of unification. The fragmented self must become unified around some center of personal loyalty. His often cited definition of conversion reflects this concern: "the process, gradual or sudden, by which a self hitherto divided, and consciously wrong, inferior and unhappy, becomes unified and consciously right, superior and happy, in consequence of its firmer hold upon religious realities."[57]

However, interest in wholeness antedates James. Psychosomatic medicine, the practice that stresses the interconnections between psychological (*psyche*) and physiological (*soma*) roots of illness, reaches back into the late eighteenth century. In 1799 Pierre Cabanis, friend of the mental hospital reformer Pinel, published a pioneering work entitled *Traite du Physique et du Moral de l'homme*. In the book Cabanis developed the thesis that pathological physiological states could derive from "moral" (by which he meant psychological) phenomena. The idea captured little attention until the rise of modern scientific psychology and until psychiatry began to be included in the curricula of medical education. In the interval between Cabanis and the mid-twentieth century, medical doctors seemed to become "so laboratory-minded, so scientific, and so impersonal, that they forgot, or felt entitled to ignore, the patient as

---

[56]Josef Goldbrunner has written a suggestive little book with this title: *Holiness Is Wholeness*, Stanley Goodman, trans. (New York: Pantheon, 1955).

[57]James, *The Varieties of Religious Experience*, 186. Cf. also, 163-65.

a person."[58] The attitude that medicine is concerned exclusively with physiological disorder may still be found, but the psychosomatic concept was rediscovered during the 1930s, 1940s, and 1950s, and increasingly the medical profession has taken seriously this broadened understanding of illness.[59]

In a narrow sense psychosomatic medicine has designated the diagnosis and treatment of specific diseases in which the primary causal factors appear to be emotional. Illnesses such as hypertension or duodenal ulcer have been classified as psychosomatic because their origin was psychological, although they obviously produce somatic changes. More recently, however, medicine has come to recognize that *all* physiological disorders have psychological overtones and *all* psychogenic diseases affect physiological functions. In this sense illness itself is psychosomatic. Psychosomatic medicine then has evolved to include not only the diagnosis and treatment of a restricted class of diseases that appear to be psychogenic, but also the careful consideration of interconnections between psychic and somatic factors in illness and health. Thus the concept of the wholeness of persons has influenced the practice of those who in our society are most overtly concerned with bodily processes.

An attack upon the temptation to fragment persons into constituent parts has also come from religious circles. A particular point at which the attack has come has been the rediscovery of biblical anthropology in its Eastern contexts. As has already been indicated, the Judeo-Christian tradition has its roots in Eastern thinking, but has grown most prolifically in the Western world. In the transition Eastern ideas and concepts were filtered through new ways of thinking that were flourishing on the Aegean in the mid-first century when Christianity arrived in Europe. In the exposure of Christian faith to the new world of which it was becoming a part,

---

[58]Erwin H. Ackerknecht, *A Short History of Medicine* (New York: Ronald Press, 1968) 236.

[59]Important works are H. Flanders Dunbar, *Mind and Body: Psychosomatic Medicine* (New York: Random House, 1947) and Edward Weiss and O. Spurgeon English, *Psychosomatic Medicine: The Clinical Application of Psychopathology to General Medical Problems,* 2d ed. (Philadelphia: Saunders, 1943).

words such as "soul" were overlaid with dualistic associations derived from Greek philosophy.

Recent biblical studies have attempted to strip biblical literature of later acculturations to view the material in its initial setting. One result of this approach, especially in the study of the Hebrew Scriptures, has been an appreciation of the contrast between Hebrew and Greek ways of interpreting the psychophysical character of human beings. Early Hebrew thought did not distinguish two separate and independent entities when such words as body and soul were used. The idea of a disembodied soul, immortal and temporarily residing in mortal flesh, simply was not a part of the Eastern mind-set. Rather, by "soul" the Hebrew meant to refer to the entire person, including flesh. At creation God made man "a living being."[60] For the Hebrew, created man did not *have* a soul; he *was* soul, the distinctive handiwork of God.[61] Although the Bible does not work out a careful anthropological analysis, this basic holistic assumption underlies the biblical view of personhood. The idea of a soul somehow unfortunately imprisoned in a burdensome body anticipating the glad day of deliverance to a more heavenly home appears only after Western dualism was superimposed upon Eastern Hebrew thought.

The wholeness of personhood is an important concept for the psychology of religion, which—like theology—is about the business of rational analysis. How may anything be understood with precision without breaking the whole into its constituent parts? But precisely because of the necessity to separate in order to analyze, the discipline must continuously remind itself that the whole is more than the sum of its parts.

---

[60]Genesis 3:7.

[61]Several important works discuss this issue. A. R. Johnson, *The Vitality of the Individual in the Thought of Ancient Israel* (Cardiff: University of Wales Press, 1949) is a brief but valuable statement. A summary may be found in Rudolf Bultmann, *Theology of the New Testament*, vol. 1 (New York: Scribner's, 1951) 190-227. The impact of dualism upon the anthropology of the Apostle Paul is discussed thoroughly in W. David Stacey, *The Pauline View of Man*.

SUMMARY

For some the title of this chapter may have promised more than has been delivered. The discussion certainly has attempted more to leap over the difficulties in defining religion normatively than to wade through the plethora of definitions that have been advanced and decide which one is best. Religion is so complex, the forms it takes across history and culture so varied, and its devotees and opponents so different in their understanding of its true quality that any single normative definition will need endless qualifications. For purposes of psychological study, a phenomenological, functional approach to the definition question will suffice. This will not resolve the intricacies of theological argument, but it will enable the science of religion to move on with its task. The circumference of definition will thus be drawn broadly to incorporate all those beliefs, behaviors, and associations by which persons, past and present, attempt to bind together an otherwise disordered experience and to rehearse that meaning in personal and corporate experience. Psychology of religion takes as the subject matter of its study the entire panorama of experience that individuals and groups confess as their means for giving life coherence and meaning. In short, the agenda is "not the nature of the belief, but the nature of the believing."[62]

To approach the definition issue in this way leaves the investigator open to observe, compare, and contrast the many faces of religion, ranging from those phenomena that are clearly and consensually agreed upon to patterns that are only marginally religious in their institutional form. Neither psychologist nor theologian will be content to limit study to traditional faith, but will choose to be concerned with nuances of personal meaning, cautious about coming too quickly to conclusions from the observance of relatively static institutions. In this sense, psychologist and theologian are necessary compatriots in their common concern to understand religious phenomena in the context of total personhood and remain sensitive to pervasive, private modes and moods by

---

[62]Yinger, *The Scientific Study of Religion,* 11.

which persons find sanity when "the darkness deepens" and "other helpers and comforts flee."[63]

SUGGESTED READINGS

Clark, Walter H. "How Do Social Scientists Define Religion?" *Journal of Social Psychology* 47 (1958): 143-47. Brief and thought-provoking.

Dittes, James E. "Secular Religion: Dilemma of Churches and Researchers," *Review of Religious Research* 10 (1969): 65-81.

Ferré, Frederick. "The Definition of Religion." *Journal of the American Academy of Religion* 38 (1970): 3-16.

Goody, Jack. "Religion and Ritual: The Definitional Problem," *British Journal of Sociology* 12 (1961): 142-64.

Luckmann, Thomas. *The Invisible Religion: The Problem of Religion in Modern Society.* New York: Macmillan, 1967.

Smith, Wilfred C. *Meaning and End of Religion.* New York: Macmillan, 1962. Important footnotes trace history of definition of religion.

Stark, Rodney. "A Taxonomy of Religious Experience." *Journal for the Scientific Study of Religion* 5 (1965): 97-116. Discusses diabolic as well as divine manifestations.

Strommen, Merton P., ed. *Research on Religious Development.* New York: Hawthorn, 1971. Chapter 2 by Martin E. Marty and Chapter 3 by James E. Dittes are especially relevant. Important bibliography.

Symposium: The Problem of Attempting to Define Religion. *Journal for the Scientific Study of Religion* 2 (1962): 3-35. Three articles, each followed by discussion: J. Paul Williams, "The Nature of Religion," 3-14; Luther J. Binkley, "What Characterizes Religious Language?" 18-21; Werner Cohn, "Is Religion Universal? Problems of Definition," 25-32.

Yinger, J. Milton. *The Scientific Study of Religion.* New York: Macmillan, 1970. Chapter 1 an excellent summary of the problem.

---

[63]The language is drawn from Henry F. Lyte's hymn, "Abide With Me."

CHAPTER TWO

THE SCIENTIFIC
STUDY OF RELIGION

A distinguished contemporary psychologist, Abraham Maslow, has been convinced that "the classical philosophy of science as morally neutral, value free, value neutral is not only wrong, but is extremely dangerous as well."[1] This evaluation may be excessively harsh, and it contradicts popular and professional assessments regarding the potentials of scientific methods for an adequate study of persons. The affirmation, however, brings into sharp focus the second methodological question confronted by the psychological study of religion. The researcher who proposes to examine religion must decide not only upon what is to be included under the rubric, but also upon the suitability of the scientific method itself for the study of religion. In short, the psychology of religion introduces in specific terms the long-standing general question of the relationship between science and religion.

---

[1]Abraham H. Maslow, *The Farther Reaches of Human Nature* (New York: Viking Press, 1971) 21.

Unfortunately the value-avoiding model of science challenged by Maslow has often been indulged in by religionists who tend to place science in a compartment rigidly separated from religion. Accordingly, such words as "soul" and "spiritual" have been used to tag an "unobservable" and "unmeasurable" dimension of human experience. This is to assume that science cannot explore these deeper reality levels. Sometimes the gulf has been widened by scientists who accept the judgment that religion is beyond their methodology and decline to enter the sanctuary. Psychology of religion simply cannot survive such a separation. Although the character of the material may condition one's approach to it, scientific study may not be declared illegitimate simply on the grounds that religion is too religious or holy or complex for "secular" examination.

Nor is it appropriate to conclude that scientific study can fully explore the intricacies of religious meaning. Any methodology, including both science and theology, sees phenomena from a particular perspective and therefore refracts that point of view.[2] To assume that a single approach tells the entire story is to commit the error of the blind men examining the elephant. One feels the leg and gets an "accurate" impression that the animal resembles a tree; another feels the ear or the tail or the trunk and arrives at a different conclusion. None of them is wrong but each needs the other to describe adequately his part of the elephant!

Psychology of religion presupposes the interdependence of science and theology. The scientist who assumes that his method will say all that is to be said about a phenomenon is to that extent a poor scientist; the theologian who avoids or denies the data of science by appealing to divine authority is to that extent a poor theologian. Each needs to be informed by the other, and neither awe nor modesty should be lost in the interest of supposed methodological respectability. Revelation and reason are methodological companions.[3] The development of an acceptable alliance between

---

[2]Also science has its own value structures and code of behavior and, since these are matters of morality, they are subject to being scrutinized and informed by theology.

[3]For a theological interpretation of this relationship see H. Emil Brunner, *Revelation and Reason: The Christian Doctrine of Faith and Knowledge,* Olive Wyon, trans. (Philadelphia: Westminster, 1946).

psychologist and theologian raises at least three crucial questions: (1) What is meant generally by scientific method and specifically by the psychological study of religion? (2) How do these types of study relate to the study of religion? (3) What problems are implicit in the use of scientific and psychological methodologies in the study of religion? Each of these questions needs to be discussed with some care.

THE SCIENTIFIC AND PSYCHOLOGICAL METHODS

The scientific method has become so much a part of Western thinking as to be commonplace.[4] The step-by-step process may be set forth with familiar words: (1) description, (2) analysis, (3) hypothesis-making, and (4) testing. First, a phenomenon is accurately described in all its constituent parts. Then the parts and their relationships to each other are analyzed. Hypotheses for describing the connections between the parts are formulated, and subsequently the hypotheses are tested in various situations to come finally to reasonable and dependable statements. In this sense, science is about the business of theory-making. The formation of theories expresses the fundamental concern of science to explain. "Truth" or "reality" are those theses derived from broad and scrupulous observation and tested in enough situations to give reasonable confidence in their dependability.

Such description of the scientific method, however, is much too simple. The fields of science are so numerous and varied in the way they do their work that a common description seems nearly impossible. Can a single tag cover the diverse procedures used by the biologists with elaborate machinery in the laboratory, the anthropologist carefully cataloging the behavior of tribesmen, the archaeologist reconstructing the history of a tell, and the physician evaluating symptoms in an air-conditioned office? Can the same methods be employed for studying both human and nonhuman behavior? Or does the multifarious behavior of the human animal yield itself to a universal method? Some have been inclined to answer these questions negatively and therefore have been reluctant

---

[4]The discussion here draws heavily upon Morris R. Cohen and Ernest Nagel, *An Introduction to Logic and Scientific Method* (New York: Harcourt, Brace and World, 1934) 391-403.

to talk about *the* scientific method. To their resistance has been added the argument that *all* thinking ought to proceed from the orderly and accurate observation of facts and thus it is highly artificial to separate scientific from nonscientific thought. Certainly these arguments carry weight and support the contention that it is no longer meaningful to talk about scientific method as if a single examination style could cover the wide variety of scientific procedures or the diversity of personal and corporate behavior.

Generalizations about the scientific method are made even more difficult by the historical division of science into the natural sciences and the social sciences. Methodologically the two areas overlap, but there are important distinctions between the two fields. The natural sciences have a much longer history and have therefore developed a "body of commonly accepted laws with theories of explanatory power, capable of yielding precise and reliable predictions."[5] The social sciences do not yet have a history extensive enough to have produced such a theoretical backlog. Additionally, the natural sciences are concerned with physical matter that yields itself to concrete measurement and precise analysis, but the human data with which the social sciences work do not as easily lend themselves to the exactness that may be found in the natural sciences. The farther advances of the natural sciences have resulted in tension between the two, and it may be with some defensiveness that areas in the social sciences seem intent on emulating the natural sciences, so that statistics resembles mathematics and psychobiology is closely akin to physiology. Certainly the line between the two areas is unclear, making the description of the scientific method even more problematic.

The psychology of religion obviously meets science at the point of one of the social sciences. But psychology also has many faces. Some divisions study the human animal; others concentrate upon the nonhuman, either assuming or not that transfer of information to the human can be made. Psychologists are clinical or experimental or psychometric or statistical in their interests. Some are concerned with sensation, perception, feeling, thinking, learning;

---

[5]Merton P. Strommen, ed., *Research on Religious Development* (New York: Hawthorn, 1971) xviii.

others attempt to apply psychology to practical areas of economics, industry, family relations, vocation. Still others are eclectic, selecting from the many studies those that seem relevant to their concern. The catalog of areas within psychology is as endless as one of those within religion.

Sometimes these segments of psychology live peaceably with each other, but often the truce is made uneasy with considerable disagreements on the data, how they are to be studied, and what hypotheses are to be used to explain them. In short, the plethora of interests and orientations makes it difficult, if not impossible, to generalize upon the method of psychology.

What can be said from this maze of relationships? Is there any common methodological ground for doing psychology of religion? Certainly psychologists may not be expected to speak uniformly and consistently about religion. The careful student will quickly develop a healthy suspicion of generalizations that begin, "Science says . . . " or "Psychology says . . . " and will arrive at conclusions slowly and tentatively, aiming to discount none of the data. Nonetheless, some operational guidelines seem common to the scientific enterprise and are shared by the hosts who call themselves psychologists. These principles should become part of the working creed for the psychological study of religion.

Observation and Description. The scientist at large, and the psychologist specifically, gives first place to careful observation. Knowledge is to be derived from the facts as they yield themselves to observation, classification, and organization. Statements of fact are to be judged by their conformity to circumspect observation. The painstaking scientist is careful with his observations and with his statements about those observations. Intuition, conjecture, subjectivism, and opinion are neither to be confused with nor substituted for prudent observation and accurate description.

This is not to say that intuition and speculation have no place in the work of scientists. These in fact may play a major role in formulating the direction of their work. For example, the scientist may surmise on the basis of observations of students and their post-college careers that high academic performance in college does not guarantee success in business. Impressions might stimulate an investigation of the issue, but the scientist would not presume that surmise was correct until techniques for measuring success in business had been devised, college grades had been studied, and correlation between success and grades had been determined. Intuition and speculative imagination might have set disciplined observation in motion; but after the study had begun, the scientific method would attempt to exclude all personal elements. If the intuitive thesis could not be explored through observation and organization, then it would be considered outside the domain of science and judged to be unverifiable opinion. Even educated guesswork is not the goal. For the scientist knowledge thus rests on observation and experiment, rather than on opinion, belief, or intuition.

Systematic Analysis. A second general principle by which science operates is systematic analysis; that is, observations are collected, organized, and classified in such ways as to arrive at dependable propositions. Limited and isolated data are relatively useless to the scientist because they may be used, advertently or inadvertently, to support personal bias or so narrowly selected that the evidence is insufficient for building verifiable hypotheses. The sample must be broad enough to establish some confidence that one's statements are likely to be correct.

Further, to be productive, observations must be organized around a purpose. Random observations may pile up in such disordered array as to make no sense. Observing human behavior at large may produce a kind of common sense about how people act, but such observations are frequently vague and difficult to fit into a pattern or system of propositions for understanding human behavior. For science to exist beyond common sense, some principles of order and organization must be discovered. Isolated or general observation must have some possibility for classification and orderly analysis.

The systematic labors of science over many years have produced a system with identity. Theses that stand together in mutual support and as a coherent whole have emerged out of careful, systematic analysis. The system itself not only provides science with identity but also protects against rashness. The disciplined scientist is suspicious of a lonely thesis, not to protect a closed system but to assure that the maverick concept results from systematic analysis. This mentality gives science a healthy conservatism. Change in the system occurs slowly, but it can occur. Such caution both preserves the scientific concern for systematic analysis of data and lends support to a cohesive system of hypotheses. As Cohen and Nagel have observed, "It is this systematic character of scientific theories which gives such high probabilities to the various individual propositions of a science."[6]

Accuracy, Exactness. A third premise common among those using the scientific method is an insistence upon scrupulous exactness. Accuracy is the mortar that holds together the propositional bricks of a scientific system. Accuracy demands that observations be made and recorded with precision and that limits of statements about those observations be clearly defined.

Concern for accuracy creates an emphasis upon *control.* The conditions under which observations are made and propositions formulated must be managed, not to produce a pre-decided result, but to eliminate as many variables as possible. The fewer the variables, the more accurate the conclusions.

The psychologist develops techniques to maintain these ideals of the scientific method. Available procedures are numerous. The psychologist, for example, may analyze statistical frequencies in terms of their correlation with validated norms, or administer standardized projective tests, or devise experiments in which a single variable may be measured in a controlled environment. He may apply a model of personality development to personal case history, or rate personality variables along the continuum of an established scale, or interview through questionnaire or formal conversation, or combine a number of these or other procedures.[7] But whatever techniques are used, the principles are the same: to observe faithfully and classify precisely according to systems of organization that permit dependable prediction in identical or similar circumstances. The ideal, more easily formulated than achieved, is to eliminate personal prejudice and sloppy methods that might distort observations, interpretations, and predictions. And above all

---

[6]Cohen and Nagle, *An Introduction to Logic and Scientific Method,* 395.

[7]A useful introduction to the application of scientific procedures to the study of religion may be found in Purnell H. Benson, *Religion in Contemporary Culture: A Study of Religion through Social Science* (New York: Harper, 1960) 78-115.

else the scientist remains open to new insight by a calculated reluctance to close the door to additional inquiry.[8]

SCIENCE AND THE FIELD OF RELIGION

The application of scientific method, sometimes disciplined and sometimes haphazard, has produced dramatic additions to the field of religious studies. Over the last century a number of subdisciplines have developed, each contributing significantly to the treasury of information about religion. Among these are the history of religion, the phenomenology of religion, the sociology of religion, and the psychology of religion, each of which has in some measure developed its own identity as a method for examining religion. These "new" disciplines have expanded methods and provided additional tools for understanding the nature of religion. These developments in the scientific study of religion broaden the base from which theology may do its work. The new disciplines are neither opponents of nor secondary or ancillary to theology, but important associates whose discoveries are necessary to understand and appreciate complex faith.

The story of the development of psychology of religion belongs largely to the last century and a half and to the Western academic tradition.[9] It is deeply rooted in increased contact between the Christian and nonChristian faiths and the expanding frontiers of knowledge about nonChristian religions. The comparative study of religion was born out of a one-world mentality that placed the major living religions in intimate touch with each other. Scholarship over the last two centuries has made accessible the texts of sacred writings from nonChristian traditions.[10] These basic literary materials have been supplemented by data from archaeological, historical, and anthropological research. Using the results of this work, comparative religion has been able to arrive at a chronology

---

[8]Cf. Strommen, *Research on Religious Development*, xviii.

[9]A useful, brief discussion of these matters may be found in Ninian Smart, "Scientific Studies of Religion," in F. G. Healey, ed., *What Theologians Do* (Grand Rapids MI: Eerdmans, 1970) 171-92.

[10]For example, see the monumental multivolume work edited by F. Max Müller, *The Sacred Books of the East* (Oxford: Clarendon Press, 1879-1884).

of historical development for separate religions, to translate and interpret their Scriptures, to study their doctrines and rituals, and subsequently to compare these items among various religious traditions. Unfortunately, comparisons were often done from the bias of one faith, usually Christianity, often to show the inferiority of all other faiths. Partly as an attempt to overcome such bias, the history of religion has come to define its purposes in terms of the appearance, growth, and function of religion itself.[11] One religious system is not taken as a norm to which others may be compared, but all systems, including Christianity, are considered to be manifestations of human religious concerns. Although history of religion remains interested in interconnections and intersections, it has become more hesitantly comparative than its predecessor.

The concern of the history of religion to stand outside the bias of one religion and view all religions dispassionately has encouraged attention to *meaning* in religious expression. Precise cross-cultural analysis of manifestations that on the surface appear to be quite different often reveals that they carry identical or similar functions. The subdiscipline that centers its attention upon the meaning level of religious manifestations is generally referred to as phenomenology of religion. The seminal contribution to this approach may perhaps be traced to Rudolf Otto, who in his *Idea of the Holy* expressed the view that overpowering creature-consciousness in response to that which is supreme above all creatures is at the heart of religion. The phenomenologist gives first place to meaning levels of experience; he compares and classifies religious expressions according to kindred meanings.[12] The goal is to de-

---

[11]Mircea Eliade and Joseph Kitagawa, eds., *The History of Religions: Essays in Methodology* (Chicago: University of Chicago Press, 1959) provides descriptions of this approach.

[12]Cf. Gerardus van der Leeuw's discussion of sacred time and place as universal notions in *Religion in Essence and Manifestation* (London: Allen and Unwin, 1938) 655-57. See also Mircea Eliade, *The Sacred and the Profane: The Nature of Religion*, Willard R. Trask, trans. (New York: Harper, 1961). The work of the psychoanalyst Carl Gustav Jung bears remarkable similarity to these concerns with common or kindred meanings. He states, "Every religion is a spontaneous expression of a certain psychological condition." *Psychology and Religion* (New Haven: Yale University Press, 1938) 108.

velop and use a typology that makes it possible to sort out common meanings across religious systems. The phenomenologist is therefore likely to use nonsectarian language in preference to traditional religious words. Rather than speak of conversion, for example, the phenomenologist might discuss initiation rites, a larger category to include various rituals that carry kindred meanings.

The sociology of religion shares the attitude of phenomenology, but focuses its concern upon the function served by religion in preserving corporate life. Its agenda is the "system of norms and usages designating 'right' behavior to the members of a society."[13] Historically, sociology of religion has centered considerable effort on understanding primitive religion. F. Max Müller, sometimes called the father of the science of religion, illustrates the case of a number of nineteenth century sociologists who undertook to discover the essence of religion in the simple experience of early, preliterate peoples.[14] Evidently, pioneer sociologists believed that the essential functions of religion were more easily isolated in the uncluttered experience of early culture than in later, more refined, and highly organized religious expressions. Preoccupation with primitive models continued in the work of Emile Durkheim, one of the most influential twentieth-century figures in sociology of religion.[15] However, researchers of the past several decades seem to have lost their fondness for primitive religion, converging instead upon the fluid and pluralistic character of religion in contemporary dress.[16] The body of data from the sociological analysis of religion in its contemporary setting has grown incredibly during recent years and continues to multiply.

---

[13]J. Milton Yinger, *The Scientific Study of Religion*, (New York: Macmillan, 1970) 5.

[14]See Müller, *Sacred Books of the East.*

[15]Emile Durkheim, *The Elementary Forms of the Religious Life,* J. W. Swain, trans. (New York: Free Press, 1965).

[16]See for examples, Will Herberg, *Protestant-Catholic-Jew* (Garden City NY: Doubleday, 1960); Lenski, *The Religious Factor* (Garden City NY: Doubleday, 1961); Max Weber, *The Protestant Ethic and the Spirit of Capitalism,* Talcott Parsons, trans. (New York: Scribner's, 1958); Yinger, *The Scientific Study of Religion* (New York: Macmillan, 1970).

Psychology of religion belongs to this family of scientific studies of religion. Its demarcation, especially from sociology of religion, has not always been exact because obviously individuals function as social beings.[17] Like love and marriage, individual and group behavior go together; study of one inevitably spills over into the other. Generally, psychology of religion has concentrated its attention upon personal experience rather than corporate institutions, but, since persons live in a community and are influenced by their neighbors, sociological features must necessarily be considered for a thorough understanding of individual "varieties of religious experience."

Thus psychology of religion is one among several ways in which the scientific method is systematically applied to the study of religion. Each subdiscipline has made a substantial contribution to our information about a complex subject, and daily the horizons are extended. The areas of scientific study of religion are mutually interdependent, together saying more than any one could say separately.

The birth of the psychology of religion entailing the serious application of scientific principles to understanding religious behavior has come with struggle and sometimes pain. Especially in the days of early psychoanalysis, psychology appeared to uninitiated clergy as unduly antagonistic and possibly destructive. Often religionists judged their faith to be too inward, too subjective, too personal to be explored by a discipline scrupulously dedicated to precise measurement and prediction. Consequently, a wall of separation was sometimes built between psychology and theology as if the two were independent and irreconcilable. Encounters between psychology and religious studies have subsequently fluctuated between spirited antagonism and passive indifference.

In the mid-1920s Sigmund Freud affirmed that religion is an illusion that survives on the strength of infantile wishes, serving well

---

[17]Freud's *Totem and Taboo,* in *Basic Writings of Sigmund Freud,* A. A. Brill, trans. and ed. (New York: Random House, 1938) attempts to apply his psychoanalytic model of personality development to the sociological origin of religion, but with little success. See below, 71-76.

as growth occurs but best discarded in the interest of maturity.[18] Reaction among the clergy, skilled in theology but untrained in the application of scientific method to their discipline and unimpressed by the immodesty of Freud's statement, was predictably vigorous and emotional. Dialogue between psychology and religion over the subsequent three decades preserved large amounts of the hostility generated from this exchange. Psychological study crept into seminary curricula very slowly, and not until the mid-1950s did the American Psychiatric Association include a section on religion at its annual meeting.

Gradually hostility generated by the Freudian confrontation was dissipated with growing mutual respect. The point at which reconciliation began to occur was the care and therapy of persons. Psychiatrists, clinical psychologists, and clergymen all had more people coming to them for help than they could serve. Each welcomed assistance from whatever quarter and slowly began to explore relationships with other helping persons. In theological circles the use of the old term "pastor" was recovered under the labels of pastoral care and pastoral theology, now augmented by new skills introduced from psychology. The publication of the journal *Pastoral Psychology,* with an editorial board composed mostly of religionists, was begun in 1950. Psychologists and psychiatrists were concerned to reserve the terms "counseling" and "psychotherapy" for those professionally trained in these techniques, but willingly referred persons with "religious" problems to the clergy. In a few urban areas pastoral counseling centers were established to supplement psychological clinics and psychiatric services or to provide a resource where these were unavailable. Seminary curricula were expanded to include numerous undergraduate courses, as well as graduate programs, in psychology of religion with chief emphasis upon pastoral care and counseling. In short, during the 1920s, 1930s, and 1940s, American psychology of religion (and American was about the only kind there was) was transformed into practical questions surrounding persons with "religious" problems. Psy-

---

[18]This view appears in *The Future of an Illusion,* W. D. Robson-Scott, trans. and James Strachey, ed. (Garden City NY: Doubleday, 1964).

chologists and religionists each began to stake out territory and responsibility and learned to live with each other as friends.

This resolution, however, was satisfying to neither the theologian nor the psychologist. Grounds for the division of labor were difficult to establish. Was the minister to counsel only when a parishioner described his problems with religious words? What personality disruptions do not involve religious values at their deepest levels? Is not the clinical psychologist or psychiatrist better equipped to aid some persons with religious problems? Or the clergy those with nonreligious difficulties? But, more significantly, the translation of the fundamental relationships between psychology and religion into practical matters of care and counseling produced few and feeble attempts to understand interconnections other than techniques that might be used by both pastor and psychiatrist. Theologians and psychologists learned to respect each other, but exchanged little serious conversation beyond matters of practical operation. The situation, as already noted, led some to declare that the psychology of religion was dead.[19]

Since mid-century, however, both the war and the truce seem to be passing with psychology and religion increasingly committed to the rigorous disciplines of scientific method as one avenue for understanding religion, a way of reaching beyond the practical use of psychology to assist the clergy. The appearance of the *Journal for the Scientific Study of Religion* in 1961 signaled a willingness to examine religion with the tools of social science. The journal has tilted toward sociology of religion, but it has included numerous psychological studies. The impact of the eminent Paul Tillich, who treated psychology of religion seriously in his development of a systematic theology, has been incalculable. A bibliography is beginning to develop.[20] Psychology of religion seems on the move again after its

---

[19]See above, pp. 5-6.

[20]The list could be extensive, but the following are especially helpful: Peter Homans, ed., *The Dialogue between Theology and Psychology*, vol. 3, Essays in Divinity series, Gerald C. Brauer, ed. (Chicago: University of Chicago Press, 1968); Edwin R. Goodenough, *The Psychology of Religious Experiences* (New York: Basic Books, 1965); Peter Homans, *Theology after Freud* (Indianapolis: Bobbs-Merrill, 1970); William A. Sadler, Jr., ed., *Personality and Religion: The Role of Religion in Personality*

quiescence. The development of an organized system of data comparable to other bodies of scientific knowledge still lies in the future, but the promise for movement in that direction seems brighter now than several decades ago. Certainly the hostility and passive friendliness of the immediate past seem to have given way to a more creative and productive encounter.

THE FUNCTIONAL STUDY OF RELIGION

The developing identity among the scientific subdisciplines of religion, including psychology of religion, represents a variety of attempts to apply scientific analysis to religion, and each colors the scientific method with its own hues. Each carves out an area of the large body of religious data and focuses its work there. All, however, share a common concern with *function*. Psychology of religion specifically focuses upon "the full range of consequences" of religious acts and ideas for the preservation and maintenance of character and culture.[21] In this manner religious belief and behavior become accessible to the psychologist. The gods may not be empirically available, but the human experience of the gods—confessed ideas and rituals in which the ideas are given concrete form—is observable, measurable, and subject to analysis. To be sure, such a functional approach limits the evaluative conclusions of the psychologist; the method circumscribes judgments about the nature of ultimacy. The psychologist as psychologist is not as essentially concerned with the authenticity of religion as he is with the way religion operates in the maintenance of persons and the group or groups to which they belong. In contrast to the theologian, the psychologist does not inquire about the nature of ultimacy, but critically examines what individuals and groups *do* with their sense of ultimacy.

Development (New York: Harper, 1970); Paul W. Pruyser, *A Dynamic Psychology of Religion* (New York: Harper, 1968); Wayne E. Oates, *The Psychology of Religion* (Waco TX: Word Books, 1973); Richard D. Kahoe and Mary Jo Meadow, *Psychology of Religion: Religion in Individual Lives* (New York: Harper, 1984).

[21]Yinger, *The Scientific Study of Religion*, 5.

For example, consider the use of the term "God."[22] Theological concerns with the term center upon the nature of God and demonstration that the idea of God is a valid means for understanding human life and destiny. The logic or reasonableness of the idea is paramount. The functional approach, on the other hand, inquires as to how the term serves persons either within a specific religious system or across several religions. In various religious systems the name may be filled with theological content according to the time, place, and preference of those who are committed to the system. Functionally, however, God (or Brahman or Mana or Om) serves to identify the being, process, or reality in and through which persons transcend all the life-negating forces of human existence. When persons employ the God-word, they articulate that which they conceive to be the explanation of human life and destiny in the face of trial and tribulation. The word, and ideas that accrue to it, *function* across religious communions as a way to manage the horrendous and awesome aspects of human experience. The psychologist views the ritualistic and ethical forms through which the devotee "practices the presence of God" as keys to unlock the functional significance of the God-concept.

Several interrelated issues spin off from the functional approach to religion. First, the truth or error of a religious system is not at stake. Whether religious ideas or beliefs properly describe reality does not necessarily determine their economy for self-survival. For example, a devotee confesses belief in a God who cares for him. The functional question does not ask whether God is, nor argue whether "caring" is an accurate category for describing God. These are not really the *psychological* issues. Rather, the confession is taken at face value; it is accepted as a behavioral event that has valid function in the devotee's system of personal organization. How then does the confession serve the individual in his efforts at survival? What *need* does it satisfy? In answering these questions the functionalist may seem to omit vital aspects of religion by remaining faithful to method.

---

[22]The illustration here is taken from W. C. Tremmel, *Religion: What Is It?* (New York: Holt, Rinehart and Winston, 1976) 161-62.

Second, the functional approach easily lends itself to drawing the phenomenological circumference of religion quite broadly. One using this approach is not so concerned to limit the understanding of religion to traditional forms and places. In any given historical or social context, religion is narrowly defined by the cue words that are by consensus understood as religion. As already pointed out, these consensus symbols are culture-bound, reflecting particularized ways that a specific group expresses devotion. The psychologist proposes both to explore the function of these culturally conditioned and consensually agreed upon symbols and to understand the role of expressions of the same values in ways that are not typically entitled religion.

The theologian may see this aspect of the psychologist's work as the erosion of meaning by including too much. Do not all items that satisfy needs merit inclusion under the religion umbrella? In terms of our example, should not belief in fate or survival of the fittest be classified as religion?[23] Erich Fromm's definition reflects a willingness to include so much that it excludes very little. He states that religion is "any system of thought and action shared by a group which gives the individual a frame of orientation and an object of devotion."[24] The functional approach may protect against the charge of provincialism, but it may "liquidate the religious phenomena by defining it out of all specificity."[25] The psychologist who studies religion, however, must be granted this risk in the interest of permitting persons to identify what to them carries religious weight.

Third, although functional study serves a scientific utility, it also has an intrinsic ideological implication that is too often unrecognized. To discuss religious meaning in terms of its function may be taken to imply that meaning is confined to the context of human need and satisfaction. Peter L. Berger is a researcher who has written with great insight regarding the function of American reli-

-----

[23]The popular phrase, "That's his god," reflects this attitude.

[24]Fromm, *Psychoanalysis and Religion*, 21.

[25]Peter L. Berger, "Some Second Thoughts on Substantive versus Functional Definitions of Religion," *Journal for the Scientific Study of Religion* 13 (1974): 129.

gion.[26] He refers to this as "a quasiscientific legitimation of the avoidance of transcendence."[27] To work devotedly with the functional approach is to run the risk of accepting, perhaps unintentionally, this presupposition. This is an assumption of no little theological weight. Insofar as religion incorporates transcendence in any sense, it will remain suspicious of the reduction of meaning to human terms. Again Berger may be cited: "Within the framework of science the gods will always appear in quotation marks, and nothing done within this framework permits the removal of the quotation marks. Anyone engaged in the scientific study of religion will have to resign himself to this intrinsic limitation—regardless of whether, in his extra-scientific existence, he is a believer, an atheist, or a skeptic."[28]

PROBLEMS IN THE PSYCHOLOGICAL STUDY OF RELIGION

The psychological study of religion, for all its promise, is not without its difficulties. Some of these problems are fairly superficial, such as interdisciplinary competition and jealousy, and may be resolved through the disbursement of information, mutual respect, and sensitive appreciation. Other problems are more native to both scientific and theological pursuit of religious meaning. They are not so much issues to be solved and dismissed as enduring questions demanding consistent diligence. Four such problems constantly gnaw at the relationship between psychology and religion.

Language

One obvious difficulty in doing psychology of religion is language. The problem is evident on two levels. On the surface the language problem is to understand the refined and specialized meanings that psychology and theology each assigns to its own professional vocabulary. Professional usage in neither field neces-

---

[26]Peter L. Berger, *The Sacred Canopy: Elements of a Sociological Theory of Religion* (Garden City NY: Doubleday, 1967).

[27]Berger, "Some Second Thoughts," 125.

[28]Ibid., 125-26.

sarily corresponds to usage in the street. Further, the same or similar words may mean one thing in psychology and something quite different in religion. Often words are not only defined differently, but also loaded with dissimilar emotionality.

A sample will illustrate ambiguities often built into professional language. Psychology defines "conversion" as the misdirection of psychic energy often manifesting itself in a bodily symptom such as paralysis or a tic. The experience carries "bad" connotations in the sense that such diversion is an unhealthy method for managing burdensome anxiety. Hence the psychologist would aim to assist the person to find other means to resolve anxiety and thereby make conversion unnecessary. In religious circles, however, conversion is desirable and constructive experience in which loyalty finds a new or more intense focus of devotion. Various religious traditions may debate the form that conversion ought to take, some offended by a volatile, expressive, emotional outburst and others suspicious of gradual, nontraumatic awakening. But conversion itself is commonly considered as something "good" to be sought and treasured. In this case only the idea of redirection is common to psychological and theological usage; as the assigned meanings become specific, the words drift farther apart. Additionally, the value associations are incompatible. And similar ambiguity may be observed in the use of dependence, authority, suffering, passivity, and a host of other words carrying differing definitions and value connotations.

Diversity of usage, however, creates no problems for psychological study of religion that may not be surmounted by careful definition and continuous conversation between psychology and religion. More serious and abiding difficulties may derive from the nature of language itself. Words are symbols from which speakers and hearers abstract meaning, a process so complex that it is difficult to understand how persons ever understand each other. From the simple and concrete symbol "cat" may be abstracted meanings as diverse as "soft, cuddly pet" and "dude with pegged pants and twirling chain." Religious language may be even more opaque and problematic.[29] Ultimate realities are considered to be beyond the

---

[29]These variations suggest the severe limitations of questionnaire survey methods that depend upon word associations, especially the type that occasionally

reach of descriptive categories, sometimes beyond language itself. Therefore, the devotee attempts to use metaphor and simile to explain what is in fact inexplicable. Whatever the religious system, Western or Eastern, religious language is thus marked by high levels of abstraction, metaphorical and analogous usage. To interpret such language behavior the hearer must attempt to see through the finite symbol to apprehend the infinite meaning, to understand what Langdon Gilkey calls the double intentionality of religious language. He says,

> A religious symbol points, on the one hand, to an ordinary object, event, or person and thus intends that "matter of fact": a storm, a birth, an historical event, a man, a scriptural document, an institution. But it is *religious* precisely because, in this case, this verbal sign for a finite referent also points beyond its finite object to the dimension of sacrality, of infinity, ultimacy, unconditionedness, to a holy that is manifest in and through this finite medium. And all religious language has this multivalent character.[30]

Attitudes toward language in T'ien T'ai and Zen Buddhism and, to a lesser extent, in Christian glossolalia cults caricature the problem of using finite words to convey the holy. These groups see language not only as inadequate but also as inappropriate, judging traditional forms to be impediments to apprehending ultimacy. In their view, words are products of human, analytic reason and belong to a different order than the divine. Their use actually distorts and impedes the comprehension of deity, who comes more through intuition than reason. Thus the Zen master advises silence about the One; to say anything is to frame misleading concepts and

---

appears in popular magazines. To use these techniques effectively the researcher must exhibit extreme care to assure that the subject is in fact answering the question that is asked!

[30]Langdon B. Gilkey, *Naming the Whirlwind: The Renewal of God-Language* (Indianapolis: Bobbs-Merrill, 1969) 290-91; Paul Tillich, *Systematic Theology*, vol. 1 (Chicago: University of Chicago Press, 1951) 211f; Mircea Eliade, *Patterns in Comparative Religion*, Rosemary Sheed, trans. (New York: Sheed and Ward, 1958) 158, 421; and Paul Ricouer, *The Symbolism of Evil*, Emerson Buchanan, trans. (New York: Harper, 1967) 11.

thereby indulge one's illusions. Likewise, glossolaliacs, those who "speak in tongues," forsake typical language forms as they consider themselves to be grasped by the inexplicable God. Both the Zen master and the glossolaliac aim to overcome language they regard as a rational hindrance to genuine encounter with the sacred.

Even if language is accepted as a vehicle for religious communication, its meanings must be abstracted. Consider, for example, the Christian affirmation, "God is love!" What does the expression mean? The basic content of love is derived from experiences of love (with parent, child, friend, mistress, pet, pickles). When the statement is heard, few would suppose that it incorporates all species of love. Selectivity occurs. Aspects of love are intended to be included in the religious affirmation; others are to be excluded. Certain characteristics of care and concern are abstracted from the total human experience and used to allude to the character of God. Thus "God is love" is interpreted only in restricted and qualified ways. In this sense the statement contains both truth and error (a point on which the Zen master should be heard).

In the Judeo-Christian tradition the metaphorical and analogous nature of religious language is underscored by the stature granted to biblical materials. The Bible, especially the Hebrew Scriptures, uses anthropomorphic imagery extensively in its "descriptions" of God.[31] Regard for these materials often leads many devotees to treat the materials as if the symbols are the realities and thereby short-circuit a critical point in biblical interpretation, namely, evaluating what abstraction is intended. A sizable portion of theology's business is refining the semantic analog—biblical and extrabiblical, clarifying what meanings are to be included in the symbols. If God as the Father does not refer to a male human being, Western, older, and bearded, what are the abstractions to be included and how do they relate to other ideas in the system? Variations in such abstraction is one of the matters out of which differing theological points of view are made. Psychology properly recognizes this character of religious language both within formal theological circles, and also among the theologically naive who may

---

[31]Compare as a bold example the Yahwistic materials in Genesis 2:4b-3:24.

abstract whimsically in terms of their own personal needs and aspirations. Theological words do not always mean what they appear to mean, and methodologically psychology of religion must be wary of assuming the obvious meaning or assuming that words consistently mean the same thing.

Objectivity

A second perennial issue in the psychological study of religion has to do with objectivity. Scientific procedures aim to eliminate personal bias that distorts interpretations of data, a worthy objective never to be forsaken. Control in research is important to distinguish between value judgments colored by personal experience and the objective interpretation of the facts. However, one of the most profound problems of the scientific method lies precisely here, and it is particularly applicable to the social sciences. The questions are two. First, can objectivity be achieved? And second, is objectivity desirable?

The answer to the first question seems to be both positive and negative. Certain data yield themselves easily to categorization and create no particular problems. Statistical materials, for example, may be gathered with few concerns beyond the sample's being broad enough to prevent distortions. But interpretation, explanation, and theory-building make objectivity more illusive. Are not all methods, descriptions, tools, and theories the creation of quite human researchers? Can they, even with the most refined techniques, *absolutely* avoid subjectivity? Would not Freud, for example, have framed his theories about religion quite differently had he belonged to a matriarchal rather than a patriarchal social order? Scientific laws are not data, but ways of looking at data. As such they are conceived by the researcher as cogent and cohesive interpretations and thus are subject to the foibles that characterize encounters between the interpreters as human beings.

Let it be emphasized beyond possible misunderstanding that attempts at objectivity are not to be denigrated; objectivity must be maintained as a scientific goal highly treasured and diligently sought. Compromise of this aim is a violation of both good scientific procedures and sense of fairness. Vigilance in the scrutiny of research techniques to avoid intentional or unintentional manipulation of the data is demanded. Nor does the problem belong distinctively to those using scientific research tools. Statements made by theologians are also ways of looking at data and not the data themselves.

Hence objectivity ought not be romanticized. It is more illusive ideal than ideal achievement. Neither theologian nor social scientist is delivered from subjectivity; it is even demanded of the scientist who attempts to conjecture possible outcomes of envisioned experimentation. Further, when scientist and theologian project conclusions about the nature and destiny of persons, they are likely to draw upon their own goals, motives, and commitments to ideals. Langdon Gilkey may have put the issue too boldly, but he nonetheless makes the point clearly:

> Most books of the sciences of man, in their "scientific" sections, portray man as determined by economic, political, social, and ethnic forces that determine his behavior along lines strictly devoted to his own well-being and security and that of his group, and that makes his ideals epiphenomenal at best. But in their "prophetic" sections at the ends of their books, when they discuss human destiny and the possible uses social scientific knowledge can offer toward the eradication of human evil and the improvement of the human situation, these same authors tend to see man as rationally motivated by their own liberal ideals of general well-being and social progress.[32]

The disciplined scientist will remain both sensitive to his personal involvement in structuring his methodology and drawing conclusions and scrupulously committed to procedures for correcting subjective distortion by virtue of necessary involvement. The dynamic interplay between subjectivity and objectivity is so complexly intricate that claims for value-free conclusions ought to be made with modesty. Here psychology and religion stand on common ground.

What about the second part of the question: Is objectivity desirable? As already suggested, a certain type of subjectivity gives birth to scientific examination and the revision of explanatory theories. Science is immobilized until the researcher can envision sub-

---

[32]Gilkey, *Naming the Whirlwind*, 387-88a.

jectively new possibilities in the relationships and meanings of data. But beyond subjective imagination some have suggested that continuous subjective involvement in religion may enhance understanding.[33] Accordingly, insights into religion develop more easily from participation than detachment. Although it is certainly not necessary for one to be a believer to understand religion, devotion may make persons more sensitive to the values that their religion claims and thereby place them in a better position to understand religion as a viable option for explaining human experience. This line of argument assumes that both participation and detachment represent personal stances and the former is preferable because subjective insights are themselves data to be considered in arriving at conclusions. Stained glass windows are best seen from the inside, and no one assumes that "the analysis of paint, painter, and patron exhausts the meaning of art."[34]

The point here is not that the participant has a more valid perspective on religion than the nonparticipant. Certainly some things about religion may be said only by the participant observer, but it is equally true that the believer may be blinded by faith and require the observation and judgment of the outsider. Descriptions of lead and glass, design and composition, brushes and pigments may cast important light upon windows and art. Neither the inside nor the outside view may say that it has no need of the other. The devotee must be especially cautious about assumptions that private experience is normative or that it stands outside the purview of complete examination by psychology.

Additional light is cast on the subjective-objective issue in the classical distinction between sign and symbol made by Paul Tillich.[35] For many persons the term symbol carries the connotation of nonreal, partially due to the identification of reality with objective data. Religious symbols, however, reach beyond empirical real-

---

[33]See Geddes MacGregor, *Introduction to Religious Philosophy* (Boston: Houghton Mifflin, 1959) 2-21. Compare also Wilfred C. Smith, "Comparative Religion: Whither and Why?" in Eliade and Kitagawa, eds., *The History of Religions: Essays in Methodology.*

[34]The metaphors come from Yinger, *The Scientific Study of Religion*, 1-2.

[35]See Tillich, *Systematic Theology*, 1:239-41.

ity. Unlike a sign, which "bears no necessary relation to that to which
t points, the symbol participates in the reality for which it stands.
The sign can be changed arbitrarily according to the correlation
between that which is symbolized and persons who receive it as a
symbol."[36] In short, religious symbols are "double-edged." They are
directed toward the infinite that they symbolize and toward the finite through which they symbolize it.[37] In this sense the use of religious symbols necessarily entails the interplay between objectivity
and subjectivity.

Robert Bellah's warning against either secular or religious absolutism may serve as a fitting summary of the objectivity issue. The
"religiously orthodox," says Bellah, have often felt that their belief
system represents objective reality as it is and thus all others must
be false, either absolutely or in some degree. The "secular orthodox" has also been an absolutist, believing that all religion is subjective, that is, based upon emotion, wish, or faulty inference, and
therefore false. Bellah decries both types of absolutism and appeals
for "symbolic realism," an attitude that sees religion

> as a system of symbols which is neither simply objective nor simply
> subjective, but which links subject and object in a way that trans-
> figures reality or even, in a sense, creates reality. For people with
> this point of view the idea of finding more than one religion valid,
> even in a deeply personal sense, is not only possible, but normal.[38]

Some may judge that Bellah too seriously erodes personal commitment to a single faith, but his caution against the danger of idol-
izing objectivity in either religious or secular modes must be taken
seriously.

Oversimplification through Reductionism

An indispensable phase of the scientific method is the analysis
of the larger unit by breaking it into its constituent parts. The goal

---

[36]Ibid., 239.

[37]Ibid., 240.

[38]Robert N. Bellah, "Religion in the University: Changing Consciousness,
Changing Structure," in Claude Welch, ed., *Religion in the Undergraduate Curriculum* (Washington DC: Association of American Colleges, 1972) 17. See also his
"Christianity and Symbolic Realism," *Journal for the Scientific Study of Religion*, 9
(1970): 89-96.

is to move systematically toward simpler components on the assumption that the smaller elements are more easily understood and that the whole is explained when the parts have been described. Thus water is analyzed as hydrogen and oxygen, each having its own distinctiveness but becoming water when they are combined in certain proportions. Psychology of religion shares this orderly disposition in doing its work. Attempts are made to break complex religious phenomena into smaller, manageable units. Prayer, for example, may be reduced to the combination of ceremonial body postures (kneeling, bowed head), stylized phraseology (Our Father, Amen), and typical attitudes and moods (petition, contemplation).

Psychology of religion could accomplish little without reducing the whole into constituent parts, but the method risks building theory about the larger unit on the basis of too few of its components. Wayne Oates cryptically calls such reductionism the "nothing but" fallacy—prayer is nothing but kneeling and saying, "Amen." Reductionism thus oversimplifies complexity in ways comparable to the mental behavior of the child who translates an idea into concreteness. The child who cannot manage "caring" as a concept can manage "mother hugs me," and hence the larger concept becomes the smaller episode. The smaller unit conveys the larger "theory," but caring is certainly larger than hugging.

Oversimplification through reductionism has often characterized the psychological study of religion with the result that complicated occurrences have been described as if they were single, homogeneous patterns. Consider, for example, what happens in worship. People gather at an appointed time and place and perform certain stylized acts. The building has windows, pews, pulpits, altars, shrines—architecture that suggests that people found here are likely to be engaged in religious exercise. On cue, participants stand, kneel, bow, genuflect, posture, laugh, weep, meditate, parade, sing, listen, address, dance. The list is endless, and the possible combinations from religion to religion or within a single religion are numerous. Additionally, worshipers may participate on a variety of levels and for a variety of motives. Some come to be seen; others for private meditation. Some are passive; others aggressive, active. Dependence, release of hostility, acceptance, personal worth, guilt, habit, escape, and countless other personality dynamics may be satisfied from person to person or even for the same person from time to time. So what does worship mean? Obviously any response that attempts to include all the possible components is likely to be too general to be meaningful. But it is equally true that identification of worship with only one or two of its parts will miss its creative design. Its complexity makes it relatively impossible to say that worship is nothing but this or that. Thus the researcher who would understand worship must avoid "hasty monism"—assuming that the complex phenomenon is reducible to universal explanation in terms of one of its features. In religion few things are *simply* anything!

Popular religion, especially in the conservative format used by just plain folks, is consistently plagued by reductionism. The commitment character of faith may be perceived to run counter to critical attitudes toward the forms through which the commitment is expressed. Expressions such as "spiritual" and "will of God" are easily given a kind of literalism that makes God's purpose and the provincial perception of that purpose identical. To return to our example, worship becomes "what *we* do." As a snake-handling preacher was heard to say in an unguarded remark to his congregation, "If other folks don't do it like we do, then it ain't servin' God." A reductionism that cuts perplexing human issues (and their answers) down to manageable size undoubtedly in some measure accounts for the absoluteness and urgency with which Fundamentalism holds to precisely defined doctrines.

Discrediting through Explanation

A fourth danger in applying scientific method to the study of religion (and sometimes a screen for religionists against the insights of contemporary psychology) is the assumption that religious values are somehow eroded when intelligible and cohesive explanations of experience are offered. Theologically the view that explanation is the enemy of the divine rests upon a position of dualistic moralism that assumes an explicit separation between the sacred and the secular and assigns moral superiority to certain dramatic and therefore sacral acts. It seizes upon the expectation that divinity is revealed in extraordinary events, overwhelming the devotee with awe and mystery. Expression through the ordinary world of persons and things is unexpected. In fact such contact, including explanation for supposed supernatural items, may be judged to desecrate the holy.

The experience of a late-adolescent college freshman occurs frequently and reflects the attitude that explanation by way of dynamic factors takes away the "spiritual" content of his encounter with God. As a pre-theology student, he arrives on campus with an intense sense of "the call of God" to minister in the church. His explanations are simple with no attempts to justify his direct and immediate experience of divine presence. Psychological, sociological, or even theological categories simply have no place in his explanations. Directly and simplistically he "knows" that he has been "called" by God. However, his college curriculum begins to expose him to explanatory theories about the authority role of parents and pastor and the influence of powerful unconscious factors in decision-making. He becomes sensitive to ways in which his experience satisfies quite natural personal needs and to how his decision has been reinforced by the positive response of persons who are important to him. In brief, his uncomplicated, relatively naive, and reductionistic explanations begin to become more rational and sophisticated. He now is equipped to understand, according to quite specific theses, an experience formerly couched in mystery. Unfortunately, the next step in the sequence occurs with enough frequency to be considered fairly typical—the sense of God's call loses much of its "spiritual" quality. The prospective minister is likely to feel that explanation has discredited the religious character of his vocational decision. Scientific explanation has secularized his sense of destiny.

But why should it be assumed that deity works only through extraordinary experience? May it not be reasonably expected that divine mystery may be discovered in ordinary bushes, sheep herdsmen, Palestinian peasants, or an old man trudging under a burden? The mythology of religion is marked by the dramatic, but it is also characterized by the ordinary. The idea is conceptualized as incarnation, the understanding that the divine may be discovered in the mundane, the extraordinary in the ordinary. Incarnational themes are important in Hinduism, Judaism, and Buddhism and central in Christianity. The Jewish and Christian Messiah was a figure in whom there was nothing remarkable to the eye of the common man. He had "no form or comeliness" nor beauty to make him desirable,[39] but "in him the whole fullness of deity dwells bodily."[40] For Kierkegaard the genius of religious insight is its ability to see the divine in the ordinary.[41] And if our college freshman can come to appreciate this, he may still speak of being "called by God." In fact, information derived from sociological, psychological, and theological sources may enrich his understanding of the marvel of God's work.

The problems of language, objectivity, reductionism, and explanation are not solvable in the sense that they may be corrected and forgotten. Rather, they always lurk in the shadows as threatening issues demanding constant attention. The researcher, aware that it is impossible to be delivered completely from personal bias, systematically and regularly must "attempt to identify that bias and temporarily suspend it."[42] Implicit assumptions, value systems, and personal convictions are not abandoned, but set out of action, temporarily disconnected, put in brackets.[43] Mature modesty must characterize the work of the scientist. Further, constant attention is given to methods that are being employed in the light of possible distortions. This is not always easily done; the researcher often becomes as protective of methods as of bias. It is nonetheless essential, especially in circumstances where one's personal relations to religious faith and institution may not be favorable.

Also, the limitations of psychological research may provide ready excuse for the religious devotee to avoid psychological insights necessary to understanding personal religion. Both psychol-

---

[39]Isaiah 53:2.

[40]Colossians 2:9.

[41]Søren Kierkegaard, *Concluding Unscientific Postscript* in Robert Bretall, ed., *A Kierkegaard Anthology* (Princeton: Princeton University Press, 1951).

[42]R. B. MacLeod, "Phenomenology: A Challenge to Experimental Psychology," in T. W. Mann, ed., *Behaviorism and Phenomenology* (Chicago: University of Chicago Press, 1964) 54.

[43]Edmund Husserl, *Ideas: General Introduction to Pure Phenomenology* (New York: Collier, 1967).

ogy and religion must willingly accept the parameters without demanding superiority of one over the other.

SUGGESTED READINGS

Scientific Methods

Braginsky, Benjamin M., and Dorothea D. Braginsky. *Mainstream Psychology: A Critique.* New York: Holt, Rinehart and Winston, 1974. Appeals for psychology to examine its value-laden presuppositions.

Cohen, Morris R., and Ernest Nagel. *An Introduction to Logic and Scientific Method.* New York: Harcourt, Brace, and World, 1934. An old but standard description of the scientific method and its pursuit of logic.

Kuhn, Thomas S. *The Structure of Scientific Revolutions,* 2nd ed. Chicago: University of Chicago Press, 1970. Philosophy of science.

Weiner, Irving, ed. *Clinical Methods in Psychology.* New York: John Wiley and Sons, 1976. A survey of modern methods for the practicing psychologist.

Theological Methods

Eckardt, A. Roy, ed. *The Theologian at Work: A Common Search for Understanding.* New York: Harper, 1968.

Healey, F. G., ed. *What Theologians Do.* Grand Rapids MI: Eerdmans, 1970. An introduction to the main features of religious studies.

Kaufman, Gordon D. *An Essay on Theological Method.* Chico CA: Scholars Press, 1975.

Nygren, Anders. *Meaning and Method: Prolegomena to a Scientific Philosophy of Religion and a Scientific Theology.* Philip S. Watson, tr. Philadelphia: Fortress, 1972.

Te Selle, Sallie M. "Parable, Metaphor, and Theology." *Journal of American Academy of Religion* 42 (1974): 630-45.

Wiebe, Don. "Explanation and Theological Method." *Zygon* 11 (1976): 35-49.

Science, Psychology, and Religion

Barbour, Ian G., ed. *Science and Religion: New Perspectives on The Dialogue.* New York: Harper, 1968. Similarities and dissimilarities between science and religion.

_____. *Myths, Models, and Paradigms: A Comparative Study in Science and Religion.* New York: Harper, 1974.

Gilkey, Langdon B. *Religion and the Scientific Future: Reflections on Myth, Science, and Theology.* New York: Harper, 1970.

Hodges, Daniel L. "Breaking a Scientific Taboo: Putting Assumptions about the Supernatural into Scientific Theories of Religion." *Journal for the Scientific Study of Religion* 13 (1974): 393-408.

Hosinski, T. E. "Science, Religion, and the Self-Understanding of Man." *Religion in Life* 42 (1973): 179-93.

Johnson, Roger A., et al. *Critical Issues in Modern Religion*. Englewood Cliffs NJ: Prentice-Hall, 1973.

Narramore, Bruce. "Perspective on the Integration of Psychology and Theology." *Journal of Psychology and Theology* 1 (1973): 3-18.

Schilling, Harold K. *The New Consciousness in Science and Religion*. New York: United Church Press, 1973.

Teihard de Chardin, Pierre. *Science and Christ*. New York: Harper, 1968.

Journals

Journal for the Scientific Study of Religion (1961 to present)

Journal of Psychology and Theology (1973 to present)

Zygon: Journal of Religion and Science (1966 to present)

PART II

PSYCHOLOGICAL INTERPRETATIONS OF RELIGION

Although systematic attempts to analyze religion have been in short supply over the last century, hardly a psychologist has completely avoided the subject. Either by major books on religion or by incidental reference or by inference, religion has attracted attention. How could it be otherwise for those who are concerned with understanding the whole range of human experience, particularly those forces that move persons into action? Our task now is to review what has come out of this discussion. What has mainstream psychology had to say about religion?

Over the course of its history, scientific psychology has been characterized by three dominant intellectual currents: psychoanalysis, behaviorism, and humanistic psychology. For many years psychoanalysis, that treatment procedure and personality theory traced to Sigmund Freud, was ascendant. A second comprehensive theory has emerged under the inspiration of John B. Watson and B. F. Skinner. A host of behaviorists defined psychology as the scientific study of behavior, narrowly understood, and discarded references to mind and consciousness. Their interests have centered upon predicting and controlling the acts of persons without being bothered by concepts such as personality, intention, states of mind, or autonomy. More recently, a third group has begun to coalesce around their common reaction against both psychoanalysis and behaviorism. This tradition is commonly labeled humanistic psychology; it is also regularly called "third force" psychology. A comprehensive theory of personhood has not yet emerged from the research of this group, although they seem to rally around the thought of Abraham Maslow and share unmitigated optimism regarding human potential. Part II focuses upon what each of these psychological traditions has contributed to our understanding of the role of religion in personhood.

CHAPTER THREE

PSYCHOANALYSIS AND RELIGION

In 1859 when Charles Darwin's *Origin of Species* was published, Sigmund Freud was three years old. These two men are towering figures among those who have influenced Western life and thought to such an extent as to have helped to determine its thrust and direction. More than any others, they gave form to the new scientific spirit destined to captivate Western mentality during the twentieth century. Prior to the mid-nineteenth century, persons had been considered independent of the scientific searchlight by virtue of special endowments separating them from all other creation. Freud and Darwin, however, turned the methods of science toward the human animal as one among many species, all subject to the scrutiny of naturalistic inquiry. Their work has been so widely influential that the status of persons in relationship to an emerging scientific spirit was altered, and contemporary Western culture both enjoys the benefits and suffers the risks of the modified position.

The emergence of psychoanalysis as a method for treating certain types of illness and as a theory about the nature of personality is an intimate part of the shifting status of persons in relation to science, and those working in this tradition have written extensively on religion. Freud himself wrote several books and numerous articles on the subject, and those who follow Freud inevitably get around to religion. Their interpretations have generated considerable vigorous response, both positive and negative, and therefore need to be examined with care.

THE GREAT MASTERS

A distinguished Dutch authority, Heije Faber, delineates two periods in the history of psychoanalysis.[1] The first came to an end with the death of the two great masters of the movement, Sigmund Freud and Carl Jung. These pioneers set ajar the door for examining religion in the context of personality development and laid foundations upon which others built. The second period, the age of second generation psychoanalysis, had already begun while the founders were still alive. This stage is marked by upheaval and discontinuity, but also by slowly growing self-identity and increasing clinical concern. A brief look at the giants of the first period will help us better understand the second.

Sigmund Freud: Religion as Illusion

In infancy Sigmund Freud (1856-1939) was taken by his parents to Vienna, Austria, where he spent most of his life and practiced his profession. The young Freud was trained to be a physician, specializing in the treatment of "nervous disorders" when the treatment of such illnesses was generally scientifically unsophisticated and uninformed. Through experience, especially in the treatment of hysteria in women, the perceptive doctor discovered that these disorders were helped considerably by talking-out methods (catharsis). Through catharsis certain connections and motivations were systematically brought to the level of awareness, and thereby personal resources were mobilized toward judging, deciding, and changing. Psychoanalysis was born as an attempt to employ catharsis with system and intent: developing techniques that would bring unconscious factors to consciousness, foster intellec-

---

[1]Heije Faber, *Psychology of Religion* (Philadelphia: Westminster, 1975) 66-72.

tual and emotional insight, and promote subsequent personality changes. Influenced by Jean M. Charcot, a French neurologist and one of his earlier teachers, Freud experimented with hypnosis, free association, and dream analysis in the treatment of hysteria and kindred disorders; and over the decades between his early experiments in the 1880s until his death in 1939 at the age of eighty-three, he evolved psychoanalysis.

Freud's Approach to Personality. Psychoanalysis came into being as a method of treatment, not as personality theory. Naturally and inevitably, however, attempts to purify and standardize therapeutic procedures produced a psychoanalytic theory of personality. The scientific bent of Freud, his concern not only to develop procedures that work efficiently but also to understand why and how they work, produced a theoretical underpinning for the therapeutic process. Both the techniques and the theory-base have come to be identified as psychoanalysis. The long professional career of Freud is the story of a gradually building personality theory through the disciplined clinical treatment of patients. Throughout his career Freud remained able to reevaluate and reconstruct his theories, even after he had reached eighty years of age! Yet running throughout his theory formulations are some enduring consistencies. Karen Horney, a practicing neo-Freudian analyst writing in the year of Freud's death, suggested that three interconnected ideas of Freud were pivotal in his work and his legacy to psychoanalysis.[2]

First, "actions and feelings may be determined by unconscious motivations."[3] As commonplace as it sounds, a key to unlock Freud's thought is the idea that behavior is two-dimensional. It has a *surface* meaning that is obvious; it also has a *depth* meaning often hidden from awareness.[4] The latter is as important as the former, and often

---

[2]Karen Horney, *New Ways in Psychoanalysis* (New York: W. W. Norton, 1939) 18f.

[3]Ibid., 18.

[4]Thus the use of the term "depth psychology," often as a synonym for psychoanalysis. "Depth psychology" is the broader term designating a variety of branches of thought that owe their vitality to basic Freudian ideas, but that develop in their own unique ways. "Psychoanalysis" is usually reserved for the tradition that preserves relatively intact both Freud's therapeutic approach and his personality theory.

more determinative in creating pattern and coherence in personal experience. For example, consider a simple slip of the tongue in terms of this basic psychoanalytic premise. The act initially has a surface meaning and may be described in observable and mechanistic ways. A person because of fatigue or lack of concentration or similarity of sounds uses the "wrong" word. The slip may be so out of place that it sounds humorous. The speaker may attempt to explain his slip on the level of awareness, "I really meant to say. . . ." Psychoanalytically, however, the act is also to be understood on a deeper level of personal meaning. The slip is an occasion when the unconscious darts into consciousness. Attached to the behavior and giving it more dynamic significance are personal associations largely hidden from consciousness. The slip is not *really* an accident, but more basically a revelation of personhood that contains both conscious and unconscious elements. The momentary act that appears accidental and inconsequential is essentially a symbol to which meanings have accrued through the processes of growth, meanings that reside largely in areas of the unconscious. In this sense they are personal in character and must be unraveled, often tediously, through systematic cathartic methods. That behavior has both obvious and hidden meaning is foundational for the Freudian superstructure.

A second fundamental tenet of Freud is "that psychic processes are strictly determined."[5] No psychic act is capricious. It has its antecedents that determine its form and energy. Freud, impressed by the new physics of his day that stressed the conservation of energy, believed that human behavior, like matter itself, possessed this quality.[6] Psychic processes are as strictly determined as physical processes. Meanings attached to a phenomenon are never lost, continually expressing themselves in various ways, attaching themselves to new and sometimes surprising episodes. Hence, understanding any particular act demands questions about antecedent behavior from which the present act derives its meaning. Un-lay-

---

[5]Horney, *New Ways in Psychoanalysis*, 18.

[6]Freud was directly influenced by the German physicist Hermann Helmholtz, who advanced the idea of the conservation of energy. See Calvin S. Hall, *A Primer of Freudian Psychology* (Chicago: World, 1954) 4.

ering such meanings was a major goal of Freudian psychotherapy. Thus the orientation of psychoanalysis is toward the past, and the earliest stages of infantile behavior receive considerable attention as setting the pattern for subsequent activity.

Third, Freud concluded "that the motivations driving us are emotional forces."[7] The operational word here is "emotional," denoting the principle that personality is dynamic. Freud gave wide berth to instinctual, impulsive, passionate drives in personality—drives that demand satisfaction in either acceptable or unacceptable ways. Specific behavioral acts are accordingly to be understood as resolutions of conflicts between raw selfhood (libido) and all those social forces that would bring it under control.

Freud spent his professional career devising and purifying techniques for helping persons manage their determined, dynamic, and often unconsciously controlled behavior. Further, he attempted to develop a theoretical framework within which such behavior could be understood. Although it is too simplistic to reduce Freudian psychoanalysis to a few categories, several concepts in his theory system seem to be basic for understanding his approach to religion.[8]

Freud thought of personality as composed of three interacting systems, traditionally labeled id, ego, and superego, but perhaps better thought of as It, I, and over-I. *Id* is the raw stuff of which persons are made, a kind of primordial energy directed toward unhindered expression. Id is impulsive, irrational, asocial, and self-seeking, guided only by pleasure. But id cannot always have its way. Avenues for immediate satisfaction may not be available, or uncontrolled expression may create more anxiety than can be comfortably borne. Thus through threats of tension and pain, the real world of interrelationships inevitably thwarts id's unhindered expression and demands compromise between id's demands and society's standards. Reality regularly impedes pleasure and requires adjustments in patterns by which satisfaction is achieved, a development

---

[7]Horney, *New Ways in Psychoanalysis,* 18.

[8]See Hall, *A Primer of Freudian Psychology,* for a quite useful secondary summary of basic Freudian concepts.

crucial in the emergence of religion. In this situation two psychological control systems emerge. *Ego* and *superego* attempt to control the unhindered expression of id to avoid or at least reduce the threat of tension and pain. Through dynamic processes of postponement and discovering new patterns, ego buys enough satisfaction for id's needs to enable the person to survive in the real world. Superego acts as a moral sentinel in the process, keeping before the personality either ideal goals (ego ideal) or socially expected standards (conscience). All of the systems operate unconsciously and may be discovered only in disguise. Dreams, wit, and errors are especially helpful in unveiling the activity of id, ego, and superego.

According to classical psychoanalysis, personality emerges as the interaction of these three systems. Freud proceeded to describe various dynamic patterns by which the systems operate and ways in which both pleasure and pain are managed. The crucial context for id, ego, and superego development was for Freud the infantile family situation. In the early relationships of father-mother-son (Oedipus complex) the child confronts rudimentary expressions of id and its earliest frustrations. The most typical pattern in the Oedipus situation consists of the desire of the son for his mother, placing him in competition with his father. The father's superior strength thwarts the son's immediate fulfillment of id desires, and the frustration sets in motion the development of ego and superego controls. Freud gave considerably more attention to the masculine experience of the family triangle, reflecting the patriarchal emphasis of his own cultural and personal background, but he also discussed Oedipus from the perspective of the little girl. Theoretically, the daughter is subject to the same dynamic process, but in reverse order (Electra complex). She desires father and must learn to manage the repression of these desires, as well as her fear and hate of mother perceived as threat.

Complex family relationships may distort the Oedipus situation, but in its simplest form—child desires parent of opposite sex and is threatened by parent of same sex—is the crucible out of which personhood is born. In attempting a resolution of the early infantile conflict between desire and threat, both males and females use an assortment of "mechanisms"—identification, sublimation, displacement, repression, projection, reaction formation, fixation, regression. These are methods by which the growing person attempts to overcome or adjust to the frustration, conflict, and anxiety implicit in the early family environment. The mechanisms operate unconsciously, and the patterns by which they do this are the stuff of which personality is made. In this way personality is deeply rooted in the Oedipus or Electra situation; in infancy and childhood, personality patterns are firmly fixed. Subsequent growth and development are largely a replay of enduring infantile designs. Hence, Freud sought to return his patients to the infantile situation and restructure id, ego, and superego in such ways that they could survive without being overwhelmed by anxiety, tension, and pain.

Freud's Understanding of Religion. Freud interpreted religion, particularly the psychological origins of God, within the context of his personality theory. Throughout his long career he maintained an interest in religion, but the recovery of his views is somewhat complicated. As a creative thinker he used several models to describe religion, and these are not easily woven into a single pattern. Sometimes Freud spoke of religion as an obsession.[9] At other times he saw it as fulfillment of infantile wishes.[10] On still other occasions, he referred to it as illusion.[11] These models overlap considerably, but they are not easily made into a single theoretical structure.

Also, Freud's personal attitude toward religion sometimes creates suspicion that the scientific Freud occasionally yields to the polemical Freud, leading him to draw conclusions beyond the evidence. This charge has often been leveled at *Totem and Taboo,* a book in which Freud assumes that the Oedipus situation is replicated in the experience of the race and explains in large measure the historical origins of religion. That sociologists and anthropologists find little or no evidence for the existence of cultural phe-

---

[9]See Freud, "Obsessive Acts and Religious Practices," in *Collected Papers,* vol. 2, Joan Riviere, trans. (London: Hogarth, 1949) 25-35.

[10]See *New Introductory Lectures,* W. J. H. Sprott, trans. (New York: W. W. Norton, 1933) 219f.

[11]See *The Future of an Illusion,* W. D. Robson-Scott, trans., and James Strachey, ed. (Garden City NY: Doubleday, 1964) 47-53.

nomena that Freud conjectured casts some suspicion on the formulations. The personal religious orientation of Freud and some "loose" methodology have led some religionists to reject his interpretation without serious attention. And with some justification they see Freud's definition of religion as quite narrow, restricted to beliefs and practices associated with the idea of a transcendent God operating in an authoritarian relationship to believers.[12] He seems to have been unaware that religion comes in many forms and to have been content to treat threatening authoritarian religion as the entire picture.

In spite of these irritating difficulties, however, Freud surely is one of the most seminal interpreters of religion to appear in the last century and cannot be dismissed without a careful hearing. For him religion was a subject for serious study, and his theoretical formulations must be evaluated for what they may add to a broad scientific understanding of religion.

For Freud religion, as any other pattern of behavior, was to be understood dynamically, that is, within the context of personality growth and development. The significant questions about religion were not those having to do with the truth or reality of God, but those having to do with religion as a psychic phenomenon. How do religious ideas and acts, that like all behavior are loaded with depth content, function in the maintenance, survival, and growth of persons? Insofar as psychoanalysis focuses upon this dimension of meaning, it is, as Freud says in a letter to his friend, the Swiss pastor Oskar Pfister, "neither religious nor the opposite."[13]

Freud's view of religion is capsuled in an often cited statement made early in his career:

> Psychoanalysis has made us familiar with the intimate connection between the father-complex and the belief in God; it has shown us that a personal God is, psychologically, nothing other than an exalted father, and it brings us evidence every day of how young people lose their religious beliefs as soon as their father's authority

---

[12]See *New Introductory Lectures* 216-24, and *Civilization and Its Discontents*, James Strachey, ed. (New York: W. W. Norton, 1962) 13.

[13]Cited in Ernest Jones, *The Life and Work of Sigmund Freud*, vol. 3 (New York: Basic Books, 1957) 352.

breaks down. Thus we recognize that the roots of the need for religion are in the parental complex; the almighty and just God, and kindly Nature, appear to us grand sublimations of father and mother, or rather as revivals and restorations of the young child's ideas of them.[14]

Freud wrote these words in 1910, predating the publication of his major works on religion. *Totem and Taboo*, published in 1913; *The Future of an Illusion*, in 1927; and *Moses and Monotheism*, in 1939, are significant elaborations of the fundamental thesis that Oedipus and God are intimately related. The psychological origins of God reside in the continuous replay of the infantile drama of collision between parent and child. Like other forms of culture, religion is a human attempt to cope with both instinctual demands and threats of pain and death written on a cosmic screen. As the infant adjusts, however reluctantly, to a father both desired and feared, so the adult accepts culture to avoid the fear of extinction and/or intolerable deprivation. "The central thrust of Freud's psychology of religion . . . rests on a conception of man as a creature whose demand for personal survival will not brook disappointment."[15] A person's strongest unconscious wishes are focused upon the avoidance of pain in the fulfillment of raw personal desires. Religion in all its complexity rests on this foundation, and its various expressions are consensus devices for the management of these urgent Oedipal conflicts.

Crucial to Freud's interpretation of the psychological origins of God is his understanding of object relations. Accordingly, objects, particularly the father, carry heavy emotional weight. In the Oedipus environment the infant incorporates into self those elements necessary to personal survival, that is, parental imagos. Even after the resolution of the Oedipus complex, the personal significance of father, and in some sense mother also, lives on in these parental imagos. The imagos survive in the subsequent experience of the in-

---

[14]Freud, *Leonardo da Vinci and a Memory of His Childhood*, Alan Tyson, trans. (New York: W. W. Norton, 1964) 73.

[15]Peter A. Bertocci, "Psychological Interpretations of Religious Experience," in Merton P. Strommen, ed., *Research on Religious Development* (New York: Hawthorn, 1971) 14.

dividual although they may be modified under the impact of other significant objects.

"The birth of the living God" occurs precisely in this context.[16] For the growing person God is the representation of these images, chiefly parental, as they have been colored by relations with other significant objects. In this sense God is a kind of illusion and religion is a kind of public neurosis. Both god and religion originate in the need to find a comfortable compromise between instinctual demands and threatening reality. What persons cannot satisfy directly, they satisfy by creating God as the representation of parental images. This God serves a double psychological function. He rewards those who renounce their raw humanity (heaven for good service) and he reassures against capricious threat (loves even the sinner). God is the kind of father a person wants and needs,

> born from man's need to make his helplessness tolerable and built up from the material of memories of the helplessness of his own childhood and the childhood of the human race.[17]

Functioning in this way, religion is a powerful force in human life and ought to be valued as a socialized means for managing otherwise unbearable fear, threat, and anxiety. But it bears no other relation to reality. Religion is an illusion in that it is created out of infantile wishes for satisfaction and security and thrives only insofar as it is continuously fed by childish helplessness.

What is the future of this illusion? Certainly there is little hope in theological explanation. For one thing, the voice of the intellect is weak indeed when compared to the strength of wishes rooted in the Oedipus situation. But more importantly, attempts to give rational support to the illusion will erode the very basis for its survival. Religion is valuable as an illusion; however, its value is affective, not rational. Rational defense of religion saps the strength of its emotional appeal. Since religion thrives on its emotional confirmation of the repressions of hatred and fear growing out of the

---

[16]The phrase is the title of a valuable book by Ana-Maria Rizzuto, *The Birth of the Living God: A Psychoanalytic Study* (Chicago: University of Chicago Press, 1979). See especially 29-37, 54-84.

[17]Ibid., 25.

Oedipus situation, theological argument justifying God on any other grounds does nothing more than weaken religion's vital function. Freud puts the matter bluntly:

> Since men are so little accessible to reasonable argument and are so entirely governed by their instinctual wishes, why should one set out to deprive them of an instinctual satisfaction and replace it by reasonable arguments?[18]

Religion affords affective outlet and ought not to be taken away by force of argument. The behavior would not allow this, and "even if it did succeed with some, it would be cruelty."[19]

Thus for Freud religion as an illusion should and would survive as a useful instrument in the growth process. But outside its value as an illusion to buttress humans against otherwise intolerable circumstances, religion, according to Freud, is not only useless but detrimental to growth. Persons "cannot remain children forever; they must in the end face education to reality."[20] Sublimated expressions of infantile forces (as in religion) serve only to delay the maturation process in which growing persons confront reality directly and depend upon their own rational resources. It is not likely that the human race will attain that ideal state where intelligence is primary over instincts, all illusions are renounced, and earthly existence made tolerable. Hence religion might be temporarily indulged, but, since as illusion it is a significant and widespread hindrance to the ideal goal, religion must be renounced by those few who are able to live without it. Heaven must be left to angels and sparrows![21]

Although Freud was overtly skeptical of religion's role in the experience of mature persons, he held optimistic hope for direction from science. He did not anticipate the quick arrival of that utopian day when the human race could live without its illusions,

---

[18]Ibid., 77.

[19]Ibid., 80.

[20]Ibid., 81.

[21]Freud quotes the couplet from Heine's poem *Deutschland* in *The Future of an Illusion*, 82.

but these needed to be de-emphasized. And science was the vehicle for moving toward that goal. A telling statement concludes *The Future of an Illusion.*

> No, our science is not illusion. But an illusion it would be to suppose that what science cannot give us we can get elsewhere.[22]

Basically then, Freud sees religion as an illusion in that its enduring character comes from the deeply embedded, dynamic force of repressed conflicts between instinctual and social demands. Infantile wishes for ideal resolution to these conflicts are projected upon the screen of ultimate reality and read back as "God." Second, as an illusion religion is a valuable, sublimated way of survival, but ought not be supported on grounds that it is either an accurate interpretation of reality or the right, moral, and mature way to face life. Third, growth demands that dependence upon the illusion vanish in favor of science, whose efforts are directed toward the clarification of the real world that always takes precedence over the wishful world.

Carl G. Jung: Religion as Archetype

The work of Sigmund Freud quickly attracted a circle of associates, most of whom became close friends of the psychoanalytic grand master. These included such stalwarts as Otto Rank, Alfred Adler, Ernest Jones, Theodor Reik, and Oskar Pfister. Among these early Freudian disciples, Carl Gustav Jung (1875-1961), the son of a Swiss clergyman, stands out above all the others, especially for psychology of religion. As a practicing psychiatrist in Zurich, Jung came in contact with Freud's work, and the two developed a warm friendship until a breach in 1913 accentuated earlier tension and broke their personal relationship. Evidently, the point of contention was Jung's advancing interest in parapsychological phenomena and his mythological interpretation of symbolism. These interests led Jung to question the fundamental Freudian thesis that trauma in the Oedipal situation was the sole cause of repression. Freud evidently was suspicious of Jung's procedures as too subjective and speculative and therefore a violation of good scientific

---

[22]Ibid., 92.

methodology. According to Jung's account, the great master like a dominating father placed his personal authority above truth, insisting upon the preservation of his Oedipal theory intact.[23] Whatever the real causes for their theoretical and personal disagreements, the breach went unhealed and Jung went his own way.

Although Jung's work has not been as widely influential as Freud's, his attitude toward religion has made him generally more acceptable to religionists. One of the most often cited quotations from Jung appears toward the end of his *Modern Man in Search of a Soul:*

> Among all my patients in the second half of life—that is to say, over thirty-five—there has not been one whose problem in the last resort was not that of finding a religious outlook on life.[24]

The statement is often taken as an affirmation of religious truth, but like Freud, Jung interprets religion apart from the question of its theological authenticity. His generally sympathetic attitude needs closer examination.

For Jung religion was a quite significant item in both individual and racial history, and ideas on the subject are found throughout his writings. Four works stand out as particularly important: *Modern Man in Search of a Soul* (1933), *Psychology and Religion* (1938), *Answer to Job* (1954), and especially the chapter entitled "Late Thoughts" in the autobiographical *Memories, Dreams, Reflections* (1963). In these books both Eastern and Western religion are interpreted around several key concepts that are the core of Jungian psychology.

Collective Unconscious. Jung begins with the basic formulation in psychoanalytic thought that behavior is to be understood in terms of both its surface and depth meaning. Like Freud he sees a primordial tension between conscious and unconscious life, but there is a fundamental difference in the way the two conceptualize the

---

[23]See Carl G. Jung, *Memories, Dreams, Reflections,* Aniela Jeffs, ed., and Richard Winston and Clara Winston, trans. (New York: Pantheon, 1963) 146-69.

[24]Jung, *Modern Man in Search of a Soul,* W. S. Dell and C. F. Baynes, trans. (London: K. Paul, Trench, Trubner, 1933) 264.

unconscious. For Freud the unconscious is individual, dynamically composed of all those instinctual and repressed materials associated with the anxiety of Oedipus. For Jung the unconscious is personal and far more. Over and above the personal sphere of individual drives, memories, and repressions is the deeper stratum of the collective unconscious that incorporates universal material. The collective unconscious is:

> the all-controlling deposit of ancestral experience from untold millions of years, the echo of prehistoric world-events to which each century adds an infinitesimally small amount of variation and differentiation.[25]

Just as persons share common body structures containing vestiges of earlier developmental stages, they share a common psychic history in the collective unconscious.

For Jung the collective, not the individual, unconscious is the seat of religion.[26] The basic processes of religion arise from the collective unconscious and are real in the sense that they are psychic facts. Specific forms of personal religion, as well as the larger religions of mankind, are temporal and spatial expressions of underlying collective unconscious. Religious dogma, ritual, and myth, whether primitive or modern or from whatever tradition they come, derive not from personal needs as infantile wishes but from reality existing over and above individual constructs.[27] Matters such as religious conversion place individuals in contact with a wide reservoir of ancestral experience constantly intruding on personal consciousness. Thus religion is not for Jung a vestige of infantilism to be disposed of therapeutically, but an avenue of contact with the highest potentialities of personhood as preserved across the cen-

------

[25]Jung, *Contributions to Analytic Psychology*, H. G. and C. F. Baynes, trans. (London: Routledge and Kegan Paul, 1928) 162.

[26]Jung, *Psychology and Religion* (New Haven: Yale University Press, 1938) 5-6, 111-12.

[27]Many interpreters have pointed to similarities between Jung's concepts and Rudolf Otto's ideas of *numinous* as expressed in his classic, *The Idea of the Holy* (New York: Oxford University Press, 1926), and Jung himself in *Psychology and Religion*, 4, acknowledges his dependence upon Otto.

turies of human history in collective unconscious. It opens the depths of the human soul, often with an intelligence and purposefulness superior to conscious insight. Its vehicle for doing this is the archetype.

Archetypes. Jung believed that the collective unconscious was continued from generation to generation through archetypes, archaic and universal images that have existed from remotest times. He observed striking parallels in symbols used by otherwise diverse personalities and religious groups and accounted for the similarities in terms of the archetypes. People across cultures and historical periods have in common the collective unconscious that manifests itself in universal patterns and motifs. In the words of Jung, archetypes are "forms or images of a collective nature which occur practically all over the earth as constituents of myths and at the same time as autochthonous, individual products of unconscious origin."[28] These are latently present in all persons and will be given symbolic expression according to the historical situation to which individuals belong.

Archetypes in the Jungian scheme are the "stuff" of all religion. Through intensive study of mythology and comparative religion, Jung concluded that fixed themes regularly appear.[29] These archetypical concepts take symbolic form in various religious expressions and illustrate core solidarity among the various religious traditions of human history. All religions are repositories of archetypical images, and the purpose of ritual is to place persons in meaningful contact with these transpersonal categories.

Jung's view of archetypes and their relationship to religion is illustrated in his interpretation of God.[30] He carefully avoided the affirmation of the existence of God, except as an archetypical image. (In Jungian thought God and God-image are synonymous.) God for Jung was essentially a psychological event, an archetype that could be affirmed. He spent considerable time in his writing

---

[28]Jung, *Psychology and Religion*, 63.

[29]A helpful article on this subject is Henry C. Brooks, "Analytic Psychology and the Image of God," *Andover Newton Quarterly*, New Series 6 (1965): 35-55.

[30]Jung, *Psychology and Religion*, 74.

delineating the character of the God-image, especially emphasizing the need to incorporate femininity, which he believed had unfortunately been too little regarded in the Christian emphasis upon
the masculine Trinity.[31] But whatever its content, the God-image is
a real but subjective phenomenon; the psyche creates its manifestation of the God-image that is residual in the collective unconscious as archetype. Nonetheless, God has not been invented by
individual persons; it must be remembered that archetypes have a
life of their own, identity beyond the personal. Thus the experience of the God-image comes upon persons spontaneously. Religious affirmations and creeds are so many ways of attempting to
bring into consciousness the archetype God whose fundamental
realness belongs to the collective unconscious.

Individuation. Individuation is a term used by Jung in connection with the processes by which persons come to terms with personal and collective unconscious. Growth and maturation are to be
compared to an acorn becoming an oak. Each person, according to
Jung, is in touch with an archetypical self, his *imago Dei,* and self-
realization is the ultimate goal in life. Individuation as "the unfolding and integration of human individuality . . . is a lifelong process
by which what is potential in a human being is brought to realization and is integrated into the wholeness of a mature life."[32] The
process occurs as the collective unconscious becomes increasingly
a part of an integrated whole with the consciousness of persons.

For Jung individuation *is* the religious pilgrimage. In his autobiography he describes himself as "a splinter of the infinite deity"
and reflects upon his own pilgrimage as the discovery of this fact.[33]
Primarily through dreams, and always disguised in symbols, the
unconscious bombards consciousness with "knowledge of a special
sort;"[34] the divine life within strives towards awareness. This dis-

---

[31]Ibid., Chapter 11. Cf. Joan C. Englesman, *The Feminine Dimension of the Divine*
(Philadelphia: Westminster, 1979).

[32]Brooks, "Analytic Psychology and the Image of God," 50.

[33]Jung, *Memories, Dreams, Reflections,* 4.

[34]Ibid., 311.

covery is individuation, the genuine movement toward selfhood and the telling issue of life. Jung concludes:

> As far as we can discern, the sole purpose of human existence is to kindle a light in the darkness of mere being. It may even be assumed that just as the unconscious affects us, so the increase in our consciousness affects the unconscious.[35]

Such sketchy description of Jung's thoughts on religion obviously makes too simple these items that he examined in their complexity. Nonetheless, the brief discussion illustrates an approach to religion both akin to and different from Freud's. Moving within the same framework of depth understanding of behavior and maintaining an emphasis upon the crucial character of infancy, Jung saw religion as more than neurotic facade. It is not veiled wish fulfillment, but part of the nature of things. Its efficacy depends on enduring archetypes present in the psychological heritage of persons and whose discovery is human destiny. For many psychologists Jung is too subjective and romantic in his methodology, and for many religionists he is too naturalistic in his theology. Even so, his interpretation of religion along lines of collective unconscious, archetypes, and individuation gave to him a pattern for a unified understanding of religion across sectarian lines. In so doing, he may have both contributed to the ecumenical spirit and opened the door of reconciliation between psychoanalysis and religion.

SECOND - GENERATION PSYCHOANALYSTS

The great masters of psychoanalysis were both pioneers and prophets. As such they are to be evaluated not so much by the details of their theories as by the types of inquiry that they set in motion. More scrupulous theory building belongs to second generation psychoanalysts, both more carefully scientific in their procedure and more clinical in their concerns.

A discussion of this period, however, faces some difficulty. Contemporary psychoanalysis is no more unified than were the founding fathers. It is therefore impossible to select one or two persons who represent what has happened in psychoanalysis. Di-

---

[35]Ibid., 326.

vergence and upheaval still characterize the movement. Thus the selection here of Erich Fromm and Erik Erikson is not meant to suggest that their work sets forth the character of contemporary psychoanalysis, but both Fromm and Erikson typify recent advances in psychoanalysis. Fromm has addressed the religious issue directly, and Erikson has structured a model of personality growth with clear religious overtones.

Erich Fromm: Religion as Human Love

Erich Fromm (1900-1980) was born, educated, and spent his early professional career in Germany. He came to the United States in 1934 and subsequently gave his attention to a system of treatment that he chose to call "humanistic psychoanalysis." Fromm belongs generally to a group labeled "neo-Freudians" (including Karen Horney, Harry Stack Sullivan, and Abram Kardiner). Fromm was not particularly happy with the term neo-Freudian, but he worked in the analytic tradition. He described himself as "a pupil and translator of Freud who is attempting to bring out his most important discoveries in order to enrich and to deepen them by liberating them from the somewhat narrow libido theory."[36] To achieve this goal Fromm drew heavily upon the social sciences, especially in his interpretation of religion. His basic works include *Escape from Freedom* (1941), *Man for Himself* (1947), *The Sane Society* (1955), *The Art of Loving* (1956), *The Dogma of Christ* (1970), and *The Anatomy of Human Destructiveness* (1973), all of which have ethical and religious overtones and implications. Fromm's short *Psychoanalysis and Religion* (1950) is his systematic analysis of religion.

God Is I. Fromm's view of religion is deeply rooted in his humanistic view: all persons are intrinsically religious in the sense that the need for "a system of orientation and devotion" is universal.[37] In Fromm's words,

There is no one without a religious need, a need to have a frame

---

[36]Richard I. Evans, *Dialogue with Erich Fromm* (New York: Harper, 1966) 59.

[37]Erich Fromm, *Psychoanalysis and Religion* (New Haven: Yale University Press, 1950) 24.

of orientation and an object of devotion. . . . The question is not *religion or not*, but *which* kind of religion, whether it is one further-ing man's development, the unfolding of his specifically human powers, or one paralyzing them.[38]

Thus the fundamental human problem is unfolding human pow-ers, discovering the freedom implicit in human existence. Persons must never yield to the temptation to "escape from freedom" by re-turning to the secure womb of animal existence. Primary ties with nature must be severed, alienation overcome, and anxiety over po-tential freedom mastered.

How may these high goals be achieved? Two things are crucial. First, any authority that promises security at the expense of free-dom must be rejected. Whether from father, state, or religion, standards *imposed* from outside destroy human potential. Second, persons must tap their human resource to love. Persons lay hold on their genuine humanity through love as care, responsibility, and respect. Love is deeply rooted in human beings and the channel through which they may experience oneness with themselves and other persons. "The aim of life is to unfold man's love and reason and . . . every other human activity must be subordinated to this aim."[39]

For Fromm religion is to be understood in the context of this human potential to love. The historical religions are symbol sys-tems that, like politics or psychoanalysis, serve their correct pur-pose when they support the humanistic enterprise. Fromm states without equivocation that "there is no spiritual realm outside of man or transcending him . . . no meaning to life, except the meaning man himself gives to it."[40] Therefore, for Fromm Freud's criticism of the idea of God is correct to a point, but it must be carried fur-ther. The logic of "good" religion itself demands the negation of the concept of God. The mature person accepts God as a symbol in which humanity, at an earlier stage of evolution, has expressed a

---

[38]Ibid., 25, 26.

[39]Erich Fromm, *The Sane Society* (New York: Holt, Rinehart and Winston, 1955) 173.

[40]Erich Fromm, *The Art of Loving* (New York: Harper, 1956) 72.

consummate striving for love, truth, and justice. For such a person "God is I, inasmuch as I am human."[41] When persons become adults, they must put away childish things and affirm their own humanity, the highest virtue.

Authoritarian versus Humanistic Religion. Quite obviously, all people do not recognize this as the goal of religion, continuing in infantile fashion to think of God as a helping, controlling father. Fromm labels the religion of immaturity as *authoritarian.*[42] Power, control, surrender, and obedience characterize this type of religion. Personal freedom is sacrificed through surrender to a transcending power. But worse, that power is considered to be *entitled* to obedience. Obedience is its main virtue; disobedience its cardinal sin. Over against the awesome God of authoritarian religion persons are conceived as powerless, insignificant, and dependent, a view that violates their worth and strength as human beings. In this way authoritarian religion sacrifices the freedom and integrity of individuals for the feeling of being protected by an overwhelming power. For Fromm the price is too high.

Humanistic religion, on the other hand, promotes optimum freedom and inner strength.[43] This type of religious experience centers around human possibilities. Virtue is self-realization, not surrender and obedience. "Inasmuch as humanistic religions are theistic, God is a symbol of *man's own powers* which he tries to realize in his life, and is not a symbol of force and domination, having *power over man.*"[44] Faith is an affirmation of one's own thought and feeling, not assent to authoritative propositions. The mood of humanistic religion is joy; not sorrow, shame, and guilt. The humanistic religious attitude thus frees persons to be themselves and thereby lays claim to religion in the deepest sense of the word.

Fromm saw authoritarian religion illustrated in Calvin's theology and, in secular form, in Fascism. Illustrations of humanism are early Buddhism, Taoism, and the teachings of Isaiah, Jesus, Soc-

---

[41]Ibid., 70.

[42]Ibid., 34-37.

[43]Ibid., 37-42.

[44]Ibid., 37.

rates, and Spinoza. He was particularly attracted to mystical trends in both Eastern and Western religious tradition. The types of religion that Fromm described are easily observed in a religious environment that includes absolutist systems from Protestant Fundamentalism to Shiite Islam. His work is a startling reminder that religion may thwart human beneficence, denying the very end that the founder intended. But Fromm too easily overgeneralizes about religious systems. All Islam does not carry the Shiite authoritarianism, nor is all Christianity extractive of human freedom. A humanistic Isaiah could hardly sense the holy god "high and lifted up" and confess of himself, "Woe is me! for I am lost; for I am a man of unclean lips."[45] Nor would a humanistic Jesus have called God his Father and admonished his followers to become as children.[46] Fromm's rather casual dismissal of theistic religion as authoritarian, however, ought not cloud his valid point that certain brands of religion violate the fundamental worth of God's creation and risk being used as vehicles of authoritarian control.

Erik Erikson: Religion as Epigenetic Virtue

Probably the most widely discussed and influential psychoanalyst in recent years has been Erik H. Erikson (1902-), another emigrant from Europe to the United States who brought with him a psychoanalytic background and critical thinking about basic Freudian concepts. For many years Erikson has taught at Harvard University and written extensively in a style comprehensible to the intelligent layman. His ideas, especially on the dynamics of adolescence, have been widely disseminated through numerous books and journal articles, as well as more popular interpretation. Erikson's key concepts may be found in *Childhood and Society* (revised, 1963); *Insight and Responsibility* (1964); *Identity: Youth and the Life Cycle* (1959); and *Youth: Change and Challenge* (1963), a collection of essays edited by Erikson for which he wrote the lead article.[47] In two

---

[45]Isaiah 6:1, 5.

[46]Cf. Matthew 18:1-4; Luke 18:15-17.

[47]The last book was reissued in 1965 under the title *The Challenge of Youth* (Garden City NY: Doubleday, 1965).

significant biographical studies, *Young Man Luther* (1958) and *Gandhi's Truth* (1969), Erikson applies his personality theory to the development of two outstanding religious figures.

The Eight Stages of Man. The primary contribution of Erikson to the advancement of psychoanalytic theory is his understanding that all of life is dynamic. He accepts the Freudian view that infancy is crucial in personal development, but he also sees later stages as having their own developmental significance. Adolescence, adulthood, and old age are in their own right creative periods in which personality begun in infancy continues to be reshaped. These later stages are dependent upon earlier infantile developments, but they contain more than the replay of Oedipal resolutions. Erikson suggests an eight-stage model within which personality development is to be understood. These are set forth in the revised and enlarged edition of *Childhood and Society* and provide the framework for subsequent elaborations and clarifications.[48] Each of the stages has its own psychodynamic tension, the resolution of which produces its own "virtue," that is, character strength. The unfolding of these stages is described by Erikson as his "epigenetic diagram:"[49]

STAGE	PROBLEM	VIRTUE
1. Oral-Sensory	Trust vs. Mistrust	Hope
2. Muscular-Anal	Autonomy vs. Shame and Guilt	Will Power
3. Locomotor-Genital	Initiative vs. Guilt	Purpose
4. Latency	Industry vs. Inferiority	Competence
5. Adolescence	Identity vs. Role Diffusion	Fidelity
6. Young Adulthood	Intimacy vs. Isolation	Love
7. Adulthood	Generativity vs. Stagnation	Care
8. Old Age-Maturity	Ego Integrity vs. Despair	Wisdom

Epigenetic Virtue. Crucial to Erikson's model are the twin concepts of epigenesis and virtue. By epigenesis he means the emer-

---

[48]Erik Erikson, *Childhood and Society,* rev. ed. (New York: W. W. Norton, 1963) 247-74. See also, Richard I. Evans, *Dialogue with Erik Erikson* (New York: Harper, 1967) 11-58.

[49]See Erikson, *Childhood and Society,* 48-108.

gence of one stage out of the other. The eight stages develop in sequence; the psychological resolution of the issue of one stage prepares the way for the emergence of the successive stage. Resolution at each stage produces a basic human strength, that is, a virtue. Here the word carries no necessary religious content, but designates a psychosocial attitude, a vital strength of character that emerges out of the struggles typical of each of the eight stages. The virtues are "built into the schedule of individual development as well as into the basic structure of any social order."[50] Thus human growth is understood as a series of eight connected stages, each growing out of the preceding one and each characterized by its own tension. Out of the struggle of each period to manage its tension emerges a peculiar strength of character, a virtue, that enables a person to move to the subsequent stage.

A discussion of the first stage will illustrate the pattern of Erikson's interpretation. During the first year of life, the infant is obviously incorporative, taking in food, warmth, and attention. In this relationship to the environment, primarily in the form of mother, the rudimentary tension between trust and mistrust is present. In the crucible of simple relationships the infant learns that features of the environment can be trusted—mother feeds, cuddles, reassures. But mistrust is also essential to psychosocial development. The child must learn what in the environment cannot be trusted. Realistic relations to the world are born out of the balanced exposure to these opposing experiences; neither trust nor mistrust is inherently "good" or "bad." According to Erikson, "a certain ratio of trust and mistrust in our basic social attitude is the critical factor."[51] Out of the interplay between trust and mistrust in which the two are counterbalanced, virtue emerges. In the first stage the virtue is *hope*, a confidence that one knows what to expect from the surrounding world. Hope for Erikson is not something invented by theologians to placate fear but the confidence that the infant derives from the balanced struggle between trust and mistrust. Religion may sanctify hope and provide rituals to give it visibility, but it is born and transmitted in basic parent-child relationships.

---

[50]Erik Erikson, *Insight and Responsibility* (New York: W. W. Norton, 1964) 175.

[51]Evans, *Dialogue with Erik Erikson*, 15.

Hope is the basis ingredient of all strengths. As it emerges, the way is prepared for the next stage (epigenesis) with its own distinctive problems and possibilities. Erikson's work has focused upon the conceptual elaboration of the eight stages. His attention to adolescence has been particularly influential, stimulating considerable professional and popular discussion of identity and identity crisis. Erikson understands the basic adolescent struggle to be between identity and role diffusion. As the adolescent discovers who he is, the capacity for fidelity to some ideological point of view emerges. The connections here with religious conversion seem fairly obvious.[52]

Luther, Identity, and Fidelity. In the quite important book *Young Man Luther,* Erikson applies his psychoanalytic method to the experience of the young reformer. The book purports to evaluate the entire life of Luther but focuses upon the identity crises of his adolescence, the period when he was attempting to "forge for himself some central perspective and direction, some working unity, out of the effective remnants of his childhood and the hopes of his anticipated adulthood."[53] Erikson proceeds with caution, realizing the limitations of interpretations based upon written documents without corrective face-to-face contact.

Erikson makes no claim to understand totally the religion of Luther but proceeds on the assumption that he can shed light upon the processes by which Luther arrived at a clearer consciousness of his identity and at an ideology that supported that identity. The book's thesis is that Luther's day offered religion as an ideological option that the young man exercised in resolving the psychosocial conflicts that belonged to his infancy, childhood, and adolescence. From limited records Erikson attempts to unravel the complex patterns by which Luther derived from his mother an experience of basic trust, resolved a disruptive relationship with his father, wrestled with diffusion of identity, moved toward his own identity, and formulated a revised religious ideology to support that identity. For

---

[52]John J. Gleason, Jr., *Growing up to God* (Nashville: Abingdon, 1975), too briefly but suggestively attempts a developmental psychology of religion following Erikson's model.

[53]Erikson, *Young Man Luther* (New York: W. W. Norton, 1958) 14.

Luther personal growth and religious pilgrimage were so inter-
laced as to make them inseparable. As Erikson puts it, "The characteristics of Luther's theological advance can be compared to
certain steps in psychological maturation which way man must
take."[54]

According to Erikson's analysis, Luther's entrance into the
cloister was a crucial episode in his psychological and religious
growth toward identity. This illustrates society's willingness to allow the adolescent a moratorium in his identity crisis and afforded
the young man Luther a protective environment for his struggles
with diffusion of roles. Obedience to whom? To God, to the Pope,
or to Caesar? To his natural father or to his Father in heaven? Luther's monastic experience was characterized by "a fierce . . . struggle in him between destructive and constructive forces, and between
regressive and progressive alternatives."[55] Nonetheless, the struggle occurred in the "best organized, most sincere, and least cor-
rupted parts of the Church."[56] Erikson carefully delineates how the
cloister provided a maternal environment replicating the basic trust
of infancy and a religion that fostered identity selection. The healing aspects of monastic life were adequate enough to allow for the
future greatness of Luther, although episodic crises continued to
reawaken infantile and adolescent conflicts. In Luther the solution
of the adolescent identity crisis was partially unsuccessful and fragmentary, but enough resolution occurred to allow growth to proceed.

Erikson's intriguing engagement with Luther's pilgrimage
demonstrates a sympathetic application of a psychoanalytic model
to religious experience. Like his psychoanalytic predecessors, Erikson adds to our appreciation of the intimate connections between
psychosocial growth and faith commitments, each serving the other
in a common configuration. The Dutch theologian Heije Faber reflects upon the religious implications of Erikson's approach to personality and concludes:

---

[54]Ibid., 213.

[55]Ibid., 99.

[56]Ibid., 129.

> To become adult is to become man in the sense of self-realization; and this self-realization is "divine" in kind; it can be termed a realization of God in us.[57]

Erikson himself does not speak so boldly, but clearly the view that maturation in terms of the emergence of personal virtues is man's religious destiny belongs to Erikson's perspective.

Obviously Fromm and Erikson have not spoken the last word for psychoanalysis. The movement continues in dynamic ferment as illustrated in the suggestive work of Robert J. Lifton. Lifton sees the movement of psychoanalysis from Freud to Erikson as a healthy revolution and aims to press the revolution still further. He argues for his own "half-formed suggestion" that a new psychoanalytic paradigm be developed with a central emphasis upon death and the continuity of life.[58] Lifton advocates forsaking the defensive-compensatory models of Freud and moving beyond the longitudinal views of Erikson still tied too closely to infantile origins. Rather, a formative process ought to characterize the new paradigm. In religious terms this formative process is most often symbolized around death and the continuity of life. For Lifton the death-continuity symbol stresses continuous transformation, the basic psychological process. For psychoanalysis Lifton and others like him illustrate a psychological movement that continues to grow.

SUMMARY

As a pioneer on the blurred border between science and religion, psychoanalysis unquestionably has much to offer the psychology of religion. It has stimulated new ways of viewing and discussing old phenomena and broadened the base upon which religious experience is to be understood. Singularly important, undoubtedly the most significant contribution of psychoanalysis, is the concept that factors outside the realm of awareness influence the formation and continuance of religious life. As a matter of course,

---

[57]Faber, *Psychology of Religion*, 122.

[58]Robert J. Lifton, *The Life of the Self*, (New York: Simon and Schuster, 1976) 50. This book is an elaboration of Lifton's ideas about the future of psychoanalysis.

psychoanalysis asks how and to what extent behavior is to be understood beyond its plain meaning. Faber translates this fundamental analytic issue into a religious question, "How far is every religion not, in part or in whole, the defense mechanism of particular human conflicts?"[59] Psychoanalytic theory has generally been skeptical that religion is anything other than a socialized method for managing personal conflict and anxiety, and certainly some types of religion fit the psychoanalytic mold. It would be a grave mistake to deny that religion both inhibits and consoles. Most religion does demand the sacrifice of instinct to some extent and lightens the burden of the sacrifice by offering rewarding compensation.

But psychoanalysis is not without its limitations. If psychoanalysis is to construct "a royal road to the unconscious" dimensions of religion, several restrictions in its method must be recognized. First, psychoanalysis has emphasized the depth meaning of behavior to the virtual exclusion of its surface meaning. Cannot the significance of large blocks of human behavior be discussed without resorting to depth language? Does a slip of the tongue *necessarily* and *always* communicate hidden meanings? Is psychoanalysis now mature enough to swing the pendulum back toward center? At the same time that sensitivity to the uncanny and inobvious is maintained, it seems appropriate to let some meanings be *primarily* surface.

Second, psychoanalysis has served well in clarifying "natural" religion, that is, that kind that emerges from within the inner character and resources of persons, but has not managed revealed religion very well. Psychoanalysis tacitly assumes that faith belongs to persons by virtue of their nature, that it is born in the primal relationships of infancy, and accordingly its value is reduced to its function. Such a thesis does describe one dimension of religion beyond which many practitioners never advance. Yet other believers grow beyond these natural levels of belief and practice. Persons not only attempt by nature to arrive at a sense of the "inexhaustible cohesion of life,"[60] but also feel themselves grasped by revelation

---

[59]Faber, *Psychology of Religion*, 70.

[60]Ibid., 71.

and encounter. Revealed religion often works with imagery whose content is meant to be mythical and poetic. Certainly this rich imagery ought not be treated as literalism, and to maintain conversation with religion, psychoanalysis must make room for revealed religion.

Third, by stressing the past as causative in human behavior, psychoanalysis risks giving persons a way to escape responsibility. Certainly this is not the intention of psychoanalysis. Freud and his successors actually enlarge human responsibility. "So you mean, Mr. Freud, that I am responsible for my dreams?" "If not you, then who is?" Yet psychoanalysis offers to irresponsible persons a kind of "moral out." How can persons be held accountable for their behavior when powerful forces outside their control move against them? By emphasizing the dynamic past, psychoanalysis may make it more difficult for persons to accept responsibility for the present. In secular terms blame may be shifted to society or parent; in religious terms it is "the devil who made me do it" or "the woman you put here with me"[61] who must shoulder the responsibility.

These limitations, however, ought not dim the important light that psychoanalysis has shed upon religious faith and ideas, and religionists can ill afford to allow the findings to go unnoticed. Among those concepts that seem so well documented as to be incontrovertible are (1) that human beings are characterized by impulse and energy driving them toward security and satisfaction and may in this sense be considered *Homo religiosus;* (2) that religious behavior is akin to all other behavior, carries the weight of depth meaning, and therefore may be partially understood in functional terms; (3) that parental relationships pour form and emotion into one's rudimentary understandings of God; (4) that defensive reactions, particularly repressed sexuality or aggression or fear, may give religion a quite unhealthy hue; (5) that God and religion are often illusion, frequently made out of the demands of psychic needs; and (6) that authoritarian religion can inhibit the full development of human potential and thwart the human capacity for reason and compassion. Any religious system that intends to purify the faith of its ad-

---

[61]Genesis 3:12.

herents must take seriously these data from psychoanalysis. Oscar Pfister, a Swiss pastor and personal friend of Freud, wrote to him in a letter dated 24 November 1927 (the year in which *The Future of an Illusion* was published):

> Psychoanalysis is the most fruitful part of psychology, but it is not the whole of the science of the mind, and still less a philosophy of life and the world.[62]

Pfister's attitude is not a bad one to emulate!

SUGGESTED READINGS

General

Browning, Don S. *Generative Man: Psychoanalytic Perspectives*. Philadelphia: Westminster, 1973.

Faber, Heije. *Psychology of Religion*. Philadelphia: Westminster, 1975. Emphasizes Freud, Jung, Fromm and Erikson; attempts overview of religion from psychoanalytic perspective.

White, Victor. *God and the Unconscious*. Chicago: Regnery, 1953. Compares Freud and Jung with sympathy toward Jung.

Freud

Freud's primary works on religion are listed on page 73.

Bettelheim, Bruno. *Freud and Man's Soul*. New York: Knopf, 1983.

Gay, Volney P. *Reading Freud: Psychology, Neurosis, and Religion*. Chico CA: Scholars Press, 1983.

Hall, Calvin S. *A Primer of Freudian Psychology*. Cleveland: World, 1954. Introductory.

Homans, Peter. *Theology after Freud*. Indianapolis: Bobbs-Merrill, 1970. Advanced.

Küng, Hans. *Freud and the Problem of God*. Edward Quinn, trans. New Haven: Yale University Press, 1979. A helpful companion to the Homans volume.

Lee, Roy S. *Freud and Christianity*. London: James Clarke, 1948.

Lewis, Helen B. *Freud and Modern Psychology*, New York: Plenum, 1981.

Ricouer, Paul. *Freud and Philosophy: An Essay on Interpretation*. New Haven: Yale University Press, 1970.

---

[62]Oscar Pfister, *Psychoanalysis and Faith: The Letters of Sigmund Freud and Oscar Pfister*, Heinrich Menz and Ernst L. Freud, eds., and Eric Mosbacher, trans. (New York: Basic Books, 1964).

Rizzuto, Ana-Maria. *The Birth of the Living God: A Psychoanalytic Study*. Chicago: University of Chicago Press, 1979.

van Herik, Judith. *Freud on Femininity and Faith*. Berkeley: University of California Press, 1982.

Wollheim, Richard, and James Hopkins, eds., *Philosophical Essays on Freud*. New York: Cambridge University Press, 1982.

Jung

Jung's primary works on religion are listed on page 77.

Cox, David. *Jung and St. Paul*. New York: Association Press, 1959. Relation of justification by faith and concept of individuation.

Hall, Calvin S. and Vernon J. Nordby. *A Primer of Jungian Psychology*. New York: Taplinger, 1973.

Hanna, Charles B. *The Face of the Deep: The Religious Ideas of C.G. Jung*. Philadelphia: Westminster, 1967.

Homans, Peter. *Jung in Context: Modernity and the Making of a Psychology*. Chicago: University of Chicago Press, 1979.

_____."Psychology and Hermeneutics: Jung's Contribution," *Zygon* 4 (1969): 333-55. Good summary.

Jacobi, Jolandi. *The Psychology of C. G. Jung*. New Haven: Yale University Press, 1968. Seventh edition. Old but standard.

Schaer, Hans. *Religion and the Cure of Souls in Jung's Psychology*. R. F. C. Hull, trans. New York: Pantheon, 1950.

Fromm

In addition to Fromm's works listed on page 82, see his *The Dogma of Christ* (New York: Holt, Rinehart and Winston, 1963); *You Shall Be as Gods* (New York: Holt, Rinehart and Winston, 1966); and *The Anatomy of Human Destructiveness* (New York: Holt, Rinehart and Winston, 1973).

Evans, Richard I. *Dialogue with Erich Fromm*. New York: Harper, 1966. Transcription of conversations.

Glen, J. Stanley. *Erich Fromm: A Protestant Critique*. Philadelphia: Westminster, 1966.

Hammond, Guyton. *Man in Estrangement*. Nashville: Vanderbilt University Press, 1965. Compares Fromm and Paul Tillich.

Erikson

Erikson's primary works are listed on page 85.

Evans, Richard I. *Dialogue with Erik Erikson*. New York: Harper, 1967. Transcription of conversations.

Gleason, John J., Jr. *Growing up to God*. Nashville: Abingdon, 1975. Application of Erikson's stages to Christian education.

Film: "Everybody Rides the Carousel." 90 minutes, color, animated. Order from: Mass Media Ministry, 2116 N. Charles Street, Baltimore MD. 21218.

CHAPTER FOUR

BEHAVIORISM AND RELIGION

The psychoanalytic tradition in psychology has come under attack from two quarters. A few religionists have rejected it as an illegitimate method for studying phenomena whose meaning lies beyond human experience, and others have seen its theories as too narrowly conceived to shed much light on religion. Some psychologists have likewise been suspicious of psychoanalysis, seeing it as the residue of the philosophical tradition in psychology. These tend to evaluate psychoanalysis as too unscientific, too subjective, too historical-hypothetical, and too oriented around anecdotal evidence.[1] They insist that psychology as a social science needs to purify its methodology by learning directly from its natural science kinsmen and, therefore, becoming more empirical and experimental in its analysis of human behavior.

---

[1]See, for example, Benjamin Beit-Hallahmi, "Psychology of Religion, 1880-1930: The Rise and Fall of a Psychological Movement," *The Journal of the History of the Behavioral Sciences* 10 (1974): 84-90.

The tradition that has most vigorously challenged psychoanalytic approaches to behavior and insisted upon more objective methodology has been generally labeled behaviorism. Those who work as behaviorists are not identical in methodology, but they do share a common outlook on the nature of persons and the purposes of psychology. All varieties of behaviorism are unqualified in their suspicion of consciousness as a useful category and discard references to mind or psyche or soul. Human beings, like lower forms of life, are moved into action by environmental forces and respond as physiological entities. The observation, prediction, and control of this behavior are the tasks of psychology. B. F. Skinner puts the issue bluntly:

> We do not need to try to discover what personalities, states of mind, feelings, traits of character, plans, purposes, intentions, or other prerequisites of autonomous man really are in order to get on with a scientific analysis of behavior.[2]

The patron saint of behaviorism, or its chief knave, according to one's point of view, has been John B. Watson, an American psychologist who early in the twentieth century set the movement in motion. Since its introduction by Watson, behaviorism has "gotten on with" its analysis of behavior, developing refined techniques for observing behavior in controlled environments, for quantifying animal responses, and for predicting behavior patterns. Procedures such as the controlled experiment, factor analysis, correlation studies, content analysis, and precise measurement of neurological responses in one way or another have come out of this tradition. Behaviorism is deeply embedded in American psychology, perhaps the most extensive influence.

Unsurprisingly, behaviorism has not given a great deal of attention to religion. Strict behaviorists, even if they were sympathetic to religion, have tended to either reject or neglect religion in their work. Their assumption that religious behavior is, like all behavior, the result of basic processes of physiological response leaves little room for the metaphysical underpinnings of most religion.

---

[2]B. F. Skinner, *Beyond Freedom and Dignity* (New York: Bantam Books, 1971) 15.

Hence, academic psychology dominated by the behavioristic orientation rarely deals seriously with the topic of religion; typically its textbooks make no more than passing references to the subject. Extensive and systematic treatments of religion from among these psychologists who stress the biological, the experimental, the measurable are almost impossible to find. Nonetheless, this tradition is relevant to the development of a comprehensive psychology of religion, both because religious behavior has occasionally been interpreted from this point of view, and also, perhaps more importantly, because behaviorism makes assumptions about human beings that carry weighty theological overtones.

Here several streams of thought in contemporary psychology are brought together, not because they represent a single, unified tradition, but because each derives its vitality from the behavioristic stance. In common they view persons through the spectacles of behavior and are concerned with precise description and measurement, reliable prediction, and efficient control. First, conditioning theory lies at the heart of behavioristic psychology, and William Sargant and B. F. Skinner illustrate those who have attempted to interpret religious phenomena as conditioned behavior. Second, Edwin B. Starbuck and two California researchers, Charles Y. Glock and Rodney Stark, represent those who attempt to understand religious behavior through the application of statistical methods to its study. Empirical studies in either laboratory or field contexts is a third variation on the behavioristic theme and, finally, the method reaches its ultimate application in psychobiology, a developing interest in modern academic psychology. Although behaviorism narrowly refers to those who work with conditioning theory, these kindred spirits may be considered to belong to the larger family because they share the measurement-prediction-control perspective.

CONDITIONING THEORY

Of all theoretical formulations by psychologists, conditioning theory in either its classical or operant forms must rank near the top in acceptance and popularity. It has acquired an unmatched status as an explanatory theory and has been particularly influential in contemporary philosophy and practice. Classical conditioning was discovered through twenty-five years of experimentation by Ivan Pavlov, a Russian physiologist who achieved fame for work in digestion and blood circulation but who is more widely known for his ideas on conditioning. Pavlov's salivating dogs are familiar far beyond scientific circles.

Conditioning is a term that designates the process whereby neurological patterns become sufficiently established to make a response more frequent or predictable as a result of reinforcement. In the classical Pavlov experiment, a dog was placed in a carefully controlled environment and presented with a "controlled stimulus," the ringing of a bell, followed by "reinforcement," the presentation of food. The experiment was repeated until salivation, originally the "unconditional response" to the presence of food, became "conditioned," occurring at the sound of the bell without the reinforcement. The strength of conditioning was assessed in terms of the amount of salivation with the bell, but without the food. Later conditioning theory built upon this originally simple formula. In 1927 Pavlov's major work on the subject was translated into English.[3] This, combined with support of the theory from the American behaviorist, John B. Watson, fostered research interest in and increasing popularity for conditioning as an explanatory theory. It has been commonly applied to the study of animal behavior, but later elaborations, chiefly under the influence of B. F. Skinner, have led to its application to human behavior as well.

William Sargant:
Classical Conditioning and Conversion

To what extent does conditioning theory influence psychology of religion? Directly, not much; indirectly, quite a bit. No researcher, to this writer's knowledge, has attempted to use classical conditioning theory to develop a comprehensive psychological interpretation of religion. A British psychiatrist, William Sargant, has intimated that such a model is possible and offers a fascinating but narrow theory of conversion in the Pavlov tradition. In his book *The Battle for the Mind* Sargant adopts Pavlov's twin concepts of transmarginal stimulation and transmarginal inhibition to discuss con-

---

[3]Ivan P. Pavlov, *Conditional Reflexes*, F. C. Aurep, trans. (Oxford: Clarendon Press, 1927).

version phenomena. Pavlov experimented with excessive stimulation of his animal subjects in order to test the limits under which the simple conditioning mechanism was effective. He discovered that such stimulus bombardment could be traumatic for the animal's neurological system, producing bizarre reaction patterns; that is, transmarginal stimulation produced transmarginal inhibition. By transmarginal stimulation he meant excitement beyond the threshold of the animal's capacity for conditioned response. Prolonged arousal of this type eventually dulled or distorted established reaction patterns, a phenomenon that Pavlov labeled transmarginal inhibition. Expected conditioned responses under excessive stimulation were replaced by unanticipated reactions evolving through three phases: (1) In the *equivalent* phase the animal's neurological system responds equally to strong or weak stimuli. (2) In the *paradoxical* phase the nervous system responds more vigorously to weak rather than strong stimuli. (3) In the *ultra-paradoxical* phase the conditioned response changes from positive to negative or negative to positive.[4]

Sargant assumes that human beings react according to these same patterns and interprets religious conversion accordingly. Prolonged transmarginal stimulation and inhibition may finally result in "a state of brain activity which can produce a marked increase in hysterical suggestibility . . . so that the individual becomes susceptible to influence in his environment to which he was formerly immune."[5] Sudden and dramatic conversions are explained in this fashion. Sargant sees imagined terrors, such as burning in hellfire, created in intense religious revivals as situations of "artificially induced states of intense emotional excitement."[6] These are comparable to Pavlov's transmarginal inhibition; that is, the usual patterns of conditioned behavior collapse, creating a situation of hysterical suggestibility. In religious terms, converts are released

---

[4]Discussed by William Sargant in some detail in *The Battle for the Mind* (London: Heinemann, 1967) 11-14, 29-30, and in *The Mind Possessed: A Physiology of Possession, Mysticism, and Faith Healing* (London: Heinemann, 1973) 8-13.

[5]Sargant, *The Mind Possessed*, 13.

[6]Ibid., 7.

from their sinful past and opened to persuasion about the new life that they ought to lead. Their openness to suggestibility makes it easier for them to accept uncritically a new set of beliefs and practices.[7]

Although he does not thoroughly develop the idea, Sargant hints that the Pavlovian concepts of transmarginal stimulation and inhibition translated into hysterical suggestibility may also be used to explain other religious phenomena, such as snake handling cults.[8] On a visit to the United States, he was impressed by snake handlers around Durham, North Carolina, and saw their trancelike states as instances of religious possession induced by the intensely emotional practices of the snake handling ritual. The rhythmic and boisterous music, vigorous dancing, pogo stick jumping, paroxysms, swaying, and clapping characterizing the ritual serve to increase emotional excitement and to become transmarginal stimulation. The high moment of taking up the poisonous serpents comes when conditioned control collapses, appropriately referred to by the practitioner as "being in the Spirit." Typically, those who participate in the practice say that they "are scared to death" of snakes, except when "the Spirit moves." During these episodes of transmarginal inhibition, the suggestibility of the worshipers is considerably raised, making them easy subjects for manipulation by a charismatic leader.

Obviously Sargant has not constructed a comprehensive model for understanding religion, nor even the many varieties of conversion. His flair for the dramatic causes him to emphasize those extreme types of experience that belong to only a negligible percentage of devotees. Nevertheless, his treatment of conversion experience as a neurological response is a reminder that intense religious phenomena involve a physiological dimension and, as such, merits a hearing.

B. F. Skinner:
Operant Conditioning and
Religious Reinforcement

In recent years behaviorism and B. F. Skinner have become virtually synonymous. Practically every psychological laboratory has a

---

[7]Ibid., 53-54.

[8]See *Battle for the Mind*, 217-19; *The Mind Possessed*, 182-86.

"Skinner box," an isolated, soundproof, and controlled environment used by Skinner in his experiments with pigeons and rats. For several decades Skinner has been an overpowering figure in scientific circles, and those who discuss learning theory sooner or later must reckon with his main ideas. Skinner's writings, especially *Beyond Freedom and Dignity* (1971) and *About Behaviorism* (1974), have stirred both ardent support and vehement attacks.

Operant Conditioning. Skinner made a major modification in the classical Pavlovian theory of conditioning. He preferred to discuss operant conditioning, a concept that is the key to his thought and for which he is perhaps best known. Operant conditioning, like its classical predecessor, is built upon the thesis that reward causes behavior to be repeated. But a distinction between the two forms is made at the point of their relationship to the environment. In classical conditioning the environment is controlled in such a way that a stimulus may be forced upon the subject according to the desire of the experimenter. Action chosen by the outsider is reinforced by rewards, food pellets for example. In operant conditioning, as Skinner sees it, the subject acts upon the environment, behaving in those ways that are most likely to produce reinforcement. Whereas in classical conditioning the environment operates upon the organism, in operant conditioning the organism operates upon the environment. Responses are instrumental in changing the environment to assure satisfaction. A rat in a box pressing a lever to produce food and a person preparing lunch share the same order of behavior. Both act upon the environment according to conditioned patterns that have in the past relieved hunger by supplying food.

Skinner believed that human behavior is regularly explained by operant conditioning. Persons consistently elicit from their environment those consequences that either satisfy a positive experience or reduce a negative experience. The hungry person behaves to bring food into sight. Or a shoe is removed to relieve a pinched foot. The satisfying quality of both activities increases the probability that the behavior will be repeated. All human behavior is to be understood in these terms. Skinner's work has been largely an elaboration and application of the subtleties of this formula. Accordingly, the only real question is how to control and manipulate the conditions under which responses can be altered. Social institutions, including those of religion, are means whereby groups have learned to manage human behavior.

Religion as Reinforcer. Skinner's approach to religion must be discussed with caution. Like Sargant, he offers in his writings no systematic treatment of the subject, and it would be unfair to abstract hints and attempt to mold them into a system. Nonetheless, Skinner's behavioristic stance is the context for a variety of undeveloped but explicit hints about the nature of religious behavior. Foremost among his observations is that religious thinking, knowing, and talking are to be reduced to behavioristic terms. These, like other acts, are devices whereby the behaving animal by operant conditioning learns to live in a world of rewards and punishments. "Feelings" and "states of mind" are no more than convenient ways of verbalizing operant behavior. "I feel like going to church" must be translated into behavioristic categories that describe the experience of churchgoing as an act of positive or negative reinforcement. The stance of Skinner is made clear in the following reference:

> What behaviorism rejects is the unconscious as an agent, and of course it rejects the conscious mind as an agent, too. A biography of Mohammed asserts that "it is obvious to non-Muslims that . . . the voice of Allah was in fact the voice of Mohammed's unconscious." But if anyone spoke, it was Mohammed himself, even though he did not observe himself doing so. It was Mohammed as a person, with a history responsible for his being Mohammed, not some fragmentary inner agent, to whom he must turn to explain his behavior.[9]

Thus Skinner rejects both internal and external mechanisms as vehicles for explaining religious experience. "I feel like going to church" is a deceptive explanation until one abandons any idea that feeling causes action or Allah (or unconscious) causes feeling. It is more to the point to know what happened to the person when he went to church in the past, what satisfying experience he was attempting to repeat, and what things from the past or present environment were now inducing him to go to church as opposed to

---

[9]B. F. Skinner, *About Behaviorism* (New York: Alfred A. Knopf, 1974) 158.

somewhere else. In Skinner's view religious acts are repeated because they have been reinforced as tension-reducing behavior. Any other explanation is little more than "a primitive myth that has long outlived its utility."[10]

Skinner also comments on religious institutions. These are among those social "isms" generated by "prevailing contingencies of reinforcement."[11] One lifetime is too short for a person to be exposed by direct experience to all possibilities for reinforcement. Social institutions preserve customary behaviors of a people, and the child is born into these as surely as into a physical environment. Persons respond to the contingencies embodied in institutions and contribute to their preservation in the ways in which they respond. The reinforcers that appear in a culture are its values; what a given "group finds reinforcing as the result of their genetic endowment and the natural and social contingencies to which they have been exposed" is called good.[12] A religious institution is a special form of social order in which "good" and "bad" become "pious" and "sinful."[13] Contingencies for reinforcement are made into laws, maintained by specialists and reinforced by ceremonies and stories. Such order is supported, not because of commitment and loyalty to the values themselves, but because the institution has arranged special reinforcing contingencies. Skinner states the issue candidly:

> A person does not support a religion because he is devout; he supports it because of the contingencies arranged by the religious agency. We call him devout and teach him to call himself devout and report what he feels as "devotion."[14]

Thus institutions thrive because of their function as agents of reinforcement. Religious bodies have the additional advantages of holy sanction.

---

[10]Benjamin M. Braginsky and Dorothea D. Braginsky, *Mainstream Psychology: A Critique* (New York: Holt, Rinehart and Winston, 1974) 45.

[11]Skinner, *About Behaviorism*, 148-49.

[12]Skinner, *Beyond Freedom and Dignity*, 122.

[13]Ibid., 110.

[14]Ibid., 111.

In his controversial *Beyond Freedom and Dignity*, Skinner approaches both freedom and dignity in the same way. Freedom does not come about through the human will to be free, nor is dignity the recognized worth of another human being. Both are products of behavioral processes characteristic of the human organism. Freedom describes attempts to escape from and avoid those experiences that do not provide positive reinforcement; dignity is praise and commendation toward those that have been reinforcing.[15] A major part of the human problem rests upon the failure to accept behavioral meanings of freedom and dignity and move toward their careful and scientific management. In fact, the latter end would be better served if psychologists could move away from the unscientific language of freedom and dignity in the interest of the scientific accuracy of behaviorism.

Skinner's comments on religion are specific enough to make clear his consistent judgment that religious practices are explainable simply in terms of conditioning and conditioned behavior. He leaves no room for "freely acquired convictions" and rejects the possibility of unselfish motive.[16] He disbelieves in freedom and dignity except in operant terms but confesses an unwavering faith in behaviorism as both theory and method. Skinner presupposes that human behavior is continuous with that of rats and pigeons, that persons are victims of forces that move around them, that human beings consistently behave to avoid or reduce tension, that the decisive human question is the efficiency of conditioning, and that behavioral engineering is the road to the good society. His optimism is unbounded. In 1948 Skinner published *Walden Two*, a fascinating fictional work depicting an ideal society produced through the careful scientific management of behavior. In the introduction to *About Behaviorism*, he states that the "major problems facing the world today can be solved only if we improve our understanding of human behavior."[17] He concludes that same work with the hopeful

---

[15]See Skinner, *Beyond Freedom and Dignity*, Chs. 3, 4.

[16]Bernhard Häring, *Ethics of Manipulation: Issues in Medicine, Behavior Control and Genetics* (New York: Seabury, 1975) 115.

[17]Skinner, *About Behaviorism*, 6.

affirmation, "In the behavioristic view, man can now control his own destiny because he knows what must be done and how to do it."[18]

Accommodation between Skinnerian behaviorism and a religious viewpoint will be difficult to achieve. Many will appreciate the meticulous care with which he studied rats and pigeons and his confidence that human behavior can be modified to good ends. At the same time, few religionists, Eastern or Western, will share Skinner's optimism that the human predicament may be so simply resolved, agree that the resolution ought to come by way of behavior manipulation, concede that commitment and selflessness are to be written out of the presuppositions, or believe that operant conditioning is a theory comprehensive enough to encompass the "humanness" of human behavior.[19]

MODIFIERS AND COUSINS

Statistical Analyses of Religion

Behaviorism in the most exact sense refers to the theory, methodology, and language of the Pavlov-Watson-Skinner tradition. Several additional areas of psychology are, however, close intellectual kin to mainstream behaviorism. Although these researchers are often dramatically different from the behaviorists, they are also similar in their assumptions. They either share suspicion of or choose not to work with concepts such as mind or consciousness, but concentrate their attention upon overt behavioral acts instead, confident that careful observation and measurement unravel meaning. Included in this wider family of behaviorism are those who use statistical methods to measure and analyze the explicit and formal aspects of religion. Their work ranges from simple counting of frequencies to highly complex mathematical calculations of

---

[18]Ibid., 251.

[19]The bibliography evaluating Skinnerian behaviorism is fairly extensive. Daniel N. Robinson, *Psychology: A Study of its Origins and Principles* (Encino CA: Dickenson, 1972) and *The Enlightened Machine: An Analytic Introduction to Neuropsychology* (Encino CA: Dickenson, 1972) contain balanced and fair treatments of the movement. The suggested readings at the end of this chapter include works both favorable and unfavorable to Skinner.

correlation and probability. Using carefully worded and standard-ized questionnaires, these researchers survey samples of the pop-ulation chosen so as to be representative of the general populace. Occasionally interviews are used to clarify or supplement the data. The technique has been employed to determine frequency ("How often do people go to church?"), to discover correlations ("Are church attenders more or less prejudiced than nonattenders?"), and to examine the role of isolated factors ("How important is church attendance to you?"). Two illustrations of the approach are cited here, one from early American psychology of religion and one from social psychology.

Edwin D. Starbuck: Adolescence and Conversion. When he was a student under the famous William James at Harvard, Edwin D. Starbuck proposed a "statistical inquiry into the religious ideas and experiences of the circumambient population."[20] Initially the pro-posal received "faint praise" from the teacher, but the project cul-minated in *The Psychology of Religion.*[21] This work received James's unqualified praise and subsequently came to be regarded as one of the classics in psychology of religion. Starbuck's book is subtitled "An Empirical Study of the Growth of Religious Consciousness," reflecting the intention of the author.[22] Starbuck was convinced, evidently with less than enthusiastic support from his teacher, that psychology could tabulate data and from them analyze the prin-ciples by which religious growth occurred. In this endeavor he stands out among the pioneers who around the turn of the twen-tieth century explored new methods for bringing science and reli-gion together.

Starbuck composed eleven questions to which his subjects were to respond autobiographically, outlining their perception of their

---

[20]Edwin D. Starbuck, *The Psychology of Religion* (New York: Scribner's, 1899) vii.

[21]Starbuck's book was published in 1899, but it was preceded by two significant articles: "A Study of Conversion," *American Journal of Psychology* 8 (January 1897): 268-308; and "Some Aspects of Religious Growth," *American Journal of Psychology* 9 (October 1897): 70-124.

[22]Howard J. Booth has written a valuable treatment of the career and influ-ence of Starbuck, justifying his role in psychology of religion. See his *Edwin Dillar Starbuck: Pioneer in the Psychology of Religion* (Lanham MD: University Press of America, 1981).

own religious growth. He then cataloged the responses in an attempt to discover the roots and laws of sequence in personal religion from childhood to maturity.[23] Starbuck's subjects emphasized their conversion experience, a fact that might have been expected. American religion still bore the marks of several Great Awakenings, and revivalism kept conversion alive as an intense, emotional experience often rushing upon persons without prior notice and changing the direction of their lives. The religious climate assured that Starbuck's questions about conversion would not be ambiguous; few would ask what was meant by the word. Further, those asked to describe their religious pilgrimage were most likely to begin with that sudden and dramatic event that had been decisive for their relationship to religious faith. Starbuck's definition reflects this cultural heritage: "Conversion is characterized by more or less sudden changes of character from evil to goodness, from sinfulness to righteousness, and from indifference to spiritual insight and activity."[24] He proceeded to study the manifestations surrounding the apparently sudden episode.

Starbuck's conclusion that conversion is largely understood in terms of its relationship to adolescent phenomena is his lasting contribution, and his 1899 classic stands as the broadest empirically based study to substantiate this claim.[25] In his sample, incidents of conversion began to occur at ages seven to eight, gradually increased to ages ten or eleven, rapidly increased to age sixteen, then fell away rapidly to age twenty and became rare after age thirty. Generally, frequency among females was slightly earlier than among males. The statistical evidence thus led Starbuck to the conclusion that the experience was in some way associated with the

---

[23]Starbuck, *The Psychology of Religion*, 4.

[24]Ibid., 21.

[25]Howard J. Booth, "Pioneering Literature in the Psychology of Religion: A Reminder," is an unpublished paper delivered to colloquium on psychology and religion, University of Lancaster, England, January 1976. Starbuck's conclusions were in a certain sense refinements upon G. Stanley Hall's extensive studies of adolescence. Although Hall's monumental work, *Adolescence*, vols. 1-2 (New York: Appleton, 1904) was not published until 1904, he had done research on adolescence for over two decades. Hall and Starbuck were colleagues during part of this period.

emotional intensity of adolescence, a thesis borne out in numerous subsequent studies.[26]

Starbuck's survey, in descriptive research style, further isolated a variety of emotional states that subjects associated with their conversion. Periods of dejection and sadness were reported, as well as times of joy and peace. Feelings of incompleteness, fear of death and hell, and visions of a new life appeared in the descriptions in varying frequency, but a sense of sin was regularly present. From his analysis of these reports Starbuck distinguished two types of conversion.[27] One group saw their sin as overwhelming, and for them conversion was an "escape from sin." For others conversion involved "spiritual illumination," a positive struggle toward a larger life. The "type of conversion which is accompanied by the feeling of incompleteness is more common than that which is accompanied by the sense of sin."[28]

This capsule presentation of Starbuck's findings illustrates a pioneering attempt to understand religion through questionnaire and statistical methods. The conclusions to which he came were conditioned by what the methods he used revealed, and his questionnaire (referred to by James as "the question-circular method") was not as sophisticated and standardized as some later devices. Even so, the care with which Starbuck did his work and accepted the limitations of his methodology justifies his place as a central character in early psychology of religion.

Charles Y. Glock and Rodney Stark: Studies in Christian Piety. Since the early work of Starbuck, much more extensive and refined procedures in understanding religion through statistical methods have been developed. Charles Y. Glock and Rodney Stark illustrate a host of scholars whose extensive research belongs to that hazy area where

---

[26]Michael A. Argyle, *Religious Behavior* (Boston: Routledge and Kegan Paul, 1958) reviews the statistical study on conversion done in the first half of this century. Some of these criticize some of Starbuck's conclusions, but generally they imitate his use of the questionnaire, sometimes supplemented by other methods, and confirm his findings.

[27]Starbuck, *The Psychology of Religion*, 85ff.

[28]Ibid., 87-88.

sociology and psychology overlap.[29] These two specialists have worked under the auspices of the Research Program in Religion and Society of the Survey Research Center based in Berkeley, California. They have addressed the question of patterns in American piety. Their work has focused upon numerous issues, but three fundamental questions dominated one phase of their research:[30]

1. What is the nature of religious commitment?
2. What are the sociological and psychological sources of religious commitment?
3. What are the sociological and psychological consequences of religious commitment?

Some of the findings of Glock and Stark have been reported in two books, *Religion and Society in Tension* (1965), and *American Piety: The Nature of Religious Commitment* (1968). Both books are dependent upon data drawn from an elaborate questionnaire study of three thousand church members in northern California and a national sample of almost two thousand adult Christians. The California sample was exclusively white, and the national sample included too few non-Christians and nonaffiliated persons to be statistically significant. Thus, the Glock and Stark studies have to do with the religious stance of white American Christians weighted heavily in the direction of northern California.

A capsule presentation of some features in the reports illustrates the character of their research.[31] On the basis of their overview of the sample, five dimensions of religious commitment are conceptualized: religious beliefs (the ideological dimension), religious practice (the ritualistic dimension), religious feeling (the ex-

---

[29]The presence of social psychology in academic circles, sometimes assigned to sociology and sometimes to psychology, testifies to interconnections between the two disciplines.

[30]Rodney Stark and Charles Y. Glock, *American Piety: The Nature of Religious Commitment* (Berkeley: University of California Press, 1968) 3.

[31]A more recent volume edited by Glock, *Religion in Sociological Perspectives: Essays in the Empirical Study of Religion* (Belmont CA: Wadsworth, 1973) contains twenty-one essays on empirically based studies exemplary of the broad concerns of the Research Program in Religion and Society of the Survey Research Center.

periential dimension), religious knowledge (the intellectual dimension), and religious effects (the consequential dimension).[32] *American Piety: The Nature of Religious Commitment* examines each of these in terms of what the research sample shows. The findings on religious feeling are particularly relevant for the psychology of religion.[33]

According to Glock and Stark, the conceptual proposition that is common in the statements with which people describe their religious feelings, from the vaguest to the most frenzied, is that "religious experiences . . . constitute occasions defined by those undergoing them as encounter—some sense of contact—between themselves and some supernatural consciousness."[34] These "encounters" or "contacts" fall into four general types. In the *confirming* type, the human actor simply notes the existence of the supernatural actor without assuming that the divine acknowledges the human. In the *responsive* type, mutual presence is acknowledged and the supernatural actor is believed to respond to the presence of the human actor. Awareness of presence is replaced by an affective relationship, such as love or friendship, in *ecstatic* religious encounters. Finally, *revelational* religious experiences denote those in which the persons perceive themselves as confidants or partners with the divine. Glock and Stark then further divide each type into subtypes aiming toward an orderly "taxonomy of religious experience."[35]

These researchers were surprised that the frequency of religious experience was much higher than they had expected from the earlier Starbuck studies. Starbuck's questionnaire asked about conversion, and in his religious climate he was able to pinpoint an intense emotional upheaval, a dramatic encounter that characterized

---

[32]Cf. Stark and Glock, *Religion and Society in Tension* (Rochester NY: Ward, 1965) 18-38.

[33]Stark and Glock, *American Piety*, 125-40.

[34]Rodney Stark, "A Taxonomy of Religious Experience," *Journal for the Scientific Study of Religion* 5 (1965): 99.

[35]See Glock and Stark, *Religion and Society in Tension*, 39-66; Stark, "A Taxonomy of Religious Experience," 97-116.

no more than thirty percent of Americans.[36] Glock and Stark correctly saw that this narrowed interpretation of religion was not broad enough to cover "American piety," a limitation in Starbuck's work already noted in such studies as those of Klineberg with Swedish children[37] and the Elkinds with Massachusetts adolescents.[38] Since Glock and Stark were more interested in a broader definition of piety than Starbuck's, they intentionally structured their inquiries more neutrally to avoid words that might call attention to crises or highly mystical experiences. Instead of the Starbuck question about conversion, they asked about "a feeling that you were somehow in the presence of God." They had expected about twenty percent to acknowledge such a sense of presence, but discovered that seventy-three percent of Protestants and sixty-six percent of Roman Catholics responded affirmatively. One wonders at their surprise, however, since the general character of the question would allow a person to identify almost any religious sensitivity as "a sense of the presence of God." If the Starbuck approach eliminated too much, Glock and Stark eliminated too little. Their data on this point does hardly more than affirm the general census report of the number of Americans who believe in God.

This study points up one of the particular limitations of questionnaire-survey methods in the analysis of religious behavior, namely, finding a language with a meaning common to researcher and subject. Accurate results are directly dependent upon the ability of the researcher to manage this problem. Some have criticized Glock and Stark for too easily having come to conclusions about the possible relationships between two factors.[39] To oversimplify the problem, to say that one variable is correlated with a second may

---

[36] Argyle, *Religious Behavior*, 60.

[37] See Göte Klineberg, "A Study of the Religious Experience in Children from Nine to Thirteen Years of Age," *Religious Education* 54 (1959): 211-16.

[38] See David Elkind and Sally Elkind, "Varieties of Religious Experience in Young Adolescents," *Journal for the Scientific Study of Religion* 2 (1962): 102-12.

[39] See, for example, Allen H. Barton, "Selected Problems in the Study of Religious Development," in Merton P. Strommen, ed., *Research on Religious Development* (New York: Hawthorn, 1971) 840-42.

overlook the possibility that a third variable underlies both or that several prior variables may contribute to each. Questionnaire-survey methods, even when the questions are constructed with the greatest of care, cannot produce these kinds of discrimination. This fact demonstrates the research truism that the presence of factors side by side does not necessarily indicate a cause-effect relationship. With these limitations of methodology aside, however, Glock and Stark, and the Berkeley Research Program in Religion and Society with which they have been associated, have made important contributions in applying statistical methods to the study of American religion. Their work has certainly been a major factor in advancing statistical techniques to study religion beyond simple distinctions between Protestants, Catholics, and Jews or between regular and irregular churchgoers. Since the late 1950s, they have been outstanding spokesmen for studies that intend more precise concepts of religiosity, emphasizing the need to understand the kind as well as the degree of religious commitment.

Experimental Studies

Experimental psychology is another area of the discipline that shares with behaviorism the affinity to expose meaning through careful observation and description of behavior. Experimentalism attempts to develop more sophisticated methods than statistical survey in order to speak more accurately about cause and effect in human behavior. Complex procedures, utilizing mathematical theories of correlation and probability, are structured to permit precise judgments regarding the influence of a single factor.

The experimental method is at its heart an experience in *control*, and its life blood is the *variable*. The intention is to test the influence of a single variable by manipulating it while keeping all other variables constant. The experimenter attempts to design research in such ways as to exclude unanticipated intrusions and to guard against the researcher's biases and limitations of memory, observation, and reasoning. A typical design establishes two groups: a control group in which variables are unchanged and an experimental group in which the variable being tested is manipulated. By comparing the behavior of the two groups the impact of the altered variable may be isolated, observed, and measured. By this method the researcher hopes to control the experimental environment enough to study the influence of the single variable upon behavior. Control is essential. In this way the experimental psychologist aims to create and sustain a laboratory world with little room for surprising outcomes.[40]

The creation of an ideal, controlled environment is obviously easier in a laboratory with rats or pigeons than in natural social settings with human beings, hence limiting the use of unmodified experimental methods to study human behavior. Yet psychologists have been highly successful in circumventing the artificiality inherent in laboratory research with people (laboratory studies) and also in adapting experimental techniques to the study of social phenomena in their natural settings (field studies). Laboratory studies more easily preserve control, but tend to be artificial. The knowledge that their responses are being studied may itself have an impact upon the research subjects. Field studies have the advantage of naturalness, but control is more difficult. In both procedures standardizing the instruments of measurement, the careful use of control groups, and the replication of the experiment to test and retest the results with more than one group are necessary to assure that conclusions are in fact accurate.

Both laboratory and field varieties of experimental studies of religious phenomena have been fairly numerous and cover a broad range of interests.[41] Yet little has been done to synthesize these findings into a composite overview.[42] The method itself does not encourage comprehensiveness; in fact, it promotes the opposite.

---

[40]For a more detailed description of this procedure, see O. L. Lacey, *Statistical Methods in Experimentation* (New York: Macmillan, 1953). A helpful summary also appears in Philip Zimbardo, Ebbe B. Ebbesen, and C. Maslach, *Influencing Attitudes and Changing Behavior*, 2d ed. (Reading MA: Addison-Wesley, 1977) 129-35.

[41]Articles in *Journal for the Scientific Study of Religion* regularly report studies using the experimental method. Several experimental studies may be found in L. B. Brown, ed., *Psychology and Religion* (Baltimore: Penguin, 1973) 209-342; and Benjamin Beit-Hallahmi, ed., *Research in Religious Behavior: Selected Readings* (Monterey CA: Brooks/Cole, 1973).

[42]For a significant attempt in this direction, see Michael Argyle and Benjamin Beit-Hallahmi, *The Social Psychology of Religion* (Boston: Routledge and Kegan Paul, 1975).

Out of proper concerns with controlled environment and reliable testing, the researcher tends to narrow his attention to specific religious acts and attitudes. Hence, experimentalism makes its contributions to psychology of religion largely in terms of a wealth of information about quite particular phenomena.

The use of empirical methods to investigate religion is well illustrated in a study done by A. W. Siegman.[43] The title states that the study is "an empirical investigation of the psychoanalytic theory of religious behavior," although Freud certainly would not have accepted the idea that his theory could be tested by these methods. Siegman attempts to examine experimentally three hypotheses that he correctly or incorrectly deduces from psychoanalysis. Siegman believed that, if the analytic theory of religious behavior is correct, experimental procedures should be able to demonstrate:

1. That the more religious persons have a greater tendency to project.
2. That persons' feelings and concepts concerning God correlate with their feelings and concepts concerning their father.
3. That males have a greater tendency than females to perceive God as a punishing figure.

Siegman's subjects consisted of two groups: eighty-five undergraduate students at Bar-Ilan University in Israel and seventy-nine first year medical students at the University of Maryland. All persons in the first group were Jewish; those in the second group were almost equally divided among the Protestant, Catholic, and Jewish faiths. Hence, subjects were relatively balanced between American and non-American, but weighted in the direction of Jewish adherents. The two groups were not the classical experimental and control groups, but they did allow Siegman to test his thesis in two environments.

The testing instrument for studying the second hypothesis was Osgood's Semantic Differential, a standardized device in which subjects can rate words on various scales in terms of meanings attached to those words. Siegman was particularly interested in the

---

[43]A. W. Siegman, "An Empirical Investigation of the Psychoanalytic Theory of Religious Behavior," *Journal for the Scientific Study of Religion* 1 (1961): 74-78.

meanings that his subjects gave to the words "God" and "Father," judging that, if the psychoanalytic thesis were correct, positive correlation should occur. Both Israeli and American students were asked to rate "God" and "Father" on three scales in the Semantic Differential. Siegman found that a positive correlation of statistical significance appeared only in the University of Maryland group and on one of the three scales. Among these students, feelings and concepts about God did not correlate extensively with feelings and concepts about their father. Similar procedures were followed in regard to the other two hypotheses, but neither was supported by statistically significant correlations. Siegman concluded that his study offered only attenuated support for the three psychoanalytic theses under examination.

Considerably more flexibility and less precision in the application of experimental methods is demonstrated in a field study done under the supervision of Leon Festinger, Henry W. Reicken, and Stanley Schachter. These men attempted a field analysis of the formation, growth, and breakup of a modern religious cult that had predicted the destruction of the world.[44] A number of trained observers gained admission into the group without being identified as researchers and over a period of three months recorded their observations as participants in group life. The team collected impressive data on the behavior of a small group that believed they had been forewarned of the impending end of the world. The data included anecdotal accounts of events that took place in the presence of the observers, reports to them of earlier actions of group members, factual and attitudinal information elicited in informal interviews or conversations, and the contents of speeches made by group leaders. Through analysis of literally reams of material, the researchers were able to construct to their own satisfaction the sociological and psychological "history" of a messianic cult as it reacted to both the anticipation of a cataclysmic event and the disconfirmation following the failure of the prediction to come true.

The extremely fluid situation made the procedure open-ended. The religious community met irregularly, and their activity was

---

[44]Their method and their findings are described in Leon Festinger, Henry W. Reicken, and Stanley Schachter, *When Prophecy Fails* (New York: Harper, 1956).

unpredictable. "Problems of rigor and systematization in observation took a back seat in the hurly-burly of simply trying to keep up with a movement that often seemed to us to be ruled by whimsy."[45] Such procedure-in-motion certainly risks distortion through biased or incomplete observations and frustrates the experimental purists. It may also make possible (depending upon the preparation, initiative, and insight of the observers) empathetic scientific observation.[46] In spite of the difficulties, the researchers were able to describe in some detail the personality patterns by which charismatic leaders assembled a following whose interest focused in the anticipation of destruction of the world by a great flood, to isolate the salient features of their belief system, to capture the emotional intensity of a four-day wait for imminent salvation (by way of a flying saucer scheduled to deliver the faithful from the anticipated flood), and to unravel various patterns by which the devotees managed their disappointment and dissonance when the end did not come.[47] The social scientist who maintains critical objectivity will be guarded in generalizing upon such studies, but these methods supplement other studies that are exclusively concerned with describing more easily measured behavior.

Physiological Psychology and Religion

Another area of psychological study that owes its vitality in part to behaviorism is physiological psychology. John Watson's insistence upon the limitation of the field to investigation of objective, observable phenomena encouraged the adoption of natural science methods and gave psychology a distinct physiological flavor. Those who follow in Watson's footsteps define behavior in "completely naturalistic terms as movements in time and space."[48] In so doing, they link psychology with quantification associated with the

---

[45]Festinger, Reicken, and Schachter, *When Prophecy Fails,* 245.

[46]Walter H. Clark correctly suggests a gulf between "the devout worshipper, prostrate before the high altar" and "the eager man with a pencil in the back row." See Clark, *The Psychology of Religion* (New York: Macmillan, 1958) 42-43.

[47]See below, pp.201-203.

[48]Robert M. Goldenson, *The Encyclopedia of Human Behavior,* vol. 1 (Garden City NY: Doubleday, 1970) 149.

physical sciences. Physiological psychology takes quite seriously this concern to quantify.

The central issue of physiological psychology is the relationship that exists between psychological states and physiological processes. The history of psychology is highlighted by attempts to clarify these connections.[49] Textbooks in this tradition read like introductions to biology. For example, *Elements of Psychology*, an introductory college text written by A. C. Reid in 1938, is unified around the sensory function of the human organism. Organs for seeing, hearing, tasting, smelling, and touching are described in detail, and behavior is defined in terms of the careful measurement of physiological responses. Emotion is regarded as a total psychophysiological reaction consisting of sensory experience combined with affection, itself rooted in pleasant or unpleasant sensations. This approach to behavior has enjoyed vigorous expansion in the last two or three decades in such items as refined studies of the central nervous system, cellular biology, biochemistry, and genetic engineering. Detailed and fascinating research is beginning to be reported on the stimulation of neurons to produce desired emotional states, the alteration of genetic structures even before birth, and biofeedback to control biological functions that were earlier considered automatic. Although these techniques have not made many direct comments about religion, their assumptions about human nature and the possibilities for behavior control and manipulation have profound religious and ethical implications.

Biological approaches to human behavior have naturally centered upon the brain as the master organ of the body. The bulk of research centers around the cerebral cortex, a gray mass of cell

---

[49]Among these are Descartes's mechanical conception of the body, René Descartes, *Discourse on the Method of Rightly Conducting the Reason and Seeking the Truth* (La Salle IL: Open Court, 1899); Fechner's psychoanalysis, see Gustav T. Fechner, *Elements of Psychophysics*, Helmut E. Adler, trans. (New York: Holt, Rinehart and Winston, 1966); Helmholtz on vision, see Hermann L. Helmholtz, *Treatise on Physiological Optics*, James P. C. Southall, ed. (New York: Dover, 1962); Cannon's theory of emotion, see W. B. Cannon, *The Wisdom of the Body* (New York: W. W. Norton, 1932) and *Bodily Changes in Pain, Hunger, Fear, and Rage* (New York: Appleton, 1922); and Lashley's principle of equipotentiality, see Karl S. Lashley, *Brain Mechanisms and Intelligence* (Chicago: University of Chicago Press, 1929).

bodies composing the distinctively human hemisphere of the fore-brain (cerebrum). The cortex is the most developed part of the human brain and the locus of nerve cells involved in the higher mental processes. The cerebral cortex is the major center for not only motor and sensory functions, but also elaborate associative processes that distinguish persons from other animals. "Without it we would be unable to solve scientific problems, create works of art, organize a complex society, or preserve and extend our knowledge of the world in which we live."[50]

The working units of the cerebral cortex and all other parts of the central nervous system are called neurons, cells that are in ceaseless activity. Neurons are composed of three parts: a cell body, dendrites that extend from the cell body to receive hundreds or thousands of stimuli messages, and an axon through which contact with other cells is maintained. The number of neurons in a single human brain is estimated in the billions, and each neuron is connected axon to dendrite to countless other neurons, generating minute impulses from cell to cell. Through constant interaction of the neurons, established patterns, or networks, of unimaginable complexity are formed. For the physiological psychologist this activity is the inner universe of human existence and opens the possibility for dramatic influence upon, or even engineering of, human behavior.

Advances in the biological and chemical understanding of the human animal in the last two decades have come at a more rapid pace than at any comparable period in human history. Such procedures as the use of staining dyes, electroencephalographic recording of brain waves, and the electrical or chemical stimulation of brain centers have made possible more precise "mapping" of cortical areas in which motor, sensory, and associational functions are localized. Armed with this information, the neurologist is equipped to probe the inner world of the nervous system and alter behavior patterns previously considered involuntary.

Biofeedback. In the late 1960s research began into developing processes by which persons could control internal bodily functions.

---

[50]Goldenson, *The Encyclopedia of Human Behavior,* vol. 1, 196.

The research has come to be known as biofeedback. It rests upon the principle that persons who are provided information on their physiological functions can learn to control their responses by conscious techniques. Elaborate instruments were devised to provide the subject with feedback information on such things as brain waves, heartbeat, body temperature, and oxygen intake. Experimentation has produced quite positive results. Persons who concentrate upon the correlation between their feelings and the feedback data learn quickly that certain subjective states coincide with physiological reactions, and hence are able to raise or lower their heartbeat or body temperature to desirable levels.[51] The procedure has been practical and helpful in its application to such medical problems as tension headaches, heart disease, and epilepsy. Up to this point religion has been relatively absent from the concerns of biofeedback, although some practitioners have been interested in Eastern forms of Zen Buddhism and yoga as means of concentration and meditation.

Genetic Engineering. Considerably more sophisticated and direct probing of the inner universe has occurred in the area of genetic engineering. Advances here are astonishingly accelerated; almost ninety percent of geneticists who ever lived are still alive! The development of refined instrumentality has opened cell life in ways hitherto unknown. Especially important has been the development of electron microscopes and microelectrodes that may be used to measure and record the activity of single neurons. No longer does the physiologist need to be content with the functions of large structures, composed of billions of neurons; these larger structures may be examined in terms of their detailed composition. With the help of a computer, the activity and relationships of these smaller units may be calculated.

Further, the discovery of chemical components in cells and as parts of the field within which cells operate has opened whole new fields of biochemistry. Not only has it been discovered that connections between neurons are chemical in nature, but these have

---

[51]Results of these experiments are available through an annual volume entitled *Biofeedback and Self-Control* (Chicago: Aldine, 1971-1979). The first volume appeared in 1971 reporting research during the previous year.

been identified, and possibilities for reordering behavior through the use of drugs are being explored. To the novice symbols such as DNA (deoxyribonucleic acid) and RNA (ribonucleic acid) still suggest the "awesome worlds within a cell."[52] However, these have become the common vocabulary of physiologists who are unraveling the essential process by which the likeness of parent is transmitted to offspring. The substance being examined is so minuscule that the DNA of a human body, if extracted, "would fit into a box the size of an ice cube. Yet if all this DNA were unwound and joined together, the string could stretch from the earth to the sun and back more than 400 times."[53] Even so, with a laser beam focused through a microscope, surgery can remove part of a single chromosome!

With these advanced technical capabilities, the geneticist is enabled to envision dramatic breakthroughs in controlling human reproduction and producing human beings of their own design. Until the late 1960s genetic engineering referred almost exclusively to the selection of sperm and ova for artificial insemination or fertilization. More recently, however, far more refined and complex procedures of gene and chromosome manipulation have been developed. Possibilities for adding and subtracting chromosomes, the insertion of genes or gene information into human cells at decisive moments in fetus development, asexual reproduction, and the creation of artificial placentas become more viable with each day of research. In 1973 researchers at Stanford University and the University of California School of Medicine created in a test tube a biologically functional DNA molecule that combined genetic information from two unrelated sources. The incredible work of these scientists makes Gardner Murphy's 1969 observation that "psychophysiology has become a dramatically new science in recent decades" sound like a gross understatement.[54]

---

[52]An intriguing article by Rick Gore, "The Awesome World within a Cell," *National Geographic* 150 (1976): 355-95, summarizes the geography of the cell in such a way that it may be understood by laymen. See also the more recent article by Robert F. Weaver, "Beyond Supermouse: Changing Life's Genetic Blueprint," *National Geographic* 166 (1984): 818-47.

[53]Gore, "The Awesome World," 356-57.

[54]Gardner Murphy, "Psychology in the Year 2000," *American Psychologist* 24 (1969): 524.

Psychology has been naturally engaged by the explosion of data coming from physiologists, but a search of the extensive literature of physiological psychology reveals hardly more than passing references to religious phenomena. In an article on the effects of sensual drugs on the function of the brain, Harbin B. Jones refers to twenty-seven case histories in which persons found conversion to or exercise of religion more satisfying than drug experiences. Jones hints at possible connections with "the sensations of joy and pleasure," but does not explore the sensory function of religion that he suggests.[55]

A more comprehensive neurobiological model has been advanced by Charles Laughlin, Jr., and Eugene d'Aquili.[56] These two researchers have attempted to interpret cultural universals, including religion, by way of physiological analysis. Laughlin and d'Aquili have formulated an approach to social institutions that they label "biogenetic structuralism," and in a fascinating article attempt to use their idea to explain religious ritual.[57] They assume that all human behavior functions to establish equilibrium between the central nervous system and the environment. Both abstract thought and cultural institutions emerge from this adaptive process. They are nothing more than expressions formed by fields of neural connections located primarily in the brain. The structuring of religious myths and ritual is part of this biogenetic process, "one of the few mechanisms at man's disposal which can possibly solve the ultimate problems and paradoxes of human existence."[58] Such an approach represents a new frontier in psychobiology and may in fact be a fruitless effort, but it does suggest the thoroughgoing seriousness with which physiological psychologists take their method.

---

[55]Harbin B. Jones, "The Effects of Sensual Drugs on Behavior: Clues to the Function of the Brain," in Grant Newton and Austin H. Riesen, eds., *Advances in Psychobiology,* vol. 11 (New York: Wiley, 1974) 297-312.

[56]See Charles Laughlin, Jr., and Eugene d'Aquili, *Biogenetic Structuralism* (New York: Columbia University Press, 1974).

[57]Eugene d'Aquili and Charles Laughlin, Jr., "The Biopsychological Determinants of Religious Ritual Behavior," *Zygon* 10 (1975): 32-58.

[58]Ibid., 55.

Why physiological psychology is introduced even in such sketchy fashion into a survey discussion of the psychology of religion is a legitimate question. Neither our purposes nor the competence of the author permits an elaboration of the area in all its intriguing detail. Further, physiological psychology has provided scant data on religious phenomena and is not likely to concentrate its interest on religion in the foreseeable future. Yet the theologian cannot avoid these studies that disentangle one component of the mysterious function of the human organism. Their books cannot be burned nor their facts stuffed back safely into Pandora's box in order to maintain a mythology of mind and matter. The seriously humane, and therefore theological, questions raised by the possibilities of all manipulation and genetic engineering must be faced squarely in the continuing interchange between psychology and religion.[59]

BIOETHICS

The behaviorist approach to persons, and particularly the new physiological and biological probing of man's inner universe, may well write large portions of the agenda for psychological and theological discussion in the immediate future. Possibilities for conditioning and controlling human behavior, for influencing the future of the race genetically, for cerebral biochemistry, and for artificial production of living cells astonish even the scientists themselves. And the awesome implications of their findings have also begun to plague them, producing alongside the bold and adventuresome research associated questions regarding their ethical responsibilities.[60] In the Darwinian revolution the direct kinship of human

---

[59]Two recent books have raised this issue. *Mainstream Psychology: A Critique* (New York: Holt, Rinehart and Winston, 1974) was written by brother and sister psychologists Benjamin Braginsky and Dorothea Braginsky and strongly recommends that psychology itself examine the value structure with which it works. Bernhard Häring, *Ethics of Manipulation: Issues in Medicine, Behavior Control and Genetics* (New York: Seabury, 1975) deals with ethical issues arising from manipulative procedures in medicine, behavior management, and genetic engineering.

[60]These concerns led to a 1975 meeting at Asilomar, CA at which 134 scientists called for the National Institute of Health to establish safety standards and controls for the experiments, especially with recombinant DNA. The concern has subsequently been extended to Congress and the popular press.

beings with other forms of life became unequivocably apparent. Now the study of neurological and genetic functions of the human organism in minute detail may produce a revolution of its own kind. The revolution may well hinge on the question: Are *homo sapiens* humans or machines? One researcher has put the issue bluntly in terms of brain-mind relationships. He states, "Still to be answered is that profound question that looms stark and insistent before all humankind: Is mind a mere molecular mechanism or is there in addition a transcendental quality to awareness?"[61]

On this fundamental issue psychology has not yet "made up its mind." Some seem supremely confident that behaviorism in one form or another will offer ultimate explanations of all behavior and adamantly affirm human beneficence by way of a soulless society. With eschatological enthusiasm worthy of an evangelist, these proclaim that the new day of knowledge has burst the supernatural bubble, vanished the "inane taboo, the goading yoke of superstition, and the inventive wrath of hell." Accordingly, mind is "but an ephemeral dance of atoms;" and human morality, destiny, and significance are to be found neither "in toil and patience" nor "by dream of psychic or psychotic prophets."[62] Answers lie within the human physiological makeup and by research and experiment will ultimately be unraveled.

Others are more guarded in their vision. They see behavioristic and physiological research as expanding the information base from which the humanistic dimensions of meaning may be further explored, but are not yet ready to claim that even complete description of physiological brain processes exhausts the nature and meaning of personal psychic reality, including perceptions, feelings, fantasies, or awareness of one's own behavior. For them constructs such as knowing, feeling, awareness, and judgment have meaning beyond the molecular. While new levels of deliberate and controlled modification of human behavior through physiological manipulation are envisioned, an appeal is made to value structures

[61]Robert W. Doty, "The Brain," in Francis Leukel, ed., *Issues in Physiological Psychology* (St. Louis: C. V. Mosby, 1974) 3.

[62]Robert W. Doty, "Philosophy and the Brain," in Francis Leukel, ed., *Issues in Physiological Psychology*, 18.

that take precedence over the physiological possibilities. For example, after he summarizes the data on "genetic engineering" and suggests directions that it might take in the future, Robert L. Sinsheimer, a biologist, advocates "the distinctive value of individual humanity" as a guiding principle. "As human beings we should aim to create a new mode of cooperative organization, one in which anarchic interaction is restricted not by rigid inherited structure and stereotyped response but by conscious understanding, by anticipation, by wisdom and grace and compassion."[63] Such human sensitivity introduces into the new environment of accelerated physiological exploration some quite old questions of responsibility: Who makes the decision? To what ends are selection and control used? By what methods? Who controls the controller?

Ethical issues raised by behaviorism have not gone unnoticed in either popular or professional discussions. Since Aldous Huxley anticipated the "brave new world" of fertilizing rooms and mind control, the ethical dimensions of biological manipulation have claimed attention. Recent developments serve only to make the issues more intense. Law, medicine, science, and religion have all been eager participants in the discussion.[64]

Roger Shinn, a leading contemporary ethicist, suggests that older ethical models are no match for the complexity of bioethics.[65] Appeals to traditional authority are not very helpful. Bible, church, or religious tradition contains no injunction, "Thou shalt—or shalt

---

[63]Robert L. Sinsheimer, "Genetic Engineering: The Modification of Man," in Francis Leukel, ed., *Issues in Physiological Psychology,* 41.

[64]For example, see two articles in the *Indiana Law Journal* 48 (1973): George A. Hudock, "Gene Therapy and Genetic Engineering," 533-58, and Harold P. Green, "Genetic Technology: Law and Policy for the Brave New World," 581-604. Also Seymour L. Halleck, "Legal and Ethical Aspects of Behavior Control," *American Journal of Psychiatry* 131 (1974): 381; W. A. Visser't Hooft, "Responsible University in a Responsible Society," *Ecumenical Review* 23 (1971): 252-66; Bernhard Häring, *The Ethics of Manipulation: Issues in Medicine, Behavior Control and Genetics* (New York: Seabury, 1975); Preston N. Williams, ed., *Ethical Issues in Biology and Medicine* (Cambridge MA: Schenkman, 1973).

[65]Roger Shinn, "Genetic Decisions: A Case Study in Ethical Method," *Soundings* 52 (1969): 299-310. See also Hans Jonas, "Technology and Responsibility: Reflections on the New Tasks of Ethics," *Social Research* 40 (1973): 31-54.

not—tamper with DNA." Utilitarian or pragmatic goals, the greatest good for the most people, are helpful but difficult to manage without some standard for measuring "good." Shinn sees no easy answer, but insists that questions about the nature and end of persons may not be abandoned with impunity. Theologian and scientist alike must ask, "What does it mean to be and to become human?"[66] Behind the question is the assumption that humanness is the destiny of persons. Behaviorism, including statistical, experimental, and physiological analysis of human behavior, has been an articulate spokesman for the weighty influence of social conditioning and reinforcing factors. It forewarns against easy assumptions that isolated individuals control their own destiny independent of their environment or make decisions that are not to a degree molded by their surroundings. Its descriptions are constant reminders of the sophisticated biological and chemical composition of the human animal. Who could review the intricate work of the modern neurologist or geneticist without being convinced afresh that persons are fearfully and wonderfully made?[67]

Yet the behavioristic-physiological-deterministic-positivistic tradition says too little about persons. (1) The tacit assumption that human beings are passive and inert, moved into action and shaped by mechanistic forces that are beyond conscious control, leaves too little place for self-determination. If Tillich is correct that persons become truly human only at the moment of decision,[68] then the behavioristic assumption is a basic denial of their humanity. Recognizing that persons share many features with the natural world should not disavow man's distinctiveness "from stone or cabbage or the most intelligent chimpanzee that ever was."[69] (2) To presuppose that the human organism operates in all ways to avoid or reduce tension, social or biological, makes persons too automatically self-seeking and leaves no place for the heroic. Is there no altruism

[66]Shinn, "Genetic Decisions," 309.

[67]Psalm 139:14.

[68]Paul Tillich, *Systematic Theology*, vol. 1 (Chicago: University of Chicago Press, 951) 184-85, 200-201.

[69]J. S. Whale, *Christian Doctrine* (Cambridge: At the University Press, 1941) 163.

that does not have a hidden agenda of selfishness? (3) The implied optimistic hope that human problems may be resolved by engineering and manipulation is too utopian to account for human fallibility on the part of both subject and researcher. Karl Menninger—a psychiatrist, not a theologian—challenges the overly optimistic view of human potential in a book entitled *Whatever Became of Sin?* He concludes that there are some individuals "whose sins are greater than their symptoms."[70]

Undoubtedly the behaviorist has prompted the development of precise methodology and instruments of measurements in psychology, but those working in this tradition still need to ask two questions: one about motive and the other about heritage. First, the behaviorist needs to ask to what extent the direction of his work is influenced by the popularity of "pure" science, sometimes with the implied suggestion that the social sciences are at best quasi-scientific. Is it only by chance that physiological interpretations of behavior are "psychobiology" and not "biopsychology"? Second, the psychologist needs to entertain again the philosophical tradition that gave birth to psychology. Pursuit of the question, "What is man?" produced psychology and may still have merit. If it is to be forsaken, let it be forsaken intentionally, not by methodological accident. If religion has sometimes oversimplified human significance in the direction of "soul," let not the correction be made by oversimplification in the direction of "body."

SUGGESTED READINGS

Behaviorism

The basic Skinner bibliography is noted on page 101.

Carpenter, Finley. *The Skinner Primer: Behind Freedom and Dignity.* New York: Free Press, 1974.

Evans, Richard I. *B. F. Skinner: The Man and His Ideas.* New York: Dutton, 1968.

Physiological Psychology

Leukel, Francis, ed. *Issues in Physiological Psychology.* St. Louis: C. V. Mosby, 1974. Interpretative.

---

[70]Karl Menninger, *Whatever Became of Sin?* (New York: Hawthorn, 1973) 221.

Milner, Peter M. *Physiological Psychology*. New York: Holt, Rinehart and Winston, 1970. College text.

Robinson, Daniel N. *The Enlightened Machine: An Analytic Introduction to Neuropsychology*. Encino CA: Dickenson, 1973. Brief and readable.

Sprague, James M., and Alan N. Epstein, eds. *Progress in Psychology and Physiological Psychology*. vol. 6. New York: Academic Press, 1976. One in a series of books that periodically update the data. Technical.

Weaver, Robert F. "Beyond Supermouse: Changing Life's Genetic Blueprint." *National Geographic* 166 (1984): 818-47. Popular summary of research.

Wratchford, Eugene P. *Brain Research and Personhood: A Philosophical Theological Inquiry*. Washington DC: University Press of America, 1979.

Critique

Braginsky, Benjamin M., and Dorothea D. Braginsky. *Mainstream Psychology: A Critique*. New York: Holt, Rinehart and Winston, 1974. Readable, general evaluation of behavioristic and humanistic traditions.

Gross, Martin L. *The Psychological Society*. New York: Random House, 1978. Critique of the impact of the psychoanalytic tradition on contemporary society.

Ethics

Fletcher, Joseph. *The Ethics of Genetic Control*. Garden City NY: Doubleday, 1974.

Flynn, Eileen P. *Human Fertilization in Vitro: A Catholic Moral Perspective*. Washington DC: University Press of America, 1984,

Häring, Bernhard. *Ethics of Manipulation: Issues in Medicine, Behavior Control and Genetics*. New York: Seabury, 1975.

Jonas, Hans. "Technology and Responsibility: Reflections on the New Tasks of Ethics," *Social Research* 40 (1973): 31-54. Good general statement.

Kieffer, George H. *Bioethics: A Textbook of Issues*. Reading MA: Addison-Wesley, 1979.

Menninger, Karl. *Whatever Became of Sin?* New York: Hawthorn, 1973. Personal, journalistic, insightful.

Shinn, Roger. "Genetic Decisions: A Case Study in Ethical Method," *Soundings* 52 (1969): 299-310.

Simmons, Paul D. *Birth and Death: Bioethical Decision-Making*. Philadelphia: Westminster, 1983.

Williams, P. N., ed. *Ethical Issues in Biology and Medicine*. Cambridge MA: Schenkman, 1973.

Film

"Biofeedback: The Yoga of the West." 40 minutes, color. May be rented from Hartley Film Foundation, Cat Rock Road, Cos Cob, CT 06807.

Chapter FIVE

HUMANISTIC PSYCHOLOGY AND RELIGION

During the mid-twentieth century, a third tradition in psychology began to emerge largely as a protest against psychoanalytic and behavioristic emphases and the value systems that they were perceived to represent. This movement is often referred to as "Third Force" psychology to suggest its separation from both psychoanalysis and behaviorism. But more regularly it is called "humanistic" psychology, following the nomenclature that appears in the titles of the *Journal of Humanistic Psychology* and the Association for Humanistic Psychology, two vehicles through which the credo of this tradition is best known and preserved.[1] Although humanistic themes appeared earlier, in the 1950s these forces rallied around Abraham H. Maslow, who became patron saint of the movement and its strongest voice.

Humanistic psychology has been considerably heterogeneous, including serious researchers such as Rollo May, Carl Rogers, and

---

[1]"Existential" psychology has also been used occasionally as an umbrella term under which these individuals are discussed.

Gordon Allport on one end of the continuum and rather superficial positive thinking cultists on the other. Yet the movement is held together by a common rejection of traditional psychoanalytic and behavioristic theory and method in the interest of affirming human potential. Achievement of the highest human potential is a recurring theme, undergirded with enthusiasm and optimism usually reserved for religionists. Maslow clearly reflects the humanistic attitude when he debunks the usual statistical approach to behavior. "If we want to know how fast a human being can run, then it is no use to average out the speed of a 'good sample' of the population," he says. "It is far better to collect Olympic gold medal winners and see how well they can do."[2]

The language that regularly appears in the work of these persons accentuates their high hopes for human beings. The *Journal of Humanistic Psychology,* for example, appeals for articles on the topics "authenticity, encounter, self-actualization, search for meaning, creativity, personal growth, psychological health, being-motivation, values, love, identity, and commitment."[3] Such words reflect the highly personal nature of this tradition. On the occasion of its founding Maslow said about the journal: "The *Journal of Humanistic Psychology* is being founded by a group of psychologists and professional men and women from other fields who are interested in those human capacities and potentialities that have no systematic place either in positivistic or behavioristic theory or in classical psychoanalytic theory."[4]

The selection of representatives to portray humanistic psychology is not a simple matter, since the movement includes persons with such a wide variety of interests who employ diverse methods to explore human potential. Nonetheless, those selected here need no justification beyond their standing in the scholarly world and the extent to which their writings are read and dis-

---

[2]Abraham H. Maslow, *The Farther Reaches of Human Nature* (New York: Viking Press, 1971) 7.

[3]This appeal appears on the inside cover of issues of the *Journal.*

[4]Abraham H. Maslow, "Eupsychia: The Good Society," *Journal of Humanistic Psychology* 1 (1961): 1.

cussed. William James may justifiably be considered a pioneer among those who insist upon interpreting religion in terms of personal meanings, and his *The Varieties of Religious Experience* is certainly one among the few classics in psychology of religion. Abraham Maslow has been a vigorous critic of behavioristic psychology in America and the most outspoken advocate for uncovering human potential through self-actualization. Gordon Allport, for many years a member of the Department of Psychology and later the innovative Department of Social Relations at Harvard, is identified with experimental approaches, and many experimental psychologists view him as their mentor in doing personality studies. However, he is included here because of his persistent concern with personal becoming. Throughout his distinguished career he insisted that the propelling force of human motivation "lay in the present on-moving structure of personality, not in some anachronistic conditioning of past motives."[5]

Others might as easily be selected: Carl Rogers, who gave a therapeutic turn to this tradition in his client-centered techniques; Rollo May, whose writings over the years have emphasized the importance of existence as a dimension in psychology; or Viktor Frankl, for many years the outstanding European spokesman for humanistic psychology under the label "logotherapy."[6] However, a consideration of James, Maslow, and Allport should bring the movement into focus.

WILLIAM JAMES: A PRAGMATIC VIEW OF RELIGION

During 1901-1902, William James (1842-1910), already a psychologist of repute, was appointed to give the Gifford Lectures on Natural Religion at the University of Edinburgh. The lectures were subsequently published under the title *The Varieties of Religious Ex-*

---

[5]Gordon W. Allport, *The Person in Psychology: Selected Essays* (Boston: Beacon Press, 1968) 395.

[6]See Carl R. Rogers, *Client-Centered Therapy: Its Current Practice, Implications, and Theory* (Boston: Houghton-Mifflin, 1951); Rollo May, *Man's Search for Himself* (New York: W. W. Norton, 1953); Viktor Frankl, *Man's Search for Meaning: An Introduction to Logotherapy,* Ilse Lasch, trans. (Boston: Beacon Press, 1962) and *The Unconscious God: Psychotherapy and Theology* (New York: Simon and Schuster, 1975).

perience, a pioneering book in the psychology of religion movement that was emerging around the turn of the century and a work that still must be given serious attention for its psychological insights. Others, such as Starbuck, Hall, Leuba, and Coe, were to make significant contributions to the movement.[7] James's work, along with theirs, made visible an approach that was to dominate discussion until psychoanalysis made its impact on the American study of the psychology of religion in the 1920s and 1930s and was to influence phenomenological and humanistic studies of religion until the present time.[8]

James was sensitive to the values of psychophysiology, and had he worked half a century later, he would surely have applauded the remarkable advances in the physiological study of the human organism. Yet he could never bring himself to reduce experience to the function of the nervous system. Rather, he insisted that distinctly human qualities were discoverable in the dynamic life of a person's stream of consciousness.[9] James reserved some of his most caustic remarks for those who "see 'the liver' determining the dicta of the sturdy atheist as decisively as it does those of the Methodist under conviction anxious about his soul."[10] Conversely, consciousness is the key to human aspects of experience, especially religion. "The plain truth is that to interpret religion one must in the end look at the immediate content of the religious consciousness."[11]

---

[7]Edwin D. Starbuck, *The Psychology of Religion* (New York: Scribner's, 1899); G. Stanley Hall, *Adolescence*, vols. 1, 2 (New York: Appleton, 1904); James H. Leuba, *A Psychological Study of Religion* (New York: Macmillan, 1912); and George A. Coe, *The Psychology of Religion* (Chicago: University of Chicago Press, 1916).

[8]For connections between phenomenology and James, see Hans Linschoten, *On the Way toward a Phenomenology Psychology: The Psychology of William James* (Pittsburgh: University of Pittsburgh Press, 1968).

[9]See William James, *The Principles of Psychology*, vols. 1, 2 (New York: Holt, Rinehart and Winston, 1890).

[10]William James, *The Varieties of Religious Experience* (New York: Modern Library, 1902) 15.

[11]Ibid., 13n.

The Character of Religion

James approached religious consciousness through subjective experiences reported in the works of piety and autobiography by "articulate and full self-conscious man."[12] He firmly believed that truth was to be discovered, not through logic and theoretical argument, but through observing the data of experience. Accordingly, the royal road to religious consciousness was through what persons described their experience to be. To understand the psychological importance of religion the researcher does not begin with his own scholarly categories, using them as models into which human experiences must fit, but allows the experiences to speak for themselves, taking at face value what is said as the overflow of the inner life.

Thus *The Varieties of Religious Experience* is replete with subjective descriptions of personal religious experiences from numerous affiliations and orientations. The material is heavily weighted toward intense forms on the assumption that the distinctive features of religion are more likely to be seen in exaggerated than in normal states. For some, religion is little more than "dull habit;" these people can teach us little about the nature of religion. But for others, religion is "acute fever," burning like fire in the bones; in their experience the major characteristics of religion stand out boldly. The more extreme examples yield the more profound information. From his clinical examination James concluded that three features mark the general topography of religion.

Personal. First, religion for James is intensely personal. He was so convinced of this that he chose to take the highly personal, first-hand experience of devout individuals as subject matter for *Varieties.* He conceded that in common usage religion designated systems of thought and feeling fully organized into institutions, but his study intentionally bypasses this face of religion, perhaps in part because James personally disliked religious formalities. Consequently, James's analysis deals only negligibly with the role played by institutions in the personal religion of most people.[13] Informed

---

[12]Ibid., 4.

[13]William A. Sadler, Jr., ed., *Personality and Religion: The Role of Religion in Personality Development* (New York: Harper, 1970) 12.

by the powerful autobiographical materials with which he was working, James concluded that inward piety was the primal religious expression. Note the individualistic emphasis of his definition of religion:

> Religion . . . shall mean for us the feelings, acts, and experiences of *individual* men in their *solitude*, so far as they *apprehend themselves* to stand in relation to whatever they may consider divine.[14]

One is never quite sure what is to be included or excluded in James's definition, which "is like a slow moving cloud, omnipresent no matter in which direction you turn, . . . constantly changing shape and out of reach."[15] James himself did not defend his definition as comprehensive nor apply it rigidly throughout his study. But so it is when the focus is upon individual experience. The statement underscores his perspective that the irreducible structure of religious experience is individual and personal. And in this sense particularly he sires the humanistic tradition. Theologies, philosophies, and ecclesiastical organizations may secondarily grow out of private experience, but the raw stuff of religion consists of the personal belief "that there is an unseen order, and that our supreme good lies in harmoniously adjusting ourselves thereto."[16] In short, religion for James was a "monumental chapter in the history of human egotism."[17] The gods believed in by either crude savages or cultured intellectuals are those who respond to personal calls. James concludes that "as soon as we deal with private and personal phenomena as such, we deal with realities in the completest sense of the term."[18] Religion for James was first and foremost personal.

Emotionality. Second, James was impressed more with the emotion than with the thinking of religious experience. He perceived that his documents were literally bathed in sentiment. Here an iconoclastic touch marks James's work. During the half century

---

[14]James, *The Varieties of Religious Experience,* 31-32; italics added.

[15]Sadler, *Personality and Religion,* 12.

[16]James, *The Varieties of Religious Experience,* 53.

[17]Ibid., 480.

[18]Ibid., 489.

preceding the publication of *Varieties,* scientific analysis in the form of intellectualized, theoretical formulation had become increasingly popular. The approach had been applied to religious studies, sometimes to support and sometimes to discredit them. For example, scholars had approached biblical studies from the perspective of historical analysis, structuring logical patterns for studying biblical materials. Fundamentalism reacted negatively to such analysis but nonetheless built their own schematic structures that spelled out faith in clear propositions.[19] Any dogmatic attitude in science or religion was abhorrent to James, but more importantly he did not believe that intellectual formulae adequately uncovered the nature of the religion that he found in the experience of his informers.[20] Nor was it the base from which flowed their faith. His subjects taught him that religious emotion was the foundation upon which adherents built their intellectual structures. Read his castigating caricature of theologians who faultlessly deduce the metaphysical attributes of God.

> What is their deduction of metaphysical attributes but a shuffling and matching of pedantic dictionary adjectives, aloof from morals, aloof from human needs, something that might be worked out from the mere word "God" by one of those logical machines of wood and brass which recent ingenuity has contrived as well as by a man of flesh and blood. . . . One feels that in the theologian's hands, they are only a set of titles obtained by a mechanical manipulation of synonyms, verbality has stepped into the place of vision, professionalism into that of life. . . . Did such a conglomeration of abstract terms give really the gist of our knowledge of the deity, schools of theology might indeed continue to flourish, but religion, vital religion would have taken its flight from this world.[21]

James's words are too harsh and unfair, but his overstatement makes the point clearly. He was attempting to do more than debunk the theologian or the philosopher; he was calling for a new attitude toward the feeling and intuition that he saw dominating his

---

[19]See below, pp. 301-307.

[20]James's *Essays in Pragmatism,* Albury Castell, ed. (New York: Hafner, 1948) deals with this idea generally; in *Varieties* the understanding is applied to religion.

[21]James, *The Varieties of Religious Experience,* 436-37.

clinical data. The materials told him that nonintellectual experience preceded thinking and implied that the researcher approximates the real meaning of experience when he attends to human desires and wishes. The most helpful and precise logical categories are those that emerge from the deeper, emotive levels of experience. In this most fundamental way, truth is "but a passionate affirmation of desire,"[22] and "articulate reasons are cogent for us only when our inarticulate feelings of reality have already been impressed in favor of the same conclusion."[23] James cryptically concludes, "Instinct leads, intelligence does but follow."[24]

Since feelings are the essence of religion, all religious systems share much common ground, both in kinds of emotion and in conduct derived from these emotional states. James says,

> When we survey the whole field of religion we find a great variety in the thoughts that have prevailed there; but the feelings on the one hand and the conduct on the other are almost always the same, for Stoic, Christian, and Buddhist saints are practically indistinguishable in their lives.[25]

James's approach not only challenges the cold and stereotypical attitudes of intellectualism, but also has radical implications for one's personal orientation toward life. If primary data belong to feeling, then persons must exercise their "will to believe," not in an external creed surrounding a God, but in the authenticity of their own experiences. By acting upon personal intuitions, feelings, and insights, an individual may open the possibility of human potential and discover mysteries often hidden in routine doctrinal affirmations. Here James obviously did not take into account the possibilities of self-deception (even to the extremes of neurosis and psychosis), but he did lay bare an experiential orientation toward

---

[22] James, *Essays in Pragmatism*, 94.

[23] James, *The Varieties of Religious Experience*, 73.

[24] Ibid.

[25] Ibid., 494.

religion that later would be clarified and purified by (of all people) theologians![26]

Variety. A third feature in the topography of religious experience, according to James, is its variety. The "varieties of religious experience" are practically unlimited. James raises the hypothetical question: Is the existence of so many religious sects, types, and creeds regrettable? The implied negative answer ought not surprise us because of the varieties in personality types and individual angles of vision. One might anticipate that individuality would produce experience consonant with personality. An Emerson must not be forced to be a Wesley; a Moody, a Whitman; nor a Buddhist, a Christian. James judges that "for each man to stay in his own experience, whate'er it be, and for others to tolerate him there, is surely best."[27]

James uses several categories to sort out and classify the varieties of religious experience that he observes: saintliness, mysticism, healthy-mindedness, and the sick soul.[28] The categories are neither neat nor comprehensive, but they were derived from James's observation of his case materials. The contrast that he draws between healthy-mindedness and the sick soul is particularly informative. The terms unfortunately imply health and illness, but James is more concerned with these as types of religious experience than as evaluative categories. Healthy-mindedness is the type of experience marked by a happiness that appears to be "congenital and

---

[26]James's emphasis upon the primacy of feeling over thinking anticipates subsequent existential scientists, philosophers, and theologians. Phenomenologists by definition focus their attention upon experience. See Martin Heidegger, *Being and Time,* John Macquarrie and Edward Robinson, trans. (New York: Harper, 1962); and W. A. Sadler, Jr., *Existence and Love: A New Approach to Existential Phenomenology* (New York: Scribner's, 1969) Chs. 1-4. Theologians as eminent as Paul Tillich have indicated that religious experience is primary over religious words. Compare also Michael Polanyi, *The Tacit Dimension* (Garden City NY: Doubleday, 1966). Understanding experience behind the language is one of the crucial issues in contemporary discussions of structuralism. See C. R. Babcock, *Levi-Strauss: Structuralism and Sociological Theory* (London: Hutchinson, 1975).

[27]James, *The Varieties of Religious Experience,* 478.

[28]See below, pp. 334-35.

irreclaimable."[29] These persons positively refuse to feel unhappiness, as if it were something disagreeable or wrong. They "passionately fling themselves upon their sense of the goodness of life."[30] Their "soul is of . . . sky blue tint," their "affinities are rather with flowers and birds . . . than with dark human passions," and they "can think no ill of man or God."[31] By contrast, the sick soul groans and writhes over its condition. These "seem to have been born close to the pain threshold, which the slightest irritant sends them over."[32] God, religion, and life itself are viewed with apprehension; melancholy seems always a nearby companion. For the sick soul, conquest comes only through arduous struggle, but it does come! Through travail and struggle the "sick soul" may arrive at ecstasy and joy unknown by "healthy-mindedness," which does not confront the more profound questions.

Thus, for James the range of religious response is extremely broad. He accounts for differences by use of a vaguely defined concept of temperament. Some persons seem to be born with crystallized optimism; their temperament is "organically weighted" toward healthy-mindedness.[33] Others are "congenitally fated to suffer;" their temperament makes them the sick soul.[34] James does not reflect in detail upon the nature of temperament, nor does he explore differences in personal background or environment that may contribute to the choice of religious life-style. But his case material demonstrates unquestionably the many varieties in religious experience, each heavily loaded with emotionality and each to be accepted as potentially beneficial to the individual.

The Function of Religion

Toward the end of *Varieties* James summarizes his conclusions and says pointedly, "I believe the pragmatic way of taking religion

---

[29]Ibid., 78.

[30]Ibid.

[31]Ibid., 79.

[32]Ibid., 133.

[33]Ibid., 82.

[34]Ibid., 131.

to be the deeper way."[35] This is essentially James's view of the function of religion. The crucial religious questions are not, "Does God exist?" or "What is he like?" Rather, the important issue is, "How do God and religion serve in the human pursuit of the good life?" James cites with approval Leuba's comment: "Not God, but life, more life, a larger, richer, more satisfying life, is, in the last analysis, the end of religion."[36] He examines this pragmatic interpretation from several perspectives.

Survival Theory. James rejects the idea that religion is to be understood simply as the survival of outgrown infantilism, residues of an earlier period of human development. Religion is more than an infantile "relapse into a mode of thought which humanity in its more enlightened examples has outgrown."[37] Correspondencies between the experiences of primitive and modern man may make survival theory attractive, but that explanation is too shallow. Similarities are better explained pragmatically. Religion survives and thrives because it is functional, that is, it serves important personal needs. Similar phenomena serve similar purposes, all rooted in basic human needs for self-expression and integration. If religion "opens an individual to the most fundamental dimensions and possibilities of his personality and enables him to integrate them creatively and harmoniously into his personal world,"[38] then it may be judged authentic, whatever its form or whether it is the experience of savage or cultured man. Science may not dismiss religious phenomena as merely anachronistic, better forsaken in the interest of human maturity. The criterion by which the experiences are to be evaluated runs in a different direction. Religion's utility in the personal struggle to manage life justifies its existence and is the area in which the truth of religion is to be defined.

James borrows from Leuba the phrase "faith-state" to denote this enduring function of religion. A faith-state is a biological and psychological condition in which a person's vital powers are fresh-

---

[35]Ibid., 509.

[36]Ibid., 497.

[37]Ibid., 480.

[38]Sadler, *Personality and Religion*, 4-15.

ened. It is an emotional state that imparts endurance or zest or meaning. The presence of the faith-state is one of the forces by which persons live; its absence (anhedonia) means collapse. Religious systems have the effect of stamping positive intellectual content upon faith-states, and this explains why persons are passionately loyal to even the minutest details of their creeds. Defense of creed or truth is protection of function. Since religion operates at the very heart of human meaning, it will be defended vigorously. This subjective utility is the key to religion's meaning.

A More. What does such a utilitarian approach to religion say about the reality of God? Does religion have only psychological reality? James is guarded in this matter. So far as his analysis goes, he believes religious experiences are only psychological phenomena, but he leaves the door open for a "More." The religious person identifies his real being with the higher part of himself and in doing so,

> becomes conscious that his higher part is conterminous and continuous with a MORE of the same quality, which is operative in the universe outside of him, and which he can keep in working touch with, and in a fashion get on board of and save himself when all his lower being has gone to pieces in the wreck.[39]

Thus, for James a "More" exists over and beyond the superstructures built by religious systems. Various theologies debate both the content of the "More" and methods of union with it; that is, they build their systems of over-beliefs. When one defines the "More" as the Christian God and union as the act of Jesus Christ, he structures over-beliefs that are likely to camouflage the "More," and reduce it to human experience. Whatever is on the *farther* side, James concludes, the "More" to which persons feel connected is on its *hither* side the higher self. In the religious life the connection is felt as control from outside and above the person. Since "it is the higher faculties of our own hidden mind which are controlling, the sense of union with the power beyond us is a sense of something, not merely apparently, but literally true."[40]

---

[39]Ibid., 498-99.

[40]Ibid., 503.

In sum, then, James moves away from the proposition that persons believe because they are intellectually convinced that their creeds are true. The arguments are convincing to those who already believe on emotional grounds. Religion and religions survive because they serve persons well at the heart of where persons seek meaning for their human existence. When they no longer serve this purpose, they are replaced. This is the pragmatist's understanding of religion.

The James Legacy

To measure the work of William James by contemporary research standards would be quite unfair. Its vocabulary belongs to its own day, his definition of religion omits corporate experience, social influences on private behavior are too easily overlooked, and the emotional aspects of experience may be overemphasized at the expense of intellectual or ritual behavior. James's tacit assumption that the religion of the saint and that of the ordinary devotee are out of the same fabric may need closer examination. Nonetheless, James's specific ideas and interpretations are seminal, and his approach sets a direction for future and refined examination of religious phenomena.

Not the least of his contributions was his positive attitude toward personal religion. James demonstrated that his own study had not deprived him of interest in religion in a personal sense.[41] Hence, his experience, as well as his study, helped to overcome a distrust of psychological methodology at a time when large segments of the religious community were suspicious of all scientific studies of religion. James's positive approach played a significant role in creating interest, even enthusiasm, for a new way of approaching religious studies. Yet James maintained his scientific integrity. He confessed that for him the farther reaches of existence were appropriately called God, but carefully pointed out that this was his own over-belief. Such care in separating the data from hypothetical constructs is a helpful lesson for scientists and theologians of any age.

---

[41]Seward Hiltner, "The Psychological Understanding of Religion," *Crozier Quarterly* 24 (1947): 8.

Further, James's emphasis upon the operational significance of religion erodes explanation by way of origin. The intellectual community of James's day was familiar with such works as Frazer's *The Golden Bough,* which gathered large bodies of data to portray religion as primitive people's attempt to manage fear in the presence of awesome natural phenomena. Many considered contemporary religion to be little more than the survival of primitivism, and the sooner discarded, the better. In the face of this, James handled religion as neither anachronism nor infantilism. Since each person's religion has its own functional strength, its rejection on the basis of origin is shallow and unwise. Serious study was thus encouraged because James raised questions about dismissing religion too lightly.

James's chief contribution was the new clinical direction that he gave to the psychology of religion. His insistence that the study of religion move beyond mere words and deeds to focus upon personal import of behavior remains his most important legacy. Admittedly, his emphasis underplays important considerations of the impact of social and historical forces upon personality, and the careful attention to religious ritual and myth that appears in later studies serves as a necessary addendum.[42] Yet James reminds all who study persons that the science of religion depends for its original material upon facts of personal experience. He concludes that "truth and fact well up into our lives in ways that exceed verbal formulation . . . . In the religious sphere, in particular, belief that formulas are true can never wholly take the place of personal experience."[43]

ABRAHAM MASLOW: RELIGIONS, VALUES, AND PEAK-EXPERIENCES

James's insistence upon the primary significance of the personal dimension in religious experience gave impetus to a tradition that became full-blown in the work and writings of Abraham H.

---

[42]See for example, Bronislaw Malinowski, *Magic, Science and Religion* (Garden City NY: Doubleday, 1955); Emile Durkheim, *The Elementary Forms of the Religious Life,* J. W. Swain, trans. (New York: Free Press, 1965); and Gerardus van der Leeuw, *Religion in Essence and Manifestation* (London: Allen and Unwin, 1938).

[43]James, *The Varieties of Religious Experience,* 446-47.

Maslow (1908-1970). Maslow was trained in the strict Pavlovian-Watsonian tradition and as a student and apprentice was bowled over by classical laboratory research. However, his move to New York shortly before the age of thirty brought him under the influence of persons such as the psychoanalysts Karen Horney and Erich Fromm, the Gestaltist Max Wertheimer, and the anthropologist Ruth Benedict, all of whom had in common an intuitive rejection of the Pavlovian tradition and its assumptions. For over thirty years Maslow taught (first at Brooklyn College and then at Brandeis University) and developed his own theory of human motivation.

One biographer remarks that the distinguishing mark separating Maslow from classical psychoanalysis and behaviorism is "not a disagreement about the nature of perceptions or the correct procedure for an exact science so much as his irrepressible *optimism*."[44] The characterization is accurate. Maslow was convinced that persons fail to reach their human potential because of a "Jonah complex," their sense of unimportance and insignificance. He also believed that inherent in each person were possibilities for overcoming Jonah in self-discovery and assertion. His theory of personality is built upon this optimistic confidence.

Self-Actualization

Maslow's writings are replete with their own vocabulary (eupsychia, being-needs, metamotivation, ontification, D-values, etc.), but the two terms most often associated with his name are "self-actualization" and "peak-experience." Maslow readily admitted that his conceptualizations grew out of his attempts to explain the genius of two of his teachers, Ruth Benedict and Max Wertheimer, rather than out of controlled research. He believed that his explanations could be generalized, however, to provide a base for general personality theory. Maslow was thus not so concerned with precise research as he was with careful observation and description of those persons who in fact seemed to have moved beyond being "a bunch of buggywhip makers."[45]

---

[44]Colin Wilson, *New Pathways in Psychology: Maslow and the Post-Freudian Revolution* (New York: Taplinger, 1972) 145.

[45]Maslow, *The Farther Reaches of Human Nature*, 98.

Hierarchy of Needs and Metamotivations. According to Maslow, the fully mature person is one who has attained self-actualization, that is, "experiencing fully, vividly, selflessly, with full concentration and total absorption" what it means to be "wholly and fully human."[46] How is such an ideal goal achieved? What must happen for a person to be self-actualized? The answer to these questions resides in understanding that persons have a hierarchy of needs that can be ranked from lower to higher. Self-actualization demands that the individual move up the ladder to be motivated by, and seek satisfaction of, higher needs.

First, persons must achieve some degree of satisfaction of lower instinctoid needs, those that relate to the safety and survival of the human organism. These include not only such biological necessities as nutrition, but also belonging, affection, respect, and self-esteem. Those who achieve satisfaction on this level are not guaranteed self-actualization, but sufficient gratification of the lower needs can allow higher needs to emerge.[47] Persons who do not feel anxiety-ridden, insecure, unsafe, alone, unloved, or rootless are freed for metamotivation, that is, they may devote themselves to higher, intrinsic values, those that cannot be reduced to anything more ultimate. These are values of being (B-values) and include truth, beauty, perfection, and justice.[48] The B-values behave like needs; their deprivation breeds pathology, and their satisfaction assures health.

Choice. Self-actualization occurs as persons progress up the hierarchy in the direction of B-values. The interchange at which direction is determined is the moment of choice. At specific points individuals confront choice as necessity: to lie or to be honest, to steal or not to steal, to care or not to care. "At such points there is a progression choice and a regression choice."[49] Habitual patterns

---

[46]Ibid., 45.

[47]Compare Erikson on epigenesis; see above, pp. 86-87.

[48]Maslow lists fourteen general categories of B-values, each with numerous subdivisions. See *Religions, Values, and Peak-Experiences* (New York: Viking Press, 1964) 91-96.

[49]Maslow, *The Farther Reaches of Human Nature,* 45.

in choice-making influence movement toward or away from meta-motivation and therefore toward or away from self-actualization. To make a dozen progression choices a day is to move a dozen paces toward self-actualization. So, self-actualization is not a matter of one great moment when "on Thursday at four o'clock the trumpet blows and one steps into the pantheon forever and altogether."[50] It is a process, a matter of degrees, little accessions one by one.

The self-actualized person operates by growth motivation that asserts being by making progressive choices (B-psychology), expressing innate powers, allowing for spontaneous self-fulfillment, confident in one's own ability and insight. Actualization is thwarted by deficiency, regressive choices (D-psychology), that is, those choices that aim merely to cope with problems, prepare for the future, or defend against fear and anxiety.

Desacralization, Resacralization. The process of self-actualization is continually threatened, according to Maslow, by the defense mechanism of desacralization, the reduction of persons to concrete objects and the refusal to see in human beings symbolic and internal values.[51] Maslow suggests that this represents a mistrust of the values and virtues implicit in personality, quite often associated with the adolescent rejection of authority. For persons to become self-actualized they must give up this defense mechanism in the interest of resacralization. This means having the willingness and ability to recover a sense of awe in the presence of persons as fellow human beings. Thus Maslow appeals for "fusion of facts and values"[52] in the understanding of personhood. Those moments in which such fusion is most likely to occur are peak-experiences, transient moments of ecstasy in which self-actualization is thrust forward with a jolt.

Peak-Experiences

Maslow was impressed that the truly great persons of human history had peak-experiences: those moments of ecstasy when they

---

[50]Ibid., 50.

[51]Cf. Martin Buber's discussion of "I-Thou" and "I-It" relationships in *I and Thou,* 2d ed., Ronald G. Smith, trans. (New York: Scribner's, 1958).

[52]Maslow, *The Farther Reaches of Human Nature,* 105ff.

felt at one with the universe—moments in which openness, creativity, and spontaneity were heightened and in which the entire person seemed unified.[53] Such experiences carry their own intrinsic value; even attempts to justify or describe them take away from their dignity and worth. A person "becomes in these episodes more truly self, more perfectly actualizing potentialities, closer to the core of being, more fully human."[54] In the peak-experience not only is the world seen as beautiful and life as intensely desirable, but also evil itself "is accepted and understood and seen in its proper place in the whole, as belonging there, as unavoidable, as necessary, and, therefore, as proper."[55]

Peak-experiences do not always occur in a religious context; many in fact are explicitly nonreligious. But peak-experiences are at the core of religion. Maslow is emphatic on this point:

> The very beginning, the intrinsic core, the essence, the universal nucleus of every known high religion . . . has been the private, lonely, personal illumination, revelation, or ecstasy of some acutely sensitive prophet or seer.[56]

Maslow is convinced further that religious systems at their core are the same. Variations from religion to religion are explained by localisms, or accidents of language, or ethnocentric factors. When these elements not held in common are stripped away, religions agree in principle on the promotion of peak-experiences as vehicles to full selfhood.

Unfortunately, that has not been the history of religious institutions. Maslow reserves his most vigorous castigation for religious leaders who promote their institutions at the expense of peak-experiences. Institutions have more often than not fallen into the hands of "religious organization men" who take the institution more

---

[53]An extensive description of these experiences may be found in Maslow's *Toward a Psychology of Being*, 2d ed. (New York: Van Nostrand Reinhold, 1968) 74-98.

[54]Ibid., 98.

[55]Maslow, *Religions, Values, and Peak-Experiences*, 63.

[56]Ibid., 98.

seriously than they take the experience of the original prophet. These men have risen to the top because, as in any complex bureaucracy, they support and promote the organization. By personality they are rationalistic, materialistic, and mechanistic. Habitually they have suppressed or denied their own peak-experiences, and the possibility of such experiences now threatens the order and control of the institution by which they are sustained. Thus, the hopelessly ambiguous situation of non-peakers being in charge of institutions that at the core are intended to preserve the peak-experience is created. In this sense organized religion may become the major enemy of religious experience.[57]

In the preface to a reissue of *Religions, Values, and Peak-Experiences,* Maslow qualifies his stringent position on organized religion, stating that he had come to feel that his earlier judgment on groups and organizations had been too harsh.[58] In fact, he now believed that human beings could find fulfillment for basic needs only through social groups. Nonetheless, religious institutions and their organization-oriented leaders do not encourage those high moments of religious excitement and ecstasy.

Plateau-Experience. Shortly before his death, Maslow also advanced the concept of plateau-experience, an idea that he did not have the opportunity to develop fully.[59] Plateau-experience lacks the suddenness and intensity of peak-experience. It is marked by serenity, calmness, and ongoing enjoyment and happiness in contrast to the surprising, shocking, climactic, awesome character of peak-experience. Plateau-experience always has a cognitive element about it; peak-experience usually is exclusively emotional.

The achievement of plateau-experience takes time. Living on an elevated plateau of unitive consciousness and B-values is achieved in a lifelong process of discipline and deciding. There is no way to bypass "the necessary maturing, experiencing, living,

---

[57]Maslow says this is the major thesis of *Religions, Values, and Peak-Experiences,* viii.

[58]Ibid., xiii.

[59]Maslow, *The Farther Reaches of Human Nature,* 348-49.

learning."[60] Thus, this experience usually appears in older people, as when a mother sits quietly looking at her baby or a poet reflects on a sunset, each in wonder and contemplation. One wonders whether Maslow, had he had time to do a detailed examination, might have had some kinder words for the "spiritual disciplines" of organized religion in maintaining the plateau-experience.

In sum, then, Maslow expresses supreme confidence in the higher nature of persons; they can surpass their biological order. Religion resides in the human ability to tap inner resources and transcend baser needs. Although these inherent human values "are not the exclusive possession of organized religion," nor do they "need supernatural concepts to validate them," they are identical with spiritual values.[61] A person's natural endowment includes spiritual potential, and this may be realized as each individual lays bare the deeper self, that is, becomes self-actualized through little increments of choice. But at high moments of ecstasy and insight, persons may be flooded with deeper, unifying consciousness and gain distinctive insights into their potential as human beings. It is hoped that this may entice them toward a plateau of living dominated by the highest human values. The peak-experience is the heart of personal religion, and the promotion of this process is the business of organized religion.

Maslow and the James Tradition[62]

In the editorial preface to *Religions, Values, and Peak-Experiences,* Maslow claims that this book is in the tradition of James's *The Varieties of Religious Experience,* and this is true. Maslow affirms the importance of individual experience, especially as known in intense religious expression. Like his predecessor, Maslow takes seriously the highly personal character of religious experience and willingly

---

[60]Ibid., 349.

[61]Maslow, *Religions, Values, and Peak-Experiences,* 4.

[62]The evaluation here draws heavily upon Peter A. Bertocci's critique of Maslow in his "Psychological Interpretations of Religious Experience," in Merton P. Strommen, ed., *Research on Religious Development* (New York: Hawthorn, 1971) 24-26 and his "Review of A. Maslow, *Religions, Values, and Peak-Experiences,*" *Contemporary Psychology* 10 (1965): 449-51.

incorporates his subjective observation of clinical experience into his methodology. He affirms the James hypothesis that the essence of religion is discoverable in exaggerated, "acute-fever" phenomena. He shares the feeling that organized, institutional religion may deaden the vibrancy of personal religion. In this sense he is "pursuing William James's program for a science of religion."[63]

However, Maslow departs from James at one most significant point. He rejects outright any type of supernatural over-belief, although he has his own compensation for the farther side of the "More." Peak-experience represents more than conditioning or biological reaction of any kind and more than the eruption of an undesirable or evil unconscious. It represents a "higher nature" and comes with surprise and revelation. How like the supernatural is Maslow's description of peak-experience!! But he chooses to account for the high moments on humanistic grounds.

Maslow's humanistic explanation requires at least two observations. First, persons who have had peak-experiences, especially those crucial to the establishment and ongoing of religion whom Maslow seems to admire, account for their experiences most regularly in terms of being grasped by an outside power. To explain their experience then on naturalistic or humanistic ground flies in the face of their conviction, both during and after religious episodes, that the events are connected with an Ultimate Being or God. Reaffirming James, who insists on allowing the personal documents to speak for themselves, might serve as a corrective to Maslow on this point.

Second, it must be recognized that Maslow's humanistic naturalistic approach, like any contrary proposal of supernatural explanation, is itself an interpretation of meaning open to philosophical and theological examination. Bertocci puts it succinctly,

> If Maslow's observations of human experiences are correct, they are correct. But what is open to further interpretation is his philosophical interpretation of these "naturalistically." To say that these experiences are human is not at the same time necessarily to say that they are not, or must not be conceived as joint-products of

---

[63]Bertocci, "Psychological Interpretations of Religious Experience," 24.

persons in interaction with non-natural and non-human sources of stimulation or inspiration.[64]

Whether he or James is correct in affirming or denying reality beyond human values, Maslow might well have done us a larger favor by distinguishing between his theoretical formulations about the data and his philosophical or theological over-beliefs.

Maslow's approach encourages the study of healthy individuals as the means for understanding religion, but has his concept of maturity not eliminated most persons in the street? Has his utopian definition of the self-actualized person left most persons outside? What about non-peakers? Is there no balm in Gilead for those who do not reach those ecstatic moments when their full human potential comes into view? Maslow does not manage these questions very well except to suggest idealistically that after considerable observation he is more optimistic that all persons are potential peakers. Gordon Allport's analysis seems more broadly applicable; to his ideas we now turn.

GORDON ALLPORT:
RELIGION AND PERSONAL BECOMING

For more than four decades until his death in 1967, Gordon W. Allport (1897-1967) taught psychology at Harvard University. An autobiographical essay at the conclusion of his last book, *The Person in Psychology,* reads as a perspective on psychology's coming of age on the American scene and tells as much about other psychologists as about the author of the essay. Bertocci believes that Allport "probably more than any other psychologist perpetuates the spirit of William James."[65] Allport himself did pacesetting work on personality; he taught what was probably the first course on personality in an American college, and his text, *Personality: A Psychological Interpretation* (1937), remained normative in the field for many years.[66]

---

[64]Bertocci, "Review of A. Maslow, *Religions, Values, and Peak-Experiences,*" 450.

[65]Bertocci, "Psychological Interpretations of Religious Experience," 27.

[66]Revised and reissued under the title *Pattern and Growth in Personality* (New York: Holt, Rinehart and Winston, 1961).

Allport's work is best described as eclectic. In the James tradition he willingly uses data from whatever sources are applicable to an understanding of persons. Allport says that he has not attempted to establish a "school" nor even to follow a strictly defined program of research. Moreover, his work "has to do with the search for a theoretical system—for one that will allow for truth wherever found, one that will encompass the totality of human experience and do full justice to the nature of man."[67]

Personality and Becoming

Allport's significant treatment of religion must be understood against the backdrop of his general view that every person is to be seen as an *individual* combination of factors that are in a continuous process of change. He identifies a polarity in current personality theory with psychologists tending to gravitate toward one of the extremes.[68] One tradition begins with an assumption that persons at birth are *tabula rasa* and as essentially passive in the process of becoming persons. The organism reacts when stimulated. In this tradition the "cause" factor in personality development remains external; the smaller, molecular units of personality are judged more important than the larger, molar units; and earlier impressions are considered more significant than later influences. Allport sees this emphasis as dominant in American psychological empiricism and deplores the extent to which the conceptual frame of stimulus-response has been considered an adequate explanation of individuality and growth.

According to Allport, the other end of the polarity accounts more adequately for the complex organization and growth of individual persons. This tradition emphasizes the self-propelled character of personality. Human beings to some degree make their own future and determine their own destiny. The individual is not merely "a collection of acts, nor simply the locus of acts; the person

---

[67]Allport, *The Person in Psychology*, 406.

[68]Gordon W. Allport, *Becoming: Basic Considerations for a Psychology of Personality* (New Haven: Yale University Press, 1955) 2-17.

is the source of acts."[69] Although they are influenced by powerful external forces from the past, human beings endlessly judge, comprehend, love, desire, compare, avoid. They are perennially active, striving *toward* self-preservation and self-affirmation. "To understand what a person is, it is necessary always to refer to what he may be in the future, for every state of the person is pointed in the direction of future possibilities."[70]

Hence, the concept of becoming is crucial. Personality is never to be understood solely by its beginnings, its instinctoid needs, or past environmental influences. Primarily significant are its contemporary patterns of motivation and behavior. Persons are always becoming more than being; living is an active participle more than a noun. Personhood is the stable, yet fluid "complex product of biological endowment, cultural shaping, cognitive style, and spiritual groping."[71] It always has a future reference. Allport observes that many of the words with which activity is described are future-oriented—striving, tendency, disposition, planning, expecting, intending, and many others. "People, it seems, are busy leading their lives into the future whereas psychology, for the most part, is busy tracing them into the past."[72]

The Proprium. Although personality continuously changes, each individual is marked by a peculiar unity and distinctiveness, an inner core by which the person may be identified. Allport calls this uniqueness the proprium, a concept more narrow than person or personality and broader than ego.[73] It is an individual's style of being, his sense of self. The proprium is rooted in awareness of bodily functions that are peculiarly personal, but rapidly emerges as the person recognizes thoughts and actions as those that belong

---

[69]Ibid., 12. Allport was impressed with the German Gestalt thinkers, who emphasized the existence of an active intellect and appealed for a more serious consideration of the Gestalt school by American psychology.

[70]Ibid.

[71]Allport, *Pattern and Growth in Personality*, 572.

[72]Allport, *Becoming*, 51.

[73]Ibid., 41-56.

to *him*. Proprium is personal identity, striving in the direction of self-assertion with emotions of self-satisfaction and pride.

Social interaction is an important factor in the proprium. Persons identify themselves through intimate association of their own existence with possessions and groups peculiarly theirs. Clothes or cars or families or parties or nations are peculiarly "mine." These are not merely "things" that "I own"; they are "me" and therefore take on more importance than possessions that belong to other people. With maturity the proprium may also extend to loyalties and interests focused upon abstractions and on moral and religious values, that is, it incorporates items that are ultimately not self-focused or selfish.

Allport's view then is that persons are moving, changing creatures. Each day they are different while remaining the same. Mature survival is dependent upon maintaining identity and direction through "more homogeneous systems of motivation. . . . The possession of long-range goals, regarded as central to one's personal existence, distinguishes the human being from the animal, the adult from the child, and in many cases, the healthy personality from the sick."[74]

Sentiment and Religion

Allport gives wide berth to religion as a significant factor in the ongoing process by which personality thrives. He points out that large percentages of the American public are affiliated with some religious group and an even larger number confess belief in deity. Why then should psychology textbooks devote no more than "two shamefaced pages to the subject—even though religion, like sex, is an almost universal interest of the human race?"[75] Allport responds to such a question in the quite important book, *The Individual and His Religion*, by granting religion the extensive role that it plays in the lives of people.

How then does religion serve individual personality? Allport points to an established tradition in personality theory that at-

---

[74]Ibid., 50-51.

[75]Gordon W. Allport, *The Individual and His Religion* (New York: Macmillan, 1950) 1-2.

tempts analysis in terms of small units.[76] Talk of attitudes, values, habits, faculties, dispositions, and factors illustrates this trend. Allport himself discusses the conception of "trait."[77] Yet, he believed that to these units or even clusters of them must be added larger configurations or systems by which personality is organized and motivated. These are *sentiments,* those relatively stable units of personality that entail many components and are attached to some object of value and devotion, either concrete or abstract. A sentiment incorporates both organization and motivation and prepares a person to act; it is a system of readiness directed toward and organized around some definable object of value.

Psychologically, religion belongs to the order of sentiment. It cannot be explained by a single factor, instinct, or emotion but designates a "widely divergent set of experiences that may be focused upon a religious object."[78] Allport's definition of the religious sentiment stresses its character as well-patterned system:

> a disposition, built up through experience, to respond favorably, and in certain habitual ways, to conceptual objects and principles that the individual regards as of ultimate importance in his own life, and as having to do with what he regards as permanent or central in the nature of things.[79]

The religious sentiment varies from person to person. It reflects the ideational and emotional individuality of persons as they confront their own meaning and destiny. The subjective religious sentiment of every individual is unlike that of any other person. "The roots of religion are so numerous, the weight of their influence in individual lives so varied, and the forms of rational interpretation so endless, that uniformity of product is impossible."[80] No

---

[76]See Allport, "What Units Shall We Employ?" in *Personality and Social Encounter* (Boston: Beacon Press, 1960) 111-29.

[77]Gordon W. Allport, "What Is a Trait of Personality?" *Journal of Abnormal and Social Psychology* 25 (1931): 368-72; and "Traits Revisited," in *The Person in Psychology,* 43-46.

[78]Allport, *The Individual and His Religion,* 4.

[79]Ibid., 56.

[80]Ibid., 26.

definition can possibly suggest the complexity, the subtlety, and the personal flavor of individual religion.

Further, religion belongs to those personality characteristics that are functionally autonomous, that is, they have motivational power of their own. Here Allport stands against classical Freudians, instinctual theorists, and stimulus-response psychologists for whom the "given" in human nature is causative. According to Allport, the religious sentiment may be continuous with biological factors or early conditioning, but it has momentum of its own.[81] In the mature person the religious sentiment has severed its connections with its origins and begun to provide motive power to transform personality.[82]

The individual character of the religious sentiment means that, more often than not, it functions with some inconsistency, occasionally even capriciously. Only in the religious genius is it so perfectly organized and completely under control that no discrepancy appears. Even a strongly developed religious sentiment may be overwhelmed by impulse. Religion, like personality itself, is *becoming* more than *being*. Since the religious sentiment is marked by incompleteness and inconsistency, it must be regularly measured by the criteria by which the mature person is judged—a widened range of interests, development of personal insight, and unification of selfhood.

Extrinsic versus Intrinsic Religion

The pursuit of individual phenomena led Allport to consider the function of personal religious sentiment in interpersonal relationships. Uniform patterns were difficult to discover. In the name of religion persons justify cruelty as well as kindness, authoritarianism as well as forgiveness, dogmatism as well as openness, exploitation as well as generosity. Allport narrowed these inconsistencies to the issue of prejudice, and his study of intercon-

---

[81]In functional autonomy Allport shares a perspective with the Gestaltists Kohler, Koffka, and Lewin, as well as the client-centered therapist Carl Rogers.

[82]See Allport, *The Individual and His Religion*, 64.

nections between religion and prejudice remains normative.[83] His careful analysis led him to three interrelated conclusions that are important for the psychology of religion. The first is an observation that brotherhood and bigotry are often intertwined in religion. Many pious people are saturated with racial prejudice; paradoxically, many advocates of racial justice are religiously motivated. What makes the difference? Second, churchgoers tend to be more intolerant of ethnic minorities than nonchurchgoers. Why would a person's religion seemingly condone intolerance?

Third, Allport discovered that "the relationship between religion and prejudice hinges on the type of religion that the personal life harbors."[84] Consistently, prejudice was accompanied by one type of religion and lack of prejudice by another. This led him to distinguish between extrinsic and intrinsic religion.[85] Extrinsic religion is "religion that is used." It serves to bolster self-confidence, to improve status, to defend against reality, or to sanction a way of life. Persons with this orientation find religion useful in a number of ways and emphasize its rewards over its demands. Extrinsic religion is illustrated by Norman Vincent Peale's recommendation that prayer be used to avoid ulcers and to improve one's golf game; or the business man who professes religion because "it's good business;" or the superpatriot who praises God for protecting the nation. These people may attend church or synagogue regularly but demonstrate little willingness to talk seriously about the meaning of their faith beyond its practical advantage. Extrinsic religion is instrumental and utilitarian.[86]

---

[83]His definitive work on the subject is *The Nature of Prejudice* (Reading MA: Addison-Wesley, 1954), but summaries of his interpretation of religion and prejudice may be found in *Personality and Social Encounter*, 219-67, and *The Person in Psychology*, 185-268. The latter includes articles appearing earlier in the professional journals.

[84]Allport, *Personality and Social Encounter*, 266.

[85]The scales used by Allport to measure these two types of religion may be found in his *The Person in Psychology*, 264-68. A review of the specific items in the scales will clarify the distinctions between the two types.

[86]Will Herberg in his *Protestant-Catholic-Jew* (Garden City NY: Doubleday, 1960) makes the telling point that American religion, whatever its variety, is marked by sameness, serving purposes having nothing to do with the indigenous character of the religions themselves.

Intrinsic religion, on the other hand, is a "religion that is lived." Faith is regarded as valuable in its own right, claiming commitment and transcending self-interests. This kind of religious sentiment has matured beyond the point of an egocentric view of the universe to the evaluation of habit, custom, family, and nation in terms of exterior values. It has forsaken family and land and self to seek first the kingdom. Intrinsic sentiment subordinates instrumental motives to comprehensive commitments. "Such religion does not exist to serve the person; rather the person is committed to serve it."[87] Intrinsic religion may be seen in the martyr who sacrifices self for a cause or less dramatically in the saint who spends a lifetime in social service without demand for public or private rewards.

Allport views extrinsic religion as a shield for self-centeredness, a turning to God without turning away from self. This is the kind of religion that correlates positively with bigotry. Evidently, individuals or groups who are different are perceived as rivals to personal satisfactions, and religion—understood as a device to be used—becomes a partner for protecting self-interests. Both extrinsic religion and prejudice are "useful" and thus mutually support each other. Conversely, intrinsic religion is by nature tolerant. When religion is accepted for its own value, the way is open for exploring its full meaning. Humility about one's own judgments and tolerance for the view of others are thus built into the intrinsic sentiment.

Allport understands that extrinsic-intrinsic religion describes a continuum rather than independent categories. Individuals do not fit neatly into either division in all ways and at all times. The religion-of-the-man-in-the-street tends to move toward one end of the continuum, but each type will occasionally exhibit characteristics of the other.[88] For religion after all, says Allport, is a solitary way. Its

---

[87]Ibid., 132.

[88]His overall descriptions of extrinsic-intrinsic religion are consistent with those of Gerhard Lenski found in *The Religious Factor: A Sociological Study of Religion's Impact on Politics, Economics, and Family Life* (Garden City NY: Doubleday, 1961). In an extensive study among residents of Detroit, Lenski distinguishes between those whose involvement was "communal" (for purposes of status and social belonging) and those who were "associational" (for purposes of value and meaning implicit in the faith).

configurations are intensely personal. A thousand factors may initiate the quest, growth may occur at varying speeds and degrees, and organization of the religious sentiment constantly changes. Because religion is personal and kaleidoscopic, psychology must concentrate upon "the individual and his religion." Yet the complexity, illusiveness, and individuality of the religious sentiment make it no less important. It lies at the core of personality and represents "the audacious bid" of persons to come to terms with life, "engendering meaning and peace."[89]

A NECESSARY MODIFIER

The tradition represented by James, Maslow, and Allport adds an important dimension to the psychological interpretation of religion. These men and their humanistic colleagues stress the importance and potential of the individual in evaluating religious phenomena. In a sense the humanist stands on common ground with the classical psychoanalyst or the behaviorist, who also were concerned with individual behavior. Differences lie in the willingness of humanistic psychologists to recognize and examine "the farther reaches of human nature." James's vision of individuality, Allport's functional autonomy and propriate striving, Maslow's self-actualization and peak-experience are all constructed on the proposition that personal uniqueness and integrity transcend the biological and sociological mechanisms that are inevitably entwined in developmental processes. These men are attempting to delineate "a psychology of deep personal inwardness and uniqueness, of 'what remains' when the processes of acculturation and the meeting of lower needs have taken place."[90] Humanistic psychology assigns religion to these deeper orders of human experience, granting it a generic place in the psychic life. Hence, the phenomenon of religion is not merely the product of conflict and tension, a residue of

---

[89]Allport, *The Individual and His Religion,* 142.

[90]Peter Homans, "Toward a Psychology of Religion: By Way of Freud and Tillich," in Peter Homans, ed., *The Dialogue between Theology and Psychology,* vol. 3 of Essays in Divinity series, Gerald C. Brauer, ed. (Chicago: University of Chicago Press, 1968) 72.

unresolved infantilism, but more a self-transcendence with a dynamic power of its own.

Yet those who assume the humanistic stance risk overstating the importance of the individual at the expense of powerful social forces. What leads a person to be religious? The humanistic tradition may reinforce the popular notion that religious commitments are freely chosen, personal matters between the individual and deity. But considerable psychological research suggests that individual choice operates in a social context. The contributions of the social psychology of religion remind us of the powerful influence of other people on what individuals do, think, and feel—a necessary modifier.[91] James, Maslow, and Allport would argue that mature persons must overcome these forces, refusing to be pushed by every whim of culture. Mature faith means rising above conformity. External pressures may be strong, but individuals are not powerless objects tossed about by biological and environmental forces. Their humanity is to be discovered in the willingness to assert personal resources, to attempt to manage their own behavior, and to choose according to personally selected guidelines.

SUGGESTED READINGS

Allport

Allport, Gordon W. *Becoming: Basic Considerations for a Psychology of Personality.* New Haven: Yale University Press, 1955. Brief summary of his personality theory.

_____. *The Individual and His Religion: A Psychological Interpretation.* New York: Macmillan, 1950. A significant statement.

_____. *Pattern and Growth in Personality.* New York: Holt, Rinehart and Winston, 1961.

_____. *The Person in Psychology: Selected Essays.* Boston: Beacon Press, 1968. Includes an important autobiographical essay.

----

[91]Social psychological research on this issue is extensive. Cf. Solomon Asch, *Social Psychology* (Englewood Cliffs NJ: Prentice-Hall, 1952), demonstrating conformity of judgment when a person says two lines of different lengths are the same because others in the group have said so; or Stanley Milgram, *Obedience to Authority: An Experimental View* (New York: Harper, 1969), who showed that persons under social pressure would obey destructive commands to punish. See also Michael A. Argyle and Benjamin Beit-Hallahmi, *The Social Psychology of Religion* (Boston: Routledge and Kegan Paul, 1975) 30-57.

_____. *Personality and Social Encounter*. Boston: Beacon Press, 1960.

James

Browning, Don S. *Pluralism and Personality: William James and Some Contemporary Cultures of Psychology*. Lewisburg PA: Bucknell University Press, 1980.

James, William. *The Varieties of Religious Experience: A Study in Human Nature*. New York: Modern Library, 1902. Gifford lectures delivered in 1901-1902. A classic.

_____. *The Will to Believe, and Other Essays in Popular Philosophy*. New York: Dover, 1956.

Levinson, Henry S. *Science, Metaphysics, and the Chance of Salvation: An Interpretation of the Thought of William James*. Chico CA: Scholars Press, 1978.

Maslow

Maslow, Abraham H. *The Farther Reaches of Human Nature*. New York: Viking, 1971.

_____. *Motivation and Personality*. 2d ed. New York: Harper, 1970.

_____. *Religions, Values, and Peak-Experiences*. New York: Viking, 1964.

_____. *Toward a Psychology of Being*. 2d ed. New York: Van Nostrand Reinhold, 1968.

Wilson, Colin. *New Pathways in Psychology: Maslow and the Post-Freudian Revolution*. New York: Taplinger, 1972.

Other Humanistic Psychologists

Frankl, Viktor E. *Man's Search for Meaning: An Introduction to Logotherapy*. Ilse Lasch, trans. Rev. ed. Boston: Beacon Press, 1962.

May, Rollo. *Love and Will*. New York: W. W. Norton, 1969.

_____. *Man's Search for Himself*. New York: W. W. Norton, 1953.

Rogers, Carl R. *Client-Centered Therapy: Its Current Practice, Implications, and Theory*. New York: Houghton Mifflin, 1951.

Tournier, Paul. *The Meaning of Persons*. Edwin Hudson, trans. New York: Harper, 1957.

Welch, David, George A. Tate, and Fred Richards, eds. *Humanistic Psychology: A Source Book*. Buffalo NY: Prometheus, 1978.

PART III

PSYCHOSOCIAL DEVELOPMENT AND RELIGIOUS GROWTH

Psychoanalytic, behavioristic, and humanistic psychology each probes the complexity of an experience often clothed in mystery, and each attempts to structure a model (or models) by which religion may be interpreted. These psychological trends have shed important light upon religion's function in human survival and its role in organization of the self. Each suggests a stance for evaluating religion and represents a way by which psychology and religion may come together.

Implicit in all these traditions within psychology is a serious concern to understand human growth. In fact, the developmental process seems to be emerging as a new focus of psychological studies. Certainly the last several decades have produced extensive research and insight into the dynamics by which persons grow, elaborating cognitive, emotional, and volitional aspects of the developmental process. A mass of data has been compiled regarding "stages on life's way."[1] Practical concerns to improve education have

---

[1]Søren Kierkegaard has written a book by this title.

motivated many of these studies, and so they have rather naturally leaned toward those developmental processes involved in learning. Thus, two characteristics dominate recent research on human psychosocial growth: (1) considerable attention to infancy, childhood, and adolescence as crucial periods for learning, and (2) heavy stress upon the cognitive aspects of development. But later stages of human development, as well as affective and volitional aspects of growth, are getting serious attention, making it more possible to understand religious experience in the whole context of human development.

Part III aims to take account of these materials in understanding religious experience. If it is assumed that deity speaks to people within the context of human history (an approach that theologians call incarnational theology), growth itself may become a significant religious pilgrimage of "growing up to God." Understanding the process becomes an important task for the psychology of religion. Our strategy is to describe first the large picture of human development in terms of religion and then to relate research on thinking, feeling, and deciding to specific aspects of the religious pilgrimage.

CHAPTER SIX

RELIGION AND HUMAN DEVELOPMENT: AN OVERVIEW

In 1951 Lewis Sherrill, a Presbyterian theologian and educator, published one of those tiny but important books. Entitled *The Struggle of the Soul*, it attempted to bring studies of religious development at particular stages into a comprehensive view of the entire life span. Using psychological insights and religious language, Sherrill traced religious growth from infancy to old age, discussing the encounter of the self with God and sketching possible responses to the crises involved in the human pilgrimage. He classifies religious experience broadly into that of childhood, youth, and adulthood and then describes the general character of religion in each of these periods.

Sherrill's classifications are certainly broad. Childhood defined chronologically to include both infancy and prepuberty is far from uniform and cohesive. Variations appear even between the five-year-old who is in kindergarten and the one who is not. Is it at all realistic to group together a gangling early adolescent and a college senior? And the psychosocial problems of newlyweds, couples whose children have left home, and the unmarried middle-aged adult are certainly dissimilar. None of these categories is homogeneous, and such broad classification must be prepared to discuss variations within each category.

Nevertheless, persons within each of Sherrill's classifications are similar in terms of general psychosocial tasks to be achieved. Childhood with its diversity is that experience by which separation occurs in the interest of achieving individuality, personal removal from placenta, and enough detachment from family and friends to have a name of one's own. Youth defines those many encounters by which weaning from parents and parental figures is achieved in the interest of accepting responsibility and making mature identification. Adulthood includes all those experiences by which individual responsibility is managed in socially defined roles. Sherrill perceives these tasks to give some unity to childhood, youth, and adulthood and to permit general descriptions of religious growth during these periods.[2]

THE RELIGION OF CHILDHOOD

Psychoanalytic, behavioristic, and humanistic psychologists agree that infancy and early childhood are crucially important and enduringly influential in the structures of human personality. For this reason a large body of research has singled out the early years for intensive study. The major psychosocial features of childhood demonstrated in that research clarify the form and substance of childhood religion.

Importance of Childhood for Religion

Childhood is an experience in separation. The dramatic episode of separation of fetus from womb by which a person is thrust into a strange and threatening environment caricatures "the trauma of birth."[3] The fundamental psychosocial task of childhood is to survive as a separated and separate person. The early years of hu-

---

[2]See Lewis Sherrill, *The Struggle of the Soul* (New York: Macmillan, 1950) 23-99.

[3]Otto Rank, an early psychoanalyst, believed that birth is a prime psychological crisis from which persons never fully recover. See his *The Trauma of Birth* (London: Routledge and Kegan Paul, 1929).

man life, and in some sense the later years too, are spent attempting to discover one's niche as a person whose existence is distinct from that of other people. Birth itself introduces the most human of all questions, "Who am I?" Later experience plays out the answer in terms of relationships with other people, management of loyalties, and standards of behavior. At least three factors of childhood are important in arriving at rudimentary answers to the identity question.

First, childhood is marked by dramatic, episodic change. The research of Gesell, Ilg, and Ames in the 1940s underscores this point.[4] Childhood proceeds in alternate spurts of storm and quiescence, stress and consolidation, as children struggle to find who they are in a world that they by birth have been forced to accept. This pattern itself often provides the framework for early religious development. Parents, with support from social institutions including the church, tend to sanction the calm periods and condemn the stress periods. Religion structured inflexibly on these calm-is-good patterns of early childhood may discourage spontaneity and provide little base for later experiences of disorder and upheaval. The liturgical and educational implications of this are far-reaching. Religious institutions responsible for the nurture of children must give wide berth to children's experimentation with separation and, like parents, endure with patience the storm and stress that often accompany the experimentation.

Second, the child's high capacity for learning is strategically important for religion. Especially during early childhood, the child accepts the world into which he has been born and, like a dry sponge cast into water, eagerly absorbs the surroundings. The incorporative mood of children encourages the idea that the direction of life is firmly established during these early years, expressed in the common statement, "As the twig is bent, so the tree grows." However, the "bent twig" theory of childhood seems more folklore than fact. Character and personality can be changed after the first, third, seventh, or any other supposed magical year. Learning during college

---

[4]See Arnold Gesell, Frances Ilg, and Louise Ames, *The First Five Years of Life: The Pre-School Years* (New York: Harper, 1940) and *The Child from Five to Ten* (New York: Harper, 1946).

and adult years is both more rapid and more complex than during childhood. Persons consistently demonstrate an amazing capacity to overcome childhood liabilities and deprivations.

Nonetheless, what happens to children is indeed impressive. They learn muscular control and mobility, most of the words needed in life and how to combine them in communicative order, to respond to and to create response in human relationships, to remember and to imagine, and a thousand other things involved in growing into humanness. Religion has not allowed the rapidity and extensiveness of childhood learning to go unnoticed, especially in its attempts to inculcate cognitive concepts by which religious systems identify themselves. Hebrew Scriptures, for example, enjoin parents, "Train up the child in the way he should go, and when he is old he will not depart from it."[5] This usually means imparting to the child those ideas that will assure identification with the religious tradition and guarantee its preservation. The concepts are usually quite complex and beyond a child's intellectual comprehension. Hence, acceptance or rejection will be on grounds other than intellectual understanding. Devout parents and concerned religious institutions ought not deceive themselves into thinking that children are doing more than reciting words and imitating behavior that bring approval from authorities who are important to their survival. Critical judgment of ideas may be expected only when the ability to make such evaluations has emerged. If, however, the religious expressions of children can be accepted as childhood experience on the assumption that more reflective understanding and more personal commitments will be possible later, a wealth of religious information can be passed to children during these absorbing years.

Third, by far the most important aspect of childhood concerning religion is the enduring quality of experience with significant adults. This insight is one of our most important legacies from psychoanalysis. Freud's conclusion that God is nothing other than projected parent ought not obscure his correct observation that the child's first god is parent (usually more mother than father). From

---

[5]Proverbs 22:6.

the caring, nurturing context of early parental guardianship spring fundamental "theological" experiences. During early infancy, these exist on the level of feeling and are given cognitive form as verbal and conceptual abilities emerge. These primal, emotional experiences with parents and other significant adults are the foundations upon which future religious constructs may be built. The affective quality of parent-child relationships often carries more weight than later cognitive and conscious instruction. In this sense the cliché is accurate: religion is "more caught than taught."

As John Gleason's book *Growing up to God* points out, basic theological issues may be rooted in these early stages of psychosocial development.[6] In interpersonal experiences with family, the child learns initially the emotional content of religious faith. To wit, the experience of one's first god-mother as caring and trusting or harsh and rejecting takes precedence over consciously learned attributes of God in catechism class or Sunday school. Gleason sees parallels between the psychosocial tasks and important religious concepts. He sketches the Christian doctrinal overtones that he sees in Erik Erikson's eight stages of human development: autonomy involves the religious understanding of good and evil; initiative, an appreciation of sin and redemption; industry, good deeds; identity, the doctrine of a personal relation to Jesus as Christ; generativity, an appreciation of creation; and integrity, one's view of end-time. Each of these grows out of the preceding stage, and all rest on the foundation of hope embedded in the balance of trust/mistrust experienced in initial parent-child relations. Gleason concludes that in the fundamental psychosocial epochs of development "persons learn at the deepest levels of being whether or not their gods (God?) are basically good, kindly, accepting, whether or not the world is essentially safe, whether or not they can experience their own worth as creatures quite apart from their deeds and misdeeds, and whether or not authority can be exercised in roughly equal amounts from internal and external sources."[7]

---

[6]John J. Gleason, Jr., *Growing up to God: Eight Steps in Religious Development* (Nashville: Abingdon, 1975).

[7]Ibid., 40.

The enduring character of these primal relations is what makes childhood a crucial period for religion. Later change may be possible, but whatever happens in maturation either preserves or modifies the experiences of childhood. The success of the religious pilgrimage is determined in some measure by the degree to which external pressures and internal personality structures permit and encourage persons to separate their first gods from the God of their ultimate loyalty.

The Character of Childhood Religion

Childhood religion bears the marks of childhood itself and shows the cognitive, affective, and volitional ebb and flow typical of the early struggles implicit in separation and emancipation. In birth the infant has been cut off from secure existence and has begun the long journey back. Religious development in the child is part and parcel of the struggle to evolve a real person with name and character amid an environment that often threatens to absorb or destroy personal identity. Research has not yet uncovered all the details, but enough light has been shed on religious growth to make clear the major features of childhood religion.

Egocentric Orientation. The most obvious characteristic of childhood religion is its egocentric orientation. This is strangely paradoxical because the world into which the child is thrust at birth belongs largely to others. Powerful forces surround the tiny infant, who is innocently dependent upon the generosity of those forces for survival. Rapidly, however, the environment is objectified, beginning when the infant's eyes first follow mother-object. The infant's transformation of the object-world into instruments for primal satisfaction and security is the initial start of several childhood orderings of the world and is the rudimentary matrix of religious development.

Egocentric orientation during childhood is illustrated in the well-known research of Jean Piaget on the language of children between the ages of three and seven years.[8] Piaget found that speak-

---

[8]Piaget's *The Language and Thought of the Child* (New York: Harcourt Brace, 1932) is available in English. A summary of Piaget's theory may be found in Jean Piaget and Barbel Inhelder, *The Psychology of the Child,* Helen Weaver, trans. (New York: Basic Books, 1969).

ing did not have the same meaning for children as for adults. Language for the child is not socialized, but consists rather of "monologues" and "collective monologues," that is, it is egocentric language, "less a means of communicating ideas and information than an assertion of himself before others."[9] Everyone has observed with some delight the caricature of this kind of language in the child talking to an imaginary playmate or repeating nonsensical interpretations of religious language. "The consecrated cross I'd bear" becomes "The consecrated cross-eyed bear" because communicating idea is not his intent. Language, even when it makes little sense, announces the child's presence and affirms personal importance.

Children's prayers are filtered through this egocentric orientation. Elkind, Spilka, and Long studied the conceptions of prayer among one hundred and sixty boys and girls, ages five through twelve, and delineated three stages in their development.[10] At the first stage (ages five to seven) the child vaguely linked prayer with "God" or certain learned formulae such as, "Now I lay me down to sleep," but the experience remained indistinct and undifferentiated. At the second stage (ages seven to nine) prayer came to be specifically associated with particular activity but remained concrete and highly personalized. In the third stage (ages nine through twelve) the idea of prayer as communication between the child and the divine began to appear. Only in the last stage did the content of prayer shift from egocentric wishes (candy, rabbits, toys) to altruistic and ethical concerns (peace, love everybody).

Religious systems cannot then expect childhood religion to conform to high ideals of altruism. The child's ideas of God are initially constructed in the image of parents in terms of infantile needs to cope with a threatening environment. In this context "concepts" and "ideas" are unreflective and imitative, that is, they are accepted on the basis of relationships with significant adults, rather than on

---

[9]Jacques M. Pohier, "Religious Mentality and Infantile Mentality," in André Godin, ed., *Child and Adult before God* (Chicago: Loyola University Press, 1965) 21.

[10]David Elkind, Bernard Spilka, and Diane Long, "The Child's Conception of Prayer," in André Godin, ed., *From Cry to Word: Contributions toward a Psychology of Prayer* (Brussels: Luman Vitae Press, 1968) 51-64.

the basis of their rational content and theological meaning. Parent, pastor, or priest often attach more theological content to the religious behavior of children than it merits. Religious adults must not deceive themselves into believing that children who repeat key religious words and phrases are performing more than imitative and unreflective behavior. The development of habit on these grounds is not undesirable, but when the habit has been developed, it ought not be assumed that the child has precociously escaped childhood simply because the behavior bears religious labels.

Anthropomorphic Concreteness. A second feature of children's religion is its anthropomorphic concreteness, that is, religious words and descriptions will be translated into familiar experiences, usually in the forms of known persons. Children's questions of "how?" and "why?" usually reflect infantile attempts to relate abstract religious explanations to their subjective, concrete world of experience. Two illustrations will clarify the concreteness that characterizes childhood mentality. At one time a major Protestant denomination called one of its children's groups "Sunbeams." The group's theme song was "Jesus wants me for a Sunbeam." One wonders whether children could have envisioned themselves concretely as a beam of light, but certainly the analogous comparison between a light ray and "brightening the world" by good deeds was beyond their mental comprehension. Further, their wonderful world of television might have provided a ready concrete definition of sunbeam and translated their theme song into "Jesus wants me for a toaster!" Or consider the abstract imagery incorporated in a standard prayer taught to children: "Now I lay me down to sleep. I pray thee, Lord, my soul to keep. If I should die before I wake, I pray thee, Lord, my soul to take." Death might be made concrete in terms of the death of a pet, but it is difficult to imagine how concepts such as "Lord" or "soul" might be meaningful to a child. A parent who reflected on the theological content of such a prayer, to say nothing about sending a child to bed with the idea of death before daybreak, might be indeed grateful that the child's participation is unreflective and imitative!

The concreteness of childhood mentality regularly is anthropomorphic in descriptions of God, highly influenced in Christian circles by the patriarchal orientation of biblical literature. God is thought of and literally described as father or grandfather or bearded Santa Claus. He has eyes to see, hands to hold, and tongue to speak. But these concrete anthropomorphisms also carry for the child "signification."[11] Father is kindness or threat or fear or pampering or any number of things. Anthropomorphisms thus serve as concrete conductors and preservers of meanings that otherwise might be lost because the child's reflective ability has not yet appeared.

Piaget believes that these representational functions appear quite early, perhaps as early as the second year, and serve as a base upon which may be later built an expanding edifice of thought. Although Piaget does not apply his ideas to religious development, our identification of anthropomorphism with these early mental processes grounds religious experience in rudimentary infantile experience. The connections may be either positive or negative. To describe God as father may signify for one child a pleasing, rewarding experience; for another whose father has been tyrannical the signification may be unpleasant and threatening. In either case, later theological statements are likely to reflect these early childhood significations until the meanings are modified by more mature reflection and experience.

Anthropomorphic concreteness also clarifies the function of religious mythology. The stories by which religious systems preserve and convey their fundamental values are replete with anthropomorphisms. The Hebrew God plays in the mud and makes man or, like an Eastern farmer, walks in the garden in the cool of the day. In Greece Zeus marries Hera, and in Babylon Marduk and Tiamat enter into mortal combat. In numerous traditions and literally thousands of ways, the Gods are described to behave as people, not as ways of cutting them down to size, but as means for preserving their timeless significations. These anthropomorphisms are important carriers of meaning, and a part of their genius is to lay hold of the essential character of human existence by utilizing the rudimentary experience of childhood. As Mircea Eliade says, "The myth describes the various and sometimes dramatic ir-

---

[11]See Piaget and Inhelder, *The Psychology of the Child,* 51-53.

ruptions of the sacred into the world . . . an irruption narrated in the myths, that established the world as a reality."[12] Anthropomorphic concreteness in myth serves religion in the same way that it serves childhood—to maintain values in direct and uncomplicated forms.

Experimentation, Initiative, Spontaneity. A third major feature of childhood religion grows out of experimentation with individuality, initiative, and spontaneity. As the child's world rapidly expands beyond the family circle, new facets to the issue of separation appear. The ages four, five, and six are crucial years in which the child reaches out, takes initiative, and asserts self in territory on which peer playmates and adults beyond parents also stake claims. Entrances into kindergarten and first grade are adventures into strange new worlds demanding additional experimentation with identity.

During this period, separation proceeds at a rapid pace, often leaving children floundering and searching for patterns that will enable them to survive. Freud attaches considerable importance to this period as a time when the Oedipus struggle is intense and superego develops as a means of control.[13] But more significantly the growing child learns what it means to experiment with self in new environments. Although the world still belongs to others, particularly parents and teachers, the achievement of identity that will come to fruition in adolescence makes significant strides in the creativity and spontaneity of middle childhood.

Childhood religion is likely to take on the character of experimentation and spontaneity and come out in unpredictable and individualistic theological forms. Like early crayon drawings, conceptions of God will lack rational precision. Ernest Harms in an important study refers to this period as the "fairy-tale" stage in which fantasy and emotion are key ingredients in creativity.[14] The

---

[12]Mircea Eliade, *The Sacred and the Profane: The Nature of Religion*, Willard R. Trask, trans. (New York: Harper, 1961) 97.

[13]See above, p. 70.

[14]Ernest Harms, "The Development of Religious Experience in Children," *American Journal of Sociology* 50 (1944): 112-22.

dynamic function of fantasy in searching for forms for religious expression is illustrated in a conversation between a four-and-a-half-year-old son and his father. They were driving home from Sunday School through the countryside when without warning the son exclaimed, "Look, Daddy! There's God!" The father, sharing the excitement and taking the observation seriously, responded, "Where? Where?" "There. Up in that tree." The conversation continued, not to debate with the child that God could not possibly be "up in that tree" or convince him of a more orthodox theological position, but to understand how fantasy was creating an idea. Evidently the Sunday School teacher had that morning talked about "God in heaven" in such ways that the child associated pleasantness with the talk. Since at that time climbing a tree was his most exciting accomplishment, the child in his own way had combined the enthusiasm of the two experiences and made his own theological affirmation. In short, he was experimenting with an experience in the only way in which he knew how. His statement was individualistic, emotional, and spontaneous but nonetheless full of theological import.

The anecdote also illustrates the religious importance of allowing for "the free play of emotions and fantasy" during childhood without threat or reprisal.[15] On the deep, feeling level the child must learn that it is alright to express initiative—that parent, minister, and God can bear even crude experimentation. In this context the emotional sense of belonging, acceptance, and forgiveness is learned more fundamentally through the trial and error of human relations than through formal instruction.[16]

In summary, childhood is a psychologically dynamic period for religious development. Children have an incredible ability to imitate adult behavior, and religious institutions may appropriately provide models for imitation. But responsibility of church and synagogue extends beyond this. The child's imitation of adult ideas and actions is valuable, but the more important and enduring religious experience of children occurs on a deeper, personal level and bears

---

[15]Walter H. Clark, *The Psychology of Religion: An Introduction to Religious Experience and Behavior* (New York: Macmillan, 1958) 94.

[16]Cf. Sherrill, *The Struggle of the Soul*, 45.

the marks of childhood itself: egocentricity, concrete anthropomorphisms, crude experimentation. The religious institution may
helpfully provide models and communicate materials on the child's
level, but regularly children transform what is seen and heard into
the cognitive, affective, and volitional forms that they can manage.
The acceptance of childhood religion *as the experience of children* with
freedom to participate in a religious community that includes all
ages prepares the way for pilgrimage toward maturity.

THE RELIGION OF YOUTH

The child's faltering, sometimes awkward step toward a religion of personal commitment becomes a giant step during youth—
that crucial period in which individuality takes shape as the weaning process moves toward completion.[17] The psychosocial development of young people from about nine or ten to the late teens
makes it possible for them to accept responsibility for their own behavior and to become reflectively committed to systems of their own
choosing. Thus, the period of youth is an important chapter in the
story of religious growth.

Psychosocial Development of Youth and Their Religion

The details of psychosocial development throughout youth are
beyond our purpose here.[18] But two dramatic developments occur
during this period that make possible kinds of religious experience
decidedly different from those of childhood. The young person
develops efficiency in using a new type of thinking and becomes increasingly disengaged from childhood relationships.

Cognitive Development. An extensive body of research in the religious development of youth has scored the impressive cognitive
growth that becomes possible during this period. Piaget described
this as movement from intuitive to concrete to propositional think-

---

[17]"Youth" is used here as a broader term than "adolescence" to indicate the social extension of this period beyond biological, pubertal maturation. The correlation between the sophistication of a culture and the lengthening of dependency
is so well known as to need no documentation and is accepted here as axiomatic.

[18]Any textbook survey of adolescent psychology will supply this information.

ing.[19] The impressive researcher Ronald Goldman has applied Piaget's ideas to religion, and in his book *Religious Thinking from Childhood to Adolescence,* Goldman describes the growing capacities of persons from six to sixteen years of age to manage religious concepts. Crucial to the process is the emergence of the facility to think abstractly, that is, to take from objects and experiences those qualities that are similar and dissimilar and thence to generalize upon common characteristics. Until about age eleven, thinking is limited to concrete situations, actions, and data, but after age eleven or twelve, logical thinking in symbols and abstract ideas becomes increasingly possible.

Goldman examined abstraction in religious thinking by asking two hundred persons aged six to sixteen years to interpret three biblical stories (the burning bush, crossing the Red Sea, and the temptation of Jesus). Distinct growth along the lines suggested by Piaget was observed. The younger person tended toward concreteness; the older youth in his sample abstracted concepts and drew comparisons. Goldman's study demonstrated that youth may gradually achieve efficiency, not only in exploring hypothetical interpretations, but also in seeing the relevance of abstracted truth to their own experiences.[20] In short, cognitive growth permits transition from "a religion of pure externals to one of the inner life."[21] The developmental tempo is much slower than one might assume, encompassing the entire range of late childhood and adolescence. Apparently, abstract ability does not usually appear until age eleven or twelve. Efficiency in its use may not develop earlier than the college years, and even then it may not be equally achieved.

The studies of Piaget and Goldman demonstrate clearly that cognitive development during youth takes a turn that makes think-

---

[19]See Piaget and Inhelder, *The Psychology of the Child,* 130f.

[20]See Ronald Goldman, *Religious Thinking from Childhood to Adolescence* (New York: Seabury, 1964) 60-62, 80-84.

[21]R. M. Loomba, "The Religious Development of Children," *Psychological Abstracts* 345 (1944): 35.

ing qualitatively different from that found in the child.[22] Young persons develop the capacity to construct theories and evaluate reasons behind them. They can treat their own thoughts and feelings as external objects and reason about them. The late adolescent can construct ideals and imagine situations, conceiving "as if" situations to solve problems without having to experience them directly. "It seems reasonable, therefore, to characterize the mental ability which emerges in adolescence as the capacity for theory construction and the corresponding need as the *search for comprehension.*"[23] Such cognitive growth makes it possible for the young person to leave behind an infantile religion derived basically from surroundings, to reflect upon concepts, and to move toward a religious faith that is in new ways genuinely personal.

Identity. A second issue in the psychosocial development of youth that has special relevance for religion is identity. Erik Erikson has emphasized the crisis character of youth's struggle for identity and stressed their need to come out of the struggle with enough sense of personal worth and role to relate to other persons and ideologies with fidelity. The identity crisis is created by the breakup of the child's world, and its resolution hinges upon evolving a sense of sameness and continuity in which past childhood, present youth, and future adulthood are bound together cohesively and coherently.[24]

---

[22]Cf. Göte Klineberg, "Perception-like Images in the Religious Experience of the Child," in André Godin, ed., *Child and Adult before God,* 123-34; R. V. McCann, "Developmental Factors in the Growth of a Mature Faith," *Religious Education* 50 (1955): 147-55; André Godin, "Some Developmental Tasks in Christian Education," in Merton P. Strommen, ed., *Research on Religious Development* (New York: Hawthorn, 1971) 109-54; Jean-Pierre Deconchy, "The Idea of God: Its Emergence between Seven and Sixteen Years," in André Godin, ed., *From Religious Experience to a Religious Attitude* (Chicago: Loyola University Press, 1965) 97-108.

[23]David Elkind, "The Origins of Religion in the Child," *Review of Religious Research* 12 (1970): 40.

[24]Discussions of these ideas may be found throughout Erikson's writings. See especially his *Childhood and Society,* rev. ed. (New York: W. W. Norton, 1963) 261-63; *Insight and Responsibility* (New York: W. W. Norton, 1964) 81-107; and "Youth: Fidelity and Diversity," in *The Challenge of Youth* (Garden City NY: Doubleday, 1965) 1-28.

The achievement of identity occurs amidst intense stress. Several factors converge to create for the young person a deepened sense of rootlessness and sometimes bewilderment. Abstract cognitive abilities are recent enough that the youth may not be comfortable with them; they have not yet constructed a comprehensive worldview to replace the faded securities of childhood. Biological maturity has come to pass, but it has often outdistanced opportunities for social fulfillment. Sexual outlets comparable to pubertal physical development are not always available or, if opportunities are available, moral standards may not allow for free expression. The evaluation of these new energies and the development of norms for their management may be couched in considerable uncertainty. Further, discontinuity between youth and adult values begins to appear. The highly selective and idealistic values presented to children can no longer be accepted on authoritarian grounds, and the young person is left with threatening uncertainty and ambivalence. On the one hand, communication with and recognition by the adult world are desired; on the other, roles and values coming from outside are no longer accepted automatically. Kaspar Naegle expresses a judgment shared by many researchers that the stress faced by youth exceeds that of either childhood or adulthood:

> Suspended between a "no longer" and "not yet," youth is forced to balance continuity and discontinuity. To a degree, this may be true of all ages in our era. But children have less to look back on . . . adults have fewer radically new experiences to move into . . . to youth, the present contrasts much more vividly with past and future.[25]

The management of these stresses is sometimes turbulent, sometimes peaceful, but in American society usually it is protected. Erikson refers to the extended period between the advent of genital maturity and the onset of responsible adulthood as "a psychosocial moratorium," a socially sanctioned interlude permitting youth

---

[25]Kaspar D. Naegle, "Youth and Society: Some Observations," in Erik H. Erikson, ed., *The Challenge of Youth*, 55.

to fend for their potential.[26] The extension of this period allows for the creation of a special kind of subculture, a "youth culture" with its own values, customs, and language. This culture emphasizes disengagement; it "is not always or explicitly anti-adult, but it is belligerently *non*-adult."[27] The separate culture serves as a temporary sanctuary of belonging.[28] As a psychosocial moratorium, it provides not only an opportunity to postpone adulthood, but also a more positive chance to develop "a sense of identity which will resolve the discontinuity between childhood and adulthood."[29] An implicit risk is that disengagement may be unduly idealized and preserved to avoid moving forward into adult responsibility, a datum that may explain in part the passionate acceptance of sports in America. The familiar figure of the religious worker who attempts to emulate the dress and speech habits of youth culture in order to "reach the young people" testifies to a misunderstanding of the fleeting economy of this culture. But if the culture is accepted as a creative interlude, it may provide young people an opportunity to develop their identity as adults without complete separation from the adult world.

Youth's movement toward fully developed genitality, role selection, and sense of personal identity has overtones that are obviously religious. Not until this period is it possible for the growing person to be personally committed to an ideology, an outlook, a philosophy round which life is oriented. Youth are about the business of searching for persons and causes that will bring a sense of comprehensiveness and claim their loyalty. The struggle is "often hidden in a bewildering combination of shifting devotion and sudden perversity."[30] "The most widespread expression of the discon-

---

[26]Erikson, "Youth: Fidelity and Diversity," 12. The college experience serves as a psychosocial moratorium in American society.

[27]Kenneth Keniston, "Social Change and Youth in America," in Erik Erikson, ed., *The Challenge of Youth*, 210.

[28]See David Riesman, "Where Is the College Generation Headed?" *Atlantic* 207 (1961): 39-45.

[29]Keniston, "Social Change and Youth in America," 212.

[30]Erikson, "Youth: Fidelity and Diversity," 3.

tented search of youth is the craving for locomotion" expressed in the vernacular as "being on the go" or "running around."[31] Sports, dancing, cars, and causes (sometimes faddish and often transitory) become means through which the search is expressed. Institutional establishment often has difficulty with youth. Their locomotion seems so aimless, their loyalty objects so trite, and they often test "extremes before settling on a considered course."[32] The weeding of loyalties, ranking of priorities, and development of a comprehensive point of view take time, "and sometimes the longest time for the most talented, who usually take the job most seriously."[33]

For the shifting moods and intellectual prowess of youth to reach fruition, an accepting and secure environment is necessary. In spite of the strain and discomfort often associated with this period, the potential for human growth justifies considerable patience. In a real sense the child is learning to become the adult, understanding in larger measure who he is, learning to think reflectively and responsibly, finding strength for disciplined and personal devotion. By their responses and actions the young "tell the old whether life as represented by the old and as presented to the young has meaning."[34] Sometimes the message is reassuring, sometimes disconcerting. Caught on the "isthmus of the middle state" between childhood and adulthood, youth is marked by legitimate intensity consonant with the inherent possibilities for personal identity. The institutions of society, and especially school and church, that espouse "putting away childish things" must make available to youth-in-transition the gentler virtues and provide enough security to open the door for leaving adolescence behind.

THE RELIGION OF ADULTHOOD

With the possible exception of recent interest in the aging, adulthood has received limited attention in psychological research. The rapidly increasing percentage of the population over retire-

---

[31]Ibid., 11.

[32]Ibid., 4.

[33]Keniston, "Social Change and Youth in America," 212.

[34]Erikson, "Youth: Fidelity and Diversity," 24.

ment age and the social problems deriving from these statistics have created discussion of the psychosocial needs and potential contributions of the elderly. Otherwise, the personality development of adults has not enjoyed the scrutiny given to childhood and youth.

Popularly it has often been assumed that an adult is an adult, that growth has been completed, and that—apart from occasional and eccentric shifts—adulthood is largely cut from a single pattern. On this point popular interpretations have undoubtedly been overinformed by the tradition that emphasizes the crucial and enduring influence of childhood. No more than casual observance, however, points up dramatic differences in adults. Consistent physiological change runs a predictable and irreversible course throughout life, and sooner or later even "ageless athletes" find that "timing" is gone. Parents who move through the adolescence of their own children to grandparenthood know the certainty of adult change. Vocational shifts from "building up" to "maintaining" the business illustrate the contrast by which adulthood moves from visionary enthusiasm for the future to nostalgic satisfactions with the past. In short, adulthood is characterized by its own movement through periods with their own psychosocial dynamics. Changes in religious belief, attitudes, and behavior among adults are integrally related to these changing personality structures.

Love-Care-Wisdom

Although oriented specifically around Christian and biblical imagery, Sherrill's description of adult religion in *The Struggle of the Soul* suggests a developmental format. Three chapters reflect the temper of changing adult responsibility in terms of emotional, economic, social and religious commitments. Analogous to Jesus on the Mount of Temptation, the young adult *chooses* the direction he will take, *tempted* by a variety of options. This is the period when commitments are being made and roles are being established. During the middle years (from about thirty to fifty), the adult confronts "The Burning Bush," working out his niche, developing a philosophy by which unanticipated realities are managed. The central problem during middle adulthood is to achieve a mature, integrated view of life by which consistent decisions may be made. "Into Thy Hands" labels older adulthood whose benchmark is simplification. Interests and activities are less diversified; the "less important" is discarded in the interest of elevating the "more important." Life becomes considerably less complicated and more centered upon those items that genuinely matter.

Erik Erikson's descriptions of adulthood share the developmental perspective of Sherrill, but are more easily applied across religious lines.[35] Like Sherrill, Erikson is impressed by the changing environments of adults, creating circumstances in which new and varied alterations are demanded. But more than Sherrill he uses language less tied to a specific religious tradition and concentrates upon the resolution of the psychosocial problems presented by the successive stages of adulthood.

Three of Erikson's eight epigenetic stages belong to this period. Young adulthood begins as the identity crisis of late adolescence passes. Knowing in some measure who they are, persons enter new relationships of increasing responsibility, an experience with its own inherent conflicts. The newfound self of adolescence must be related to other selves. Hence young adulthood is an experience of exploring *intimacy*, "the ability to fuse your identity with somebody else's without fear that you're going to lose something of yourself."[36] The counterpart of intimacy is *isolation*, maintaining distance between one's self and other people. Equilibrium between intimacy and isolation then is learning to lose oneself in partnership with another while preserving one's own identity. To balance these opposites is to *love* in a most genuine way. The achievement of fullness and richness in intimate relationship with another human being is the crucial task of early adulthood as illustrated most explicitly in marriage.[37] In biblical language this experience is the expression of *agape*, the highest form of intimacy that demands nothing in return. Intimacy does not threaten isolation; the two are experienced in balance.

---

[35]See his *Childhood and Society*, 263-69; and Richard I. Evans, *Dialogue with Erik Erikson* (New York: Harper, 1967) 48-58.

[36]Evans, *Dialogue with Erik Erikson*, 48.

[37]Cf. Howard J. Clinebell, Jr., and Charlotte H. Clinebell, *The Intimate Marriage* (New York: Harper, 1970).

Middle adulthood, according to Erikson's model, is the period of maximum productivity. During this period, adults share *generativity* and *creation* with society at large, participating in the establishment and direction of the next generation. To do otherwise is to *stagnate in egocentricity*. This is the age for the discovery of limits of one's abilities and adjustments in self-concept on the basis of reality and not dream. The future increasingly becomes the present, and fantasy gives way to achievement. The strength of character that emerges during middle adulthood Erikson calls *care,* that sense of concern and responsibility which values "that which needs protection and attention."[38] In religious terms stagnation and meaninglessness are avoided by interpreting one's own responsible function in perpetuating life and culture as belonging to God's intention for persons. The Genesis story of Adam contains more than a hint of this purpose for persons. Humankind shares with God the maintenance of created things.[39] Creatures who fulfill their destiny care not only about their own offspring, but also about all creation.[40]

The final stage of adulthood is old age and maturity, where the central issue is finding satisfaction that life as it has been lived has had some fulfillment and accomplishment. The sense of *integrity* derived from this reflection must at least outweigh the feeling of *despair* coming from decreasing productive abilities. A person whose physical activity has decreased, whose authority has been eroded, and who may become more dependent upon others must sense some well-being about a job well done, a life well lived. Kubler-Ross underscores this kind of transformation among persons facing their own death. Final acceptance comes in an experience of "transfer of hope," a shift from the desire for personal survival to confidence in the accomplishments of others.[41] Erikson rather loosely refers to the emotional integration of late adulthood as the achievement of *wis-*

---

[38]Evans, *Dialogue with Erik Erikson,* 53.

[39]Cf. Genesis 1:26-30.

[40]This is the psychological and theological underpinning of ecological concerns.

[41]Elizabeth Kubler-Ross, *On Death and Dying* (New York: Macmillan, 1970).

dom, not in the sense of accumulated knowledge, but in the sense of discrimination that emphasizes the more enduring and important.

From Messianism to Nostalgia

The developmental descriptions of Erikson add important qualifications to the question, "Do persons get more religious as they get older?" Some religious practices seem to decline in later years, undoubtedly influenced in part by growing infirmities of age.[42] Yet "more of the formal social participation of the elderly . . . is in church than in all other voluntary community organizations together."[43] And apparently, religious feelings become more intense as persons approach old age. A number of surveys report a higher percentage of the elderly who say that religion is an important, often the most important, item in their lives.[44]

The ambiguous evidence combined with a developmental understanding of adulthood suggests that our question needs to be restated. The issue is not so much whether adults get more or less religious as they get older as it is the changing role of religion in the experience of the adult. That the function of religion changes as adults change seems incontrovertible. The movement generally seems to be from messianic aspiration toward nostalgic reassurance. Young adulthood thrives on messianic optimism, not in the sense of absolute confidence that the world can be conquered, but in the sense that accomplishment lies in the future. What can be done is still to be done. Children are to be reared, houses to be paid for, promotions to be earned. Energy is directed toward tomorrow. In the Hebrew scriptures such confidence in the future is expressed as messianism. Yahweh, who has acted in past history, will

---

[42]Cf. Harold L. Orbach, "Aging and Religion: A Study of Church Attendance in the Detroit Metropolitan Area," *Geriatrics* 16 (1961): 535-40; and Rodney Stark, "Age and Faith: A Changing Outlook on an Old Process," in Benjamin Beit-Hallahmi, ed., *Research in Religious Behavior: Selected Readings* (Monterey CA: Brooks/Cole, 1973) 190-207.

[43]David O. Moberg, "Religiosity in Old Age," in L. B. Brown, ed., *Psychology and Religion* (Baltimore: Penguin, 1973) 191-92. This article may also be found in *Gerontologist* 5 (1965): 78-87.

[44]Cf. Moberg, "Religiosity in Old Age," 189-90.

continue to act by sending his anointed messiah to achieve his purposes. Life ahead can be affirmed not so much because the answers are in as because of the conviction that God will continuously act redemptively. The young adult is likely to appreciate and appropriate this understanding of faith as his mood. His mind set is futuristic, looking forward to participation in the future of the kingdom. He leaps with faith into the future.

Gradually, often imperceptibly, the mood of adulthood shifts. Roles become more and more established; changes tend to become cumulative and less reversible. Commitments to family, occupation, and religion stabilize character and restrict developmental alternatives.[45] Personality and life-style become more set, less susceptible to decisions that lead in radically different directions and interruptible only by major social or personal crisis.

With increasing psychosocial stability the religion of adulthood is likely to turn toward nostalgia. Unfortunately, the negative aspects of nostalgia in religion have often been emphasized.[46] Accordingly, the experience is seen as a way to escape from present responsibility, a shrinking back to past securities to avoid facing new decisions. Contemporary religion of just plain folks in the southern United States is marked by large doses of escapist nostalgia. Worship consists largely of replication of models from the frontier, and religious talk is preoccupied with the "good ole days when people were really religious." Yet, nostalgia is not necessarily just homesickness for religion as it used to be. For the aging person it may be a resource for genuine personal strength and reassurance. It may be a vehicle whereby the older adult looks to the past to select values, ideas, and activities that are reassuring and supportive. Fewer worlds to conquer lie ahead; those that have been conquered become more important. The positive nostalgic mood is illustrated by the person who says, "I used to try to garrison the whole frontier

---

[45]Paul B. Maves, "Religious Development in Adulthood," in Strommen, ed., *Research on Religious Development,* 782.

[46]See Wayne E. Oates, *The Psychology of Religion* (Waco TX: Word Books, 1973) 273-74.

of Christian doctrine; but now I find I had much better garrison my own heart."[47]

Movement toward nostalgia among the aging is supported by research that shows a tendency among older adults who are already religious to become more conservative and more intensely committed to their religious views.[48] Paul Maves lists several factors that possibly explain religious conservatism among older adults:

> that they carry the values of an earlier, more conservative period, that they might have increased difficulty of learning, whether due to decreased neural plasticity or to the conflict of new learning with established habits, that they tend to become isolated from social changes, that they may be cast into the social role of conservers of social patterns, and that they might have less energy.[49]

With specific individuals these factors may be combined in a number of ways to discourage flexibility and increase conservatism. But whatever its genesis, conservatism serves nostalgic religion and provides the older adult enough security and reassurance to survive a fleeting future.

A DEVELOPMENTAL SYNTHESIS

Human growth is indeed a dramatic pilgrimage in which interests, abilities, and philosophies continuously move. Biological, sociological, and psychological developments in personhood are the matrix for changing religious experience. The pioneering work of James W. Fowler brings together many features of this movement in his research on faith development.[50] Building upon the earlier work of Jean Piaget and Lawrence Kohlberg, Fowler interprets

---

[47]Lewis Sherrill, *The Struggle of the Soul,* 146.

[48]See, for example, Sidney L. Pressey and Raymond G. Kuhlen, *Psychological Development through the Life Span* (New York: Harper, 1957); and Moberg, "Religiosity in Old Age," 186-207.

[49]Maves, "Religious Development in Adulthood," 785.

[50]Fowler's research is reported in numerous journal articles (see the Suggested Readings at the end of the chapter) and in his book *Stages of Faith: The Psychology of Human Development and the Quest for Meaning* (New York: Harper, 1981). Fowler is one among many researchers who have discussed the relationship between religious and psychosocial development beginning as early as Sigmund Freud.

faith, like cognition and moral judgment, to develop through sequential and identifiable stages.[51] At each stage the individual's faith is related to the psychosocial patterns of that stage in both content and "the underlying structures or operations of human thought and belief."[52]

For Fowler faith is the primary orientation, the "structural core," of a person's existence. It incorporates forms by which persons think and make moral judgments, the ways they put their world into order, roles taken, the locus of their authority, the bounds of their social awareness, and ways they use symbols. These "structural competencies" converge in a series of faith stages through which the growing person normally moves:[53]

Stage 1: Intuitive/Projective Faith (about four to eight years). The world is given meaning through parents and other primary adults by intuitively projecting meaning through imitation of those adults.

Stage 2: Mythic/Literal Faith (about eight to twelve). Meaning here is derived from those groups with which a person is affiliated; faith appropriates from the community those stories (myths) which make sense of the environment, taking them literally.

Stage 3. Synthetic/Conventional Faith (from about twelve into adulthood) is conforming faith, taking direction from popular convention, but beyond Stage 2 involving personal choices among conventions. It balances various conventional demands into a workable synthesis of meaning.

---

[51]See below, pp. 272-80, for a discussion of the developmental process as described by Piaget and Kohlberg. These discussions, along with those of Fowler and Erikson, may be easily compared to the important work of Jane Loevinger on ego development. Loevinger, *Ego Development* (San Francisco: Jossey-Bass, 1976), charts ego development through eight stages, each with its distinctive style of moral control, interpersonal relationships, preoccupations, and thinking. Although Loevinger's concerns are not specifically religious, her developmental model resembles those of Kohlberg and Fowler, whose concerns are more directly religious.

[52]James W. Fowler, "Stages in Faith: The Structural-Developmental Approach," in T. C. Hennessey, ed., *Values and Moral Education* (New York: Paulist, 1976) 173.

[53]James W. Fowler and Sam Keen, *Life Maps: Conversations on the Journey of Faith,* J. Berryman, ed. (Waco TX: Word Books, 1978) 96-99.

Stage 4. Individuating/Reflective Faith (after seventeen or eighteen years) is a pattern of faith personally chosen and consciously differentiated from the expectations of others; autonomous.

Stage 5. Conjunctive Faith (usually about mid-life or later) embraces the paradoxes and discontinuities into consolidative patterns; one's own system is seen interdependent with the larger human family.

Stage 6. Universalizing Faith (late life) is the faith of the saint in which ultimacy, rather than self, is the point of reference.

Fowler's descriptions are a model for delineating the relationships between religious experience and the psychosocial emergence of personhood. Faith from Fowler's view is more verb than noun. Psychosocial development may not provide definitive answers to the theological issues of human existence, but it does clarify the forms and structures by which those issues take shape in human experience. Without consideration of the dynamic processes by which persons grow toward maturity, discussion of human nature and destiny will inevitably be incomplete.

SUGGESTED READINGS

General

Loevinger, Jane. *Ego Development.* San Francisco: Jossey-Bass, 1976. Discusses growth in terms of ego development.

McCann, R. V. "Developmental Factors in the Growth of Mature Faith," *Religious Education* 50 (1955): 147-55.

Rokeach, Milton. *Beliefs, Attitudes, and Values.* San Francisco: Jossey-Bass, 1968.

Sherrill, Lewis. *The Struggle of the Soul.* New York: Macmillan, 1951. Brief and homiletical in tone.

Strommen, Merton P., ed. *Research on Religious Development.* New York: Hawthorn, 1971. Review of research. Part 4: chs. 17, 18, 19, 20 are particularly applicable.

Childhood

Godin, André, ed. *From Cry to Word.* Brussels: Lumen Vitae Press, 1968.

_____, ed. *From Religious Experience to a Religious Attitude.* Chicago: Loyola University Press, 1965. The two Godin volumes include significant articles.

Goldman, Ronald. *Religious Thinking from Childhood to Adolescence.* New York: Seabury, 1964. Other works on cognitive development are listed in Suggested Reading for Chapter 7.

Graebner, O. E. *Child Concepts of God*. Chicago: Lutheran Education Association, 1960.

Youth

Allport, Gordon W. *The Individual and His Religion*. New York: Macmillan, 1950. Chs. 2, 5, and 6 are especially relevant to youth.

Erikson, Erik H., ed. *The Challenge of Youth*. Garden City NY: Doubleday, 1965.

Jacob, Philip E. *Changing Values in College*. New York: Harper, 1956. Studies impact of college teaching.

Ross, Murray G. *Religious Beliefs of Youth*. New York: Association, 1950. Old but dependable.

Stewart, Charles W. *Adolescent Religion: A Developmental Study of the Religion of Youth*. Nashville: Abingdon, 1967.

Adulthood

Howe, Reuel L. *The Creative Years*. New York: Seabury, 1959.

Levinson, Daniel J. *The Seasons of a Man's Life*. New York: Knopf, 1978.

Moberg, David O. "Religiosity in Old Age," *The Gerontologist* 5 (1965): 78-87.

Scudder, Delton L., ed. *Organized Religion and the Older Adult*. Institute of Gerontology Series. Vol. 8. Gainesville: University of Florida Press, 1958.

Sheehy, Gail. *Passages: Predictable Crises in Adult Life*. New York: Dutton, 1976. Popular.

Faith Development

Fowler, James W. *Stages of Faith: The Psychology of Human Development and the Quest for Meaning*. New York: Harper, 1981.

_____. "Stages in Faith: The Structural-Developmental Approach," *Values and Moral Education*. T. C. Hennessey, ed. New York: Paulist, 1976.

_____, "Faith Development Theory and Aims of Religious Socialization," *Emerging Issues in Religious Education*. G. Durka and J. Smith, eds. New York: Paulist, 1976.

Fowler, James W. and Sam Keen. *Life Maps: Conversations on the Journey of Faith*. J. Berryman, ed. Waco TX: Word, 1978.

CHAPTER SEVEN

THE DEVELOPMENT
OF RELIGIOUS THINKING

The larger developmental picture provides a background for considering more specific functions of personhood and their relationship to religious experience. Persons inevitably think, feel, and decide; often these happen in a religious context. If we assume that religious ideas, emotions, and decisions are to be understood in the same ways as in nonreligious context, then psychology should help us construct defensible ideas, dependable emotions, and trustworthy decisions. To these specific developmental issues we now turn.

The meaning of religious experience is largely preserved in cognitive forms. Ideas, concepts, and beliefs are formal statements through which the private and personal world of religion is made visible and communicable to one's neighbor. Even the Zen Buddhist or glossolaliac who insists that experience is beyond ordinary language cannot avoid cognitive activity when faith is communicated. When the devotee of any religious persuasion uses the first word to describe religious experience, doctrine enters and exploration of cognitive validity begins. Religious groups inevitably transform "faith" into a collection of cognitive statements defining "the faith," that is, experience becomes creed. Further, creed turns back upon the devotee as stimulus of new experience. "Being religious" thus becomes an issue not only of confronting the divine, but also of accepting or rejecting the traditional ways of thinking and talking about the divine. Such exchanges explain one facet of religious denominations, sects, or cults, often divided over both what is being thought and said and, how the thinking and talking is being done.

Psychological study has given considerable attention to the dynamics and development of cognition and, therefore, enlightens the processes of religious thinking.[1] The present chapter examines the relationships between cognition and religion on three levels: present-tense thinking by which religious concepts are formed, past-tense thinking by which religious concepts are preserved, and future-tense thinking by which religious concepts are imagined.

THE FORMATION OF RELIGIOUS CONCEPTS

The formation of religious ideas is closely related to the development of conceptual ability, a competence that emerges slowly and matures relatively late. Before early adolescence, the child operates on a rudimentary conceptual level, preserving those ideas made available from the environment in terms of childhood needs and abilities.[2] Children's thinking about religion is therefore concrete and imitative. Sometimes these conceptual patterns become so overladen with emotional intensity rooted in the security of childhood, that they cannot be later altered without unbearable guilt, and persist into adulthood so strongly undergirded that the hint of rearranging them is interpreted as a threat to religion.

Normally, however, newly emerging conceptual abilities enable the adolescent to broaden his understanding and appreciation of religious concepts. The young person potentially becomes more efficient in objectifying thoughts and feelings, able to reason about

---

[1]A serious attempt to apply psychological treatments of cognition to religious thinking is found in Paul Pruyser, *A Dynamic Psychology of Religion* (New York: Harper, 1968) 47-138. This chapter draws heavily from Pruyser.

[2]See David Elkind, "Origins of Religion in Childhood," *Review of Religious Research* 12 (1970): 35-42.

them as if they were external objects. Contrary-to-fact situations can be conceived and examined as if they were real. In short, the young person learns to abstract and conceptualize on levels beyond childhood, using a large number of hypotheses, relating them to each other, and analyzing reasons behind them. Religious thinking becomes increasingly possible in ways completely foreign to the intellectual capacities of childhood.[3]

Criteria for Thought Organization

The development of efficiency in organizing religious thought takes time and practice because it involves complex processes. It involves the numerous patterns by which persons organize their environment and utilize symbols to preserve meaning and value. Adequate religious thinking must be measured by the standards of good thinking in general. These standards include three that are peculiarly important for religion: a criterion of sorting, having to do with how persons break their environment into manageable units; a criterion of congruence, referring to the relationship between one's sortings and his statements about them; and a criterion of symbolism, concerned with the preservation and communication of sortings.

The Criterion of Sorting. "Good" thinking is grounded in the cognitive act of sorting out the constituent parts that make up the whole. A person enters a room and perceives furniture, walls, ceiling, light, color. Thinking about "room" begins as perceptions are grouped into categories, seen as parts of the larger unit, a cognitive process called sorting. Beyond accuracy of perception, each small unit must possess internal coherence, that is, its parts must stand together according to some common characteristic. The category must be logically consistent with other concepts already established as coherent. The criterion of sorting includes both characteristics. Good concepts are those whose internal parts bear a coherent relationship to each other and are consistent with other concepts already established as coherent.

---

[3]Developing abstract ability during adolescence underscores the need for (1) a different approach to the religious education of young people than has been practiced with children and (2) the inclusion of religion studies in high school and college curricula.

The criterion may be illustrated in a simple experiment. A paper bag containing twenty-five or thirty miscellaneous items (pens, pencils, chalk, golf tee, index card, paper clip, coins, keys, etc.) is emptied on the desk and the question is asked, "What are these?" The initial responses consist of general statements, "Items belonging to you" or "Things you have emptied from the bag." The items are then covered and the statements written on the blackboard. Participants easily perceive that apart from the now-covered items the statements have little or no meaning. The *span* of the concept was too inclusive to serve any real purpose of thought organization. The statements are too general to be false, but too meaningless to be accurate. They fail to order the data into coherent units that can convey meaning in relation to other concepts.

Biblical interpretation has a difficult time without narrowing the conceptual span through sorting. Biblical material more often oriented around fluid experience than well-ordered theological concepts, regularly offers generalizations that demand interpretative abstractions and applications. Consider, for example, the conceptual issues at stake in a sermon based on Chapter 11 in the book of Hebrews. The sermon on "faith in God" may pleasingly admonish persons to have it, yet sort out so little that hearers get the impression that faith is a good "something" without ever knowing what it is. They may, in fact, feel guilty for not having "it." The text might be cited from Hebrews 11:1: "To have faith is to be sure of the things we hope for, to be certain of the things we cannot see." Grammatically, the verse has the earmarks of definition, but what is defined? Faith is that "something" that gives assurance and conviction. Thus the statement is more a hint at the direction in which the concept faith is to be structured, rather than an establishment of conceptual boundaries. The remainder of Hebrews 11 hints by specific illustration at the ingredients of faith to be abstracted from the experiences of its heroes. In this way the chapter is very much like items poured onto the desk, a miscellany from which coherent concepts are to be abstracted; used to classify the experiences of Abel, Abraham, Moses; and built into a larger concept of "faith." The possible sortings are many (the stuff of which sermons are made), but each should be tested by its internal coherence and external consistency.

Forced to narrow the span of their conceptualization, participants in our experiment returned to the simple object-sorting problem of describing those things that had been emptied from the bag. The problem was not too complex for sophisticated observers. The obvious classes of objects were used: coins were put in one place and writing implements in another. Consensus easily validated that pens, pencils, and chalk belonged together because they could be used to write. No one felt compelled to challenge the classification; no one felt that they had experienced a grand revelation. The coherence was obvious and consistency was validated by their experience since having picked up their first crayon. Here conceptualization is still at a fairly simple level, demanding only direct abstraction of a common quality. Concept formation was no more complicated than a sermon on faith that is content to say, "Faith means trusting God." Too trite for debate; too obvious for excitement!

Rather rapidly, however, some participants, probably enamored with having fun, began to put the materials together in atypical ways—the golf tee, a pencil, a quarter, and an index card. They explained that all belonged to a golf game. "The tee is used by the player who writes his score on the index card with the pencil and wins a quarter from his opponent." In this instance, items were combined, not because of their common inherent qualities, but because their use in a common situation was conceived. Here more advanced conceptualization was taking place. One-step abstraction of common qualities gave way to two-step abstraction in which a conceived use holds together items with differing qualities. Further, a narrative was constructed to preserve the conceptualization.

The arrangement of items according to use illustrates the important function of narrative in human thinking and explains, in part, the religious role of story forms such as myth, parable, and historical narrative. Stories are not only enjoyable, but they also facilitate the preservation of ideas and enable persons to bring together and easily remember diverse items. Who has not been asked whether or not he has read a book without being able to recall, until an episode or character is mentioned? But with a point of contact established the entire story begins to unfold.[4] In like fashion a narrative about Jocasta, Laius, and their son Oedipus more easily preserves meaning than a nameless discussion of parent-child relationships. Or Adam and Eve in a garden talking to a subtle serpent makes pointed the nature of sin as rebellion against Yahweh.[5] Narrative is a vehicle through which isolated episodes and meanings attached to them are remembered and recalled.

Narrative also enhances the credibility and authority of values contained in the story. "Things that have happened" seem to carry more weight than mere "things."[6] Jesus's use of parables may be understood in this light. A man falling among thieves on the way from Jerusalem to Jericho claims attention as authoritative by virtue of its real life possibilities.[7] It seems not accidental that ancient Israel associated her God with the events of history, particularly known in crucial episodes of exodus, monarchy, and restoration from exile. A God of history is simply more credible than a God of reflection. Pruyser suggests that an important way in which Judaism and Christianity have established authority for Scripture has been to develop stories about its origins.[8] The Christian and Jewish Scriptures use narrative extensively and thereby authenticate their message. To miss this point is to miss both the significance of narration in religious conceptualization and important dimensions of Scripture itself. Religious authentication through narrative explains why incarnation becomes pivotal in the Judeo-Christian tradition. The God who comes to humanity, the story of whose coming can be told, is a believable God. The sorting has been done specifically and narrative preserves its meaning.

The Criterion of Congruence. A second criterion for measuring good concept formation is the congruency found between mean-

---

[4]For a report of an experimental study of this phenomenon, see Frank Restle et al., eds., *Cognitive Theory,* vol. 1 (Hillsdale NJ: Lawrence Erlbaum Associates, 1975) 277-83.

[5]The Yahwistic narrative in Hebrew Scriptures is marked by the skill of storytelling.

[6]Pruyser, *A Dynamic Psychology of Religion,* 99.

[7]Luke 10:30-37.

[8]Pruyser, *A Dynamic Psychology of Religion,* 99-100.

ingful sortings and statements reflecting those sortings. *In good concept formation verbal statements correspond to sortings that have been made, while maintaining enough flexibility to incorporate new sortings.* The principle has two sides to it: (1) the correspondence of statements and (2) enough flexibility to allow the inclusion of new data. In the sorting illustration mentioned above, if a person said the coins were being separated, but the dime was left because it was smaller than the others or the index card was included because one might write a check on it, the statement would to some extent be incongruent with the sorting. The conceptualization has a certain sloppiness about it because the categories are not clearly defined. The sorting boundaries are unclear and, hence cognitive statements aiming to describe the sortings lack precision. "Coins" accurately labels most of the separated items but does not include all things appropriate to the category and includes one item whose relationship is certainly opaque.

Theology is a serious attempt to introduce congruence into religious conceptualization, to sharpen the boundaries of ideas through logical processes. Yet, the destiny of theology is to be unable to complete its task. Unless one assumes that all answers are in, theological statements must leave room for revision, expansion, and updating. Paul Tillich, and many other theologians as well, see the need for flexibility to be grounded in the nature of the Christian confession that the God of ultimate reality cannot be confined to ordered propositions. Divinity cannot be reduced to concepts. Tillich believes that "the courage to be" becomes possible in the discovery of the "God above God," the God sometimes in, but always beyond, conceptual statements.[9] The same cognitive openness is preserved in meditative traditions, especially in Eastern religion, where theological statements are subsumed under openness to divine invasion.

Yet, the need for fluid and flexible conceptualizing does not free the theologian, Eastern or Western, to entertain illogical analysis. Illusive divinity, not illogical indulgence, must justify any incongruence deemed necessary to theological discussion. Unjustifiable

---

[9]See Paul Tillich, *The Courage To Be* (New Haven: Yale University Press, 1952) 186ff.; compare his *Dynamics of Faith* (New York: Harper, 1957) 30f.

incongruence appears in the often repeated Fundamentalist statement that attempts to defend Genesis 1 as a scientific description of creation, supposed to have occurred in 4004 B.C.E.: "God created old rocks to fool archaeologists." The strange combination of "creation" and "old" illustrates imprecise sortings and consequent fuzziness in the conceptual statement. Whether or not God should be theologically conceived as one out to fool archaeologists is another matter!

Religion confronts the congruence issue also in the area of defining morality. The human situation has enough built-in ambiguity to necessitate some flexibility in the rules by which behavior is governed. Few ethical decisions fit neatly into "good" or "bad" categories. "You shall not kill" is a clear-cut sorting, but its application is more difficult. The thorny ethical problems of euthanasia, abortion, death-with-dignity, war, self-defense, and slaughter of non-human animals demand additional definition and clarification. Each of these situations contains elements of the "good" or "bad" and may not be easily resolved according to a simple sorting.

Hence neat legal statements are inadequate to describe ambiguous moral situations and must give way to flexibility in the application of moral concepts, "a sophisticated blurring of conceptual boundaries."[10] After healing a man on the Sabbath, Jesus asked those Pharisees who insisted on the scrupulous observance of Sabbath laws, "If any one of you had a son or an ox that happened to fall in a well on a Sabbath, would you not pull him out at once on the Sabbath itself?"[11] They could not answer him without confessing that their rigid legal definitions, although congruent, did not recognize the ambiguities implicit in the human situation.

The principle of cognitive congruence, movement toward clear conceptual definition while leaving room for flexibility, provides an important clue for the psychological understanding of religious faith. Faith is not blind cognitive acceptance in spite of the evidence, but a pilgrimage in which faith statements become increasingly comprehensive and congruent ways for making sense of

---

[10]Pruyser, *A Dynamic Psychology of Religion*, 82.

[11]Luke 14:5.

experience. Gerhard Ebeling says, "Faith is movement and happening, it is life, fulfilled life."[12] Faith is an act of the total personality; it is not limited to a few rational statements or even to the entire cognitive process.[13] Faith is larger than reason, and in so far as religious thinking leaves open possibilities for change and expansion, it lends support to what Allport calls the heuristic character of mature religion.[14] It can be *certain* enough to act without demanding absoluteness.

The Criterion of Symbolism. Concept formation, good or bad, operates through symbols. Words, signs, rituals, and acts carry the weight of meanings assigned to them. The criterion of symbolism in good concept formation requires that *symbols permit thought to be organized and communicated clearly.* The simplest symbols used by human beings are words, but even the simplest words can be ambiguous when they stand alone. A familiar word such as "cat" may refer to a scratching, shedding animal with a peculiar odor; a soft, purring, cuddly pet; or a guy with pegged pants and a twirling chain. The specific word must be combined with others to permit more discriminating concept formation. The combination of words into sentences and paragraphs enables associations with individual words to be organized into conceptual patterns. The structure itself becomes an enlarged symbol in which individual words take on more precise meaning and all the words together mean more than the individual words.

Symbolism obviously plays a major role in religious thinking and assumes almost countless forms. Specific words (inspiration, Om, charismatic); institutions (synagogue, church, temple); literary traditions (Old Testament, Bible, Talmud, Upanishads); ritual (mass, genuflection, turning toward Mecca); and religious persons (Bud-

---

[12]Gerhard Ebeling, *The Nature of Faith*, Ronald G. Smith, trans. (Philadelphia: Fortress, 1961) 21.

[13]Tillich, *Dynamics of Faith*, 4-8. Cf. also Leland Elhard, "Living Faith: Some Contributions of the Concept of Ego-Identity to the Understanding of Faith," in Homans, *The Dialogue between Theology and Psychology*, 135-61, that from the psychological point of view discusses faith as intimate to the evolvement of ego-identity.

[14]See Allport, *The Individual and His Religion*, 72-74.

dha, Virgin Mary, Moses) achieve significance as symbols of the sacred. The extent and richness of religious symbolism may be discovered by examining any segment of the contemporary religious community.

Several observations are appropriate in understanding symbolism as a part of thought organization in religion. First, religious symbols assume their meaning, like separate words in a sentence, in a context. Simple bread and wine used in an environment of worship mean something quite different from those same items on a table in a private residence. The ringing of a bell may announce the end of a class or summons to prayer and worship. The larger social and personal context determines the value assigned to the symbol. This is the primary argument for the historical and critical study of religious literature, an approach that aims to recapture the original setting and mind set from which such statements come. The context itself provides cues to the meaning of the word symbols.

Second, religious symbols may be either too narrow or too broad to serve thought organization well. An important function of speech in the development of thought is to permit dialogue with others and with oneself to clarify the context of symbols.[15] Religion risks short-circuiting such conversation when symbols are made narrowly rigid or vaguely comprehensive. An illustration of the constricted use of symbols is Fundamentalism and other absolutist religious systems which insist that a symbol may have only one simple meaning. Thus inspiration means *only* verbal dictation of Scripture. The word is cut down to a single meaning with no leeway to consider other doctrines of inspiration.

Likewise, religious symbols may be so inclusive that meaning is lost. Consider these signs:

---

[15]The comment that "I can't hear myself think" reflects this speech function.

Appearing on a book's dust jacket they might vaguely suggest that the book is about religion, but little more. A single symbol incorporates an entire religious tradition, a generality tolerated in much popular American religion. The creed of this position is, "It doesn't matter what you believe as long as you are sincere about it." This mentality, as surely as that of absolutist Fundamentalism, erodes confidence in the use of religious symbols. If Fundamentalism is unwilling to allow symbols to remain as fluid and flexible as religious thought itself, then tolerance of generality encourages the use of symbols without content. Both thwart serious and substantive conversation about religious meaning.

Third, religious symbolism is inevitably ambiguous due of the personal dimension of symbols, the continuous inclusion of new experiences, and the nature of the symbolized data. As indicated above, the concrete symbol "cat" has attachments that are highly personalized, so that meanings may range from pet to peril. How much more difficult to find common ground for abstract theological words such as "worship" or "redemption." Further, these personal dimensions are in a continuous state of flux. Persons confront new experiences that alter understanding and grow in their ability to manage ideas cognitively. In the world of expanding experience and growth, new meaning may become attached to old symbols. This is a fact that John A.T. Robinson seemed not to take into account in his insistence that being honest-to-God demands that traditional God language be forsaken.[16] Robinson correctly points out that biblical language belongs to a flat earth cosmology, and then concludes that phrases such as "God in Heaven" say nothing to contemporary man. Robinson failed to recognize, however, that these old symbols might be given new meanings so that one might continue to speak of God-up-there simply to denote his apartness, not the space of his dwelling. Exposure to new experiences and the growth of personhood may make possible such a transformation of countless religious symbols. Hence, God-as-father is no longer an

---

[16]See John A. T. Robinson, *Honest to God* (Philadelphia: Westminster, 1963).

anthropomorphic reference, but a symbol for care, love, nurture, threat, authority, and control in all sorts of personal combinations.[17]

The ambiguity of religious symbols is also created by the nature of that which is symbolized. Paul Tillich emphasizes that man's ultimate concern *must* be expressed symbolically, not merely because of the nature of language, but more importantly, because of the character of ultimacy.[18] The finite can never fully reveal the infinite. When the timeless enters time, it must be expressed symbolically. Divinity is contained within time and space but is never identical with them. Thus, the symbol is forever inadequate to catch the full dimensions of the eternal. As the devotee becomes sensitive to this fact, he becomes less confident in the adequacy of the symbol. Since symbols cannot penetrate to the core of ultimacy, they always contain a mixture of revealing and concealing.[19] God-talk then becomes continuous clarification of the inadequacies and ambiguities inherent in symbolism. Hence, religious language has what the phenomenologists call a fringe or horizon dimension, a hazy area where the symbol becomes inadequate. Langdon Gilkey says, "Our own effort is to bring to enough provisional clarity the character of that horizon or background of totality in order to establish that character is one of ultimacy and sacrality."[20]

---

[17]This is not to say that the patriarchal language of Western religion should not change to avoid sexist connotations. It may be that in specific contexts the symbols themselves may become too narrow or offensive and therefore need to be discarded or reconstructed.

[18]Tillich, *Dynamics of Faith*, 44ff.; see also his *Systematic Theology*, vol. I (Chicago: University of Chicago Press, 1951) 108-111. Compare also Emil Brunner, *Revelation and Reason: The Christian Doctrine of Faith and Knowledge*, Olive Wyon, trans. (Philadelphia: Westminster, 1946) ch. 1; Paul Ricoeur, *The Symbolism of Evil*, Emerson Buchanan, trans. (New York: Harper, 1967) 11.

[19]The importance of symbolism is emphasized in biblical literature by the dominance of the idea of word. Dangers involved in the misuse of words led authors in crucial passages to admonish care in the use of language. See Exodus 20:7, 20; Matthew 5:33-37; Luke 6:43-45. Speaking Yahweh's word is the primary work of the Hebrew prophet and the concept of word is used in the prologue of John's Gospel (1:1-14) to indicate Jesus' significance.

Dissonance Theory and Religious Paradox

Ideally, religious thinking should be organized with perfect coherence, consistency, congruence, and clarity. However, such a hope is at best idealistic and utopian. A person's conceptual system, to the contrary, often includes ideas that by logic are mutually exclusive. Contradictory ideas may be held at the same time. Leon Festinger has referred to this phenomenon as cognitive dissonance, borrowing a concept from the field of music.[21] Two musical tones that do not blend well, that do not harmonize, are said to be dissonant. Likewise, two ideas are dissonant when they do not meld with each other, with one contradicting the other. Cognitive dissonance is present when an individual holds these discordant ideas at the same time and often with equal emotional support. Dissonance is to be distinguished from ambivalence: a term denoting the combination of two opposite affects, such as love and fear, directed towards the same object. Both ambivalence and dissonance may create a state of uneasiness, but they are not the same thing.

Religion concepts are replete with dissonance. Consider two statements from biblical literature regarding the nature of persons. The Hebrew psalmist describes the dignity of human beings:

> *Yet you made him inferior only to yourself;*
> *you crowned him with glory and honor.*[22]

Contrariwise, St. Paul, using another reference from the Psalmist as a source, describes persons as grossly sinful:

---

[20]Langdon B. Gilkey, *Naming the Whirlwind: The Renewal of God-Language* (Indianapolis: Bobbs-Merrill, 1969) 281n. An excellent discussion of the issues suggested here appears in Gilkey's "The Possibility of Religious Discourse in a Secular Age," in *Naming the Whirlwind*, 247-304.

[21]Cognitive dissonance theory was formulated by Leon Festinger in 1957 and has been the focus of much research since that time. See Festinger, *A Theory of Cognitive Dissonance* (Stanford CA: Stanford University Press, 1957); and also Philip Zimbardo, Ebbe B. Ebbesen, and C. Maslach, *Influencing Attitudes and Changing Behavior*, 2d ed. (Reading MA: Addison-Wesley, 1977) 67-85.

[22]Psalms 8:5.

There is no one who is righteous,
    no one who is wise
    or who worships God.
All have turned away from God;
    they have all gone wrong;
    no one does what is right, not even one.[23]

The two passages are dissonant. Is a person God's holy creation or a miserable and unregenerate sinner? In his *Essay on Man* Alexander Pope reflects this dissonance:

Placed on this isthmus of a middle state,
A being darkly wise and rudely great:
With too much knowledge for the Sceptic side,
With too much weakness for the Stoic's pride,
He hangs between.

In religious discussion it is common to refer to such discontinuities as *paradox*, statements that include seemingly incongruous and contradictory elements but also contain truth. Søren Kierkegaard, the mid-nineteenth century Danish theologian, argued that the paradoxical quality of Christian truth must be brought to the forefront of theological discussion.[24] The very idea of God in time, the central affirmation of Christianity and what Kierkegaard calls "the absolute Paradox," is a contradiction since God is by definition eternal. According to Kierkegaard, such is always the case "when the eternal truth is related to an existing individual."[25] As the Dane put it cryptically, and paradoxically, in his *Journals*, "It is the duty of the human understanding to understand that there are things which it cannot understand, and what those things are . . . the paradox is not a concession but a category . . . which expresses the relation between an existing cognitive spirit and eternal truth."[26] Thus

---

[23]Romans 3:10-12; compare Psalms 14:1-3.

[24]Among others, Paul Tillich underscores the importance of paradox for religious thinking. See his three-volume set, *Systematic Theology*, especially 1: 56-57, 150-52; 3: 165-72, 223-28.

[25]Søren Kierkegaard, *Concluding Unscientific Postscript*, in Bretall, *A Kierkegaard Anthology*, 219.

[26]Bretall, *A Kierkegaard Anthology*, 153.

paradox is not only legitimate, but also an essential part of theology. "As a meaningful form of discourse in religion, it presupposes that the object of discourse has a mystery and a depth which our ordinary words and propositions cannot totally explicate, and that therefore we speak about that mystery in paradoxical terms to indicate facets of it that we do understand, but which we cannot put into a comprehensive rational unity."[27]

Hence, dissonance in religious thought is an inevitable feature of paradoxical faith and does not necessarily imply the truth, or error, of one of the dissonant propositions. When one assumes the fundamental mystery involved in the affirmation of deity and the inevitable paradoxical quality of the finite experience of the infinite, then both horns of the paradox are assumed to contain both truth and error. For this reason alone, theology should not become fixed in propositions. Its business is continuous clarification.

Resolving Logical Inconsistency

Dissonance theory supposes that human beings attempt to resolve cognitive conflict sufficiently enough to maintain some sense of unity and direction. Without some resolution of dissonance the organism is likely to go "halting between two opinions," unable to act with conviction. The picture of the child with money to purchase one of two toys, both of which he wants, but unable to decide caricatures the inability to rank priorities, to decide, and to justify, internally, the choice that is made. The other option left in resolving dissonance seems to be inaction and prolonged frustration. Homeostasis, tension reduction, ego strength, and developing identity are so many ways of underscoring the importance of lowering cognitive dissonance enough to permit decision, action, and survival itself.

Bruno Bettelheim's descriptions of behavior in German concentration camps during World War II illustrate the extremes to which persons will go in resolving situations of unbearable conflict.[28] During the early stages of their confinement to these camps,

---

[27]Gilkey, *Naming the Whirlwind*, 176.

[28]Bruno Bettelheim, "Individual and Mass Behavior in Extreme Situations," *Journal of Abnormal and Social Psychology* 38 (1943): 417-52.

the prisoners attempted to maintain their preinternment ideas and values, but their traditional behavior produced severe punishment. Those who remained under these threatening conditions for as long as three years were often able to transform completely their values, accepting camp life as normative and imitating the guards in manner and ideas. Older prisoners even became apprehensive about the thought of leaving the camps to return to outside life.

What happened to the people Bettelheim studied under extraordinarily difficult circumstances, occurs in milder form in normal surroundings. Persons will attempt to reduce the anxiety and dissonance that causes stress. A wide range of cognitive techniques, rational and irrational, are available for defusing dissonance, and establishing enough comfort with discordant ideas to live with them and make decisions. Five patterns for managing dissonance regularly appear in religious thinking.[29]

1. Compartmentalization   — a way of nonthinking
2. Rationalization   — a way of biased thinking
3. Reinterpretation   — a way of metaphorical thinking
4. Apocalyptic revisionism   — a way of naive thinking
5. Paradoxical analysis   — a way of critical thinking

In and of themselves these cognitive patterns are neither good nor bad. The techniques may be used rationally or irrationally to reduce dissonance.

Compartmentalization is a way of not thinking about dissonant ideas. Thinking occurs in separate units or compartments, in such ways that concepts in one unit do not need to be related to those in another. Compartments may be constructed in terms of distinctive times and places, so that thought about an item may be different in differing circumstances. Or one may think about his own behavior in one way and the behavior of others in another way. The duress under which they lived enabled the subjects of Bettelheim's study to separate life inside from life outside the concentration camp, not

---

[29]For other ways of sorting these techniques, see Robert P. Abelson, "Modes of Resolution of Belief Dilemmas," *Journal of Conflict Resolution* 3 (1959): 343-52; and Barry F. Anderson, *Cognitive Psychology* (New York: Academic Press, 1975) 314-25.

unlike the merchant who operates according to the rule, "Religion is religion and business is business."

During the 1960s, many devout churchmen were able to dismiss responsibility for racial segregation on the grounds that these were matters of law or sociology, and not religion. Thus, with clear conscience and logic they could confess to love the black man "in his place," which meant not only "in the back of the bus" but also "in the compartment of white American thinking." In this instance compartmentalized thought was used to justify injustice and build a formidable wall of separation. Fortunately, the force of law was to break down these compartments and demand cognitive resolution of another type.

Compartmentalization as a cognitive device may be deeply rooted in the patterns of childhood thinking. Without abstract ability, children learn to resolve problems by imitation. Different social contexts may provide quite discrepant thought patterns. In school, for example, scientific designs may be incorporated through imitation, whereas a religious environment may provide different problem-solving devices. It seems possible that these separated compartments may continue into adulthood *if* abstract reflection does not make the dissonance unbearable enough to force reconstruction.

A second technique for reducing dissonance is *rationalization,* a way of biased thinking that supports a chosen position. This method is tremendously important in its implications for religion because few people come to religious commitment without alignment and loyalty. Personal history has usually established a positive or negative relationship with a religious tradition.[30] Cognitively, these persons are already in a biased position, inclined more toward rationalizing their established commitment, rather than toward objectively considering options. An unbiased stance might allow them to move from observation to conclusion, but their biased disposition encourages beginning with the conclusion, and using thought

---

[30]Gilkey, *Naming the Whirlwind,* 430ff., defends the thesis that "a basic attitude or viewpoint that is argued from and not argued to, and so which arises mysteriously out of experience itself, lies back of all our creative thinking." Compare also Michael Polanyi's *The Tacit Dimension* (Garden City NY: Doubleday, 1966).

to rationalize that conclusion. This is rationalization, arguing *from* rather than *to* a conclusion. Rationalization is not necessarily an unhealthy mechanism; one may rationalize a perfectly sound thesis or act. But when rationalization becomes so defensive that ideas and behavior must be defended at all costs, it becomes a means for avoiding the data, and a deterrent to cognitive growth.

Barry Anderson describes three types of biased thinking by which persons are apt to rationalize their religious experience.[31] "Sweet lemon thinking" intends to increase the attractiveness of a chosen alternative. Thinking of this sort emphasizes the positive aspects of one's position. An example of this would be justifying the Joshua interpretation of the bloody execution of innocents by emphasizing that the power of the Almighty enables Him to do with His creation what He desires.[32] Conversely, "sour grapes thinking" intends to debunk the alternative not chosen. Here the explanation of the Joshua story might focus upon the idea that the survival of Israel's enemies might hinder Yahweh's purpose and, therefore, they deserved to die. "Differentiation" thinking is a third kind of biased thinking. It justifies an alternative in the present situation, while holding that a different alternative might be justified in another. Execution of innocents might be understandable in war, but generous treatment of enemies, even doing them kindness, might be appropriate on other occasions.

All these patterns of rationalization reduce dissonance by adjusting belief structures to make them more compatible with established conclusions and behavior. Such adaptations occur even when a person is forced to do something that is contrary to his private opinion. If the pressure is not too much, in which case the change may be blamed on the pressure itself, persons tend to change their opinion to correspond with what has been done or said.[33] When the change is made for small reward or relief from negligible pressure,

---

[31]Anderson, *Cognitive Psychology*, 320-23, is a helpful summary upon which this paragraph draws heavily.

[32]Joshua 1:18; 6:17-21; 8:26-27; 10:35, 40.

[33]Leon Festinger and James M. Carlsmith, "Cognitive Consequences of Forced Compliance," *Journal of Abnormal and Social Psychology* 58 (1959): 203-210.

"a good deal of biased thinking is necessary to increase the attractiveness of the chosen alternative sufficiently to provide an internal justification for the choice."[34]

Another option for resolving logical inconsistency often used by religious devotees is *metaphorical reinterpretation,* a pattern by which incompatible ideas and acts are made congenial by assigning one or both of them abstracted, metaphorical meanings. A study by Sanford M. Dornbusch and his associates clearly demonstrates this process in biblical interpretation.[35] Two hundred and sixty nine students were asked to interpret and indicate agreement or disagreement with twelve passages of Scripture that supposedly contradict American middle-class values. Their answers were coded in five categories ranging from literal to very metaphorical interpretation. The results suggests a major distinction in the degree to which persons reinterpret tenets of their religious traditions. When faced with cognitive conflict between the biblical passages and current American secular themes, those who wished to agree with the passages were more likely to employ metaphorical interpretations. Those who described themselves as atheists or agnostics agreed with the passages less and were inclined to give literal interpretations to them. Evidently, metaphorical reinterpretation of the passages permitted believing Americans to accept biblical injunctions when literal interpretation might have produced too much dissonance.

Fourth, dissonance in religious thought may also be reduced through *apocalyptic revisionism,* a technique of naive thinking. Apocalyptic mentality thrives on the future, assuming a "sweet-by-and-by" when all conflicts will be resolved. Present conflicts are accepted because, ultimately, they are unreal. And this is not altogether without its blessing. Often an immediate circumstance that seems to spell disaster (as when a student receives his first failing grade), may be endured by hope derived from the possibility of redemption at some future date. Apocalyptic mentality is destructive in so far as it leaves the *entire* shape of the future to deity, with noth-

---

[34]Anderson, *Cognitive Psychology,* 322.

[35]Dornbusch et al., "Two Studies in the Flexibility of Religious Beliefs," in Philip E. Hammond and Benton Johnson, eds., *American Mosaic: Social Patterns of Religion in the United States* (New York: Random House, 1970) 100-110.

ing expected from the believer except naive trust that "everything will turn out alright." The future without the present indulges infantile wishes, and yields naive irresponsibility. The attitude is illustrated by religionists who glibly refuse to confront conflicting ideas with such statements as, "Some things are just not meant to be understood" or "We may not understand now but some day we will."

Leon Festinger and his colleagues in an intriguing book entitled *When Prophecy Fails* have examined the frustration of apocalyptic wishes and found them amazingly tenacious. What happens when an apocalyptic cult expecting the end of the world gathers at the proper place on the appointed date and nothing happens? One might expect that the group would give up their beliefs in disillusionment, but with only minor exception quite the reverse happened among those in the Festinger study. Explanations for the "delay" were immediately forthcoming, expressing newfound confidence in the old beliefs. The apocalyptic vision was revised, both to explain the delay and to prepare for a new revelation with a new timetable. Only a few believers fell away. In fact, the period of disconfirmation was followed by increased proselytizing to persuade others to join the wait for a new apocalypse.[36] Apocalyptic revisionism served well those whose hope for the coming end had gone unfulfilled.

Finally, dissonance in religious thought may be managed through *paradoxical abstraction,* a way of critical thinking. This is the most sophisticated option for handling dissonance. In paradoxical abstraction two seemingly contradictory ideas are reconciled by abstracting truth from each of them. Sophisticated conceptualization recognizes the sense in which each of the discordant statements may be true and how they may be true at the same time. Is man saint or sinner, angel or beast? Paradoxical abstraction affirms both propositions and proceeds to clarify how each side of the paradox is both true and false. The comment of Blaise Pascal illustrates the point:

It is dangerous to make man see too clearly his equality with the

---

[36]See Leon Festinger, Henry W. Reicken, and Stanley Schachter, *When Prophecy Fails* (New York: Harper, 1956) 193-215.

brutes without showing him his greatness. It is also dangerous to make him see his greatness too clearly, apart from his vileness. It is still more dangerous to leave him in ignorance of either.[37]

The use of one or more of these techniques of dissonance reduction not only enables the devotee to make logical that which is illogical, but also permits the preservation of large doses of inconsistency. Many persons utilize their theological system to protect strange and incompatible ideas. Students who wrestle with making their ideas logically whole, and professors who teach them, may imagine the utopian situation in which people move inevitably toward consistency in thinking, but in fact "for most of the people most of the time and for all of the people some of the time inconsistency just sits there."[38]

This discussion of concept formation demonstrates that human beings can organize their religious thought in many ways. The ability to sort out one's surrounding and use classes and systems of classes represents a major step forward in cognitive development. By abstracting and conceptualizing, the growing human being is able to move beyond the perceptual world to take into account a variety of viewpoints and formulate ideas on the basis of that variety. Religious thinking depends upon this process. Religious concepts must be judged not only by their theological content but also by their internal coherence and their consistency with other concepts to form a stable gestalt, their congruence with the data and openness to new experience, and their precise use of symbol systems. The discipline of religious thought according to these criteria enhances the preservation of treasured meaning as devotees continuously transform their faith into creed.

MEMORY AND RELIGIOUS CONSERVATION

A distinguishing mark of the human being is the ability to think about the past. By remembering, persons can preserve the expe-

---

[37]Blaise Pascal, *Pensées,* Introduction by T. S. Eliot (New York: E. P. Dutton, 1958) paragraph 418.

[38]Daryl Bem, *Beliefs, Attitudes, and Human Affairs* (Monterey CA: Brooks/Cole, 1970) 34 Cf. Robert P. Abelson, "Computers, Polls, and Public Opinion—Some Puzzles and Paradoxes," *Trans-Action* 5 (1968) 20-27, for a discussion of "opinion molecules."

rience of the past and recapture thinking and feeling about it. Cognitive psychologists in recent years have renewed their interest in human resources for storing information, the short- and long-term range of retention, means by which information is retrieved and reused, and countless other aspects of memory. Their extensive research has produced a vocabulary of its own and no small body of theory. Religion touches this important research at several points.[39]

Memory, Recollection, and *Chronos*

The primary function of memory is to give continuity to human experience. To accomplish this goal, memory operates with *chronos,* one of the two words used in biblical literature to refer to time. *Chronos* is measured, calibrated time. It is clock time of hours, days, months, and years. In its most rudimentary function, memory links experiences with each other *within chronos* and arranges them in some sequence. This is the point made in an important article by Stephen Crites on "the narrative quality of experience."[40] Episodes, like the notes of a piece of music, are meaningful as they stand temporally in sequence. "Without memory, in fact," says Crites, "experience would have no coherence at all. Consciousness would be locked in a bare, momentary present, i.e., in a disconnected succession of perceptions which it would have no power to relate to one another."[41] Memory enables the writer to sit at his desk and reclaim ideas from articles that have been read, conversations with colleagues, and discussions with students, using them in the construction of a narrative. The critical reader, likewise on the basis of recollections, will judge the meaning of the narrative. Without memory, neither construction nor criticism would be possible. Memory on this level functions in the same way as one seeking a lost object. By retracing one's steps, that is, by recollecting experiences of *chronos* in sequence, the item may be found.

---

[39]For introductory summaries of this material, see Frank Restle et al., *Cognitive Theory,* 1: 149-218; and Barry F. Anderson, *Cognitive Psychology,* chs. 4, 6, and 7.

[40]Stephen Crites, "The Narrative Quality of Experience," *Journal of the American Academy of Religion* 34 (1971): 291-311.

[41]Ibid., 298. One symptom marking tertiary syphillis is the inability to place things in temporal sequence; all the past is jammed into the present.

Memory as recollection of *chronos* plays an exceedingly important role in the conservation of personal religion. Paul Pruyser believes that familiar hymn tunes and words are preferred because they bring to consciousness past satisfying experiences, even when such hymns are musically inferior and often crude.[42] Why would a highly intelligent and culturally sophisticated person revert to the crude forms of brush-arbor revivalism and Stamps-Baxter gospel songs? Perhaps for no more complicated reason than that they are "old familiar tunes" and through memory recapture past experiences of religious simplicity. "I remember when" thus becomes a nostalgic confession in which the recollection of *chronos,* specific times and places, conserves religious sentiments deeply rooted in personal consciousness.

Chronos memory also is significant for corporate religion. "An enormous part of religious forms, creeds, and experiences finds its *raison d'etre* in history, rather than in the exigencies of the present time."[43] In the Judeo-Christian tradition, history is where God is discovered. Hebrews remember the Exodus from Egypt: Yahweh is God because of what he did. Collective memory preserved that belief by recollecting the events of the past. Israel's model was to remember and hence to believe. Early Christianity preserved the Hebrew theme. God was known because he entered history in the person of Jesus of Nazareth. In remembering the historical Jesus—episodes, words, personal encounters—believers established their faith. Both Hebrew and Christian identity is thus grounded in memory of historical events; recollection of *chronos* serves as the vehicle for conserving cognitive belief structures.

Memory as recollection does not always bring comfort and solace. Psychoanalysis has taught us well that the past may be an individual's worst enemy; memories may become exceedingly heavy burdens. Memory may feed neurosis by keeping traumatic experiences in the foreground. If mere recollection of those experiences would cure the patient, therapy would be far more simple. The healing of persons who feel the weight of their own *chronos* en-

---

[42]Pruyser, *A Dynamic Psychology of Religion,* 55.

[43]Ibid.

tails a more complex process of rearranging the patient's relationship to the past. And groups, like individuals, may experience the past as burdensome. Entire religious systems may be built around attempts to atone for recollected sins. Painful memories of individuals, and groups, are pointed reminders that memory is more than recollection of event. It is often encumbered by the dead weight of past meanings, and managing these associations is more a matter of reflection than recollection. Hence memory entails more than recalling episodes from *chronos;* it also activates the reconstruction of one's relationships to episodes that are recalled.

Memory, Reflection, and *Kairos*

For the most part, psychology's attention to memory has concentrated on the chronological aspects of the "experience." Research has assumed memory to be mainly the reproduction of past experience, and many questions about how the process occurs have been raised. Biological and neurological reactions have received special attention. Typical problems for experimental investigation have been the number of items available to short-term memory, the relationship of the order of items to recall, and the transfer of materials from short-term to long-term storage systems. These studies have yielded important data regarding memory as recollection of *chronos,* but, unfortunately, they miss the farther side of memory.

Memory is not only recollection, but also reflection and recreation. Remembering the past means more than retaining it. In remembering, the past is recast in the context of the present. "Memory never copies the past: it constitutes it as past by breathing new life into a bygone reality, and by placing it in a whole new context."[44] For one thing, not all of the past is remembered and items are selected as much on the basis of contemporary personal concerns as past importance. Thus a football coach, a tackle, and an uninitiated spectator might recall quite different things from the same game. Individual perspectives condition the selection of data about what happened on the field. And that which is remembered takes on a

---

[44]Louis Dupre, "Alienation and Redemption through Time and Memory: An Essay on Religious Time Consciousness," *Journal of the American Academy of Religion* 43 (1975): 673.

life and order of its own. Events of the past are retemporalized and reexperienced with both old and new associations. In this sense, memory is biography, not only recalling past experience, but reconstituting it in personal terms. Reflection brings to memory the faith, insight, imagination, and values of the present moment so that episodes are both recollected and relived. Historical event is clothed in contemporaneity. Event becomes in reflection the living moment, incorporating all the old meaning that memory can afford and all the new meaning that the replication of the episode in memory can stimulate.

The experience of a birthday is a simple illustration. "Today is my birthday!" affirms both the past and the present. Chronologically it means that three hundred and sixty five days have passed since the statement was last accurate. It also means gladness, sadness, eligibility for a driver's license, retirement, "another day older and deeper in debt," or a thousand other things poured into the memory of another year. Each birthday represents something old and something new contained in the treasury of the past. Memory functions to converge the past into the present; it includes the detached observation of a past experience and also the new experience of remembering itself.

Memory as reflection is akin to the biblical concept incorporated in a second Greek word used to refer to time, *kairos*. Whereas *chronos* is quantitative time, *kairos* is qualitative time. It is the right time, not in the sense of the correct hour or day, but in the sense of "the time is right." *Kairos* is used by Jesus to discuss the time of his suffering and death,[45] by John the Baptizer to announce the fulfillment of time,[46] and by St. Paul to describe the moment in which God had sent his son as the center of history.[47] The contrast between *chronos* and *kairos* is clearly seen in a comparison of the inquiry of Herod about "the exact time (*chronos*) the star had appeared"[48] and John's announcement, "The right time (*kairos*) has

---

[45] Matthew 26:18, John 7:6.

[46] Mark 1:15.

[47] Romans 3:26.

[48] Matthew 2:7.

come . . . and the Kingdom of God is near!"[49] Herod was asking a calendar question and John was proclaiming the significance of events. *Kairos* adds to *chronos* the qualitative dimension.

Theological discussions since World War I have made much of distinctions between calibrated time and sacred time, and insisted that both are important for understanding religions that formulate their ideas and structure their rituals around historical episodes.[50] Let us return, for example, to the Hebrew interpretation of the Exodus from Egypt, an event remembered as the crucial act of Yahweh and memorialized in the Passover (Sedar) ritual. Israel intended to recall the historical event of Exodus and remember the benevolence of Yahweh in that recollection. But more, the ritual recollection was intended also to be a reliving of the event, as if the participants in the ritual were themselves leaving Egypt for the first time. Through memory Israel reenacted sacred history, reliving an event and making it equally binding upon every generation in which the ritual was observed. The point is tellingly made in the Deuteronomic introduction to the Decalogue:

> At Mount Sinai the Lord our God made a covenant, not only with our fathers, but *with all of us who are living today.*[51]

Contemporary Judaism preserves this understanding of the Exodus and the Seder ritual. The closing scene in the modern novel *Exodus* is the observance of a Passover. The author, Leon Uris, conceptualizes the story of an American nurse and an Israeli freedom fighter of the twentieth century as a new exodus. Their return to Israel is a celebration and a recreation of "the most important moment in the history of our people . . . their going forth in triumph from slavery into freedom."[52]

The preservation of reflective memory is illustrated in Christian ritual. Communion, the Lord's Supper, the Eucharist— this

---

[49]Mark 1:15.

[50]Paul Tillich discusses the dual character of time in ontological terms. See his *Systematic Theology*, 1, 257-58.

[51]Deuteronomy 5:2-3, italics added.

[52]Leon Uris, *Exodus* (Garden City NY: Doubleday, 1958) 599.

observance aims to memorialize Christ's death and is an event held
to be crucially significant across the Christian community. Theological blood has been spilt over the specifics of the observance.
Should wine and unleavened bread be used, or may grape juice and
the commercial loaf be substituted? Do the elements change, or does
the presence of Christ in the elements sacralize the occasion? Is
grace brought to life by act of the presiding priest or in the attitude
of the communicant? These and other such questions have produced heated debate and deep divisions among Christians. Common among the contending parties, however, is the idea that more
than recalling an event goes on in keeping the ritual. Remembering Christ's death infuses the observance with contemporary grace.
Participation in the ritual of remembrance becomes itself a sacred
moment in which God speaks, acts, and reveals. The ritual is conceived to bring to life old memories with new patterns of meaning.
"Throughout the ages Christians have found meaning and consolation in the remembrance of Jesus' life and passion while sacramental rituals have made this life contemporary with their own."[53]

In the sense of the discussion here, memory and sacrament are
quite closely related. Many Protestant Christians are suspicious of
sacrament because of its associations with particular Roman Catholic doctrine that designates an act as sacramental because of its
correct performance; the authoritative priest doing the ritual correctly gains objective grace for the participant. The Reformation
tradition largely rejects this interpretation on the grounds that it is
too impersonal and too magical, and subsequently Protestantism has
largely avoided the word sacrament. However, the word needs to
be freed from its narrow, sectarian connotations (either Protestant
or Roman Catholic) to recover its larger theological and psychological sense. More fundamentally, any act that serves to mediate God's
grace to persons is sacramental. The crucial theological argument
is neither whether one, two, or seven sacraments are the correct
number, nor how sacraments are properly administered, but to
what degree does an act become the vehicle for a living encounter
with divinity.[54] The psychological experience of memory enables

[53]Dupre, "Alienation and Redemption," 677.

[54]Tillich, *Systematic Theology*, 3: 120-24.

this to occur. An act of the past may be recalled, but more, it may be relived. Past association and meanings may be brought to life again, and with additional meanings. In biblical language God may be heard to speak as he has spoken before, and we might hear with new insight and understanding. In short, an event such as the observance of Eucharist may become sacramental *kairos,* a moment of sacred time.

The conserving function of memory as recollection and reflection serves well the conservative character of religious institutions. Certainly the structures of religions are partially explained as means for conserving cherished consensual values. Innovative ideas, values, and movements are viewed with considerable caution by an institution whose life depends upon preserving established organizations, creeds, and rituals. The cognitive mood of establishment religion is memory, the tendency to look back and cherish those experiences that have proven valuable. The disposition to remember risks bondage to the past; it also enables religion to survive as a social institution.

IMAGINATION AND RELIGIOUS VISION

If memory permits persons to deal cognitively with the past, imagination allows for anticipation of the future. Thinking about the past selects experiences that have a proven significance and filters them through concerns and values of the moment. Imagination adds another dimension; it enables thinking persons to move beyond the present and anticipate a future unlike the past. "This is what man does when he takes steps to avoid world famine, irreversible destruction of the environment, or nuclear warfare, none of which he has ever experienced."[55]

To describe imagination as future thinking is not meant to separate it from the past. The human experience of time, as has already been suggested, does not fall into easy and separable categories of past, present, and future. Rather, in experience these

---

[55]Anderson, *Cognitive Psychology,* 17. Robert J. Lifton has written suggestively about the creative dimensions of remembering as a means to avoid "psychic closing off." See particularly his *History and Human Survival* (New York: Random House, 1970) 114-94.

merge into inseparable configurations. The word "imagination" itself suggests close links with the past—images preserved from past perceptions provide content for imagination. But imagination involves a peculiar use of these images. Unlike memory that recalls the past and baptizes it in new experience, imagination uses images to anticipate both constructive and destructive possibilities. As Robert Lifton suggests, remembering Hiroshima animates imagination to envision circumstances in which such tragedy will not be repeated. In this way imagination represents the attempt to envision new combinations of past experience and, thus introduces spontaneity, creativity, and responsibility into the thinking process. It enables persons to envision change and is necessary for the work of the scientist who envisions new possibilities for experiment, the artist who allows imagination to play with old forms, and to the philosopher who experiments with a wide range of conceptual possibilities.

Autistic and Reality Thinking

The paradigm structured by Peter McKellar delineates the place of imagination in the thinking processes.[56] He says that thinking ranges along an objectivity-subjectivity continuum. At one end is R-thinking (reality-thinking), in which the objective features of reality dominate thought. This is sometimes labeled "scientific" thinking. It is presumed that all personal factors should be eliminated in the interest of thinking about what is "out there." The language of R-thinking is concrete and descriptive. At the other end of the continuum is A-thinking (autistic-thinking), in which subjective elements of thought are allowed to range free from the control of external reality. Personal wishes and desires are expressed without the restrictions of objectivity; it is thinking whose meaning is essentially private. Language used to express A-thinking tends to be emotional, impressionistic, and metaphorical. The model may be graphically described as follows:

A-thinking ⟷ A/r ⟷ A/R ⟷ a/R ⟷ R-thinking
("Pure" Poetry)   ("Pure" Science)

---

[56]Peter McKellar, *Imagination and Thinking: A Psychological Analysis* (New York: Basic Books, 1957).

Thought typically moves along the continuum, combining the subjective and the objective in highly personal ways.

Lines written by the poet Wordsworth on the occasion of a revisit to Tintern Abbey, a medieval ruin in southwestern England, is a case study in the compromise of A and R processes.[57] The poem opens with R-descriptions in which the ruins themselves dominate the poet's language:

> Once again do I behold these steep and lofty cliffs,
> That on a wild secluded scene impress
> Thoughts of more deep seclusion; and connect
> The landscape with the quiet sky.
> The day is come when I again repose
> Here, under this dark sycamore, and view
> These plots of cottage ground, these orchard tufts,
> Which at this season, with their unripe fruits,
> Are clad in one green hue

In this language the ruins in their natural setting dominate the incidental reference to "thoughts of more deep seclusion." Note the inclusion of references to the observable scene. However, imagination moves the poet beyond the perceptions of the things around him:

> While here I stand, not only with the sense
> Of present pleasure, but with pleasing thoughts
> That in this moment there is life and food
> For future years.

Standing amid the ruins brings "present pleasure," but more, personal language and meaning "for future years."

---

[57]George W. Meyer, ed., *Selected Poems: William Wordsworth* (Arlington Heights IL: AHM Publishing Corporation, 1950) 36-40; valuable discussions of Wordsworth's double use of sense experience may be found in Mary Warnock, *Imagination* (Berkeley: University of California Press, 1976) 114-26, and Colin C. Clarke, *Romantic Paradox: An Essay on the Poetry of Wordsworth* (London: Routledge and Kegan Paul, 1962).

For I have learned
To look on nature, not as in the hour
Of thoughtless youth; but hearing oftentimes
The still, sad music of humanity,
Nor harsh nor grating, though of ample power
To chasten and subdue. And I have felt
A presence that disturbs me with the joy
Of elevated thoughts; a sense sublime
Of something far more deeply interfused.

Developmental psychologists have noted the place of fanciful and emotional constructs in the development of childhood religion. Harms suggests that initially the child's conception of God is a fairy-tale conception that should not be forced into rational molds.[58] Later researchers, including Piaget, Goldman, and Godin, have affirmed the important role played by imagination and fantasy in the intellectual growth of the child. But imagination does not necessarily disappear with the passing of childhood. It touches upon religious thought at two points: temptation and creative thought.

Fantasy and Temptation

Wayne Oates includes in his *The Psychology of Religion* a brief but provocative chapter in which he explores the relation between the psychological concept of fantasy and the theological concept of temptation.[59] According to Oates, fantasy and temptation are anticipatory states that are closely akin to each other. Fantasy is imagination running free, unattached to behavior and relatively unencumbered by memory. It may include simple, conscious daydreaming or the child's imaginary playmate or the complex configurations of the private world of schizophrenia. Whether simple or complex, fantasies thrive on satisfaction from "a mental activity estranged from reality."[60]

---

[58]Ernest Harms, "The Development of Religious Experience in Children," *American Journal of Sociology* 50 (1944): 112-22.

[59]Wayne E. Oates, *The Psychology of Religion* (Waco TX: Word Books, 1973) 186-93. Compare the helpful article by Lucy Bregman, "Fantasy: The Experiences and the Interpreter," *Journal of the American Academy of Religion* 43 (1975): 723-40.

[60]*Ibid.*, 187.

The Judeo-Christian tradition has tended to distrust fantasy and imagination because of their inherent potential for irresponsible behavior. Biblical literature regularly associates imagination with evil, underscoring the possibility that imagination may serve morally distorted purposes.[61] Without the balance of objective standards (R-thinking in McKellar's terms) imagination may be the vehicle for uncontrolled subjectivism, running the risk of reading autistic wishes as the will of God. As the New Testament book of James says, "A person is tempted when he is drawn away and trapped by his own evil desire."[62] When this happens, imagination is inclined to create "gods which have an increasing likeness to human beings, complete with sexual differentiation, family structures and kinship patterns, and differentiations of labor with specializations of functions akin to the social and individual characters of man."[63] Church history contains enough illustrations of bizarre ideas and inhumane actions in the name of God to justify some caution in giving too wide a berth to imagination in religious conceptualization.

But temptation is to be distinguished from behavior that might issue from it. Temptation is anticipatory thinking that may produce either good or evil results. The biblical account of the temptation of Jesus makes this distinction clear.[64] The parallel reports in Matthew and Luke both suggest considerable imagination in the experience. Jesus imagines himself turning stone to bread, floating from the pinnacle of the Jewish Temple to win popular acclaim, and seeing all the kingdoms of the world before him. Temptation came in the vision of possibilities to which Jesus might have responded responsibly or irresponsibly. Not the imagination but the subsequent response determines the moral quality of the experience. Temptation was negative only in the sense that a negative choice was possible.

---

[61]Matthew 4:1-11; Luke 4:1-12.

[62]James 1:14.

[63]Pruyser, *A Dynamic Psychology of Religion,* 62.

[64]Matthew 4:1-11; Luke 4:1-12.

Yet temptation imbedded in imagination also presents the option of right choices. The Gospel narratives of Jesus' temptation introduce his public mission with the obvious intention of portraying one who "overcame temptation" by making responsible choices. Imagination enabled him to envision radically alternative life-styles and to evaluate each one reflectively. The options could be entertained "as if" they were true. "As if" thinking has the double advantage of overcoming blind choice and permitting decisions to be made quickly and responsibly. Imagination allows decision without having to flip a coin or to test each alternative through trial and error. Possible consequences can be pictured and responsible decision may be compacted into the present moment in light of how a situation is likely to turn out. In this sense, imagination is not only important but essential to proper decision-making.

Imagination, Creation, and Theopoetics

Imagination has been put under a suspicious cloud by many religious devotees, not only because of its traditional associations with evil, but also on the grounds that giving a place to imagination reduces religion to "mere fantasy." According to this mind-set, a clear distinction is drawn between reality and fantasy with the latter being associated with distortion, illusion, and at worst hallucination. This position may be supported by a narrow Freudian interpretation that sees fantasy merely as the neurotic construction of an irrational, make-believe world. In this way fantasy is reduced to escapism, a pattern of imagination by which the painfully threatening world is avoided through images that have only private meaning.

Yet cannot Freud, and depth psychologists following him, be read more broadly? Is neurotic fantasy—the attempt at make-believe reconciliation with the threatening world—a negative illustration of a positive process with a dynamic of its own? Are dreams and Oedipus alike negative expressions of the powerful force of human imagination? May not the dream and mythmaking, two favorite paradigms for the depth psychologist, be understood positively as vehicles through which individuals function creatively—two kinds of activity employed by thinking persons to move beyond past experience to construct an idea world in new forms?[65]

---

[65]Cf. Robert J. Lifton, *The Life of the Self* (New York: Simon and Shuster, 1976)

Many recent interpreters have emphasized the creative aspects of imagination. Jung's autobiography, *Memories, Dreams, Reflections,* is an impressive effort in this direction. Jung sees his own life and work as an individual pilgrimage in personal mythmaking that was much more than private and not entirely explained by surrounding culture. In Jung's view his life story had been archetypical, placing him in touch with superpersonal and supercultural reality. He comments on one of his earliest childhood dreams:

> Through this childhood dream I was initiated into the secrets of the earth. . . . Today I know that it happened in order to bring the greatest possible amount of light into the darkness. . . . My intellectual life had its unconscious beginnings at that time.[66]

The Jungian emphasis upon creative features of imagination seems to be continued in contemporary discussions of the theology of play. A rapidly expanding bibliography perceives play as a vehicle of imagination, liberating persons from the undue bondage of seriousness and structure.[67] Although these discussions run the risk of subordinating other aspects of human consciousness, they appropriately stress that play "is one of the most characteristic expressions of the freedom of the spirit."[68] A little free play, especially if it is modified by seriousness of purpose, may open persons to dimensions of their existence simply unavailable through structured analysis.[69]

99-100, who describes dreams as possessing "an exquisite immediacy in their creative rendition of 'the state of the mind.'"

[66]Carl G. Jung, *Memories, Dreams, Reflections,* Aniela Jeffs, ed.; Richard Winston and Clara Winston, trans. (New York: Pantheon, 1963) 15.

[67]For example, Hugo Rahner, *Man At Play,* Brian Battershaw and Edward Quinn, trans. (New York: Herder and Herder, 1972); Sam Keen, *Apology for Wonder* (New York: Harper, 1969); idem, *To a Dancing God* (New York: Harper, 1970); Harvey Cox, *The Feast of Fools* (New York: Harper, 1968); Robert E. Neale, *In Praise of Play* (New York: Harper, 1972); and David L. Miller, *God and Games: Toward a Theology of Play* (New York: Harper, 1972).

[68]Tillich, *Systematic Theology,* 3:161.

[69]This is the point made by Owen Barfield, "Matter, Imagination, and Spirit," *Journal of the American Academy of Religion* 42 (1974): 621-29.

The theologian Paul Tillich writes of the role of play and art, which he calls "the highest form of play," in his own religious development. An imaginative tendency had manifested itself during his boyhood through a delight in play, and was later expressed in an appreciation of art. Play and art were thus manifestations of imagination deeply rooted in his childhood, and Tillich associates these with his most productive moments as a reflective thinker. He says,

> The difficulties I experienced in coming to terms with reality led me into a life of fantasy at an early age. Between fourteen and seventeen, I withdrew as often as possible into imaginary worlds which seemed to be truer than the world outside. In time, that romantic imagination was transformed into philosophical imagination.[70]

Tillich's early imaginative turn persisted in a lifelong delight in play that he believed supported his discovery of the creative arts, especially music, literature, and painting. These became for Tillich important vehicles for the genuinely creative realm of his religious imagination, not merely in developing an attitude of conceptual breadth and experimentation, but in producing specific theological ideas. The concept of the "break-through" that dominates his theory of revelation, for example, he attributes to his artistic contemplation of expressionistic painting, which opened his eyes "to how the substance of a work of art could destroy form and to the creative ecstasy implied in this process."[71] Later, in contemplating the transition from expressionism to realism, Tillich developed his concept of "belief-ful realism," an idea central to *The Religious Situation,* a book dedicated to an artist friend.

Thus, Tillich's pilgrimage is a case study in "practicing the religious imagination" and justifies the appeal by Amos N. Wilder for the development of "theopoetics."[72] Wilder believes that religion runs the risk of getting lost in abstraction, rationalism, and stereo-

---

[70]Paul Tillich, *On the Boundary: An Autobiographical Sketch* (New York: Scribner's, 1966) 24-33.

[71]Ibid., 28.

[72]Paul Pruyser illustrates the creative play of the imagination in the corporate experience of the religious community; see *A Dynamic Psychology of Religion,* 63ff.

type, and appeals for correction by asserting the rights of religious imagination.[73] Wilder sees a contemporary theopoetic in the form of renewal of the religious imagination as the hope for quickening established faith and confession to match "the fateful issues of our new world-experience."

As important as it is, imagination should not stand alone. Without roots and tradition, vision and fantasy are easily transformed into a cult, ends in themselves and little more than idle daydreaming. The dreamer who remains estranged from reality risks self-indulgence and contributes nothing to the vitality of religious community. Imagination, although oriented toward the future, must remain attached to the present. To be genuinely creative, imagination must be tempered by contact with a real world of people and things. Klinger's four criteria delineating how fantasy serves creativity well underscore this connection:[74]

(1) Persons must possess intellectual and personal capabilities to formulate fantasy without its being forced or artificial.

(2) The fantasy must be "at least occasionally relevant to a problem" in which the problem-solver is "immersed."

(3) A creative solution must be allowed to emerge, the difference between painting a picture and painting with numbered-pencil kits.

(4) Fantasy "must be received hospitably," including the disposition to exploit it in one's actions.

When these criteria are met, fantasy is moved out of the dream world into the arena of action and stimulates new solutions to old issues. In a religious context disciplined imagination may allow established rites and customs to be empowered by vision and ossified doctrine to be infused with new life.

---

[73]See his three articles in *Christian Century* on the general theme of "Theology and Theopoetic": "Part 1: What Forms Will a Theopoetic Take Today?" 90 (1973): 593-96; "Part 2: Renewal of the Imagination," ibid., 1195-98; and "Part 3: Ecstasy, Imagination and Insight" 91 (1974): 428-29. These articles were a prelude to his 1976 publication, *Theopoetic: Theology and the Religious Imagination* (Philadelphia: Fortress, 1976).

[74]Eric Klinger, *Structure and Functions of Fantasy* (New York: Wiley-Interscience, 1971) 219-20.

In a sense, discussion of thinking in past, present, and future tenses distorts the marvelously complex cognitive ability of persons. In any cognitive act the three tenses merge into a single configuration and may be separated only for academic discussion and clarification. Memory and imagination are inseparably joined in the present. The discussion might well conclude, then, by returning to unity—an insight that is at least as old as Augustine, who observes:

> But perhaps it might properly be said: there are three times, a present of things past, a present of things present, a present of things future. For these are in the mind as a certain triadic form, and elsewhere I do not see them: the present of things past is memory, the present of things present is direct attention, the present of things future is anticipation.[75]

SUGGESTED READINGS

Conceptualization

Anderson, Barry F. *Cognitive Psychology.* New York: Academic Press, 1975. A textbook introduction.

Festinger, Leon. *A Theory of Cognitive Dissonance.* Stanford CA: Stanford University Press, 1957. The pioneering study; definitive.

Piaget, Jean. *The Grasp of Consciousness: Action and Concept in the Young Child.* Susan Wedgewood, trans. Cambridge: Harvard University Press, 1976.

——————, and Barbel Inhelder. *The Psychology of the Child.* Helen Weaver, trans. New York: Basic Books, 1969. A summary of Piaget's ideas.

Rowland, G. Thomas, and J. Carson McGuire. *The Mind of Man: Some Views and a Theory of Cognitive Development.* Englewood Cliffs NJ: Prentice-Hall, 1971. Digested summary of several theorists.

See also works listed as Suggested Readings for Chapter 6.

Memory

Childs, Brevard S. *Memory and Tradition in Israel.* Studies in Biblical Theology, no. 37. Napier IL: Alec R. Allenson, 1962. Discusses memory in Old Testament.

Crowder, Robert G. *Principles of Learning and Memory.* New York: Halsted, 1976. Textbook summary.

Piaget, Jean. *On the Development of Memory and Intention.* Eleanor Duckworth, trans. Worcester MA: Clark University Press, 1968.

---

[75]*Confessions,* XI, xx.

Imagination

Klinger, Eric. *Structure and Functions of Fantasy*. New York: Wiley-Interscience, 1971. Complex and analytical.

Kroner, Richard. *The Religious Function of Imagination*. New Haven: Yale University Press, 1941. Brief but suggestive.

May, Rollo. *The Courage to Create*. New York: W. W. Norton, 1975.

Taylor, Irving A., and J. W. Getzels, eds. *Perspectives in Creativity*. New York: Aldine, 1975.

Warnock, Mary. *Imagination*. Berkeley: University of California Press, 1976.

Wilder, Amos N. *Theopoetic: Theology and the Religious Imagination*. Philadelphia: Fortress, 1976.

CHAPTER EIGHT

THE EMOTIONAL FUNCTION OF THE SELF AND RELIGIOUS AFFECTION

Persons are emotional animals. They feel and they feel deeply. Nonetheless, the analysis of emotion is exceedingly difficult for at least two reasons. First, it is hard to distinguish between feelings and the objects of those feelings. Except in cases of severe personality disorder, feelings are directed toward persons, things, and experiences, and it is much easier to discuss the qualities of the object to which the emotion is attached rather than the emotion itself. Saying what makes him or her desirable seems to be more simple than characterizing feelings for him or her! Hence, feelings are easily built into cognitions around emotions, and these are quickly built into stereotypes that lose the private character of emotion. Love thus becomes a set of ideas, a particular combination of cognitions that objectify emotion into a concept. Then a discussion of love becomes an experience in cognition, not affection. Talk is inevitably cognitive.[1]

---

[1]The terms "emotion," "feeling," and "affect" are illusive to precise definition and are used here interchangeably.

The major problem in isolating pure emotion, however, is ambivalence, the experience in which contrasting emotions toward the same object are held at the same time. Few, if any, emotions are without mixture. Feelings of love and fear, pleasure and displeasure, and acceptance and rejection may be combined in various proportions in a single relationship. Hence, describing how one feels in a given moment toward a specific object is likely to be an exercise in the discovery of the dominant emotion at the time, while recognizing its counterpart lurking in the shadows. Persons forced to respond to the question, "How do you feel?" often revert to generalities: "Great!" "Awful." "Like a million!" or "I can't tell you how I feel!" Ambivalence makes precision difficult. Such confusions of cognitive and affective functions leave a certain vagueness about emotion that partially accounts for psychology's more extensive research on thinking than feeling.

Generally emotions fall into two categories. One group consists of unpleasant feelings, prompting persons to avoid situations that produce them. Emotional intensity varies according to the extent of threat involved in situations that give rise to unpleasant emotion. Circumstances that are mildly threatening are likely to evoke mild emotional reaction, but sudden and serious danger tends to mobilize intense emotion and "have the effect of integrating and concentrating behavior" upon avoiding or escaping the threat.[2] Unpleasant feelings are not always destructive but serve often to preserve the person, as when fear causes one to leap to the curb to avoid a speeding automobile.

Another group of emotions is more positive and satisfying, such as the pleasure one derives from the visit of a friend. Less intensity and urgency usually characterize these feelings, but they are, nonetheless, significant in motivating persons to repeat pleasant behavior. Either pleasant or unpleasant emotion in excess may be debilitating, but when they are appropriate to the circumstances and balanced in intensity, both play an important role in self survival.[3]

---

[2]Carl R. Rogers, *Client-Centered Therapy: Its Current Practice, Implications, and Theory* (Boston: Houghton Mifflin, 1951) 493.

[3]See Robert W. Leeper, "A Motivational Theory of Emotion to Replace 'Emo-

Religious groups have expressed a variety of attitudes toward emotionality, usually overlaying emotion with moral connotations. Specific emotions, such as anger, may be judged evil and others, such as love, are called good without recognizing that one can "be angry and sin not"[4] or "love pleasure rather than God."[5] Or emotionality itself may be accepted or rejected on moral grounds. At one extreme is the synonymous identification of religion and emotion, and on the other extreme is a thoroughgoing rejection of emotionality in religion. In fact, the illusive character of feeling may easily encourage the devotee to identify emotion as the work of God. This undoubtedly explains in some measure a usage that appears regularly in traditional plain-folks religion. "I feel God (or the Holy Spirit) leading me to" is a common expression often combined with the tacit assumption that thinking about the proposition is likely to interfere seriously with the work of the Spirit. The presumed affinity between emotion and the work of the Spirit is likely to spill over into intense religious practices marked by informal ritual designed to break down inhibition and encourage uncontrolled emotionality.

At the opposite pole others systematically weed feeling out of their religious experience. These aim to develop a religion of the head in preference to a religion of the heart. Feelings, particularly those of tenderness or aggression, are seen as signs of weakness, unsophistication, or even evil. The world of ideas and concepts is judged superior to emotions; thus these persons aim to be as unemotional and as much in control as possible. In psychoanalytic terms these persons use both repression and suppression to control feelings that are unduly threatening. Unconsciously, feelings may be exiled to the farthest reaches of personality. More consciously controlled, they may be expunged until hardly a trace of them is left. The religious expressions of persons on this end of the emo-

tion as Disorganized Response,'" *Psychological Review* 55 (1948): 5-21. Many general approaches to personality, such as those represented in college psychology textbooks, treat emotion under motivation.

[4]Ephesians 4:26.

[5]II Timothy 3:4.

tional continuum are likely to be marked by rigidity, compulsion, and inflexibility.

These extreme attitudes toward emotion are reminders that religion carries heavy emotional weight for most people. The cliché about avoiding religion along with politics in polite conversation testifies that dispassionate discussion is difficult if not impossible. Yet, even when affect is overlaid with cognitive aspects of religion, emotional processes continue and are subjects for the psychological understanding of religious phenomena.

THEOLOGY'S CLAIM ON EMOTION

There has existed in Christian theology over the last three centuries an intense struggle concerning the role and relationship of thinking and feeling in religion. Is human reason sufficient to probe religious truth, or must it be supplemented by emotion? To which function does revelation belong? As the eighteenth century began, the idea that reason alone was the avenue to truth enjoyed ascendancy, especially in Western Europe.[6] Deism typified this position: God is the great watchmaker who has set all things in motion to operate according to established and ordered processes. From this point of view the chief end of humans is to use cognitive resources to explore and hopefully unlock the intricate mysteries of the world. The subtitle of John Toland's tract *Christianity Not Mysterious,* published in the seventeenth century before the heat of the controversy, states the position explicitly: "A Treatise Showing that There is Nothing in the Gospel Contrary to Reason nor Above It: And That No Christian Doctrine Can Be Properly Called A Mystery."

Unsurprisingly, the heightened respect for the power of human reason was met by a corresponding insistence upon human emotion as a substantial part of the religious life. Much of the story of Christian theology since the turn of the eighteenth century has been centered around the struggle between these two camps.[7] For

---

[6]See William A. Scott, ed., *Sources of Protestant Theology* (New York: Bruce, 1971) 161-62.

[7]For example, the issue is joined in the mid-twentieth century in attempts to restore revelation to a central place as a source of knowledge of God. See Karl Barth,

a while the struggle was intense, but by mid-eighteenth century the controversy was calm enough for the relationship between reason and feeling to be seen as one of mutual enrichment. Three names stand out prominently among theologians who claimed emotion as essential to the religious life: Friedrich Schleiermacher, Rudolf Otto, and Jonathan Edwards. Their work, although not strictly in the field of psychology, is profoundly psychological.

Schleiermacher:
Feeling of Absolute Dependence

Friedrich Schleiermacher's emphasis upon emotion is known through two primary works, *The Christian Faith* and *On Religion: Speeches to Its Cultured Despisers* (often referred to simply as *Speeches on Religion*). In these books the heart of religion is identified as "the feeling of absolute dependence." "Consciousness, the totality of being from which all determination of self-consciousness proceeds, is comprehended under the feeling of dependence."[8] Schleiermacher held that the religions of mankind, each in its own way, are manifestations of this elementary *feeling* of dependence upon God. For him religion was not derived fundamentally from either rational knowledge (contra the Deists) or moral action (contra Immanuel Kant), but from feeling, an immediate and unifying self-consciousness of the Infinite. He states, "To feel oneself absolutely dependent and to be conscious of being in relation to God are one and the same thing."[9]

In *Speeches on Religion* Schleiermacher defends this view of religion against its "cultured despisers," those who too easily would reject religion in favor of more formal and ordered cognitive systems. Originally published in 1799, the book is at once a protest against reducing religion to either ethical or metaphysical structures and also a brief positing feeling as the essence of religion. For

---

Evangelical Theology: An Introduction, Grover Foley, trans. (New York: Holt, Rinehart and Winston, 1963) for an introduction to this position. Compare also Emil Brunner, *Revelation and Reason: The Christian Doctrine of Faith and Knowledge*, Olive Wyon, trans. (Philadelphia: Westminster, 1946).

[8]Friedrich Schleiermacher, *The Christian Faith*, H. R. Mackintosh and J. S. Stewart, trans. and eds. (Edinburgh: T. and T. Clark, 1928) 126.

[9]Ibid., 17.

Schleiermacher, religion at its best was neither a corpus of moral legislation to be diligently obeyed nor a well-ordered dogmatic system satisfying the believer's intellect. Both theology and ethics are valuable to religious expression, but they are important only insofar as they are derived from contemplative apprehension of the Divine. The core of religion is thus no *idea,* but "immediate consciousness of the Deity as He is found in ourselves and in the world."[10] Schleiermacher's descriptions of feelings are somewhat vague,[11] but his insistence upon the importance of emotion is "a patent protection against formalism, ritualism, and rationalism in religion, which summed up for generations before and after him the conviction of all who demand that religious experience touch the heartstrings."[12]

Otto: Sense of *Numinous*

Rudolf Otto offered Schleiermacher's *Speeches on Religion* lofty but qualified praise. In an introduction that he prepared for a reprint of the book, Otto recognized "traces of incompleteness and amateurishness" but proclaimed the work as "one of the most famous books that history has recorded and preserved."[13] Undoubtedly Otto's high regard for Schleiermacher is partially explained by their common concern to bring self-awareness to center stage in theology and to emphasize affective qualities in that self-awareness.

In his own powerful book *The Idea of the Holy,* Otto defines his interest as an "inquiry into the non-rational factor in the idea of the divine and its relation to the rational." Otto calls the nonrational factor the sense of *numinous,* an overwhelming experience of awe in the presence of the "Wholly Other." "This mental state is per-

---

[10]Friedrich Schleiermacher, *On Religion: Speeches to Its Cultured Despisers,* John Oman, trans. (New York: Harper, 1958) 101.

[11]Psychology has been thus far unable to make the descriptions much more precise except in terms of physiological states accompanying emotion.

[12]Paul W. Pruyser, *A Dynamic Psychology of Religion* (New York: Harper, 1968) 141.

[13]Schleiermacher, *On Religion,* "Introduction," x.

fectly *sui generis* and irreducible to any other."[14] It is "creature-consciousness" or "creature-feeling," a sense of "nothingness before an overpowering absolute of some kind."[15] Creature-feeling is human reaction to the majesty, the awesomeness, the unfamiliarity of the "Wholly Other" and contains both fear and attraction. It is *mysterium tremendum,* sparking "a sense of personal insufficiency and impotence, a consciousness of being determined by circumstances and environment"[16] and one is tempted to flee from its threatening presence. It is also *mysterium fascinans,* strangely intriguing and attracting. Creature-feeling contains fear and curiosity in the presence of mystery.

Otto believed that creature-feeling exercised profound influence upon primitive religion. He suggests that the Buddhist *Om* and the Hebrew *YAH* may originally have been spontaneous verbal outbursts in the presence of *mysterium tremendum et fascinans.*[17] The sense of the mysterious has not disappeared from even the most sophisticated religions. "In every highly developed religion the appreciation of moral obligation and duty, ranking as a claim of the deity upon men, has developed side by side with the religious feeling itself."[18]

Edwards: Religious Affection

Another champion who advocated emotion in religion was Jonathan Edwards, a minister in Northampton, Massachusetts, and an astute theologian psychologist. As a minister Edwards was a major voice in the Great Awakening, a revivalistic movement that swept the eastern seaboard of the United States in the mid-eighteenth century. Edwards the preacher shared the emotional intensity of the movement and was not beyond using sensational, hellfire sermons to induce an emotional response. When he preached his famous

---

[14]Rudolf Otto, *The Idea of the Holy,* John W. Harvey, trans. (New York: Oxford University Press, 1926) 7.

[15]Ibid., 10.

[16]Ibid., 9.

[17]Ibid., Appendix 3.

[18]Ibid., 53.

sermon "Sinners in the Hands of an Angry God,"[19] which describes God holding sinful souls "over the pit of hell, much as one holds a spider . . . over the fire," it is said that hearers clutched the pews in front of them until their nails clawed into the wood. Edwards defended such use of emotion on the grounds that unregenerate men needed to be terrified into fleeing the wrath to come.

Yet Edwards was more than a sensational preacher; he was also a careful analytic thinker unwilling to indulge in emotion for its own sake. In language clearly belonging to his day, Edwards insists that the "religion which God requires, and will accept, does not consist in weak, dull, and lifeless wouldings," but is one that is "earnest, fervent in spirit," with "hearts vigorously engaged in religion."[20] But religious affection is to be distinguished from uncontrolled passion, feelings that rush upon persons more suddenly "whose effects on the animal spirits are more violent, and the mind more overpowered, and less in its own command."[21] Affections are characterized by understanding and self-control. Although Edwards was little in sympathy with the uncontrolled emotion of frenzied revivalism, he believed that emotion was a necessary ingredient of genuine religion.

Edwards further separates emotions that are positive from those that are negative. Love is "the chief of the affects, and the fountain of all other affections."[22] From it flow hope, joy, compassion, gratitude, and zeal. Although these may occur in the irreligious, they are necessary factors that move the religious person to action. They have their negative counterparts in such feelings as hatred, anger, fear, and guilt. Edwards uses extensive scriptural documentation to justify desirable emotions and to support his contention that religion and emotion fit hand in glove.

Still, religious emotion is not its own end. Affections are not to be judged by their intensity or their "great effects on the body."

---

[19]Clarence H. Faust and Thomas H. Johnson, eds., *Jonathan Edwards: Representative Selections,* rev. ed. (New York: Hill and Wang, 1962) 155-72.

[20]Jonathan Edwards, *Religious Affections,* John E. Smith, ed. (New Haven: Yale University Press, 1959) 10.

[21]Ibid., 9.

[22]Ibid., 19.

Rather, the "truly gracious and holy affections," those emotions that are pleasing to God, must incline persons to Christian practice. Edwards leaves no doubt that "'Holy practice' must be pursued with 'highest earnestness and diligence,' so that the practice of religion may be said to be eminently one's work and business. . . . Religious behaviour must persist in all times and seasons, through all changes, and under all trials."[23] Thus Edwards anticipated later psychologists who transform emotion into motivation and concentrate their attention on behavior patterns produced by emotional commitments. The fruits of emotion are more easily studied than raw emotion itself.[24]

Schleiermacher, Otto, and Edwards serve as not so gentle reminders that psychology must study religion in its emotional, spontaneous context. At those points where religion becomes dry and stilted, and too cognitive in orientation, an emotional protest may be expected. Charismatic movements in their many forms represent such a protest. Emotional revivalism in all its variety, from Billy Sunday to Billy Graham, is an attempt to reclaim a religion that speaks to the heart. Although many of their features may be cognitively offensive to their "cultured despisers," these emotional movements are likely to go on claiming adherents from across the social spectrum on the conviction that religion belongs to the heart as well as the head.

INTERFACE BETWEEN EMOTION AND RELIGION

The affective dimension of human experience gives both personality and religion warmth and flavor, liveliness and spontaneity.[25] Freud recognized that the tenacity with which people hold to religious ideas is determined by the strength of associated feelings and wishes. Yet religion has not praised emotion without qualification. To affirm the unencumbered expression of affect is to be-

---

[23]Ibid., 306.

[24]See for example, Thomas J. Coates, "Personality Correlates of Religious Commitment: A Further Verification," *Journal of Social Psychology* 89 (1973): 159-60.

[25]Compare Adrian van Kaam, *Religion and Personality* (Garden City NY: Doubleday, 1968) 68-69.

lieve that emotion is a dependable moral guide and to structure a religious universe in which self-indulgence is the highest good. Hence both corporate and private religion have been selective in their attitudes toward emotion.[26] By what standards ought such selections be made? What are the good and bad emotions? When does intensity of commitment become religious fanaticism? How does one draw the line between feeling guilty and being guilty? These are not easy questions with simple answers, and conflicting answers are easily found within religious systems. A single feeling may be condemned in one religious group and praised in another. The patient acceptance and endurance of suffering is an enviable virtue in asceticism, but is evidence of lack of faith in reassurance cults that prefer relaxation and positive thinking as ideals.

The resolution of hard questions regarding the moral quality of specific emotions and emotionality itself is a matter for continual theological discussion, but the psychology of religion can inform theological discussions of emotion at two crucial points where religion and emotion interface: gratification and guilt.

Delayed Gratification and Self-Denial

Timing Satisfaction. Psychoanalysis has demonstrated beyond question that emotions are powerful things demanding satisfaction. Yet few cultures, with the possible exception of some artificial and highly protected environment, permit the direct and immediate expression of impulses. Channels for direct fulfillment are not always available, emotional needs sometimes contradict each other, and giving full vent to feelings often places persons at odds with their neighbors. Practicality and social context demand compromise between the force of personal emotionality and the need for community living. A maturing individual simply cannot emote immediately and all over the place.

The neurotic individual insists upon unhindered and uninterrupted satisfaction of emotional needs without consideration of other persons. Sick persons tend to act out their feelings with little or no ability to defer the expression of impulses or, perhaps worse still, to camouflage their feelings so that they behave as if emotion

---

[26]Pruyser, *A Dynamic Psychology of Religion,* 147.

is absent or inherently evil. The mentally healthy person, on the other hand, is one who is able to accept emotional needs and with some efficiency adapt to the demands of the external world. Learning to be human entails the ability to rank priorities and make choices in emotional expression as well as tolerate considerable delay and modification.

Some psychologists have discussed the management of emotionality as part of the maturation process under the label of delayed gratification, "the willingness to defer immediate, less valued rewards for the sake of more valuable but temporarily deferred outcomes."[27] The crucial factor is the timing of emotional expression. Learning to delay gratification begins when the infant cannot satisfy all needs immediately. Bottle or breast is not immediately available and waiting produces frustration. Emotional maturation begins as the infant learns to wait. Later development continuously involves the timing of gratification. The development may be expected to move through three stages:

Stage 1. Little ability to delay (which, if persisting into adulthood, would be classified as infantile or even psychotic) to

Stage 2. Fear-motivated delay (which, if persisting into adulthood, would be seen as neurotic compulsion) to

Stage 3. Goal-oriented delay (which would be flexible, discriminating, and motivated by ideal images of the future).[28]

Self-Denial. The Western religious establishment has shared society's concern to control wanton emotionality and censured the indulgence of feelings for their own sake. Unfortunately, in the name of self-denial some religious groups, rather than seeing their task as helping persons express their emotions at appropriate times and places, have attempted to exile feelings, honoring the rigid control of emotionality. Repression and suppression have been encouraged on the assumption that emotional expression inherently

---

[27]Walter Mischel and John Grusec, "Waiting for Rewards and Punishments: Effects of Time and Probability on Choice," *Journal of Personality and Social Psychology* 5 (1967): 24-31.

[28]Roy W. Fairchild, "Delayed Gratification: A Psychological and Religious Analysis," in Strommen, *Research on Religious Development*, 190.

threatens genuine faith. "God is always looking for someone who is enjoying himself and then putting a stop to it." This childish expression portrays an attitude deeply rooted in the Judeo-Christian tradition. In one form or another it appears in asceticism, certain types of evangelical pietism, and positive thinking cults. Accordingly, any satisfying emotion, especially those derived from sexuality or aggression, is considered suspect and probably the work of an "Evil One," deceptively attempting to snare anyone who yields to natural desire. The attitude is often grounded in a dualistic view of personhood that strictly separates the physical from the spiritual and interprets the physical as opposed to the highest and best. In this tradition the biblical injunction to forget the self and lose one's life is misinterpreted to mean denying things to the self and especially avoiding "fleshly" pleasure.[29] Generally, these patterns of self-denial and control are supported with confidence that the future will provide what the present denies.

This type of self-denial mentality undergirds segments of Christian thought and is illustrated classically in monastic asceticism. The rigid life of the nun or monk is intended to bring under control the expression of those desires that might interfere with the development of the "good" life. If emotion can be sufficiently restrained, it is supposed, the spiritual self will flourish. In asceticism the body is rejected in the interest of the soul. In extreme cases this involves isolating oneself from the world (as withdrawing to a cave as a hermit) and severe asceticism (as self-flagellation or living on a diet of sesame seeds). In milder forms the ascetic spirit survives in varieties of contemporary evangelical pietism that have made some peace with culture but continue to define faith in terms of denying mortal flesh and preparing the soul for its heavenly home. The morality of such groups stresses avoidance of sensual sins, such as smoking, drinking, and carousing, and their ritual is oriented around hope for the "the home over there."

Advocates of mind-over-feeling in much popular religion also deny emotionality in their own peculiar way. The high priest of this movement for several decades has been Norman Vincent Peale,

---

[29]Matthew 16:21-28; Mark 8:34-38; Luke 9:23-27.

with assistance from Bishop Fulton Sheen, Rabbi Joshua Liebman, and a host of lesser lights who have learned to market this brand of religion. These persons insist that positive thinking is the royal road to the good life. "Thought conditioners," "spirit lifters," "prayers for all occasions," and "Satan control kits" are offered as devices for avoiding fear, anxiety, and other unpleasant emotions. Cognitive and ritualistic techniques are used to keep positive thoughts at the forefront of consciousness and to avoid negative emotionality as if it were unreal. As asceticism uses mortification of the body, so Peale and company use mental activity to erode the claims of emotionality.

Monasticism, asceticism, varieties of evangelical pietism, and positive thinking cults in their extreme forms overreact to the risks of emotionality with too much control; they miss the creative contributions of feelings suggested in the works of Schleiermacher, Otto, and Edwards and disavow emotionality to the extent that persons do not mature in their ability to delay gratification.

Self-Control. Several features of American life in the sixties suggested that the willingness to delay gratification was being eroded by demands for immediate emotional satisfaction.[30] The protest movements of the sixties, more permissive attitudes toward premarital and extramarital sex, greater stress upon practical emphases in education, and a resurgence of sensate religion may be partially understood as calls for immediate expression and instant fulfillment of personal desires. Future, long-term goals seem to have been sacrificed in the interest of present, short-range benefits. In ways less rebellious against the establishment, the mentality of immediate satisfaction has been preserved in the American credit system. Credit-card thinking leaves little room for conceiving satisfaction in future terms. Encouraged by persuasive advertising, Americans have learned well to complain about prices and to continue to "buy-now-pay-later." The credit system has become "a

---

[30]See Florence R. Kluckhohn and F. L. Strodtbeck, *Variations in Value-Orientations* (New York: Harper, 1961); Alan W. Watts, *Psychotherapy: East and West* (New York: Pantheon, 1961); Edward E. Sampson, "Student Activism and the Decade of Protest," *Journal of Social Issues* 23 (1967):1-33; William E. Schutz, *Joy: Expanding Human Awareness* (New York: Grove, 1967).

powerful battering ram against the older values of hard work, thrift, living within one's means, and 'saving for a rainy day.'"[31] With a billfold of credit cards average Americans need not delay the gratification that any product might bring. They may remain forever in debt, but they do not need to think very much about controlled emotions and delayed gratification.

The late seventies and early eighties, however, have brought a resurgence of conservative religion and values.[32] Does this represent a modern rebirth of asceticism or a contemporary search for control devices that take faithful account of human emotionality? Whatever the correct interpretation, the psychological task for religion is to develop an approach to emotionality that incorporates delayed gratification. Clearly, uncontrolled and indiscriminate expression of emotion gives too large a place to feelings and tends to reduce the human person to the level of animal, but the rigid denial of feeling, even in the name of God, thwarts a primary datum of human experience. Reconciliation of the extremes demands that our theological statements on self-denial be informed by psychological interpretations of delayed gratification. Several guidelines seem appropriate.

First, renunciation itself is not a religious virtue. Self-denial, like any other behavioral pattern, must be evaluated in the context of the function that it serves. "While the *ability* to delay or renounce gratification is crucial to discipleship, the 'willingness to sacrifice' per se cannot be exalted indiscriminately."[33] Neither renunciation nor indulgence of emotions is itself virtuous; either is to be evaluated by the role that it plays in a person's motivation. The theologian David Roberts says, "Whether sacrifice is a supreme manifestation of goodness depends on the manner in which the individual enters into it, and upon its connections with his ideals and his love. It can be, and often is, a means of expressing self-hatred

---

[31]Fairchild, "Delayed Gratification," 158.

[32]See Dean M. Kelley, *Why Conservative Churches Are Growing: A Study in Sociology of Religion* (New York: Harper, 1972).

[33]Fairchild, "Delayed Gratification," 165.

in the form of self-punishment. One gives himself a beating by rigorously imposing self-denial."[34]

An act motivated by fear is qualitatively different from one motivated by care; one expressing itself automatically carries different moral weight from one deliberately instigated.[35] The transformation of self-denial into self-control depends in some measure on one's ability to focus on function.

Second, self-denial becomes self-control when the so-called sinister emotions such as aggression, dependency, sexuality are consciously accepted and informed by the notion of appropriate time and circumstance for expression.[36] "Superego religion" based on oppressive laws, reinforced by arbitrary authority, and motivated by fear must surrender to "ego religion." The latter operates "in accordance with emerging goals and values and perceptions of social and religious reality."[37] It uses these standards to guide, control, regulate, schedule, and plan the appropriate expression of emotions.

Third, religious appeals for self-control must rest on a realistic acceptance of emotion as an essential part of human experience and provide guidelines for its expression in terms of both present and long-range values. Religion properly embraces emotion when it affords a vision of the future that makes sense of delayed gratification and also provides opportunity for self-expression in the here-and-now world. Without a sense of enduring values persons have no reason to delay gratification; without some present fulfillment apocalyptic visions of satisfaction in a distant future are no more than idle dreams. A perennial question addressed by religion is, "What is worth delaying gratification?"

---

[34]David E. Roberts, *Psychotherapy and a Christian View of Man* (New York: Scribner's, 1950) 139.

[35]Fairchild, "Delayed Gratification," 173-75.

[36]See discussion of *Kairos* above, pp. 212-16.

[37]Fairchild, "Delayed Gratification," 174. Fairchild borrows the labels "superego religion" and "ego religion" from Roy S. Lee, *Freud and Christianity* (London: James Clarke and Co., 1948).

Guilt, Sin, and Conscience

A second point of intersection between emotionality and religion is guilt, that peculiarly human capacity and disposition for self-judgment. The psychoanalytic interpretation of the origin of religion assigns a major role to guilt. Accordingly, religion both preserves the original Oedipus pattern that produces guilt and serves to allay the burden of threatening emotion deeply imbedded in early relationships with parents and parent substitutes.[38] Both personal and corporate religion are constructed out of childhood wishes to possess one parent and to defend against the perceived threat from the other parent. To act directly toward the threat would only increase anxiety and guilt. Religious ritual achieves indirectly what cannot be accomplished directly; it pays off the guilt debt. Substitute behavior in the form of religious acts is one of the more socially and personally acceptable channels for relieving the infantile burden.[39]

Whether or not religious origins are to be explained according to the psychoanalytic design, guilt certainly is woven into the fabric of personality development and it conditions religious experience. Religious groups differ considerably on the kind of behavior that is tolerated, but all sanction formal and informal values that may not be violated without penalty of guilt. Self estimates of guilt do not seem to vary considerably from one denomination to another.[40]

Generally religion views guilt as a negative emotion, something to be avoided by correct behavior or to be escaped by repentance and forgiveness. And guilt certainly can have devastating effects when the intensity of the emotion is disproportionate to the act to which it is attached. At one extreme are those who manifest less guilt than their deeds merit. The so-called clinical psychopath seems to have no sense of right and wrong and suffers no pangs of conscience regardless of how antisocial the behavior exhibited might

---

[38]See above, pp. 70-74.

[39]See Oscar Pfister, *Christianity and Fear* (New York: Macmillan, 1948) 151-56.

[40]Perry London, Robert E. Schulman, and Michael S. Black, "Religion, Guilt, and Ethical Standards," *Journal of Social Psychology* 63 (1964): 145-59.

be. Others manage to discount guilt by placing the blame outside themselves. Parents, social circumstances, or human nature become scapegoats for personal responsibility. These persons are adept at rationalization and can usually explain quite logically how they have been entrapped and therefore are not responsible for misdeeds. If pushed, these persons may perceive themselves as victims of a plot. Clinically they are labeled "paranoid" and, like psychopaths, avoid responsibility through rigid avoidance devices. Both psychopathic and paranoid individuals manage guilt by attempting to get rid of it and present a clinical picture of innocence disproportionate to their antisocial behavior.

At the other extreme are those who suffer unbearably over trifles. Guilt so dominates their emotionality that it wanders around in search of something to which it may attach itself. Sometimes these individuals cannot even identify a reason for the intensity of their suffering. It is not so much that they have done *acts* worthy of condemnation; *they themselves* are unworthy and merit punishment. Their guilt may even turn in upon itself so that they feel guilty about feeling guilty. The behavior of persons weighted down with excessive guilt may be marked by compulsive acts, such as continuous hand washing to obliterate the "damned spot." Or it may take the form of deep depression sometimes accompanied by a feeling of having committed an unpardonable sin. If the behavior is not severe enough to require hospitalization, persons with undue burdens of guilt make chronic confessors and are dependable statistics for the revivalist who counts the number of decisions.

Observation of these exaggerated states may easily produce stereotypes of guilt as abnormal and pathological. Yet guilt has its positive side. It does not need to be an all-or-nothing reaction to which persons either hold themselves guilty beyond the requirements of law and justice or scuttle all responsibility. It can be an impetus to creative behavior and human growth. A sense of inadequacy has driven the adolescent with physical limitation to athletic prowess, the socially shy scientist to diligence and discovery in the laboratory, and the alcoholic to humanitarian concern for a fellow sufferer. Clark observes that "it is doubtful that many of the positive achievements of modern civilization would be possible without the peculiarly human capacity for feeling guilt and the prick of that inner stimulus that we call conscience."[41]

In his extensive work with Vietnam veterans, the psychiatrist Robert Lifton observed guilt in both its negative and positive forms.[42] *Static* guilt was characterized by a "closed universe of transgression and expected punishment" from which the veterans were unable to extricate themselves. For some this took the shape of numbing, a feeling of being dead to life; others were self-lacerating, continuously punishing themselves in self-condemnation. All with static guilt seemed to be "cut off from the life process," to live in a "death-dominated condition."

Yet other of Lifton's veterans were able to make their guilt *animating,* "characterized by bringing oneself to life around one's guilt." Animating guilt propels persons forward toward "connection, integrity, movement." It engenders energy and stimulates new images and possibilities. "Above all, animating guilt is inseparable from the idea of being responsible for one's actions—so much so that we may define it as the anxiety of responsibility."

There is no necessary reason for guilt to be associated with religion for it to be creative, but if it is to encourage positive uses of guilt, religion must be concerned especially with the ways in which it defines *sin and conscience.*

Guilt and Sin. In Western society religion has traditionally transformed guilt into sin by sacralizing a legal code and associating guilt with breaches of the code. As in the public domain one is "guilty before the law" when the accepted standards of the group have been violated, so in the religious domain he is "sinful" when a code defined as the law or will of God has been transgressed. This is the ethical face of authoritarian religion decried by Fromm and the interpretation of guilt and sin eroded generally by psychoanalytic personality theory. Legal interpretations assign guilt and sin to neatly drawn categories; if the laws are explicit and if evidence proves a misdeed, then guilt may be assigned and justice adminis-

---

[41]Walter H. Clark, *The Psychology of Religion: An Introduction to Religious Experience and Behavior* (New York: Macmillan, 1958) 90-91.

[42]See Robert J. Lifton, *Home from the War* (New York: Simon and Schuster, 1973) 97-233. Note especially 126-28; the quoted phrases come from these pages.

tered. Depth psychology has taught us, however, that responsibility is not always so clear, reminiscent of a question asked of Jesus: "Teacher, whose sin caused him to be born blind? Was it his own or his parents' sin?"[43] Jesus refused to discuss guilt on these grounds, suggesting his judgment that blindness was not always explained by sin and that sin could not be reduced to linear responsibility.

The difficulty of assigning responsibility has caused the concept of sin to fall into disrepute in ever-widening circles. Accordingly, the model of persons as sinners is suspect as likely to hold persons responsible for more than they are actually accountable and has been largely replaced by "various forms of rationalism which tend to obscure man's devious and apparently inexhaustible self-interest."[44] Psychologists and theologians alike have talked more about "guilt feelings" than guilt or sin with the implication that persons are not *really* guilty, but only feel that way. Particularly those involved therapeutically with counselees whose self-esteem is shattered judge that it is better to stress their positive. creative potential than to remind them of sin.

Recently, however, some therapists and psychologists have recommended a return to the concept of sin. Notable among these have been O. Hobart Mowrer and Karl Menninger. Mowrer has chided his fellow psychologists for treating antisocial behavior too tritely by using mild and indirect words to describe harsh and unpleasant realities. He insists that therapy and health are better served by a return to negative words to label negative behavior. One, therefore, should not be reluctant to use words such as sin[45] to bring responsibility into focus. Mowrer believes "the main reason 'mental illness' has been such a mystery in our time is that we have so assiduously separated it from the realm of personal morality and immorality."[46]

---

[43]John 9:3.

[44]Fred Berthold, Jr., "Theology and Self-Understanding: The Christian Model of Man as Sinner," in Homans, *The Dialogue between Theology and Psychology*, 19.

[45]See O. Hobart Mowrer, *The Crisis in Psychology and Religion* (New York: Van Nostrand, 1962); idem, ed., *Morality and Mental Health* (Chicago: Rand McNally, 1964).

[46]Mowrer, *Morality and Mental Health*, vii.

The same note is sounded in the reflective book *Whatever Happened to Sin?* by Karl Menninger. He decries the weakened responsibility that comes from translating sin into psychological euphemisms such as "aggressive" or "self-destructive" behavior and argues that healing occurs not merely through insight but through teaching persons that they are responsible for their own actions. Menninger, therefore, appeals for a return to the use of the word "sin" as a means to realistic confrontation of the destructive elements of behavior. Thus therapy is successful to the extent that counselees decide on a responsible course of action and begin to bring it into being. Although these interpreters may leave too little room for social influences on conscience and overlook corporate aspects of responsibility, Mowrer and Menninger serve as a necessary corrective to the overemphasis upon the destructive power of guilt prevalent in psychoanalysis and the avoidance of the sin factor in contemporary psychotherapy and personality theory.

Yet, the theologian had best rejoice reluctantly that these non-theologians are returning to sin and responsibility as useful categories. Mowrer and Menninger still are talking about sin as misdeed. It may be therapeutically sound to recapture responsibility for such behavior and reconstruct behavior patterns that are ethically correct, but sin as a breach of code does not plumb the depths of human isolation and aloneness. A return to a legalistically based concept of sin may in fact deepen guilt, of which people already have more than can be borne. If the constructive functions of guilt are to be rediscovered, the definition of sin must incorporate condition, attitude, and relationship.

Christian theology, consistent with its Jewish heritage, offers an understanding of sin that is more broadly based than the concept of sin as misdeed. Sin is a condition that disrupts relationships with God and neighbor, and thereby thwarts a person's potential as a creature of God. Profound stories in Genesis 3 and 4 depict sin as rebellion against God and as violence against neighbor. These are evil not because they are evil deeds, but because they contradict the highest human potential.[47] Thus, sin is that inevitable and ever-

---

[47]See Henry J. Flanders, Robert W. Crapps, and David A. Smith, *People of the Covenant: An Introduction to the Old Testament,* 2d ed. (New York: Wiley, 1973) 74-81.

present circumstance of persons in their relationship to their potential as God's created beings. As Paul Tillich puts it, sin "is the
unreconciled duality of ultimate and preliminary concerns, of the
finite and that which transcends finitude, of the secular and the
holy. Sin is a state of things in which the holy and the secular are
separated, struggling with each other and trying to conquer each
other."[48]

Wayne Oates's provocative discussion of sin and forgiveness reflects this broadened understanding of sin.[49] He interprets sin mul-
tidimensionally. To "define sin in terms of the behavior patterns
and taboos of changing human conditions" is "a kind of idolatry of
our own ideas of right and wrong."[50] Rather, sin incorporates the
idolatry of "the elevation of a preliminary concern to ultimacy."[51]
Faith calls for launching out into the unknown in response to the
eternal, but sin describes enslavement to destructive habit, the
avoidance of one's own humanity through a childish feeling of om-
nipotence, and alienation from both God and man. Insofar as ideal
humanness is never fully achieved, sin is an inevitable part of life's
pilgrimage and forgiveness is essential to self-acceptance. Since sin
is larger than misdeed, forgiveness cannot be reduced to superficial, trite forgetting of errors. More fundamentally, forgiveness entails affirming human worth as God's creation even when persons
fall short of their possibilities. Forgiveness of this sort delivers sin
from morbidity and gives birth to striving born of grace and gratitude.

Guilt and Conscience. To see sin and forgiveness in this larger
context broadens one's understanding of conscience. Conscience is
a phenomenon of discrepancy referring to that inevitable gap between the self as it is and the self as it may become. To have conscience means to envision an ideal of life to which commitment may
be made and to recognize the gulf that inevitably exists between the
ideal and present achievement. Thus conscience thrives upon vi-

---

[48]Tillich, *Systematic Theology,* 1:218.

[49]Oates, *The Psychology of Religion,* 203-214.

[50]Ibid., 205.

[51]Tillich, *Systematic Theology,* 1:13.

sion and possibility, from which are derived feelings of inadequacy, guilt, and sin at not having arrived. Oates then is correct in following Royce to associate loyalty and conscience. "To have a conscience . . . is to have a cause, to unify life by means of an idea determined by this cause."[52] The familiar pangs of conscience at their best constitute not merely remorse over an improper act but those negative feelings rooted in the recognition that one falls short of the ideal; following the dictates of conscience results in those positive feelings associated with right behavior, that which moves one closer to the ideal.

The vision of human possibility[53] gives a lingering quality to sin and conscience. It provides a sense of oughtness, a moving of persons toward the ideal. Such a view of conscience gives the impression of universality.

> Man cannot live without some sense of right, and every society must have a sense of the rightness of its own customs. An individual may break off, call himself amoral, or feel himself as completely independent of ordinary social rules as did the Greek tyrants whom the Sophists defended—or as Hitler did. But people can do this only when they can convince themselves that popular notions of right are morally wrong, at least for the more energetic and capable spirits, and that they do a higher right in flouting them.[54]

Although the sense of rightness or oughtness seems consistently present in human experience, the "do's" and "don'ts" of conscience vary considerably from culture to culture, and even from person to person within a single culture. What behavior has not been perpetrated in the name of God and a good conscience? The idea that conscience is divinely implanted and fully equipped to guide persons to beatitude through small whispers falls quickly before such variation. Some who are strict in their observance of Sundays cannot understand others who feel that Blue Laws restrict

---

[52]Josiah Royce, *The Philosophy of Loyalty* (New York: Macmillan, 1909) 175.

[53]Compare Sigmund Freud on "ego ideal," *The Ego and the Id,* 4th ed., Joan Riviere, trans. (London: Hogarth, 1947) 34-53; and Lewis J. Sherrill on "the imagined self," *The Gift of Power* (New York: Macmillan, 1955) 38-40.

[54]Edwin R. Goodenough, *The Psychology of Religious Experiences* (New York: Basic Books, 1965) 20.

freedom. Jews might attach pangs of conscience to the Sabbath and Moslems to Friday. Conscience certainly is not a uniform guide at the point of content.

Diversity in the specific content of conscience is partially explained by the initial stages by which conscience begins to appear. Patterns of moral judgment begin long before an individual has developed reflective cognitive capacity that would permit rational decisions about right and wrong. They come out of early infancy when the child's relationship to the environment is more affective than cognitive. The psychoanalytic description of the early emergence of control devices as superego is generally accepted. Accordingly, superego represents the internalization of parental images who threaten punishment followed by rewards of being accepted, approved, and loved. From the beginning of life, the child faces repeated frustrations of desires, usually accompanied by veiled or overt threats of punishment. These are taken seriously not merely as thwarting satisfaction, but also as threatening life itself. To protect self and assure survival, the young child identifies with the threatening demands and internalizes them. This internalized control structure is superego, a primitive and impersonal device for organizing desires and weakening the external threat to existence. Thus, superego preserves the dark sanctions of the past in largely unconscious control of those acts that might produce threats from the environment.

Two points about the formation and function of superego should be made clear beyond possible misunderstandings. First, the energy for superego is emotional, not cognitive, energy. It operates without necessary regard to the moral quality of acts themselves. Superego guilt rather is the naked fear of rejection. The source of the commands of superego "do not arise from any kind of perception of the intrinsic goodness or objectionableness" of acts but "can be described positively as the desire to be approved and loved, or negatively as the fear of loss of such love and approval."[55]

Second, an individual's moral life may be dominated by an infantile superego or the superego may be revised and enlarged in

---

[55]John W. Glasser, "Conscience and Superego," in John J. Heaney, ed., *Psyche and Spirit: Readings in Psychology and Religion* (New York: Paulist, 1973) 36-37.

the direction of a more rational and conscious apparatus. Superego has a legitimate function; it is crucial in the socialization of children and provides a primitive base for the emergence of more mature moral sensibilities. But superego remains too tied to the past, equipped to replicate judgments but not very adaptable to new situations. It orients behavior around authority figures in a position to grant or withhold approval but cannot assess values in and of themselves. Thus human moral sensibility must develop beyond superego, that is, superego ought to become conscience.

One of the tasks of religion is to assist in diminishing the arbitrariness of the superego as more rational and conscious commitments to values are made. The maturing person enlarges moral function beyond superego, a structure much too narrow to cover conscience.[56] Freud spoke of the ego ideal as a way of surpassing superego, saying, "It is easy to show that the ego ideal answers to everything that is expected of the higher nature of man."[57] Erich Fromm speaks of the "humanistic conscience" that taps an individual's inner creativity and enables decisions to be made for which the person himself takes responsibility.[58] Rollo May points to the similarity between the terms "conscience" and "conscious" and insists on bringing past and present experiences together in "creative conscience"—"one's capacity to tap one's own deeper levels of insight, ethical sensitivity and awareness, in which tradition and immediate experience are not opposed to each other but interrelated."[59] Paul Tillich's term is "transmoral" conscience, "that judges not in obedience to a moral law but according to the participation in a reality that transcends the sphere of moral commands."[60] These men envision conscience to be larger than

---

[56]Joseph Sandler, "On the Concept of Superego," in Ruth S. Eissler et al., eds., *The Psychoanalytic Study of the Child,* vol. 15 (New York: International Universities Press, 1960) 128-62.

[57]Freud, *The Ego and the Id,* 37.

[58]See Erich Fromm, *Man for Himself* (New York: Holt, Rinehart and Winston, 1947) 141-72.

[59]Rollo May, *Man's Search for Himself* (New York: W. W. Norton, 1953) 215.

[60]Paul Tillich, *The Protestant Era* (Chicago: University of Chicago Press, 1948) 145.

superego, moving beyond emotional energy derived from unconscious repression to motivate the moral life. They appeal for conscience not merely as something to be tolerated as the price to be paid for orderly social living, but as something to give creative direction to emotional impulses.[61]

In sum, then, gratification and guilt are double-edged. They may cut out the heart of self-acceptance by seeking immediate satisfaction without regard to neighbor or by overwhelming with shame at trifles. Or they may dispose persons to transcend mere animal existence that demands direct satisfaction without regard to responsibility and cause them to affirm their places as responsible members of the human family.

SUGGESTED READINGS

Religion and Emotion

Edwards, Jonathan. *Religious Affections*. John E. Smith, ed. New Haven: Yale University Press, 1959. First published in 1746 under the title *A Treatise Concerning Religious Affections*.

Otto, Rudolf. *The Idea of the Holy*. John W. Harvey, trans. New York: Oxford University Press, 1926.

Schleiermacher, Friedrich. *The Christian Faith*. H. R. Mackintosh and J. S. Stewart, trans. and eds. Edinburgh: T. and T. Clark, 1928.

_____. *On Religion: Speeches to Its Cultured Despisers*. John Oman, trans., New York: Harper, 1958.

Film: "Meeting in the Air." 16 mm., color, c. 28 minutes. Available from Religious America, Yale University Media Design Studio, 305 Crown Street, New Haven CT 06520.

Guilt

Belgum, David. *Guilt: Where Psychology and Religion Meet*. Minneapolis: Augsburg, 1969.

McKenzie, John G. *Guilt: Its Meaning and Significance*. London: Allen and Unwin, 1962.

Tournier, Paul. *Guilt and Grace: A Psychological Study*. Arthur W. Heathcote, trans. New York: Harper, 1962.

---

[61]Freud states, "The price we pay for one advance in civilization is a loss of happiness through the heightening of the sense of guilt;" *Civilization and Its Discontents,* James Strachey, ed. (New York: W. W. Norton, 1962) 134.

Warlick, Harold G., Jr. *Liberation from Guilt.* Nashville: Broadman, 1976. Popular and pastoral.

Conscience

Bier, William S., ed. *Conscience: Its Freedom and Limitations.* New York: Fordham University Press, 1971.

Davies, W. D. "Conscience." In *The Interpreter's Dictionary of the Bible.* George A. Buttrick et al., eds. Vol. 1, 671-76. Nashville: Abingdon, 1962. An excellent summary of biblical concepts.

Knight, James A. *Conscience and Guilt.* New York: Appleton-Century-Crofts, 1969. A competent psychological treatment.

Nelson, C. Ellis, ed. *Conscience: Theological and Psychological Perspectives.* New York: Newman, 1973.

Pierce, C. A. *Conscience in the New Testament.* London: S. C. M. Press, 1955. Discusses biblical and Hellenistic uses.

CHAPTER NINE

VOLITION AND MORAL DECISION MAKING

In his *The Varieties of Religious Experience* the irrepressible William James reports the melancholy of a fictitious Frenchman. James later confessed this to be an autobiographical account of fear that had brought him to the edge of despair.[1] At the age of twenty-eight he had been suddenly overwhelmed with a sense of panic and near collapse characterized by "a horrible fear of my own existence." An epileptic patient, "a black-haired youth with greenish skin, entirely idiotic," whom he encountered in the hospital, became the focus of his fear. "That shape am I, I felt, potentially. Nothing that I possess can defend me against that fate, if the hour for it should strike for me as it struck for him . . . I became a mass of quivering fear."[2]

James traces his escape from the precipice of despair to his affirmation of free will. On 30 April 1870, he wrote in his diary:

---

[1] Gay W. Allen, *William James: A Biography* (New York: Viking, 1967) 165-66.

[2] James, *The Varieties of Religious Experience*, 157.

I think yesterday was a crisis in my life. I finished the first part of Renouvier's 2nd Essay and saw no reason why his definition of free will—"the sustaining of a thought because I choose to when I might have other thoughts"—need be the definition of an illusion. At any rate I will assume for the present—until next year—that it is no illusion. My first act of free will shall be to believe in free will.[3]

James became so convinced of the decisive importance of will that it occupied a significant place in his *Principles of Psychology*, and his insightful essay entitled "The Will to Believe," written in 1896, remains worthy reading.

James's report certainly raises as many questions about volition as it answers. To what extent can a person genuinely control his destiny by acts of will? In what sense is will molded by physiological or sociological factors? How, in fact, may will as a conscious act be separated from a whole complex of interpersonal and intrapersonal factors? In his later writings James spoke to some of the questions implicit in his affirmation of will, but his experience simply would not allow him to forgo will as one of the major aspects of the functioning self, often the determining factor in health and survival.

Will, or volition, adds to cognitive and affective aspects of behavior the important dimension of commitment. Human behavior involves not only thinking and feeling about open options, but also selecting a course for personal action. To discuss will is to contemplate a level of behavior in which individuals decide among the options they will follow amid counterpressures from their own impulses or from the environment. How do persons come to the place where they can make decisions regarding their behavior? To what extent may decisions that are made be considered their own decisions? These are not easy questions, and vast areas of psychology have chosen to avoid them by eliminating choice and decision and substituting instead mechanistic and deterministic models. They nonetheless are questions that lie close to the heart of religion and cannot be sidestepped by the psychology of religion.

---

[3] As cited in Allen, *William James*, 168.

FREEDOM AND DETERMINISM

At the base of any discussion of volition is the principal issue of human freedom. Before the advent of scientific psychology, the idea of will was often advanced as an affirmation of individual freedom. Will was defined as an independent faculty that enabled persons to determine their own destiny with no outside influence. But psychoanalysis and behaviorism have long since eroded the naive assumption that behavior is independent of countless drives, anxieties, fears, and impulses coming from unexpected places. Rollo May calls Freud's challenge to the futility and self-deceit of vaunted Victorian concepts of will power one of his great—if not his greatest—contributions. His evaluation is that Freud's formulation of a new image of "willing" persons "shook to the very foundation Western man's emotional, moral, and intellectual self-image. Under his penetrating analysis, Victorian 'will' did, indeed, turn out to be a web of rationalization and self-deceit."[4]

Freud correctly diagnosed a concept of unconditional will as inadequate, but he overstated the case when he completely ruled out possibilities of freedom and choice. Freud makes the point forcefully: "There is within you a deeply rooted belief in psychic freedom and choice, . . . it is quite unscientific, and . . . it must give ground before the claims of a determinism which governs even mental life."[5] He thus portrays persons as completely driven by forces beyond their control, will, and decision. Behavioristic psychology underscores this emphasis upon the determined nature of human behavior. B. F. Skinner perceives persons as largely helpless victims of operant conditioning. Free choice is impossible because all behavior results from interaction between genetic inheritance and experiences with environment. Such concepts as "freedom" and "dignity" in the sense of liberation from conditioning are no more than illusion. The best freedom for which human beings can hope, according to Skinner, is the proper management of determining forces for human beneficence.

---

[4]Rollo May, *Love and Will* (New York: W. W. Norton, 1969) 182-83.

[5]Sigmund Freud, *A General Introduction to Psychoanalysis* (New York: Perma Giants, 1948) 95.

Whether or not the approach of psychoanalysis and behaviorism contains theoretical truth and helps persons understand that they are not entirely free to choose, these approaches offer support for a pervasive tendency to avoid personal responsibility for decision. It "has become almost an endemic disease in the middle of the twentieth century" for modern man "to see himself as passive, the willy-nilly product of the powerful juggernaut of psychological drives."[6] Earlier one might have thought about a fate determined by will, but now it is more fashionable to think of the repressed mental life. "The unconscious is heir to the prestige of will."[7] Then add sociological determinism, which sees persons as the products of economic forces and a mass mentality, before imposing governmental power and nuclear energy, and will is in for a difficult psychological time. Contemporary man "so often has the conviction that even if he *did* exert his 'will'—or whatever illusion passes for it—his actions wouldn't do any good anyway."[8]

A protest against the Freudian devaluation of the will and free choice appeared early in the history of psychoanalysis. Otto Rank, a brilliant member of Freud's coterie, regarded will as a life force that had been dampened both by overly moralistic religion and by psychoanalytic subjugation of the will to the unconscious. "It is important," said Rank, "that the neurotic above all learn to will, discover that he can will without getting guilt feeling on account of willing."[9] Rank further conceived of therapy as encounter between the wills of the patient and the analyst and proposed that the goal of therapy was to develop the patient's creative will, the willing of that which one wants rather than what is expected. Rank thus counterbalances a deterministic position that writes off personal and responsible decision making.

Another interesting slant on the old problem of free will is offered by George Pugh, who attempts a physiological explanation of

---

[6]May, *Love and Will*, 183.

[7]Allen Wheelis, "Will and Psychoanalysis," *Journal of the American Psychoanalytic Association* 4 (1956): 286.

[8]May, *Love and Will*, 184.

[9]Otto Rank, *Will Therapy and Truth and Reality* (New York: Alfred A. Knopf, 1950) 9.

decision. As a scientist he rejects the extreme definitions of will either as metaphysical entity presumed to exercise ultimate control over human behavior or as an essentially predictable personality system that follows deterministic laws. Pugh prefers a model that he believes to be between these traditional extremes and calls it "the value-driven decision system."[10] Accordingly, the human brain operates as a data-processing system into which evolution has built primary values by which it operates (such as those associated with pain and hunger). It also incorporates a range of secondary values—those moral, ethical, and social principles that "are products of personal and cultural experience with the environment and with the primary human value system."[11] Guided by both primary and secondary values, the decision system considers alternatives and makes choices, that is, decides which alternative to select. This is not romantic or idealistic "freedom" because the brain is not free to select its own primary value system. But it is "choice" by virtue of its operation using decision criteria. Further, Pugh argues that neural responses in the brain are unpredictably susceptible to input from hundreds of neurons and to "minor fluctuations in temperature, chemical composition, and possibly even quantum mechanical effect."[12] He discusses these points in some detail and judges that human beings do make choices, that the choices are as free as it is theoretically possible for them to be, and that the choices are intrinsically unpredictable. Since these are issues around which free will has been traditionally discussed, he concludes that the "affirmation of free will corresponds better with reality than does its denial."[13]

Thus the idea of will refuses to go away. The concept has been largely neglected by modern psychologists and has been systematically undercut by approaches that see persons more as automatic machines, functioning without control over their interests and

---

[10]See George E. Pugh, "Human Values, Free Will, and the Conscious Mind," *Zygon* 11 (1976): 2-24.

[11]Ibid., 4.

[12]Ibid., 13.

[13]Ibid., 14.

destiny. But will persists. It survives in the volitive, future tense as an essential part of language.[14] "I shall do this" adds resolution and determination to the decision. Everyday language is a constant reminder that will is present as a responsible mover in human experience. Phenomenologically, it regularly crops up, sometimes in thinly veiled disguises labeled the unconscious or sexuality or motivation.

To be sure, psychoanalysis and behaviorism have appropriately eroded the idea of a romantic will liberated from external control and influences, one by which persons may create behavior by mere acts of that will. Anyone who has been around a mental hospital is familiar with patients who will to be well in the most strenuous ways but are unable by willing to heal themselves. Will may be short-circuited by powerful and sinister forces that make people neurotic and even psychotic. Outside the hospital as well, effort of will cannot make all things possible; it operates within the parameters of the possible options, a point made by Stuart Hampshire.[15] Hampshire distinguishes between can-possibility and will-possibility. A can-possibility is the *ability* to accomplish an action; will-possibility refers to the *desire* to act in a particular way, the intention to do something. Will sets the self in motion to achieve the possible; it may not be expected to gain the impossible.

INTENTION: THE SEAT OF WILL

Will as Intention

Will as the intention to carry a decision to completion cannot be reduced to any other facet of human activity. James's observation many years ago remains valid: "If anyone should . . . assume that intellectual insight is what remains after wish and will and sentiment preference have taken wing, or that pure reason is what then settles our opinions, he would fly quite as directly in the teeth of the

---

[14]Leslie H. Farber, *The Ways of the Will: Essays toward a Psychology and Psychopathology of Will* (New York: Basic Books, 1966) 4.

[15]Stuart Hampshire, *Freedom of the Individual* (New York: Harper, 1969) 16-17, 29.

facts."[16] If will is understood as endeavor rather than as faculty or metaphysical entity, then it is consistent with the data to speak of will as a distinctive personality function and effort of will as a behavioral act. Since will lies close to value systems and individual responsibility, its understanding is a significant feature of the psychology of religion. To recognize that persons act and react in the context of intense biological and environmental forces does not demand reducing human beings to machines that merely respond to external stimuli and conditioning. But neither does it mean that will is unencumbered by these and other powerful forces. To affirm will is to affirm human freedom in a particular way. In light of available alternatives and in the context of external pressures, persons do decide, and their decisions make a difference in the direction of their lives. The key is to acknowledge the presence of dynamic psychological and sociological factors in any decision. In short, knowing oneself in all one's dynamic makeup is the truth that indeed makes one free. Such achievement, however, is never easy nor complete. The human animal, caught in the web of powerful, determining forces, is incredibly adept at self-delusion and self-deception. Who could know one's self in all its complexity? And who has either time or patience to unravel all those factors associated with an act of will? Nevertheless, the human vocation is to will a course of action, to know enough about oneself to take responsibility for the action, and to keep self-examination open enough to decrease self-deception.

Willing then represents the marshaling of one's values, resources, and energies with enough personal insight to move one toward a possible goal. It is that system of self-organization that gives direction to personality, enabling choices to be made toward an end. Will is conscious and unconscious, selective and driven, free and bound. It involves cognition but moves beyond the formation of ideas to selecting and ordering them with some priority. Unconscious forces and repressed impulses influence but need not, except in cases of illness, victimize will. Gordon Allport points out that even the most deterministic therapists assume the relative freedom

---

[16]William James, *The Will to Believe and Other Essays in Popular Philosophy* (New York: Dover, 1956) 8.

of persons. They attempt to help their clients develop self-insight in the belief that "a patient who achieves a high degree of self-objectification, who sees his personal equation clearly written out, is at least in a position to weigh his inclinations, comprehend his limitations, and follow with some success a self-chosen course of action."[17]

Will sometimes operates aggressively and directly upon a set of circumstances; at other times it seems more passive and indirect. The psychiatrist Leslie Farber writes of this as the "two realms of will."[18] In one realm will designates the movement of the total person in a certain direction. Human capacities form a seamless pattern while thrusting the self forward, or backward, without the full consequences in view. This willing is characterized by freedom and relaxation and may be recognized as *willing after the fact*. It is illustrated by W. H. Auden's comment in *The Dyer's Hand:* "When I look back at the three or four choices in my life which have been decisive, I find that, at the time I made them, I had very little sense of the seriousness of what I was doing and only later did I discover what had seemed an unimportant brook, was, in fact, a Rubicon."[19] William James had earlier argued that some behavior is ideomotor action, that is, movement that follows unhesitatingly and immediately upon the mere thought of it. A "fiat, decision, consent, volitional mandate, or other synonymous phenomenon of consciousness"[20] produces behavior without awareness of anything between the conception and the execution. Only after the fact do persons reflect upon the full implications of a choice that has been made.

The second realm of will is directly experienced during the event itself. It is willing *before and during the fact*. In this case will thrusts itself obtrusively into an experience so that persons are as aware of its presence as they are of their arms or legs. "Unlike the joined totality of the first realm, the course of the will in this realm is rela-

---

[17]Allport, *Becoming*, 84.

[18]Farber, *The Ways of the Will*, 1-25.

[19]W. H. Auden, *The Dyer's Hand* (New York: Random House, 1962) 103.

[20]James, *The Principles of Psychology*, 2:522f.

tively isolated."[21] It presses toward a peculiar object and anticipates a specific end—as when the student studies to pass a test. A vast range of getting, achieving, winning, possessing, doing, and owning represents the operation of this realm of will.

Farber's categories may fail to emphasize sufficiently the ways in which unconscious factors may influence will and choices. Nonetheless, his description highlights intention as a central activity of will, in fact the very core of the process. According to Gordon Allport, a peculiar kind of activity associated with one's personhood is "propriate striving," a way of connecting intending and acting. "At low levels of behavior the familiar formula of drives and their conditioning appears to suffice. But as soon as the personality enters the stage, . . . we are . . . forced to postulate motive of a different order, motives that reflect propriate striving."[22] Thus, conduct that is propriate differs markedly from behavior that is not and reflects values intimate to personality itself. Rollo May echoes the same theme and spends two chapters in his *Love and Will* analyzing will and appealing for renewed attention to intentionality as a viable category for describing human experience and practicing therapy.[23] All three of these writers, while acknowledging the presence of causative forces, conceive intention to be the seat of will, the heart of consciousness, and the essence of the human capacity to form, mold, and give direction to experience. "Man, in all that is distinctive of his species," says Allport, "is a creature of intentions."[24]

Characteristics of Intention

Intention is a behavioral act that asserts humanness and brings the force of will to bear on options that are open to persons. It serves a vital function in maintaining personality and preserving personal values. Several features characterize the intending experience.

First, intention is a means to resolve conflict. As the word itself implies, intention means being "in tension" with at least two viable

---

[21]Farber, *The Ways of the Will,* 11.

[22]Allport, *Becoming,* 48.

[23]May, *Love and Will,* 223-72.

[24]Allport, *Personality and Social Encounter,* 59.

alternatives, that is, intention and conflict fit hand in glove. Obviously, the intensity of conflict may vary considerably and may decrease for no other reasons than earlier resolution. Some intention is primary and produces a series of movements that are in some measure self-perpetuating For example, once a student has made a decision to enter college, many steps in enrolling, selecting courses, and meeting requirements issue from the original decision with little conflict. Subsequent action naturally proceeds from the original intention with minimal consideration of choices. Eight o'-clock classes may create some difficulty, but generally the student does not decide whether he will attend each class as if attendance were an independent and new choice. But suppose that on registration day the student had the option of taking one of two courses, each desirable and each possible. Now an additional operation of intention is necessary; conflict between two options creates the necessity for an effort of will. The demand for conscious intending may be even more evident if one option contains "desire" and the other "ought."[25] Course A has the easier professor, makes less demands, and is more fun. On the other hand, course B, although not as immediately desirable, is a requirement for graduation or necessary for vocational preparation. In the selection of course A or B intention serves both to relieve present conflict and to cue future behavior (attending the class, doing the assignments, etc.).[26]

Second, intention decisively influences one's perception of the environment. An example offered by Rollo May so clearly illustrates the point that it is repeated here as the discussion of this idea:

> This afternoon, for instance, I go to see a house in the mountains. Suppose, first, that I am looking for a place which some friends can rent for the summer months. When I approach the house, I shall question whether it is sound and well-built, gets enough sun, and other things having the meaning of "shelter" to me. Or suppose that I am a real-estate speculator: then what will strike me will be

[25]See John Howie, "Is Effort of Will a Basis for Moral Freedom?" *Religious Studies* 8 (1972): 345-49.

[26]One who has either registered or taught students senses the need to allow student intention to act in the former to enhance performance in the latter. Research might affirm or deny these impressions.

how easily the house can be fixed up, whether it will bring a price attractively higher than what I shall have to pay for it, and other things meaning "profit." Or let us say that it is the house of friends I am visiting: then I shall look at it with eyes which see it as "hospitality." . . . Or, if this is a cocktail party at the house of friends who have snubbed me at a party at my house, I find myself seeing things that indicate that anyone would prefer my cottage to theirs . . . Or, finally, if this afternoon I am outfitted with my watercolor materials and bent on doing a sketch, I shall see how the house clings to the side of the mountain, the patterns of the lines of the roof leading up to the peaks above and sweeping away into the valley below, and indeed, now I even prefer the house ramshackle and run down for the greater artistic possibilities this gives me.[27]

In all cases the stimulus and the perceiver are the same; the variable is what the observer intends to see.

A third characteristic of intention is its orientation toward the future. Freudianism has demonstrated that intention is never a purely conscious phenomenon free from the irrational and often demonic forces of the past. But psychoanalysis has been so tied to the past that both present and future are made subordinate to it. Present and future acts have been interpreted as ways of "de-tensioning" disturbances deeply rooted in the past. Behavioristic approaches have likewise depreciated the future by orienting thought around the past. Their focus has been upon expectancy, or what may be reasonably expected as likely on the basis of past experience.

Such maximizing of the past deals with only half of the problem.[28] "Addiction to machines, rats, or infants leads us to overplay those features of human behavior that are peripheral, signal-oriented, or genetic. Correspondingly, it causes us to underplay those features that are central, future-oriented and symbolic."[29] Intending keeps the future alive. Willed behavior becomes more than tension reduction; it also preserves cherished, long-range goals and values. Intention is not merely wishing that the future will be dif-

---

[27]May, *Love and Will*, 224.

[28]See Allport, *Becoming*, 65-68, 87-88; and *Personality and Social Encounter*, 60-66.

[29]Allport, *Personality and Social Encounter*, 65.

ferent; it incorporates personal resolve to make it so. Future then is not simply a state of time that is coming to pass, but it contains the sustained strivings to bring into being one's values. Unlike fleas and flamingos, human beings make promises, and the most significant ones are those that they make to themselves.

Fourth, crucial to the intending process is self-image: the good parent, the good scientist, the good student, the good Christian. Self-image may be adequately or inadequately informed, but it is nonetheless an ever-present factor in motivation. The importance of self-image as a motivational factor is hinted at in Freud's concern that ego be strong enough to overpower the restrictive superego and in "field" approaches that give preference to the contemporary context of personality rather than the unchanging id or earlier conditioning.[30] Some who evaluated the ability of the soldier in World War II to endure the strain of combat concluded that the man who stood the strain best was the one who wanted to "stand with his outfit, to support his commander, to win a victory for democracy."[31] The young man who saw himself as a good soldier was able to perform accordingly, even under dire circumstances.

Lecky's analysis of childhood thumb-sucking illustrates the importance of self-image for intention:

> Certainly the child who sucks his thumb gives the act plenty of exercise and gets enough satisfaction from it to fix it indelibly. Therefore if the habit theory is true, we should be able to predict absolutely that the child will continue to suck his thumb for the rest of his life. But what really happens? Every year millions of children who have industriously sucked their thumbs since birth, and who have successfully resisted every effort to force them to change their behavior, quit the practice spontaneously when they are five or six years old. The reason is that they are beginning to think of themselves as big boys or girls, and they recognize that thumb-sucking is inconsistent with the effort to maintain this new idea.[32]

---

[30]See Kurt Koffka, *Principles of Gestalt Psychology* (New York: Harcourt Brace, 1935); Kurt Lewin, *Field Theory in Social Science* (New York: Harper, 1951).

[31]Allport, *Personality and Social Encounter,* 40.

[32]Prescott Lecky, *Self-Consistency: A Theory of Personality* (Fort Myers Beach FL: Island Press, 1945) 122f.

Modifying the behavior of the thumb-sucking child, or the delinquent, the criminal, the alcoholic, or Joe Christian often hinges more upon altering the self-image than on changing habits.

A fifth characteristic of intention, and one that is most important for the psychology of religion, is its function in maintaining meaning and commitment. To inquire about the intent of the law is to ask about its meaning, the goal toward which it is directed, the end toward which it is committed. Intending should be read not as a kind of mentalism that itself achieves a goal, but rather as the focus of one's resources and energies toward a chosen end. Thus, intention incorporates both the value attached to an item and the inclination of the self toward that item. Intention organizes experience around valued items that are selected for attention and pursued in purposeful ways.

Both classical and modern Roman Catholic theology have given a large place to intention as a strategic variable for Christian ethics and participation in the sacraments. According to this point of view, it is reasonable to expect devotees to refine their ability to judge what is correct behavior and to discipline drives and impulses into correct behavior patterns. By intentional acts of will persons propel themselves, as it were, to seek goodness. Not only the behavior itself but also the intention moving a person to act determines the moral quality of experience. Roman Catholic theology thus makes intending a decisive factor in establishing the moral content of behavior.

The same application is made to validation of the sacraments. What makes a ritual sacramental? Suppose a person approached a clergyman for a demonstration of baptism. He did not intend to be baptized but wished merely to know the procedure. The minister, likewise intending to do a demonstration and not to baptize, proceeds to pour the water and repeat the associated words. The ritual is repeated and the formula pronounced, but the baptism did not occur because neither participant intended the demonstration to be a baptism. Here intention is the difference between a demonstration and a holy act.

The significance of intention is also preserved in Protestant circles. Søren Kierkegaard was a vigorous Protestant spokesman for the moral decisiveness of will as intending. In his classic *Purity of*

Heart, will is interpreted as central to Christian devotion. Human beatitude is continually interrupted by the separation of sin. "Each day, and day after day something is placed in between: delay, blockage, interruption, delusion, corruption."[33] In a real sense sin for Kierkegaard is disruption of intention, distraction from willing commitment. Its resolution is to will commitment without reservation. "Willing one thing" is "purity of heart," the key to repentance, confession, and genuine personhood. Such willing turns aside all distraction to enable a person to center upon a unifying commitment to God.[34] Purity of heart is to will one thing. In moving words at the opening of the book (and repeated at its closing), Kierkegaard prays for the gift of will:

> So may Thou give to the intellect, wisdom to comprehend that one thing; to the heart, sincerity to receive this understanding; to the will, purity that wills only one thing. In prosperity may Thou grant perseverance to will one thing; amid distractions, collectedness to will one thing; in suffering, patience to will one thing. Oh, Thou that giveth both the beginning and the completion, may Thou early, at the dawn of the day, give to the young man the resolution to will one thing. As the day wanes, may Thou give to the old man a renewed remembrance of his first resolution, that the first may be like the last, the last like the first, in possession of life that has willed one thing.[35]

RESPONSIBLE DECISION MAKING

Good intention is no more than idle wish until it is given form and structure of positive action. Intention that remains in the area of wish paves the proverbial way to a hell of frustration, inaction, and futility. Intention that moves beyond wish marshals personal resources for the achievement of the intended goal and generates power for moving the self toward the fulfillment of intention. In order for this to occur, persons must decide on a course of action

---

[33]Søren Kierkegaard, *Purity of Heart Is to Will One Thing* (New York: Harper, 1956) 31, 218.

[34]Ibid., 215.

[35]Ibid., 31, 218.

and take responsibility for the decision that has been made. The end of intention is responsible decision making. As the etymology of the word suggests, to decide is "to cut off" debate about available options and to set in motion patterns of action to achieve the selected goal. Deciding puts one on record with self and others that a particular end is desired and that personal resources will be directed toward that end.

What makes a decision a responsible act? How can one be sure that a decision has been the correct or best decision? Rarely, if ever, is it possible for persons to be absolutely certain, but some guidelines for deciding are important. First, responsible decision making accepts the unavoidable boundaries within which decisions must be made, without blaming the decisions on circumstances. Wayne Oates lists four limits regularly present in entertaining alternatives: (1) limits of data, (2) limits of time, (3) limits of prior decisions, and (4) limits of available alternatives.[36] On "the computer level of decision-making" data are gathered in an attempt to get all the facts before arriving at a judgment, but all the facts can never be known and personal characteristics such as age, maturity, intelligence, and health may interfere with the interpretation of the data. Responsible decision making moves on the available data but continually remains open to new light and revised interpretation.

Time also limits decision making. To procrastinate indefinitely, whether waiting for additional data or for other reasons, often results in the decision being made simply by the passing of time itself, as when one passes a deadline for paying a bill or taking a test. Also, prior decisions limit future options. To marry one person determines the range of additional decisions regarding marriage; to be committed to one God in monotheistic religion precludes allegiance to another God. In this sense, making decisions proscribes one's absolute freedom. Jesus' statement of the idea is, "You cannot serve both God and money."[37] Decisions are also limited by the available alternatives. Here all the limitations imposed by genetics and upbringing, by preparation and training, and by opportunities

---

[36]Oates, *The Psychology of Religion,* 197-99.

[37]Matthew 6:24.

that are open apply. Responsible persons are those who can decide within the parameters established by these limitations of data, time, previous decisions, and alternatives without feeling that they have been victimized by the boundaries.

Second, responsibility accepts the risks inherent in deciding for one option over another. "The perfect choice is a fantasy, a dream, a substitute for action."[38] Persons routinely choose between alternatives that each contain truth and attractiveness. To decide in one direction is at the same time to exclude the unchosen possibility and risk that the rejected option in the long run might have been the better one. As Paul Tillich says, "Every decision is, in some respect, absolutistic. . . . It is a risk, rooted in the courage of being, threatened by the excluded possibilities, many of which might have been better and truer than the chosen one."[39]

In the Sermon on the Mount, Jesus advances an approach to morality that incorporates risk. The Pharisees and law teachers whose ethical system he challenged attempted to define good behavior by rules that eliminated risks. Their legal codes contained a hidden agenda of safety: requirements for the moral life were reduced to knowledge of the law and resolve to keep it. In contrast, Jesus recognized that responsibility, although aided by law, could never be fully contained in precepts, no matter how endless their multiplication. Kingdom righteousness demands more than keeping regulations: "You will be able to enter the kingdom of heaven only if you are more faithful than the teachers of the Law and the Pharisees in doing what God requires."[40] The member of God's kingdom is not satisfied merely to keep the law but evaluates action on the deeper, more illusive, and more risky levels of ethical principle.[41] An ethics of law may be more precise and certain than an ethics of principle and hence provide for dependent individuals more security. But an overly legalistic moral code may also produce

---

[38]Oates, *The Psychology of Religion,* 201.

[39]Tillich, *Systematic Theology,* 1:152.

[40]Matthew 5:20.

[41]Compare Crapps, McKnight, and Smith, *Introduction to the New Testament,* 103-104.

inhibitions strenuous enough to abet procrastination. When sin lurks around every corner and persons are surrounded with too many taboos, "any activity becomes so danger-laden that one has to minimize action for comfort."[42] The element of risk may be eliminated, but the unfortunate result of a legalistic morality of safety is often inaction, procrastination, and even withdrawal. The responsible person, however, recognizes the ambiguity in a moral decision and takes the calculated risk that the decision may be wrong or contain implicit danger, but the risk is preferable to perennially "halting between two opinions." Nothing ventured, nothing gained.

The acceptance of risks is closely related to a third feature of responsibility: namely, the ability to act without demanding absolute certainty. Gordon Allport suggests that mature religion is inevitably heuristic.[43] The mature individual fashions religion in full consciousness that the structures are human and inadequately contain the full measure of the infinite God. The living God can no more be reduced to propositions than to idols of wood and stone. Even cherished doctrines and rituals are understood as potential idols if they are absolutized. Hence, heuristic religion holds its beliefs tentatively until they can be confirmed, clarified, or replaced by more valid beliefs. Revised beliefs then become the basis for decision, but they remain heuristically affirmed. In this sense doubt is the constant companion of faith, reminding the devotee of the limited and therefore tentative character of religious constructs.

Heuristic religion is to be distinguished from skeptical doubt that indulges questions for their own sake. Chronic doubt, like moral absoluteness, may produce indecision and inaction. Although absolute certainty is impossible, responsible commitment must engender sufficient certitude to move life forward. Allport makes the point clearly:

> What many unbelievers do not realize is that the mature believer's eyes are wide open. The latter knows that he is finally uncertain of his ground. But he feels, reasonably enough, that in a world where optimistic bias and faith are largely responsible for human accom-

---

[42]Pruyser, *A Dynamic Psychology of Religion*, 251.

[43]Allport, *The Individual and His Religion*, 72-74.

plishment, it would be silly for him to lapse into unproductive skepticism, so long as he has a chance of being correct. . . . The believer, banking on a probability, slight though he may deem it to be, finds that the energy engendered and the values conserved prove the superiority of affirmation over indecisiveness.[44]

The mature, responsible individual continuously examines the propositions to which commitment is made, revises commitments in the light of new and corrective insights, and thereby both strengthens faith and keeps doubt in proper perspective.

Fourth, an act becomes responsible to the degree that it transcends immediate and personal considerations. The biblical form in which this issue is posed takes the format of a question: "Where is your brother, Abel?"[45] Any given moment is replete with self-oriented desire, drives, and impulses demanding satisfaction. Yet decisions regarding personal fulfillment also occur within a nexus of relationships with other significant human beings. A theological and psychological base for understanding persons as responsible beings is their capacity to be their fellow's keeper, to transcend their own experience by taking into account the best interests of other persons and groups. Hence, responsibility is a quite personal word. Responsible persons who function in a complex network of dynamic relationships with other people ultimately focus upon themselves. The words of Paul Tillich make a necessary point: "The word 'responsibility' points to the obligation of the person who has freedom to respond if he is questioned about his decisions. He alone must respond, for his acts are determined neither by something outside him nor by any part of him but by the centered totality of his being. Each of us is responsible for what has happened through the seat and organ of his freedom."[46]

Responsible acts also are those that transcend the present; they neither disregard the past nor borrow from the future. Consider, for example, an act that seems blatantly irresponsible—driving an automobile a hundred miles per hour down a well-traveled high-

---

[44]Ibid., 73.

[45]Genesis 4:9.

[46]Tillich, *Systematic Theology,* 1:184.

way. Why is this irresponsible behavior? It obviously is a decision made without regard for others on the roadway and it flies in the face of all probability statistics regarding past accidents and speed. It is a decision made for the pleasure of the moment, without due consideration of the future of self or survivors. But suppose the vehicle is an ambulance rushing a victim to the hospital emergency room. Questions might still be raised about the appropriateness of the behavior, but the added factors of human welfare and saving a life make one more inclined to think of the behavior as responsible. Responsible individuals made decisions while attempting to balance past, present, and future considerations and while taking into account the values of others.

MORAL DEVELOPMENT

The capacity to will and the ability to make responsible decisions are intimately entwined with the complex process by which human beings move from infancy to old age. Moral development has to do with those features of growth that bear upon a person's emergent ability to make choices that are psychologically and theologically mature. Generally, healthy moral development moves from fear-oriented to goal-oriented controls. Volition that is fear-oriented operates according to threats of detection and punishment and depends heavily on external sanctions. It is characterized by high levels of obedience to external authority and little ability to delay gratification. Goal-oriented volition, however, is marked by independent, internal sanctions and conscious selection of ends. As growth occurs, important transformation from "must-consciousness" to "ought-consciousness" may be observed.[47] External sanctions give way to internal ones. Experiences of prohibition, fear, and "must" give way to experiences of preference, self-respect, and "ought." And specific habits of obedience give way to broad schemata of values that confer direction upon conduct. Two important researchers, Jean Piaget and Lawrence Kohlberg, stand out among those who have clarified these shifts.[48]

---

[47] Allport, *Becoming*, 73.

[48] The "stages" approach typifies the work of many researchers, including Er-

Jean Piaget:
Rules and Moral Judgment

Over several decades Jean Piaget, a professor at the University of Geneva, Switzerland, has studied the origins and transformation of moral judgments in children. His book *The Moral Judgment of the Child* was first published in 1932 and has become a point of reference for later research on moral development. In this work Piaget develops the thesis that "morality consists in a system of rules, and the essence of morality is to be sought for in the respect which the individual acquires for those rules."[49] Piaget centers his analysis upon the rules for children's games and intensifies the broad steps in the child's perception and practice of game rules through the first twelve years of life. His studies led him to conclude that there is a close parallel between moral and intellectual development. "Logic is the morality of thought just as morality is the logic of action."[50] Norms, as the logic by which behavior is to be measured, are not innately a part of the human equipment but emerge out of the attempt of the growing person to bring equilibrium to human relationships. Piaget examined the process by which moral judgment emerges from two points of view: (1) *the practice of rules,* ways in which children effectively adapt themselves to rules, and (2) the *consciousness of rules,* the extent to which rules are accepted as restraint.

From Heteronomy to Autonomy. From his observations and conversations with children playing marbles Piaget concluded that moral judgment moves along a continuum from heteronomy to autonomy. Heteronomy is characterized by relations of constraint; rules are perceived as imposed from outside. Regulations against "damaging property, lying, or stealing are not seen as procedures established for the smooth functioning of the group or community, but are perceived as arbitrary rules, like 'laws of the gods' that

---

ikson (see above, pp. 85f.); Fowler (see above, pp. 186-87); and Loevinger (see her *Ego Development* [San Francisco: Jossey-Bass, 1976]). Piaget and Kohlberg, however, talk specifically in terms of moral judgment and decision making.

[49]Jean Piaget, *The Moral Judgment of the Child* (London: Kegan Paul, Trench, Trubner, 1931) 1.

[50]Ibid., 404.

one must not transgress."[51] Rules are accepted as static systems arising from authority and demanding unilateral respect.[52] Gradually, heteronomy diminishes in favor of autonomy; cooperation develops on the basis of ideal norms behind the rules. Rules come to be accepted, not because they are laid down by significant authorities, but because they are perceived as requirements for cooperation and worthy of respect as the products of free decision and mutual consent. In this sense, moral judgment is "a collective product," "the fruits of reciprocity," the consciousness of the self in a social context.

In individual cases the transformation from heteronomy to autonomy may be by spurts and jumps, but the impression of steady advance may come from observing many individuals. The general direction of moral development can "be observed by schematizing the material and ignoring the minor oscillations that render it infinitely complicated in detail."[53] The development occurs in four stages. The first stage is *motor* and *individual* in character. Before the age of two the child acts at the dictation of desires and motor habits. Although some ritualized patterns may appear, play at this stage is purely individual with no consciousness of collective rules. The second stage is *egocentric*. Between the ages of two and six the child imitates rules and rituals without attempting to unify different ways of playing. Even when playing with other children, those at this stage operate for their own ends, conscious of rules that govern play but unaware that rules relate to relationships with peers. In this context rules are highly impersonal and may be treated as sacred and inviolable. The child senses an obligation to the rules but does not possess cognitive abilities that permit advancement beyond imitation and blind obedience.

In the next two stages children move closer to autonomy. The stage of *incipient cooperation* appears around the age of seven or eight. Marble players become concerned with winning and hence

[51]Ronald Duska and Mariellen Whelan, *Moral Development: A Guide to Piaget and Kohlberg* (New York: Paulist, 1975) 8.

[52]Piaget, *The Moral Judgment of the Child*, 402.

[53]Ibid., 17.

insist that the rules be mutually understood in the interest of fair play. Although rules for one game may be agreed upon, understanding of "rules in general" remains vague. When questioned separately, opponents may give disparate and often contradictory accounts of the rules. Finally, between the ages of eleven and twelve the *codification* of rules begins. In this stage rules become a code for universal application. Aided by cognitive abstraction children become interested in rules for rules' sake and "frequently spend more time legislating for every possible event than they spend in actual play."[54] But the rules are not absolute. The purpose of rules to promote social harmony makes them important, so they can be changed to fit that purpose. Hence the child's acceptance of peers as equals is crucial at this stage. Relationships between children and adults, even when they are open and generous, are insufficient to get beyond a morality of constraint; peer relationships are more significant. Piaget is direct and to the point: "Now, criticism is born of discussion, and discussion is only possible among equals: cooperation alone will therefore accomplish what intellectual constraint fails to bring about."[55] For Piaget, then, peer relationships are crucial to moral development.

From Moral Realism to Intention. According to Piaget's analysis, moral rules fall into the same classification as game rules; children develop respect for moral regulations and their application in decision making in the same ways that they grow in their use of game rules. Piaget discusses moral growth as movement from moral realism to intention, terms that parallel heteronomy and autonomy. During the period of moral realism, rules are considered sacred and the practice of them is egocentric. Before the age of eight or nine a child's sense of duty is heteronomous; it is spelled out in commands that are judged as good and binding because they come from adults.[56] The rules of obligation are literally and concretely accepted and penalties are judged by the material size of the consequences. Piaget illustrates moral realism by getting children to react

---

[54]Duska and Whelan, *Moral Development,* 11.

[55]Piaget, *The Moral Judgment of the Child,* 409.

[56]Ibid., 105ff.

to stories containing dilemma situations of clumsiness, lying, and stealing. One pair of his stories demonstrates both his procedure and findings:[57]

A. There was once a little girl who was called Marie. She wanted to give her mother a nice surprise, and cut out a piece of sewing for her. But she didn't know how to use the scissors properly and cut a big hole in her dress.

B. A little girl called Margaret went and took her mother's scissors one day when her mother was out. She played with them for a bit. Then as she didn't know how to use them properly she made a little hole in her dress.

Children were told the stories and subsequently questioned about which little girl was the naughtiest. Moral realism is seen in the conversation with Const, age seven:

"Which of them is naughtiest?"
"The one who made the big hole."
"If you were the mother, which would you have punished most?"
"The one who made the big hole."
"Let's pretend that it was you who made the big hole so as to give your mother a surprise. Your sister is playing and makes a little hole. Which ought to be punished most?"
"Me."
"Are you sure or not quite sure?"
"Quite sure."[58]

Here Const maintains persistently that naughtiness is measured concretely and realistically by the size of the hole. Older children, however, take intention into account. Corm, age nine, heard the same stories and concluded that the one who cut the smaller hole was the naughtier: "She oughtn't to have taken the scissors to play with. The first one didn't do it on purpose. You can't say that she was naughtier." Piaget found that the average age for judgment on the basis of intent was nine years old and that not a single child over ten judged according to moral realism. He therefore

---

[57]Ibid., 118.

[58]Ibid., 123.

concludes that developmental movement from moral realism to intention is completed by age ten.

Heteronomy and autonomy, moral realism and intention thus describe the process by which the child frees moral judgment from uncontrolled influence of external forces, enabling responsible decision making to occur. Piaget believes that the struggle between the extremes remains as part of the adult moral experience. Heteronomous submission in such forms as obeying traffic laws or following church rules simply becomes habit. Heteronomy may unify social organizations, including religious institutions, around specific rules and practices, but normally heteronomous behavior should decline as persons grow up to responsibility, making their decisions with increasing autonomy and intention.

Piaget's research lends support to a theological approach to morality that moves beyond legalism. The older child, and the mature adult, is able to see intention behind the rules and adapt the rules according to their purposes. Theologically, morality is broader than law. It includes the whole range of experience by which persons actualize their freedom and destiny. "A moral act . . . is not an act in which some divine or human law is obeyed but an act in which life integrates itself in the dimension of spirit. . . . Morality is the function of life in which a potentially personal life process becomes an actual person."[59] Piaget, therefore, may be read as a commentary on the necessarily fluid character of rules associated with moral development. In this context he has much to teach.

Lawrence Kohlberg:
Listen To Reasons

The research of Lawrence Kohlberg, professor of education and social psychology at Harvard, complements that of Piaget. Kohlberg's doctoral dissertation was entitled "The Development of Modes of Moral Thinking and Choice in the Years Ten to Sixteen,"[60] and his professional career has followed that interest.[61]

---

[59]Tillich, *Systematic Theology*, 3:38.

[60]Kohlberg (Ph.D. diss., University of Chicago, 1958).

[61]Kohlberg's work is known through numerous journal articles and chapters

The Heinz Dilemma. Kohlberg's research method is similar to Piaget's; he tells his subjects a series of stories, each containing a moral dilemma, and then elicits their recommendations for a solution and their reasons for the recommended solution. A familiar dilemma story used by Kohlberg is that of Heinz:

> In Europe, a woman was near death from a special kind of cancer. There was one drug that the doctors thought might save her. It was a form of radium that a druggist in the same town had recently discovered. The drug was expensive to make, but the druggist was charging ten times the amount the drug had cost him to make. He paid $200 for the radium and charged $2,000 for a small dose of the drug. The sick woman's husband, Heinz, went to everyone he knew to borrow the money, but he could only get together about $1,000, which is half of what it cost. He told the druggist that his wife was dying and asked him to sell it cheaper, or let him pay him later. The druggist said, "No, I discovered the drug and I'm going to make money for it." So Heinz got desperate and broke into the man's store to steal the drug for his wife. Should the husband have done that? Why?[62]

A single subject was asked to resolve several problems of the nature of the Heinz dilemma. The reasons behind the resolutions were examined with probing questions, and responses were classified according to a scoring system devised by Kohlberg. Repeated examination of these issues over many years and many subjects has enabled Kohlberg to describe a pattern by which moral development occurs through six states.

---

in collected works. Among these are "Moral Education in the Schools: A Developmental View," *School Review* 74 (1966): 1-30; "Early Education: A Cognitive-Developmental Approach," *Child Development* 39 (1968): 1013-62; "A Cognitive-Developmental Approach to Moral Education," *The Humanist* 32 (1972): 13-16; with Carol Gilligan, "The Adolescent as a Philosopher: The Discovery of the Self in a Preconventional World," *Daedalus* 100 (1971): 1051-86; "Development of Moral Character and Moral Ideology," in Martin L. Hoffman and Lois W. Hoffman, eds., *Review of Child Development Research*, vol. 1 (New York: Russell Sage Foundation, 1964) 383-427; with Rochelle Mayer, "Development as the Aim of Education," *Harvard Educational Review* 42 (1972): 449-96. A valuable summary of his work is found in Duska and Whelan, *Moral Development*, 42-79.

[62]This and other research stories are included in Appendix 2, Duska and Whelan, *Moral Development*, 121-23.

Kohlberg's Stages. Kohlberg identified three major levels, each with two stages, through which persons move in their moral development.[63]

Level I. *Premoral Judgment.* On this level the child responds to forces of power exerted from the outside in terms of either physical or hedonistic consequences.

Stage 1. *Obedience and punishment orientation.* This stage is characterized by unquestioning deference to superior power and aims to avoid trouble without considerations of meaning and value.

Stage 2. *Naively egoistic orientation.* Here the orientation is toward exchange and reciprocity. Concern for others may appear, but fairness or sharing are understood as means to personal ends. Right action toward others is not a matter of rules of justice, but a means for exchanging one good deal for another.

Level
II. *Conventional Role Conformity.* The distinctive mark of this level is the recognition and unquestioned acceptance of social norms and loyalty to those norms as incorporated in the standards of social groups—family, church, and nation. It includes two stages.

Stage 3. *"Good-boy" or "nice-girl" orientation.* Behavior at this stage is guided by stereotypical images of roles. Approval by the group to which one belongs becomes important and conformity to expectations is the price one pays for acceptance by the group.

Stage 4. *Law-and-order orientation.* Here respect for authority and maintaining social order become important for their own sake. Behavior is motivated by "doing one's duty."

---

[63]The summary here draws upon Kohlberg, "Moral Education in the Schools;" "Stages of Moral Development as a Basis for Moral Education," in Clive M. Beck, Brian S. Crittendon, and Edmund V. Sullivan, eds., *Moral Education: Interdisciplinary Approaches* (Toronto: University of Toronto Press, 1971) 86-88; and Duska and Whelan, *Moral Development,* 45-47.

Level
III. *Self-Accepted Moral Principles.* At this level the person sur-
passes conformity as the mode of morality and defines
principles that carry moral weight apart from the authority of persons and groups who hold them and apart from
individual needs and associations. Here the person recognizes that norms of culture are socially conditioned and
therefore not absolute.

Stage 5. *Legalistic contract orientation.* Duty is defined as
contract; principles have been examined and
agreed upon by all who are involved. The contract may be altered when it is socially demanded,
but changes must follow mutually accepted procedures. In regard to either the standards themselves or the procedures by which they are
defined, majority will and welfare must be followed.

Stage 6. *Universal ethical principle orientation.* At this stage
morality is a matter of abstract universal principles, not rules. The principles must be judged
by their logical consistency and comprehensiveness. Respect for the equality, rights, and dignity
of human beings occupies a key place in this highest stage of moral development.

Kohlberg also suggests a seventh stage that he has not yet integrated into his scheme. Even the attainment of stage six, the
awareness of rational universal human principles of justice, inadequately explains commitments in truly outstanding individuals
who seem to adopt cosmic perspectives in their moral judgment.[64]
These seem to be motivated by "contemplative experience of non-
egoistic or nondualistic variety."[65] The essential characteristic of
stage seven is "the sense of being a part of the whole of life and the

---

[64]Martin L. Hoffman, "Development of Internal Moral Standards in Children," in Strommen, *Research on Religious Development*, 218.

[65]Ibid., 230ff.

adoption of a cosmic as opposed to a universal humanistic (stage 6) perspective."[66]

Kohlberg concluded that persons move through these six (or seven) stages in order and without exception. No one takes the steps two at a time but passes through stage one to get to stage two, through two to arrive at three, and so forth. Further, persons are cognitively attracted to the stage immediately above their own but cannot comprehend moral reasoning at a stage beyond their own. Also, Kohlberg's extensive studies have demonstrated few subjects at the upper level of his scheme, probably accounting for the lack of attention to the conjectured stage seven. In short, moral development is growth and, like all growth, comes painfully slow. The slow movement occurs as an individual's moral stance is unable to cope with moral dilemma. Accordingly, moral growth is understood as finding additional and more adequate ways to resolve complexities in the moral life. No disequilibrium; no growth. Frustration at the lower levels of moral development is the occasion for readjusting the framework within which more adequate moral decisions may be made. Moral development is basically experimental. Persons recapitulate in their cognitive statements those resolutions that have been discovered in experience.

Kohlberg and Religion. Kohlberg's studies advance the understanding of moral growth an important step beyond Piaget's emphasis on the consciousness and practice of rules. More than Piaget, he stresses ethical complexities and the need for judgment based upon principle. Within Kohlberg's model the vision of moral ideas takes on an importance that is suggestive for religions concerned to broaden the base upon which their constituents practice morality. Personal autonomy and responsibility are more discernible in each passing stage and become most visible at level three. Unfortunately, most religious communicants remain at stages three and four, encouraged by institutions that embody social norms given religious sanction. Consequently, Kohlberg speaks to those reli-

---

[66]Hoffman, "Development of Internal Moral Standards in Children," 213. See also his "Childrearing Practices and Moral Development: Generalizations from Empirical Research," *Child Development* 34 (1963): 295-318.

gious systems that are concerned with autonomous decision making surpassing obedience to establishment rules and beliefs.

Persons may develop morally quite apart from a religious context, but religion may promote the moral pilgrimage in two complementary ways: (1) to keep before persons the complexity of ethical situations, thereby frustrating solutions that are too simple and (2) to enliven the vision of ultimate principles while at the same time maintaining grace and forgiveness at intervals along the way to perfection. Kohlberg's research constantly reminds religion that immature stages are not the ends of moral growth and that moral principles are not to be romanticized so that they are unrelated to growing persons.

SUGGESTED READINGS

Will and Decision

Farber, Leslie H. *The Ways of the Will.* New York: Basic Books, 1966. Readable.

Festinger, Leon. *Conflict, Decision, and Dissonance.* Stanford CA: Stanford University Press, 1964.

James, William. *The Will to Believe.* New York: Dover, 1956. Old, but still valuable.

Kaufman, Gordon D. *The Context of Decision.* Nashville: Abingdon, 1961. A theological analysis.

May, Rollo. *Love and Will.* New York: W. W. Norton, 1969.

Freedom

Brehm, Jack W. *A Theory of Psychological Reactance.* New York: Academic, 1966. Psychological reactions when freedom is assaulted.

Ellul, Jacques. *The Ethics of Freedom.* Geoffrey W. Bromiley, trans. and ed. Grand Rapids MI: Eerdmans, 1976. Voluminous theological treatment.

Franklin, R. L. *Freewill and Determinism.* Atlantic Highlands NJ: Humanities, 1968. Summary of traditional philosophical views.

Wicklund, Robert A. *Freedom and Reactance.* New York: John Wiley, 1974. Elaboration of Brehm.

Intention

Irwin, Francis W. *Intentional Behavior and Motivation.* Philadelphia: Lippincott, 1971. A cognitive theory in a broad sense.

Meiland, Jack W. *The Nature of Intention.* New York: Methuen, 1970. A comprehensive philosophical theory; psychologically suggestive.

Moral Development

Duska, Ronald, and Mariellen Whelan. *Moral Development: A Guide to Piaget and Kohlberg.* New York: Paulist, 1975.

Fowler, James W. "Toward a Developmental Perspective on Faith," *Religious Education* 69 (March-April 1974) 207-19. Proposes a provisional description for six stages in faith development. See also his *Stages of Faith: The Psychology of Human Development and the Quest for Meaning.* New York: Harper, 1981.

Gilligan, Carol. *In a Different Voice: Psychological Theory and Women's Development.* Cambridge: Harvard University Press, 1982.

Kohlberg, Lawrence. "Stages of Moral Development as a Basis for Moral Education." In *Moral Education,* Clive M. Beck, Brian S. Crittendon, and Edmund V. Sullivan, eds. Toronto: University of Toronto Press, 1971.

Lande, Nathaniel, and Afton Slade. *Stages: Understanding How You Make Moral Decisions.* New York: Harper and Row, 1979. Popularizes Kohlberg.

Lickona, Thomas, ed. *Moral Development and Behavior.* New York: Holt, Rinehart and Winston, 1976. Comprehensive articles by leading theorists.

Piaget, Jean. *The Moral Judgment of the Child.* London: Kegan Paul, Trench, Trubner, 1931. Standard.

RELIGIOUS LIFE-STYLES

Cognitive, affective, and volitional functions are part-processes that converge in every behavioral act. People think about options, decide, and feel that their decisions are correct; or they decide on the basis of feeling, and then state reasons to account for what they have done. The part-processes have substantive meaning only in relationship to each other. Affective states are expressed in cognitive beliefs, and volitional judgments are made about what constitutes correct decisions or good feelings. The continual interplay of thinking, feeling, and deciding means that an analysis of the parts inevitably leads to a consideration of a whole, those intricate systems by which affection, cognition, and volition operate with consistency and consequence. Single behavioral acts are thus episodes in a larger drama with its own plot and movement.

General personality designs have been seen as contexts for understanding specific wishes, acts, beliefs, and expectancies and have attracted the attention of numerous researchers. In the Gestalt tradition an organizing principle is perceived as the key to personality, a focus for patterns or systems that give cohesion to a wide variety of acts and ideas. James Miller calls such personality structures "general behavior systems" and defines them as having a single boundary, continuous in time and space, with recognizable functional interrelationships.[1] Such organizations are like a flotilla of ships in touch with each other by radio.[2] Individual units may seem to function independently and the design may vary from time to time. Nonetheless, ships in convoy are parts of an overall configuration that moves in the same general direction. Each part serves the other in mutual protection and support. Likewise, personality has its wholeness. Isolated acts may appear to be eccentric, but over a period of time and across many acts and ideas general patterns will appear.

These unifying processes may be described as ego development. With human development the "ego, originally in the service of the drives, becomes increasingly also a precipitate of experience as development goes on."[3] Ego is in touch with both the inner world of drives and the outer world of environment and acts as "the administrative and tactical agent" to negotiate the harmony of the two worlds.

> It effectuates a synthesis between the various realities that are relevant to life: the reality of cell and tissue needs; the reality of psychic wishes, feelings, and capacities; the realities of the physical environment; and the reality of social and cultural opportunities and threats. And if one would contemplate apart from these a cosmic reality, the ego would certainly have to take it into account as another party with which transactions have to be made.[4]

The synthesizing function of the ego thus brings order out of the chaos of part-processes and gives a certain sameness to a person's life.

---

[1]James G. Miller, "Toward a General Theory for the Behavioral Sciences," *American Psychologist* 10 (1955): 513-31.

[2]Ibid., 515.

[3]Pruyser, *A Dynamic Psychology of Religion* (New York: Harper, 1968) 206. The idea of ego development has been discussed extensively by Jane Loevinger, *Ego Development* (San Francisco: Jossey-Bass, 1976).

[4]Pruyser, *A Dynamic Psychology of Religion*, 205.

Although these general behavior systems may develop with it, religion may afford structures by which persons may unify their understanding of themselves and the world, or even the cosmos. In this sense religion may become an organizing principle and one can speak of a religious life-style, that relatively uniform system built up over a long period of time that expresses at any given moment a person's reading of both internal and external worlds. It is the profile of religion, the general direction or thrust of the religious life. It incorporates attitudes and ideas that may be inferred from what persons do and say, as well as what they confess to be their beliefs and values. Observing one's religious life style would permit a prediction as to how a person would be likely to act in new and different circumstances.

Primarily, a religious life-style enables individuals to use meaning to bring differentiated parts of their experience into a cohesive whole. "I am religious" is translated into a whole, a gestalt, a pattern that is considerably more specific and identifiable. Being religious means being Baptist or Roman Catholic, conservative or orthodox. Sudden or radical shifts are discouraged; a single pattern promotes consistency and continuity. There may be episodic exceptions within the design, and over an extended period changes in the general configuration may gradually emerge. Occasionally a dramatic crisis (sometimes under the label of conversion) may precipitate a sudden shift in life-style. But more often alterations occur slowly and with consistency and continuity taking shape over a long period of time.[5]

The histories of the great religions of the world reflect at least three general patterns by which persons practice religion. Each has numerous sub-types and follows a varying intensity. They may be briefly described:

— *Religion of authority* is a religious life-style oriented around specific historical forms and structures that are assumed to carry the weight of God's redemptive presence in the world.

---

[5]Allport's data regarding the more regular occurrences of gradual (71% in Allport's sample) as opposed to sudden conversions illustrates the reticence toward sudden shifts in religious life-styles. See *The Individual and His Religion*, 33-34.

— *Religion of becoming* is a religious life-style oriented around the processes of history that calls the good life into being.

— *Religion of spontaneity* is a religious life-style oriented around neither form nor history, but around the conviction that God moves directly upon the human spirit.

The thesis in part four is that one of these patterns will tend to unify the experience of an individual and serve as what Robert Bellah tabs "a superordinate meaning system," which is a complex of "symbolic forms and acts which relate more to the ultimate conditions of his existence."[6] Since religious life-styles are psychological organization systems, their dynamics operate across the broad spectrum of personality. Typical patterns in the religious life may also be expected to appear in a person's political outlook or approach to economics. Individuals who are close-minded in their religion will also likely be close-minded in politics; those open-minded in one area of their life are likely to be open-minded in others.[7] Psychologically, the patterns of personality organization are apt to function throughout the personality with religious, political, and economic manifestations.

Part four examines each of these religious life styles and describes their chief characteristics to illustrate patterns in contemporary religious systems.

---

[6]Robert N. Bellah, "Religious Evolution," *American Sociological Review* 29 (1964): 359.

[7]Milton Rokeach, *The Open and Closed Mind: Investigations into the Nature of Belief Systems and Personality Systems* (New York: Basic Books, 1960) 109-31. Numerous studies have demonstrated these connections. For example, see Dean R. Hoge, "College Students' Value Patterns in the 1950s and 1960s," *Sociology of Education* 44 (1971): 170-97; E. T. Gargan, "Radical Catholics of the Right," *Social Order* 11 (1961): 409-19. S. M. Lipset, "Religion and Politics in the American Past and Present," in Robert Lee and Martin Marty, eds., *Religion and Social Conflict* (New York: Oxford University Press, 1964); Anthony M. Orum, "Religion and the Rise of the Radical White: The Case of Southern Wallace Support in 1968," *Social Science Quarterly* 51 (1970): 674-88.

CHAPTER TEN

RELIGION OF AUTHORITY: THE WAY OF OBEDIENCE

The religious life of an individual may be oriented around the conviction that specific historical forms and structures are vehicles for the purposes of God in the world. These persons devote energy and religious exercise to preserving those sacred forms. Since authority is vested in sacralized structures, their religious life may be designated *a religion of authority*. Those who are characterized by this religious style affiliate with institutions that they assume carry the weight of God's presence and are loyal to authorized order.

THE CONTOUR OF RELIGION OF AUTHORITY

A religion of authority is dominated by conceptions of power and control.[9] Its distinguishing manner is to build and maintain re-

---

[8]For other attempts to conceptualize patterns by which persons organize their religious life, see Robert H. Bonthius, *Christian Paths to Self-Acceptance* (New York: King's Crown Press, 1948); Rodney Stark, "A Taxonomy of Religious Experience," *Journal for the Scientific Study of Religion* 5 (1965): 97-116; Donald Capps and Walter H. Capps, *The Religious Personality* (Belmont CA: Wadsworth, 1970); and Heije Faber, *Psychology of Religion* (Philadelphia: Westminster, 1975) 143-325.

ligious structures to which allegiance may be given. The essential mood of religion of authority is obedience. External authority is conceived to have the right to command loyalty, and the primary virtue is willing surrender of the self to its control. Creeds and rituals are envisioned as means for extending divine control. Within this general design considerable variation may exist. The authority's strength may be perceived as mild or absolute; power of control may derive from the Bible, the church, a moral code, a tradition, or more than one of these in combination; acceptance and allegiance may be unreflective and naive or the end of rational judgment. But amid the variations the contour of authoritarian religion is dominated consistently by perceptions of a higher power that transcends human experience and demands full loyalty and obedience.[10]

In Western culture religion of authority has traditionally been associated with masculinity and an assumption of the dominant role of male figures. Traditional images are regularly patriarchal in character. God is the father and his subjects are the obedient children. The Judeo-Christian tradition was born and nurtured in a patriarchal environment and consequently its basic ideas were typically expressed in masculine forms. Christianity is heir to many of these usages as is clearly illustrated in the trinitarian formula: "Father, Son, and Holy Spirit." Hence, Western religion may yield to this tradition when religion is built upon authority patterns. Preserving the "male dominance" image thus becomes crucial to preserving the faith. In those situations where sacred associations are made with the images themselves, it is exceedingly difficult to recognize that the figures are more expressive of cultural context than theological reality and to subsequently transcend masculine anthropomorphic metaphors.

Jung was aware of the dominance of masculine imagery in Christianity and suggested the addition of a fourth category to the

---

[9]"Religion of Authority" and "authoritarian religion" are used synonymously in the discussion here without any intention to debunk.

[10]Classical theological models have tended to be monarchical and hierarchical, therefore encouraging authoritarian forms of religious expression. This tendency has been a point of protest in contemporary process theology.

Trinity, the "Mother God."[11] Jung's resolution, however, is not radical enough since it still maintains stereotypical definition of masculinity and femininity. Have we not come far enough in our psychological understanding to no longer make dominance and aggression father traits and tenderness and submission mother traits? Do not enough cultural variations appear (both culture to culture and within a single culture) to justify interchange in social roles? Both questions should be answered affirmatively and should inform the label "religion of authority." The distinctive feature of religion of authority is the acceptance of control by external authority whether masculine or feminine. The authority may be domineering and aggressive; it may also be caring and nurturing.[12]

A religious life-style built upon loyalty to either masculine or feminine authority may be found in most religious traditions. The overly scrupulous Puritan, the inflexible Roman Catholic, the legalistic Pharisee, the Protestant biblicist, the Islamic fundamentalist, and the conservative Jew are not identical in their beliefs. Some in each group are likable; others in each group can be quite unpleasant. Tolerance or intolerance is not the private possession of any one of them. Some appeal to the Bible as authority, others to the church or synagogue, and still others to law or Torah. Doctrinal differences are easily discernible. But psychologically these diverse groups share a common approach to religion. They all travel the way of obedience, defining their faith in terms of structures external to themselves that in some fashion rightfully demand loyalty and submission. Several features dominate the contour of their religious territory.

Authority

P. T. Forsyth asserts that "the question of authority, . . . in its religious form, is the first and last issue of life," and it is certainly a

---

[11]Carl G. Jung, *Answer to Job,* R. F. C. Hull, trans.(Princeton: Princeton University Press, 1973) 165-78.

[12]Heije Faber, *Psychology of Religion,* 157-90, appropriately perceives that it is more profitable to use Erikson's psychoanalytic model emphasizing infantile relationships with both father and mother to discuss the psychoanalytic understanding of religion, rather than depending upon Freud, whose association of the origin of religion with the Oedipal period too strongly stressed the role of the father.

psychological truism that authority is an inescapable issue.[13] "Every living soul has to come to terms with authority, power, and responsibility. These three categories are charged with affect; they are integral to religion and conversely, religions have a good deal to say about them."[14] Personalities and religious systems may be totally different in their intent to espouse or escape from an external power that proposes to control their life and destiny. Although the issue of authority encompasses relationships beyond religion, religious experience necessarily entails the question of authority and to describe a religious life-style as "the way of obedience" brings the issue sharply into focus. To whom and under what circumstances will persons abdicate initiative for their own behavior?

The exploration of this question needs to begin with the recognition that many characteristic features of religion foster the adoption of willing obedience. Issues at stake in religion are not incidental, but are those that deal with the issues of life and death. Those things about which authority figures speak are not remarks to unconcerned or faddishly interested onlookers. They are instructions to active participants who are concerned with ultimate matters. Religion provides an "overarching ideology" within which detailed instructions carry an added weight.[15] Religion also legitimates ranking authorities in the persons of priests, ministers, teachers, shamans, rabbis, and even God. Hence, religion in a sense encourages the sacrifice of initiative, and it rewards those who surrender with a strong sense of having done the right thing.

Second, obedience to authority embraces the pressure to conform. The ease with which adolescents conform to peer culture illustrates how persons may succumb to the wishes of a group to avoid the stigma of standing out as different. But the pressure extends beyond adolescence. The phenomenon is demonstrated in the research of Solomon Asch, who conducted an experiment in which

[13]P. T. Forsyth, *The Principle of Authority in Relation to Certainty, Sensitivity and Society* (London: Independent Press, 1952) 1.

[14]Pruyser, *A Dynamic Psychology of Religion*, 262.

[15]Stanley Milgram, *Obedience to Authority: An Experimental View* (New York: Harper, 1969) 142.

groups of six people were shown a line and asked which of the three other lines matched it in length.[16] All but one of the subjects were secretly directed to give the incorrect answer. The uninstructed person, under the pressure of the incorrect statements, regularly conformed to them rather than report the obvious evidence. The need to conform is intense and, like obedience, sacrifices personal responsibility for the reward of belonging.

Obedience, however, moves beyond conformity.[17] It operates in a hierarchical structure in which the person or thing above has the right to prescribe behavior for the person below. Further, obedience involves explicit orders and commands coming from a superior, not merely conforming to the group. Compliance to an order or command, not imitation of the subject, is the criterion by which obedience is judged. And most importantly, conforming persons tend to belittle and underplay external influences on their behavior, whereas obedient persons willingly embrace an authority as the explanation of their actions.

Religion of authority is an act of obedience, not merely conformity. It encourages obedience by vesting authority in specific, concrete, and external objects. Power and responsibility may be vested in organizational structures that are strictly hierarchical, as in the Roman Catholic Church where the highest officer is seen as God's divine representative on earth. Starting with the Pope, authority is dispensed from the top downward. Or, the organization may be more informal but carry no less authoritarian weight, as in sectarian Southern Baptist churches in which particular patterns of worship, fund-raising, or records-keeping are overlaid with sacredness. Authoritarian religion may also vest power in ideas, particularly as expressed in Scriptures, doctrines and creeds, or legalistic codes. Authority may be granted to religious leaders either by placing them in an authoritative institutional position or by accepting their judgments as final. The success of religion of authority rests upon its ability to fortify these roles and to incite persons to surrender por-

---

[16]Solomon E. Asch, "Effects of Group Pressure upon the Modification and Distortion of Judgment," in Harold S. Guetzkow, ed., *Groups, Leadership, and Men* (New York: Russell and Russell, 1963) 177-90.

[17]Milgram, *Obedience to Authority*, 14-115.

tions of their personal autonomy to regulation by persons, institutions and/or codes of higher status.

Stanley Milgram, one of the important contemporary interpreters of authority, has demonstrated an amazing staying power that typifies vested authority. In his book *Obedience to Authority* Milgram reports on extensive experimentation with persons who were asked to administer electric shocks of increasing severity to protesting victims. He discovered that ordinary people, even when they were asked to carry out actions incompatible with their moral standards, and though the destructive results of their actions were made plain to them, generally did not have the personal resources to resist authority. Milgram concluded that the key to the destructive behavior of his subjects was "not in pent-up anger or aggression, but in the nature of their relationship to authority."[18] Certainly, religion of authority does not uniformly produce destructive behavior. Quite to the contrary, the ends are generally more beneficial to one's fellows than destructive. But Milgram's experiments teach something significant about the life-style of obedience. Those who follow this path give themselves up to the wishes of the authority. Once the transfer has been made, it is difficult to break free. Milgram refers to this relationship as the "agentic state," that condition in which an individual sees self as an agent for carrying out the intentions of that which has been vested with authority.[19]

Third, religious authority may be either good or evil, advantageous or disadvantageous. A naive but willing person may accept the controlling function of authority without regard for its inherent value or right to control. A student who unquestioningly accepts a statement as true merely because it is written in a book or spoken by a professor practices this type of submission and opens possibilities to being manipulated by those who consciously or unconsciously enjoy the exercise of power. In a religious context these persons uncritically accept ideas and practices imposed from the

---

[18]Ibid., 168.

[19]Ibid., 132-134.

outside, a religious style deplored by Erich Fromm as uniformly immature and undesirable.[20]

On the other hand, religion of authority may serve worthy ends. Acceptance of external authority is not always at the expense of personal worth and does not inevitably lead to the exploitation and devaluation of individuality. Consider for example the function of religious funeral rituals that carry intense social approval. The bereavement trauma may neutralize an individual's personal resources for managing the disruptions that come with intense grief. Obviously, unscrupulous morticians and ministers alike may exploit for their own purposes the confusion of bereaved persons. The rituals themselves may be crude, exploitative, or theologically unsophisticated. Nonetheless, participating in accepted, authorized ritual may foster movement through the grief. At a time when personal disorganization threatens, surrender to previously structured authoritative forms may serve personal survival well until equilibrium is restored. In milder forms those students who depend upon the judgment of their professor or strength from peer culture may be served well by established forms, pending the development of more autonomous authority systems.[21]

Priestly Order versus Prophetic Disruption

In religion of authority the emphasis upon the authority of religious forms is allied with an insistence upon priestly order and de-

---

[20]Erich Fromm, *Psychoanalysis and Religion* (New Haven: Yale University Press, 1950) 42ff.; cf. Schubert M. Ogden, "The Authority of Scripture for Theology," *Interpretation* 30 (1976): 242-61; and "Sources of Religious Authority in Liberal Protestantism," *Journal of the American Academy of Religion* 44 (1976): 403-16. Ogden distinguishes between *de facto* authority, a type that parallels Fromm's authoritarianism, and *de jure* authority that derives its power from beyond itself, justifying its right to attention and control.

[21]The issue here touches upon cybernetics, a field concerned with the science of control, including the physiological and psychological systems that direct human behavior. Helpful introductions to this field may be found in W. Ross Ashby, *An Introduction to Cybernetics* (New York: Wiley, 1958); Gordon Pask, *An Approach to Cybernetics* (London: Hutchinson, 1961); and C. R. Evans and A. D. J. Robertson, *Cybernetics* (Baltimore: University Park Press, 1968). One of the pioneers in the field, Norbert Weiner, has commented on "certain points where cybernetics impinges on religion" in *God and Golem, Inc.* (Boston: MIT Press, 1964).

corum. Since authority is vested in formal and informal organizational structures, those charged with keeping the forms intact are honored. Across religious traditions, priests have been given the responsibility to sustain those institutional customs, practices, and organizations that unify and preserve the values of a religious community, and that have come to be traditional authority vehicles. Proper maintenance of worship, education, enlistment, and service has been entrusted to those who practice the priestly function, whether or not they are called priests. Often detailed rules specify the correct structures, and the good priest is one who is familiar with the regulations and carries them out correctly. Neither imagination and creativity nor the eccentric priest enjoys a favorable place in authoritarian religion, which prefers the stability of everything being "done in a proper and orderly way."[22]

The religious life-style of obedience likewise leans toward priestly approaches to doctrine. Creeds, confessions of faith, and catechisms are important. They reduce illusive experience to clear, concise, and tangible statements and provide for priest and people cherished objects toward which loyalty and obedience may be directed. They function explicitly to identify a religious tradition and serve as vehicles for priestly conservation. Among noncreedal groups the Bible is sometimes accorded this function. When the authority of a biblical interpretation is derived from the institutional status of the interpreter or its conformity to a traditional interpretation, or when selected verses are recited to support existing institutional forms, then Scripture is subordinated to institution and cast in a priestly role.[23] Those who follow the way of obedience find it easy to give a dominant role to creeds, confessions, statements of

---

[22]I Corinthians 14:40.

[23]Paul Pruyser points to several patterns by which the authority of the Bible may be maintained: (1) legalists who find authority along the lines of an ultimate code, (2) literalists who take the authoritarianism of the letter and forget the spirit, (3) modernists who look for relevant gems of instruction and inspiration, (4) demythologizers who distinguish between medium and message and seek new media, and (5) those who develop their ideas independent of the Bible and then seek out proof texts to add authority. See Pruyser, *A Dynamic Psychology of Religion*, 268-69.

faith, and the Bible, which are seen as means to make clear how obedience may be exercised.

Undue allegiance to priestly order and decorum runs the risk of fostering a closed and intolerant religious system. Clear and oversimplified definitions of creed and cultus cultivate a spirit of "having the truth" and thereby encourage ingroup commitments. Organizational patterns and doctrinal affirmations within one's own sect or denomination are taken as normative, thereby promoting separation from other groups and from culture itself. The trend is supported by David Moberg's study of sixty-six Protestant churches in a Midwestern American city. Moberg found "that theological conservatism is characteristic of sectlike religious bodies and theological liberalism of those that are churchlike."[24] Those sectlike groups that intentionally separated themselves from culture were unable to entertain change in their creedal and cultic forms. Separation and stability go hand in hand. Although cause and effect are not clear in Moberg's exploratory study, it seems reasonable to judge that tolerance of change would vary proportionately to the intensity of commitment to establishment forms.

Religion of authority has a difficulty making peace with the prophet, who fulfills a function in the Judeo-Christian tradition as a necessary complement to the priest. The priest aims to maintain religion through the established vehicles of institutional life; the prophet owes no allegiance to the establishment and often sees his role as disruptive. The prophets of ancient Israel were not iconoclasts concerned to tear down religious institutions merely for pleasure in the destruction. But neither were they protectors of the *status quo*. "The prophet who is properly so called was a man who knew God in the immediacy of experience, who felt an inescapable constraint to utter what he was profoundly convinced was the word of God. . . . He was a true prophet in the measure of his experience of God, and the measure of his experience was the measure of his receptiveness and of his response to it."[25] He spoke the word of God

---

[24]David O. Moberg, "Theological Position and Institutional Characteristics of Protestant Congregations: An Exploratory Study," *Journal for the Scientific Study of Religion* 9 (1970): 57.

[25]H. H. Rowley, *The Servant of the Lord and Other Essays on the Old Testament* (London: Lutterworth, 1952) 128.

as if it were "fire in his bones," convinced that the message was the single way to purify motivation, deepen devotion, and renew creed and cult.

The peaceful coexistence of the priestly and prophetic functions is difficult if not impossible; "they are rarely combined in one person, with the result that there tends to be a polarization in organized religion between priestly and prophetic typologies of men and priestly and prophetic styles of religious life."[26] Religion of authority clearly tilts in the direction of the priest. In its milder forms this religious life-style cherishes the establishment, resists change, appeals to the past, and relies on nostalgia for authoritative support. In its more radical forms, however, authoritarian religion defends the faith more vigorously. Change itself may be considered evil. No room can be made for the individual or the congregation that is different. Religion of authority vigorously preserves the office of the needed priest, but also risks killing the prophet or stoning the messenger of God who comes with a corrective word.

Integrative Affiliation

A third characteristic of religion of authority is its emphasis upon affiliation with religious groups. Any religious life style may derive considerable support from identifying with like-minded persons, but such associations seem particularly crucial for those who obey authority. Religion for them seems chiefly corporate, not private. The sociology of religion has been concerned with such affiliations, concentrating upon the influence of social factors in the formation and maintenance of group life. Persons voluntarily involve themselves in organized life, secular or religious, to avoid "excessive fluidity of our social culture" and "to gain a degree of routinized and recognized fixity."[27] Apparently the value of such associations increases proportionately to the person's involvement in the organization. Will Herberg argues further that participation in religious

---

[26]Pruyser, *A Dynamic Psychology of Religion*, 266.

[27]Clyde Kluckhohn and Florence Kluckhohn, "American Culture: Generalized Orientations and Class Patterns," in Lymon Bryson, Louis Funkelstein, and R. M. MacIver, eds., *Conflicts of Power in Modern Culture* (New York: Harper, 1947) 249.

organizations may meet integrative needs even better than participation in nonreligious organizations.[28]

But persons also belong to groups for deeply personal reasons.
They find in their affiliation with consensual institutions a sense of
community for their individual life styles. Thus, affiliation is a psychological as well as a sociological matter. Participation in religious
groups is socio-psychologically integrative, affording not only social order and consistency, but also gestalts within which private experiences find affirmation and support. In a suggestive article,
Donald Capps has traced the changes in the religious affiliation of
a certain Orestes Bronson from this point of view. He sees Bronson's successive associations with Congregationalism, Methodism,
Presbyterianism, Universalism, Socialism, Transcendentalism, and
finally Roman Catholicism as a search for the mitigation of early
personal frustrations.[29] Childhood deprivation and the search for
a reliable authority were decisive factors forcing him into affiliation
with religious bodies whose style fit his personal needs.

For such personal affirmation to occur a high degree of congruence of beliefs must be present. Persons organize their social
world according to the degree to which the beliefs of others are
congruent or incongruent with their own.[30] Preference seems to be
given to persons with similar belief systems over other factors. This
organizing principle is more important than race or ethnic group-
ings, for example, in determining affiliation patterns. "If race or
ethnic categorizations are important, it is because they are convenient symbols that stand for complexes of beliefs which to one de-

---

[28]Will Herberg, *Protestant-Catholic-Jew* (Garden City NY: Doubleday, 1960) 31.
Herberg's judgment is confirmed by William F. Sweiker, "Religion as a Superordinate Meaning System and Socio-Psychological Integration," *Journal for the Scientific Study of Religion* 8 (1969): 300-307.

[29]Donald Capps, "Orestes Bronson: The Psychology of Religious Affiliation,"
Journal for the Scientific Study of Religion 7 (1968):197-209.

[30]Rokeach, *The Open and Closed Mind,* 35 ff., notes that an individual's belief
system includes two independent parts: those things believed and those things
disbelieved. Disbeliefs are not merely the opposite of belief, but include all items
rejected whether or not they disagree with accepted propositions.

gree or another are seen to be similar to and different from our own."[31]

The dominance of belief in patterns of social affiliation is significant for the psychological dynamics of the religious way of obedience. Attaching authority to explicit and concrete religious ideas and insisting upon their proper preservation in the ministrations of the priest, correct belief offers practitioners large amounts of certainty and therefore security. These devotees *know* in whom they believe and what they believe. They are intensely creedal and will tolerate little if any diversity. Those who do not confess agreement with established beliefs are likely to be labeled nonbelievers, and those who agree may come to consider themselves *the* religious community. For them affiliation not only makes a difference, but also lies close to the heart of religion.

A Legalistic Ethic

At no point is the certainty of religion of authority more in evidence than in ethics. In his provocative argument for "situation ethics" Joseph Fletcher states that ultimately persons have only three alternatives in making ethical decisions: (1) the situational approach in which "right" is abstracted from the total circumstances in which a decision is to be made, (2) the antinomian approach which operates without moral principles or maxims, and (3) the legalistic approach in which rules and regulations are taken as absolute guidelines.[32] In keeping with its spirit of allegiance to external structures religion of authority adopts the third of these options and evolves a legalistic ethical system that intends to spell out plainly all issues of moral responsibility.

All living religions have groups that stress ethical legalism, but the approach has been especially prevalent in Judaism and Christianity. Legalism triumphed among the Jews after the Babylonian exile when the Hebrew community became predominantly a people of the Torah. After a long interval in which the Law had moved in the shadows, post-exilic Judaism recovered the Torah as the fo-

---

[31]Ibid., 391.

[32]Joseph Fletcher, *Situation Ethics: The New Morality* (Philadelphia: 1966) 17-39.

cus of religious faithfulness and sought to apply its instruction to every aspect of daily life. The result was not only the resurrection of the Torah but also an emergent system of interpretation, the "tradition of the elders," that under the tutelage of scribes, rabbis, and certain Pharisees developed into an elaborate and codified system. It was hoped that no situation might occur in which there was not some law or interpretation of law to guide conduct.

David Bakan believes that psychoanalysis has most directly appropriated the habit of mind found in traditional Judaism, the

> tendency to subject every aspect of life, every aspect of thought and behavior to the minutest scrutiny . . . there is perhaps no psychological approach today which subjects each action and each thought of the individual to such minute scrutiny, with the exception of psychoanalysis. The Jews all through the centuries had learned how to engage in close scrutiny, . . . this role of close scrutiny is picked up by psychoanalysis substituting intrinsic guides rather than the extrinsic guides of rabbinic law.[33]

Freud's personal background in Judaism probably justifies Bakan's claim, but Judaism does not stand alone in imposing the "yoke of the Law." In Christianity both Roman Catholics and Protestants have comparable ethical systems. Roman Catholic ethicists have attempted to build ethical rules upon natural law, spelling out rational regulations that could be considered universally applicable and therefore valid guides for behavior. Henry Davis, a Jesuit theologian, summarizes this position:

> There is a body of law, Divine, Natural, Ecclesiastical, and Civil, which has to be explained. The quarrel with a juristic system should logically be a quarrel with the Ten Commandments; indeed, it should be a quarrel with human nature itself, for nature forbids certain human acts, because human reason reveals to man a lawgiver who has imposed laws on human beings, and reason imposes on man certain obligations as from a Supreme Lawgiver.[34]

---

[33]David Bakan, "Psychoanalysis in the Interpretation of Judaism," unpublished address to American Jewish Congress, Chicago, 1962, as cited in Joseph Havens, ed., *Psychology and Religion: A Contemporary Dialogue* (New York: Van Nostrand, 1968) 97.

[34]Henry Davis, *Moral and Pastoral Theology*, 4th ed. (New York: Sheed and Ward, 1943) 3.

Protestantism has tended to give a biblical turn to the attitude. Accordingly, ethical regulations are drawn from the words and sayings of the Bible, usually in one of two ways. A literalist approach to the Bible selects certain sayings and isolates them as moral precepts. The Bible is made a kind of "manual of discipline" containing preset answers to both simple and tough issues. The ethical task then is largely a matter of checking the index and looking up the answer. Billy Graham's advice-giving newspaper column, revealingly called "My Answer," illustrates this technique. Consistently, a verse or verses from the Bible are recited to clue the answer to the inquirer's question. A second way in which the Bible is typically used in Protestant legalism is proof-texting. Here the ethical stance is derived from a nonbiblical source, usually the mores, and given religious sanction by reciting selected Scripture. Both techniques tend to disregard the context and hence to reduce the Bible to a code of moral instructions.

As diverse as rabbinic Judaism, rationalistic Catholicism, and biblicistic Protestantism are, they share a common outlook, all attempting to generate a clear and explicit moral code to which obedience is due. On the surface legalism appears to be a difficult and complex approach to ethics. How might one be expected to master and remember, much less obey, the massive bulk of rules and regulations designed to control the entire range of behavior? The task certainly seems ponderous; consequently large portions of the energy of this religious life must be spent in popularizing the demands of the code, in keeping its regulations updated, and in reinforcing loyalty to its rules. Psychologically, however, this ethical style is easy ethics. It tends to simplify complex and ambiguous ethical problems. Few situations demanding ethical decisions may be resolved so neatly. Whereas most ethical decisions are cast in gray, legalism assumes they are cast in black and white. These systems shift the focus of moral responsibility from persons to codes. The legalist makes persons responsible not so much for reflecting upon the moral quality of their own actions, as for remembering and following a code. Sin and righteousness in this context depend on how adequately the code has been served.

Hence Pharisaic legalism, biblical proof-texting and literalism, and naturalistic ethical codes alike make the management of guilt,

a key function of religion, easier by oversimplifying the ethical task.
When the code is clearly and concretely stated in rules and regulations, guilt can be specified. One knows when the law has been
broken and the important questions are those of justice and forgiveness. Has the law been broken? If so, what is the punishment
prescribed in the law? Are there additional rules by which the consequences of breach may be avoided? The lines are clear and persons can manage the pattern. If sufficient mercy can be written into
the rules, legalistic ethics has the advantages of simplicity, clarity,
and directness. However, this method of religious obedience side-
steps the questions of ambiguity found in most ethical situations,
allows dimensions of corporate responsibility to go unrecognized,
and too easily pretends that moral principles can be reduced to laws.
It may be easy to decide on legal grounds whether or not murder
or adultery has been committed, but it is more problematic to observe love of neighbor beyond the commands of the law. Religion
of authority may faithfully follow the prescribed codes of goodness
without being too helpful in the weightier matters of ethical responsibility.

FUNDAMENTALISM:
A CASE STUDY IN CARICATURE

When Erich Fromm debunks authoritarian religion and its primary virtue of obedience, he fails to recognize the constructive possibilities of this style of life. If in fact it does not run roughshod over
humanistic values, this practice of religion may serve society and
some individuals well. Communal living demands some compromise between individual and corporate needs, and authority is one
pathway along which the compromise may be achieved. Religion as
a system of social organization serves this need in that it provides a
type of social authority structure to which obedience may be given.
Or, to put it in our nomenclature, religion of authority functions
positively to the degree that it serves functions of socialization and
supports individual pursuit of meaning.

Further, a religious life-style of obedience may remain theologically positive and idealistic. The authority may be humane and be-
nevolent; conservative institutional forms may preserve values that
merit saving, and ethical rules and regulations may direct action to-

ward morally worthy ends. Yet the risks are high. Vested power is no less dangerous in religious circles than in politics or economics. Authority easily becomes domineering and manipulative. Priest or pastor, parent or code may usurp power that rightfully belongs only to God and assume responsibility that rightfully belongs to individuals. Both the assets and liabilities found through the way of obedience may become visible in those for whom religion of authority is a consuming way of life.

The Fundamentalist Movement

Fundamentalism as a specific religious movement is a caricature of the way of obedience.[35] A detailed history of Fundamentalism is beyond our purposes here, but we need to understand the intensity of its commitment.[36] Basically, Fundamentalism arose as a defense against what was perceived to be a major threat to the integrity of religious faith during the last half of the nineteenth century. In the wake of the Darwinian revolution beginning in mid-century, the question of the relevance of scientific mentality and method as it stood in relation to religious thought became a burning theological issue. Segments of Christianity saw new and positive possibilities to reside in the encounter between science and religion and attempted to accommodate the new spirit to enrich their understanding of faith. Out of their efforts came exciting new possibilities for interpreting the Bible through literary analysis,[37] for redefining the processes of Christian education along lines of human growth,[38] and for refined understanding of the meaning of religious experience. The budding disciplines of psychology and

---

[35]The word "fundamentalist" is sometimes used to designate a devotee who is ultra-conservative, but strictly it should be reserved for those who belong to a specific historical movement.

[36]A brief but helpful introduction to this movement appears in Arnold B. Rhodes, ed., *The Church Faces the Isms* (Nashville: Abingdon, 1958) 45-67. More thorough treatments are listed in Suggested Readings.

[37]Julius Wellhausen published his classical exposition of the literary origins and development of the Hexateuch in 1885.

[38]Horace Bushnell's classic *Christian Nurture* (rev. ed. [New Haven: Yale University Press, 1916]) was first published in 1847.

sociology were taken as new avenues for broadened and updated understanding of religious meaning.[39]

However, all Christian believers did not view the new spirit with favor. Some saw the rise of science as the birth of a new and false god and the application of the scientific method to religion as an erosive and intolerable compromise of Christian witness. Honorable believers felt sincerely and intensely that their religious faith was threatened by the rising popularity of scientific approaches to human problems, particularly in the application of analytical and descriptive methods to the study of the Bible. For them the crucial battleground was biblical interpretation and the nature of Jesus as God's Christ. Innovations on the basis of scientific method threatened the traditional ways of talking about these basics; and, out of a genuine concern to preserve the faith, Fundamentalism was born. Across denominational lines champions arose to defend the established focuses of authority in religion. A series of Bible conferences rallied defenders of the faith, gave them an institutional identity, and culminated in the formation of an informal but authoritative creed.

By the end of the nineteenth century the creed of Fundamentalism was beginning to take shape around several concepts:

1. The inerrancy of the Bible,
2. The virgin birth of Christ,
3. The substitutionary atonement of Christ,
4. The physical resurrection of Christ,
5. The anticipated bodily return of Christ to earth.

These simple propositions came to be considered the heart of Christianity by Fundamentalists and were elaborated in a series of twelve volumes published over five years between 1910-1915 under the title *The Fundamentals: A Testimony to the Truth*. With the creed firmly established, Fundamentalists set out in a fire-eating campaign to condemn the new scholarship in every form and to promote their beliefs as the only basis of being a Christian.

---

[39]Recall that William James's work on religion was done toward the end of the century.

The Fundamentalist movement claimed adherents across denominational lines and has ebbed and flowed in intensity during the twentieth century, reaching one of its crescendos in the vigorous evolutionary theory debates of the 1920s. Its identity has been maintained largely through vocal charismatic leaders such as J. Frank Norris, John R. Rice, and Carl McIntyre. It has also become institutionalized in such interdenominational organizations as the World's Christian Fundamentals Association and such schools as the Moody Bible Institute and Bob Jones University.

One point should be made explicitly beyond any possible misunderstanding; the Fundamentalist does more than emphasize the crucial importance of the Bible and Jesus for the Christian faith, an affirmation that is shared by many conservative evangelicals. The Fundamentalist insists upon the absoluteness of *one* doctrinal interpretation of the Bible and Jesus. For the strict Fundamentalist one *must* believe in the inerrancy of what the Bible says to believe in the Bible and, further, believing in the Bible in this way is essential to being a Christian. Likewise, accepting atonement as a substitutionary act is the *only* way atonement may be genuinely confessed. And all of the fundamentals must be affirmed. Thus, Fundamentalism in its original form and among many of its contemporary adherents is an absolute and closed system with the faith clearly and securely defined.

Over the years some elements of the movement have moderated so that contemporary Fundamentalism does not present as vigorous and united a front as it did in the years of some of its founders and early advocates. A naive and pietistic element in the movement simply accepts the tenets without reflection. These people see no need to draw connections with modern thought. This level of experience appears among those who emphasize experience over ideas and accept compartmentally the experiences that they have had. For them biblical inerrancy means little more than affirming a love for the Bible. Also, more reasonable Fundamentalism has selected from the world of scholarship those elements that dovetail with their theology without creating undue conflict and anxiety. Thus, the movement has produced some quite reputable and competent biblical scholars in the area of textual criticism who do their work in confidence that the "original" documents of the Bible, none of which are available, are inerrant.

Modern American popular religion also embraces extensive samples of prostitute Fundamentalism, a brand practiced for pay. Charlatans have seen an opportunity to exploit this mentality for their own financial gain and have learned to play a Fundamentalist game. They fill radio and television space with tirades against straw men and they "give away" books, records, tapes, and assorted religious trinkets to those who send in "free-will" contributions. Such are those who "sell the needy for a pair of shoes" and use religion to fill their own coffers. But this illegitimate Fundamentalism is not our primary concern here. The popularity of Fundamentalism makes the work of the charlatan possible, but the latter is more in business than in religion.

However, countless persons are sincerely and firmly committed to Fundamentalism because they find it a satisfying, religious lifestyle. The militancy, exclusiveness, and aggression typical of the early movement remains with many of them; some are ready to call down fire from heaven to purify college and seminary classrooms, and to save church and country. And why should they not be intense when their theological conviction is that the very cause of God is at stake? About them it is appropriate to inquire, "What makes Fundamentalism appealing?"

Fundamentalism as Life-Style in Caricature

What can be said about the dynamics of Fundamentalism as a religious life-style? What service does this pattern offer in the preservation of selfhood? Initially, it must be observed that Fundamentalism is an instance of religion of authority with little mixture. Its hallmarks are clarity and simplicity. Lines of authority are explicitly drawn, beliefs are specified without ambiguity, rules of conduct are direct and relevant, and rewards and punishments are known. Devotees are clear on what gets them to heaven or sends them to hell. Confession itself has its own rules; grace and forgiveness are dispensed according to specific regulations. Gordon Allport sees this religious style as an illustration of extrinsic religion that thrives as an escape from the complexities of life. He states, "They do not seek so much to preserve the *status quo* as to return to a former, simple small-town or agrarian way of life where individual achievement and responsibility are the only virtues. God has an important role in this ideology as a dispenser of rewards for individual achievement."[40]

Fundamentalism's clarity and simplicity offer the believer reassurance and security. God, morality, and religious institution are built into a simple edifice of absoluteness. But this is a high risk construction. Although absoluteness offers security, it risks collapse when confronted by a complexity that cannot be resolved by a simple answer. This helps us understand why the Fundamentalist insists that every verse of the Bible must stand equal with every other verse. What is at stake is not the authenticity of the Bible, but the very existence of a religious structure carefully knit together in absoluteness. The Fundamentalist correctly senses that if one brick is removed, the entire building collapses.

The absoluteness of Fundamentalism in its extreme form is quite similar to compulsive behavior. In compulsive behavior large amounts of free-floating anxiety come to be focused upon a specific act that when done faithfully has the effect of relieving anxiety. The behavior may be quite socially acceptable (as with the workoholic), or trite and seemingly unrelated to anything significant (as avoiding stepping on cracks in a sidewalk). In either case the compulsive act is fed by intense shame and guilt that demand ready relief. For the extreme Fundamentalist an absolute, closed system may serve the same function. Scrupulous preservation of an absolute and specific system clearly defines the channel for the relief of anxiety.

Cognitively, Fundamentalism caricatures conceptual neatness through concreteness. Loose ends are neatly tidied up; nothing is left to chance. As Paul Pruyser indicates, even those who are quite capable of abstract thinking do not use that ability in this pattern of religion.[41] The Bible becomes a thing and its phrases admonitions to be followed to the letter. Such concreteness limits imagi-

---

[40]Gordon W. Allport, *The Person in Psychology: Selected Essays* (Boston: Beacon Press, 1968) 231.

[41]Pruyser, *A Dynamic Psychology of Religion*, 93.

nation by leaving little room for metaphorical interpretation. Six days is six days and blood is blood. The Fundamentalist insists that "every word of the Bible is true" and that one "tampers with Scripture" by taking it any way other than literally. It should be noted, however, that the Fundamentalist himself is unwilling to follow his hypothesis to its logical conclusion. Images such as a "door" or "light" in reference to Jesus are not so easily taken concretely and literally.

Small wonder that the early Fundamentalists had such difficulty with Darwin, who showed that life, even in its biological forms, is in a continuous state of movement and change. This thesis has been reaffirmed in many ways and in numerous contexts since the mid-nineteenth century. It lies at the heart of personality theory, which understands persons as growing creatures whose being is discoverable in their becoming. Dynamic psychology and dynamic religion alike refuse to accept the *status quo*, believing that the "absoluteness" of any given moment denies the very character of life itself.

Fundamentalism not only challenges many data of science but scientific mentality as well. It in essence rejects the view that life is a pilgrimage, moving into the future. Rather it yields to the temptation to follow a backward path to discover and preserve an earlier, and presumably purer, form of the sacred. Since the contemporary Western experience incorporates the forward movement of the scientific spirit, Fundamentalism often finds itself in open conflict with contemporary culture and claims its adherents from among those who reject responsible living in a real world. Religion of authority does not inevitably become Fundamentalism, but those who follow the way of obedience would do well to be warned by extremism in defense of God, exhibit extra care in attaching undue authority to man-made constructs, and incorporate a little modesty in their rubrics of obedience.

SUGGESTED READINGS

Authority

Bryant, Robert H. *The Bible's Authority Today.* Minneapolis MN: Augsburg, 1968.

Campbell, Dennis M. *Authority and the Renewal of American Theology.* New York: United Church Press, 1976. Brief, readable examination of five periods of authority in American theology.

Cragg, Gerald R. *Freedom and Authority: A Study of English Thought in the Early Seventeenth Century.* Philadelphia: Westminster, 1975.

Flacks, Richard, ed. *Conformity, Resistance, and Self-Determination.* Boston: Little, Brown and Company, 1973. A collection of significant articles.

Jenkins, Daniel T. *Tradition, Freedom, and the Spirit.* Philadelphia: Westminster, 1951.

Kirscht, John P., and Ronald C. Dillehay. *Dimensions of Authoritarianism: A Review of Research and Theory.* Lexington: University of Kentucky Press, 1967.

Manschreck, Clyde L., ed. *Erosion of Authority.* Nashville: Abingdon, 1971. Contains an important article by Roger Shinn.

McKenzie, John L. *Authority in the Church.* New York: Sheed and Ward, 1966. A Roman Catholic view.

Milgram, Stanley. *Obedience to Authority: An Experimental View.* New York: Harper, 1969.

Moore, Robert L. *John Wesley and Authority: A Psychological Perspective.* Chico CA: Scholars Press, 1979.

Rokeach, Milton. *The Open and Closed Mind: Investigations into the Nature of Belief Systems and Personality Systems.* New York: Basic Books, 1960.

Fundamentalism

Barr, James. *Fundamentalism.* Philadelphia: Westminster, 1978. Basic.

Cole, Stewart G. *The History of Fundamentalism.* Hampden CT: Archon Books, 1963.

Feinberg, Charles L. *The Fundamentals for Today.* Grand Rapids MI: Kregel, 1961. Papers defending Fundamentalist positions.

Furness, Norman F. *The Fundamentalist Controversy, 1918-1931.* New Haven: Yale University Press, 1954.

Gasper, Louis. *The Fundamentalist Movement.* Hawthorne NY: Mouton, 1963.

Herbert, A. Gabriel. *Fundamentalism and the Church.* Philadelphia: Westminster, 1957.

Marsden, George. *Fundamentalism and American Culture: The Shaping of Twentieth Century Evangelicalism, 1870-1925.* New York: Oxford University Press, 1980.

Sandeen, Ernest R. *The Roots of Fundamentalism: British and American Millenarianism, 1800-1930.* Chicago: University of Chicago Press, 1970.

CHAPTER ELEVEN

RELIGION OF BECOMING: THE WAY OF AFFIRMATION

When ancient Israel was carried into Babylonian exile in the early sixth century B.C.E., she left behind a way of life. Not only was the nation exiled from a territory, but also from those authoritative forms upon which she had come to depend as upon a father. The Jerusalem Temple and its cultus, the center of her traditional patterns of obedience, was like an empty wilderness; the Davidic king, like the nation itself, was uprooted. Established religious structures of temple, king, and land were gone; and Israel's faith, which had been a religion of authority, was in shambles. Indeed, as the Hebrew poet perceives, it was an occasion of genuine crisis:

> By the rivers of Babylon we sat down:
>   there we wept when we remembered Zion.
> On the willows nearby we hung up our harps.
> Those who captured us told us to sing;
>   they told us to entertain them:
>   "Sing us a song about Zion."
> How can we sing a song to Yahweh in a strange land?[1]

---

[1]Psalm 137:1-4.

The Jewish experience of Babylonian exile is a parable in what can happen regularly in the ongoing drama of religion. Established forms and structures regularly become outmoded or irrelevant or unworkable and the community of faith confronts the necessity of finding new alternatives to old life-styles. What happens to those who live by the waters of Babylon and desire to go on singing Yahweh's song when the old tunes seem strangely off-key? In Babylon it is no longer possible to worship in Jerusalem, but are there other options than cursing God or becoming as the Babylonians? Many have found, as the early Jews did, that new forms of piety serve as well as old ones and have come to revise the old patterns in terms of God's contemporary acts in history. This is done in superlative confidence that human capacity can discover and relate to what is happening in the here and now. Affirmations of faith shift from forms of the past to new and revised forms for the present.

THE CHARACTER OF RELIGION OF BECOMING

Psychologically, religion of becoming often emerges out of the ashes of religion of authority. The gods, like those of the ancient world, continually die to be born again. Society's establishment forms become inadequate for numerous and inevitable reasons. History moves on, and social institutions and vocabularies attached to past situations become outdated. New data become available and demand more refined understanding than expressed in old forms. Persons and religious communities mature, changing their relationships to cherished authorities. The fluid character of experience sometimes produces new vigor among those committed to the way of obedience to reinforce and maintain the establishment. For others old authority forms are divested of their power, and new structures replace the old. But more than replacement may occur. Change itself may become the heart of religious experience. Attention becomes focused upon reality behind forms, both old and new. Being religious becomes a pilgrimage in which process itself is the agenda. This is the stuff out of which religion of becoming is constructed. Religion is here built upon the conviction that the good life is being continuously called into being. It affirms the processes of history and the significant role that persons have in bringing divine purposes to pass.

In the United States the affirmative mood has permeated mainline denominations and been prominent in the outlook and structure of numerous sectarian groups. The emphasis appears in various shapes and degrees of intensity. Religion of becoming includes those who seriously apply ethical principles to the social structure to assure every person the right to a full life, as well as those who promote self-confidence to achieve peace of mind or gain material rewards. Included also are denominationalists who tacitly assume that they can devise organizations and programs, on a scale that often rivals Madison Avenue, to assure the Kingdom's arrival. In all its various forms, however, three emphases dominate the religious life-style: self-affirmation, an incarnational view of history and science, and humanistic ethics.

Self-Affirmation

Religion of becoming is the way of affirmation. The practitioner of this religious life-style affirms that a peaceful, abundant life can be the possession of persons who diligently pursue it with the personal resources at their disposal. They operate upon the conviction that life can be increasingly harmonious, whatever the circumstances, because God is in the present scene effecting radical changes in persons and groups. In contrast to religion of authority that places a supreme confidence in validated forms, religion of becoming trusts human potential and aims to avoid interruptions on the way to fullness that persons as divine creatures can achieve.

The religious life-style of affirmation is described by Robert Bonthius as "the meliorist pathway" which in Christian terms is

> preeminently that Christian view which thrills to the indeterminate possibilities not only of man but of his world under God. It envisions great and beneficent changes open to man by virtue of his real, if limited, freedom. And, seeing man thus surrounded by manifold resources, all within a harmonious universe and dependent in part upon his effort for development, meliorism endeavors to awaken him to the realization of these possibilities. It stresses the importance of man affirming himself and adapting what he has at

hand, and above all it occupies itself with the elaboration of the positive means by which man can realize this greater beatitude.[2]

Religion of becoming is simply illustrated in Eastern religion. Although Hindu India has its ascetic and doctrinaire elements, these are not nearly so pronounced as her "willingness to explore and exploit the full magic of mankind's psychosomatic nature" and to find within the self intimations of the divine Brahman, that universal reality permeating everything.[3] The "tales of fabulous lore and holy men of wondrous powers" found in the Hindu tradition "allow a new sanctification of the romantic faculties of marvel in days of minimalized belief—no wonder of India is greater than that of the divine presence within."[4]

Yet religion of becoming has found its most productive soil in the West, particularly in the Protestant experience of the United States. Western Catholicism, from St. Francis to Hans Küng, has had numerous representatives of Christian optimism and human possibilities, but the fundamental concepts by which Catholicism is defined center in traditional forms and structures and thereby discourage eccentric individualism. Protestantism, although not without its emphasis upon tradition, has thrived on protest and individualism, and in America joined itself with powerful secular forces to promote the idea of human potential. The birth of the United States occurred on the frontier, and the "good" person was the one who faced the arduous tasks of frontier life with heroic faithfulness. This frontier mentality and its first-born offspring, the self-made man, provided American Protestantism with a pervasive model for emphasizing twin concepts that were at the heart of its understanding of religious faith: the importance of the individual

---

[2]Robert Bonthius, *Christian Paths to Self-Acceptance* (New York: King's Crown Press, 1948) 74. The emphasis here is similar to contemporary process theology in the tradition of Alfred North Whitehead and Charles Hartshorne. Helpful introductions to this theological perspective may be found in Robert Mellert, *What Is Process Theology?* (New York: Paulist, 1975) and John Cobb, *A Christian Natural Theology* (Philadelphia: Westminster, 1965).

[3]Robert S. Ellwood, Jr., *Religious and Spiritual Groups in Modern America* (Englewood Cliffs NJ: Prentice-Hall, 1973) 217.

[4]Ibid.

and doing one's moral duty in the social order. Hence religious embellishment easily fused with the frontier spirit to idealize the self-made man.[5]

The frontier spirit has continued in America even after the passing of the frontier. Attitudes underscoring human potential have come to full flower under the impact of twentieth century scientific advancement and large segments of American religion have baptized the mentality. The idealistic hope for human accomplishment is expressed, for example, by E. Stanley Jones, a Methodist minister whose writings were popular during the pessimistic days of World War II. Jones speaks in glowing terms about Christianity tapping the deepest human resources to bring persons to their full potential: "The unity of the material and the spiritual, the secular and the sacred, the personal and the social—the unity of all mankind under a single government—with God as Father and men as brothers. Deepest of all it brings a man into unity with himself, delivering him from all resentments, all fears and anxieties, all self-centeredness and all guilts and complexities and inferiorities."[6]

The most prominent feature of religion of becoming is this confidence in human capabilities. Humanness is not something to be overcome through denial or rigid control, but something to be affirmed as positive and creative. To be sure, persons are capable of decay and corruption, but these violate the nobility of their creation. The end of faith, according to this orientation, is "to understand ourselves truly and set free the forces within us that make for growth."[7] The individual as an autonomous soul capable of a loving, personal relationship with divinity is the central conviction in religion of becoming. It therefore encourages free and responsible

---

[5]The discussion here touches upon Max Weber's thesis, developed in *The Protestant Ethic and the Spirit of Capitalism*, Talcott Parsons, trans. (New York: Scribner's, 1958) that the spread of Calvinism encouraged and sometimes sanctified the accumulation of wealth.

[6]E. Stanley Jones, *Is The Kingdom of God Realism?* (New York: Abingdon-Cokesbury, 1940) 282.

[7]Harry C. Meserve, "Religion without Dogma," in Harry B. Scholefield, ed., *A Pocket Guide to Unitarianism* (Boston: Beacon Press, 1954) 3.

exploration of the self in full confidence that God's handiwork is to be found in the process.

Those remembering the psychology of Abraham Maslow will recognize immediately the continuity between his thought and this religious stance.[8] Maslow was not concerned to defend one religion against another, but he did intend to express boldly his certainty that human beings were capable of asserting their inner nature, even if only a little at a time, and that such affirmation was for human beneficience. Nothing is more important than human experiment in self-discovery. Maslow says, "No social reforms, no beautiful constitutions or beautiful programs or laws will be of any consequence unless people are healthy enough, evolved enough, strong enough, good enough to understand them and to put them into practice in the right way."[9]

But how does one become good, strong, and healthy enough? Maslow's advice is simple, perhaps too simple: "When in doubt, be honest rather than not."[10] By this he meant not circumspection in regards to a moral code of rightness, but openness without guise. Most people play posing games, putting forth a self that is "dishonest." Personal maturity is better served by ripping away false faces, masks, and pretenses, allowing for no evasions or excuses that prohibit or interrupt straightforward, open honesty.[11] Although Maslow acknowledges that such openness has its liabilities and must be practiced in moderation, his candid appeal to honesty expresses his unqualified confidence in human potential.[12]

---

[8]See above, pp. 142-50.

[9]Maslow, *The Farther Reaches of Human Nature*, 19.

[10]Ibid., 46.

[11]J. L. Moreno built an entire therapeutic procedure on this hypothesis. In psychodrama the assignment and exchange of roles are intended to strip away defenses and to deal forthrightly with the enacted reality.

[12]Transactional analysis originated with Eric Berne in 1966. See his *Principles of Group Treatment* (New York: Grove, 1966). The emphasis is remarkably similar in concept to Carl Rogers's earlier client-centered therapy whose non-directive techniques aimed to liberate self-expression. TA and client-centered therapy aim to assert positive personal values more than to probe the hinterlands of the psyche. The mind-set of TA is reflected in the title of T. A. Harris's book *I'm OK, You're OK* (New York: Harper, 1969).

A serious religious turn on the values of individualism is Unitarianism, a denominational fellowship that aims to be "religion without dogma." Two emphases clearly place Unitarianism in the camp of religion of becoming: its rejection of formal creeds and its promotion of human reason. The group traces its origin to the antitrinitarians of the Protestant Reformation. Over subsequent centuries it has preserved a healthy suspicion of formal belief statements. Creeds are judged to be products of the times and places from which they originate and are not worthy to be elevated as objects of faith. More important than sacralized creed and tradition is the preservation of the freedom of mind and spirit to pursue illusive truth. The liberated human spirit can be trusted to discover life's highest meaning through clear and reverent reason.

The Unitarian's reluctance to state belief in explicit terms, except to affirm the freedom and integrity of the human spirit, has sometimes been interpreted by outsiders as nonbelief. It would be fairer—and more accurate—to say that Unitarians, especially those of humanistic bent, recognize that life's most profound questions are unanswerable and prefer to leave them unanswered. They rather center their energy on engaging the problems of contemporary life. A Unitarian ministers states, "One world at a time. I am interested in the world where I am now, in the moral purposes and meanings which the human mind has infused into it, and in the achievement of such ethical goals and ways of life as are possible."[13]

Unitarianism affirms the self by assigning human reason an exceedingly important role. Faith must incorporate the power of rationality, not to produce authoritative creeds and propositions, but to explore continuously the ponderous questions implicit in human existence. There are no absolutes, only widening knowledge that can deepen religious understanding. The Unitarian poet James Russell Lowell in "The Present Crisis" asserts,

> *New occasions teach new duties; Time*
> *makes ancient good uncouth;*
> *He must upward still, and onward,*
> *Who would keep abreast of Truth.*

---

[13]Meserve, "Religion without Dogma," 4.

The human vocation is to pursue truth wherever it may be found, and since it is illusive and faith is exploratory, no one may presume to have received the final word. No single way of religion is *the* way. All religious traditions share the interpretation of universal religious truth and preserve their dignity insofar as they keep open free and bold inquiry.

Thus, Unitarianism is distinguished from other religious groups not by a particular dogma or set of dogmas, but by its confidence that unencumbered rational examination will reveal truth when supernatural revelation cannot always be expected to do so. In this sense it is "pure" religion of becoming. Only in the human situation can divine truth be found and only through reason can it be unraveled. Again, the position is clearly stated by a Unitarian minister: "If, after patient, honest and bold thought, you stand in disagreement with scriptural teachings, trust your own reasoning powers. Never be blindly subservient to the past. At all costs honor your own mind."[14] One could hardly be more forthright in honoring human rationality.

Others have found the introduction of Eastern religious cults into Western life to be their vehicle for enacting self-affirmation. The Vedanta Society, the Self-Realization Fellowship, and the Transcendental Meditation movement that follows Maharishi Mahesh Yogi represent imports from the East which stress that the individual is a segment of the divine soul. These and kindred groups exercise techniques for directing personal energy toward the realization of one's true nature. The confession of the novelist Christopher Isherwood upon his conversion to Vedanta illustrates this point of view:

> Psychologically, this (Vedanta) was of the greatest importance to me *because of my fear and hatred of God as the father-figure*. . . . Vedanta began by telling me that I was the Atman, and that the Atman was Brahman; *the God-head was my own real nature,* and the real nature of all that I experience as the eternal, surrounding universe. Having taught me this, it could go on to explain that this one immanent and transcendent Godhead may project all sorts of divine forms and incarnations. . . . I could now think of the gods as

---

[14]Scholefield, *A Pocket Guide to Unitarianism,* 37.

mirrors in which man could dimly see what would otherwise be quite invisible to him, *the splendor of his own immortal image*. By looking deeply and single-mindedly into these mirrors, you could come gradually *to know your own real nature*.[15]

Self-affirmation appears not only in thoughtful, reflective judgments on human potential, but also in naive and banal appeals to raw self-interests of greed and power. American religion of just plain folks is dotted with groups led by charismatics who promise that God will reward with money and status those who assert themselves. Religion of becoming, like religion of authority, has charlatans who have learned that selfish religion—properly merchandised and advertised—is big, profitable business. The Georgia prophet, Rev. Ike, and a host of others brazenly claim that God returns blessings in direct proportion to remitted offerings. Such selfish appeals are of the same psychological order, but they are prostitutions of sane and serious attempts to affirm human possibilities as a way to open the secrets of existence.

Incarnation

A second feature of religion of becoming as a religious life-style is its incarnational view of science and history. Stated categorically, two points of view have dominated both Christian and non-Christian theology: the transcendental and the incarnational. From the transcendental standpoint faith transcends human experience and comes to persons as a free gift. Nothing can be done by persons to acquire it. Faith is delivered, as it were, from the outside; and the human problem is to receive the gift and preserve it from contamination. Religion of authority represents a transcendental approach to theology. The excessively transcendental person is likely to be a defender of the faith and suspect that history and science threaten religious integrity. Historical hypotheses regarding the origins of Christian or scientific theories about creation are not only unnecessary, but jeopardize the purity of faith that has been once and for all delivered to the saints.

---

[15]In John Yale, ed., *What Vedanta Means to Me: A Symposium* (Garden City NY: Doubleday, 1960) 51. Italics added.

On the other hand, incarnation emphasizes the involvement and nearness rather than the remoteness of deity. Faith comes not by delivery but by permeation. History is the arena where God works and the vehicle through which he may be discovered. "The 'incarnation' theologian wants to touch with his own hands the historical embodiment of faith and, accordingly, he does not shun history, but only bad historians."[16] The historical growth of the church, Scripture, and dogma is traced and relished because of the conviction that these processes depict divinity at work and humanity responding to it. Likewise, science is welcomed as an essential aide in describing the encounter between the human and the divine. The incarnationist endorses the claim that, "The Word became a human being and, full of grace and truth, lived among us."[17] It is further assumed that the "living word" becoming flesh continues in the ongoing historical process.

The two tendencies can be neatly described on paper and in practice occasionally harden into opposing camps. But transcendence and incarnation are not necessarily mortal enemies. In fact, contemporary theology is marked by dialectical exchange between the two viewpoints, each informing and balancing the other. Religion of becoming, however, clearly tilts toward incarnational themes with a corresponding openness toward science and history. "The conviction is that the more clearly man understands his world and himself through the varied means at his disposal—science, art, music, friendship, and most of all, religion—the more possible it becomes for him to realize the fullness of God."[18] Hence this religious life-style acknowledges no divisions between religious and nonreligious truth. Those data coming through science and history are as sacred as religious facts. Whatever persons learn about themselves and the universe to which they belong enhances human potential and needs no further authentication.

The primary thrust of the ethics of religion of becoming emanates logically and predictably from its central affirmation. Morally

---

[16]George H. Tavard, *The Pilgrim Church* (New York: Herder and Herder, 1967) 28.

[17]John 1:14.

[18]Bonthius, *Christian Paths to Self-Acceptance,* 81.

correct behavior promotes those cherished human values that permit the full expression of selfhood—freedom, equality, unity, love, understanding, and confidence. Conversely, evil consists of distortions and interruptions of human potential. Human beings are not fallen creatures whose goodness is to be restored through obedience, but divine creations whose image needs to be uncovered. Even human appetites such as hunger and love are not inherently evil, as if the flesh were locked in a war against the spirit. The ethical task consists in the noble use of one's total being, including impulses and appetites, to rise to the full potential of a completed person. The optimistic view that persons are fundamentally holy and redeemable insofar as their natures can be affirmed stands in marked contrast to the view that persons are depraved and so caught up in their sinful nature that their only hope lies in intervention by a transcendent deity.

By virtue of its emphasis upon the importance of the individual, religion of becoming occasionally deteriorates into an ethics of self-indulgent hedonism, with the pursuit of pleasure as its highest moral good. But this is not its usual pattern. More typically, the lifestyle insists upon both personal and corporate responsibility. Human dignity belongs to all persons; therefore, the believer must act responsibly toward self and respect the worth of others. As one advocate states, the "impact of religion on individual human life and on society must be ethical—or it would be worthless. The power and truth of our religion is to be judged, not by the church we belong to or the beliefs we profess, but by what we are and what we do."[19]

A candid expression of the ethical attitude that typifies religion of becoming appears in Horace Bushnell, a Congregational minister whose work spanned the fourth, fifth, and sixth decades of the nineteenth century. Bushnell was particularly repulsed by the enthusiastic revivalism of his day, a mode that seemed "to produce a first crop of sin, and then a crop of holiness."[20] By its actions, said Bushnell, the Church assumed "that men are to grow up in evil, and be dragged into the church of God by conquest. The world is to lie

---

[19]Scholefield, *A Pocket Guide to Unitarianism*, 5.

[20]Bushnell, *Christian Nurture*, 2.

in halves, and the kingdom of God is to stretch itself side by side with the kingdom of darkness, making sallies into it, and taking captive those who are sufficiently hardened and bronzed in guiltiness to be converted."[21]

Bushnell challenged the promotion of human sinfulness and in his classic *Christian Nurture,* published in 1847, recommended as axiomatic that "the child is to grow up as a Christian, and never know himself as being otherwise."[22] The nurturing function of the home and church was to foster spiritual renewal whereby a child would seem "to have loved what is good from his earliest years." Although Bushnell did not accept the unqualified goodness of human nature, he rejected austere Calvinism and represented a confidence in human capacities to grow into rightness. His outlook has influenced segments of the Christian community over many years.

In religion of becoming the humanistic bent toward ethics is not confined to an individualistic understanding of humanity. Responsibility is also understood in social terms. Irving Taylor describes this attitude as "transactualization,"[23] "a person-environment system in which the person alters the environment (rather than being altered by it) in accordance with self-actualizing forces."[24] In transactualization social organizations are designed to stimulate the creative person's internal systems rather than impose external controls. In short, persons are conceived as creators of the environment rather than reactors to it. The good society is an extension of human values; ethical responsibility in social terms aims to maintain those structures that mirror the best of humanness. Since religion of becoming stresses individualism, it takes seriously those social evils that hamper self-fulfillment, and its ethics include earnest work toward the creation of a society that justly promotes individual well-being.

---

[21]Ibid., 27.

[22]Ibid., 4.

[23]Irving A. Taylor, "An Emerging View of Creative Actions," in Irving A. Taylor and J. W. Getzels, eds., *Perspective in Creativity* (New York: Aldine, 1975) 300-303.

[24]Ibid., 301.

Again, Unitarianism provides an example of how this religious life-style emphasizes the importance of the individual through a concern for social betterment, a position shared with humanistic religionists across many groups. One of them says, "We believe in people, in *all* people. In the practice of our religion, we would be sensitive to all human suffering. We would learn to suffer when others suffer—anywhere. We would become courageous in the service of others."[25] Such deep compassion for fellow human beings is reason enough to work toward the transformation of society according to humanitarian designs. Put candidly, "A person seeking his own selfish good necessarily helps other people whether he wishes to or not. Conversely, the person seeking to be altruisitic and to help other people must then necessarily reap selfish benefits."[26]

These three features, then, are marks of religion of becoming, a religious way oriented around the here and now. It looks for its motivational power, not to a remote deity speaking from outside humanity or contained in abstracted and authoritative forms, but to contemporary manifestations of human need. The emphasis upon humanity may be so intense that God becomes an unnecessary component, but insofar as he is needed, he is discovered in the human face. Religion of becoming affirms individual, personal values and perceives society's needs as extensions of those values. Its dynamic component, its "habitual center of personal energies," is the affirmation of one's own potential with its power continuously reinforced by reassurance in sermon and the printed word that this is the highest loyalty. The religious way of affirmation thrives on the hypothesis that one true to self must thereby also be true to other persons and to divinity.

POSITIVE THINKING:
A CASE STUDY IN CARICATURE

Over several decades positive thinking groups have served dramatically to preserve religion of becoming as an American reli-

[25]Homer A. Jack, "Action for Social Betterment," in Scholefield, *A Pocket Guide to Unitarianism*, 23.

[26]Maslow, *The Farther Reaches of Human Nature*, 20.

gious life-style. These groups do not necessarily represent the best in the self-affirmation tradition, particularly in their tendency to overlook or discount ethical responsibility, but they present boldly the significant features of this life-style. The positive thinking movement has been in evidence in many brands, some of which have appealed to the assertion of personal powers to achieve success, prosperity, and wealth. In its most blatant forms self-affirmation cults make sweeping claims for "success plans" summarized around religious clichés and directly attached to many gifts that supposedly produce the desired happiness and material prosperity. The claim is simple and straightforward: persons can have anything that they have the faith to ask for. For example, Frederick J. Eikerenkoetter II, a flamboyant black minister commonly known as Rev. Ike, overtly claims that "you can't lose with the stuff I use" and offers a simple three-step procedure for achieving one's desires: believing, giving, and prosperity. The "blessing plan," in the words of Rev. Ike, "is the idea of success and prosperity, working in your mind, moving you to give." The general design is reenforced by a series of "success ideas of the month" offered on regular radio and television broadcasts that are amply sprinkled with testimonies of those who have reaped the tangible rewards of their methodological faithfulness.

Rev. Ike represents the rococo face of a movement that during the 1940s and 1950s isolated religion's traditional consolation function and made it a prominent feature of American religion. The chief spokesman for the positive thinking tradition since the early 1940s has been Norman Vincent Peale, minister of the Marble Collegiate Church in New York City, who is more moderate and sophisticated in his approach, but no less certain than Rev. Ike that persons can resolve their problems through affirmative action. The tenets of positive thinking have been promoted extensively through the printed page; Peale's two most popular books, *A Guide to Confident Living* (1948) and *The Power of Positive Thinking* (1952), have sold millions of copies. The attitude is also advanced by Rabbi Joshua Liebman in *Peace of Mind* (1946) and Monsignor Fulton Sheen in *Peace of Soul* (1949), but the "high priest" of the movement for four decades has been Peale.

Through the years positive thinking has clearly and consistently put forward the same themes: human problems are no more than temporary hindrances to full selfhood and are rooted in negative thinking about one's capabilities. These may be steadily overcome by positive thinking that produces unqualified self-confidence and brings to fruition human potential. Nothing is more helpful in maintaining a positive attitude than religion, especially prayer, church attendance, and the recitation of selected Scripture verses. Random quotes from Peale's *A Guide to Confident Living* illustrate the attitude:

> Keep your mind free from confusion and all the creative ideas you need will be yours.
>
> ··
>
> You do not need to be haunted by fear. Your religion can help you. It acts as medicine, releasing power in your mind, the power of faith which drives away fear.
>
> ··
>
> Take time every day to affirm that the re-creative process is taking place in you, in your body, in your mind, and in your spirit.
>
> ··
>
> By changing your thoughts you can also change situations and changing some situations is a requisite to success and happiness.
>
> ··
>
> Change your thoughts (spiritually) and everything changes.[27]

These are representative citations and could be replicated from throughout Peale's writings. *The Power of Positive Thinking* opens with the admonition: "Believe in yourself! Have faith in your abilities! Without a humble but reasonable confidence in your powers you cannot be successful and happy. But with sound self-confidence you can succeed." The book proceeds to offer illustrations and guidelines for "a peaceful mind," "prayer power," "the happiness habit," and "the health formula," by avoiding negative thoughts of defeat and embracing faith in one's self. The recommended formula is "(1) prayerize, (2) picturize, (3) actualize."[28]

---

[27]Norman V. Peale, *A Guide to Confident Living* (Englewood Cliffs NJ: Prentice-Hall, 1948) 87, 137, 181, 243, 247.

[28]Norman V. Peale, *The Power of Positive Thinking* (Englewood Cliffs NJ: Prentice-Hall, 1952) 55.

The bold presentation of Pealeism here is not intended merely to debunk this religious life-style. Countless individuals are destroyed through unwholesome depreciation of themselves and some have found a measure of self-esteem through practicing the suggested formulas. Insofar as positive thinking coincides at all with the data, it is certainly preferable to negative thinking. In this movement, however, both advantageous and disadvantageous features of a religious pilgrimage that gives primary place to self-affirmation are caricatured. What does this bold expression say about religion of becoming and its psychological economy in the human experience?

The limits of Pealeism are easily found. Theologically, positive thinking cuts divinity to an exceedingly small size, making God a convenient vehicle for self-help. It takes a Job's friends approach to human suffering, assuming that all problems derive from sin—here clearly seen as the unwillingness to confess negative thoughts and practice techniques that automatically produce positive attitudes. Little room is left for the suffering of the righteous or the inability to change unpleasant circumstances. There is no room for patience in tribulation and nobility in enduring inescapable suffering. Positive thinking assumes that all problems are surmountable through mentalism and overlooks the possibility for the genuinely heroic. Concern with ethics, especially in the area of social responsibility is relatively absent.

Psychologically, Pealeism fails to appreciate the ambiguity that often exists between wanting to change and the ability to change. It is simply untrue that circumstances can be changed by thinking change. Persons are often caught in psychological webs from which they cannot extricate themselves, especially by such simple formulas as repeating "I believe" three times each morning or going to church every Sunday for three months.

In short, positive thinking is both theologically and psychologically naive. In emphasizing the resources of persons, it elevates human beings to the place of worship and leaves no room for the sacrificial and the heroic. In setting forth far too simple self-help plans it reduces both maturation and salvation to thinking processes. Positive thinking promises more than it can deliver. Peale states candidly, "An inflow of new thoughts can remake you regardless of every difficulty you may face now, and I repeat—*every difficulty.*"[29] What happens when one prays, thinks positively, and goes to church, but the baby dies anyway?

Less exaggerated expressions of religion of becoming may take warning from positive thinking cults. Self-affirmation runs the risk of overconfidence in human potential, of fostering a romanticizing of the inner world to facilitate self-discovery at the expense of corporate, social responsibility. Why tamper with social structures when problems are essentially private? If religion of authority jeopardizes individual freedom for the reward of security, religion of becoming risks loss of authority, realism in hardship, and social responsibility for the reward of personal liberty and creative power.

In spite of its theological and psychological limitations, however, the religion of positive thinking has served well a coterie of devotees. First and foremost, in its utter simplicity this style of religion brings faith within reach of the common person. Clergy and classroom theologians may be sensitive to dialectical ideas and the intricacies of theological argument, but average believers are concerned with a religion that speaks to immediate, individual problems and harmonizes with their deep-rooted attitudes.[30] Particularly in Western industrialized culture the idea that complex problems can be resolved by human ingenuity and industry with the aid of scientific methods is deeply ingrained. Modern persons have grown accustomed to asking profound humanistic questions in a desacralized context. Issues of energy, pollution, population, and hunger are easily translated into how-to problems. The energy or hunger problem is then simply a matter of using human ingenuity to develop enough energy sources or to produce sufficient food. That these are complex problems whose resolution may entail altered life-styles and careful management of present resources is an option not easily entertained.

Peale's "simple steps" and "practical formulas" fall into the same category. They make complex problems sound easily resolvable and

---

[29]Ibid., 213.

[30]J. Milton Yinger, *The Scientific Study of Religion* (New York: Macmillan, 1970) 492.

bring the resolution close at hand. Persons can *do* something about their difficulties. For those whose guilt, suffering, and confusion lie deep in personal and social structures, Peale's approach is thoroughly disappointing. But others whose problems are not so complex may relish a religious life-style that is to the point of their experience, enjoys the aura of science and religion at the slogan level, and offers direct and recurring answers. In the American environment it is not surprising "that persons who are brought up hearing claims that a change to the correct soap can revolutionize your chances for marital happiness, or reading implications that if you improve your vocabulary by twenty words a day you may become a big executive, should respond favorably to 'the power of positive thinking.'"[31] It brings God within reach and makes happiness and success readily attainable.

The positive thinking cults may also be instructive in the matter of personal commitment being intensified by a sense of participation. On this point the findings of George M. Prince, a researcher on creativity, are informative. Prince has been particularly interested in operational creativity, that is, developing procedures to foster human creativity. He was instrumental in evolving synectics, a systematic way to produce good ideas, and participated in the organization of Synectics, Inc., a business designed to invent new products and sell them to appropriate companies to make and market. In the operation of Synectics, Inc., Prince observed a pattern that was repeated often enough to be impressive. A client would pay for an invention, the invention would occur, and subsequently the invention would languish with little or no further action by the purchasing company. Prince concluded that their lack of involvement in the creative process robbed them of motivation to follow through to completion. "In contrast, the groups we worked with who did their own inventing would overcome one monstrous difficulty after another until they had a marketable product."[32] Enormous and continuous energy and commitment seemed to be derived from authorship.

---

[31]Ibid., 161.

[32]George M. Prince, "Creativity, Self, and Power," in Taylor and Getzels, *Perspectives in Creativity*, 155.

Prince's observation regarding the relationship between creativity and commitment suggests a dynamic process that seems to be at work in positive thinking cults and generally in religion of becoming. To be sure, the positive thinkers ask their followers to practice techniques devised by charismatic leaders and promoted as exterior authority forms. In this sense positive thinking resembles religion of authority, which requires obedience as the first virtue. But more forcefully, the life-style demands self-assertion. Salvation requires personal involvement, even if only on a follow-these-easy-steps level. In caricature, God is used to generate personal power. Persons participate in their own salvation; in fact, redemption hinges upon the proper thought processes. If Prince is correct in his observation, then this active involvement is likely to increase the level of religious commitment—at least in using religious devices to maintain the proper attitude. Continuous assertion of self-confidence avoids the lackey effect that robs commitment of its psychic energy. The genuine believer is indeed working out his own salvation and derives energy from his involvement in the process.

The assets of positive thinking, however, do not compensate adequately for its liabilities. In caricature the movement appropriately stresses the need for a self-image that is worthy of defense and perpetuation; religion across centuries and cultures echoes an appreciation for the worth of human beings and appeals for the reinforcement of commitment through personal involvement. But Peale leaves his optimistic view of persons untempered by realism and undisciplined by social responsibility. "Bootstrap" redemption cannot resolve complex human problems. Those whose difficulties remain after the easy steps have been executed may be plagued with additional guilt because their problems have not gone away. Self-affirmation without self-criticism and social responsibility easily becomes self-indulgence. Those who follow religion of becoming with the most profit add acceptance of frailty to confidence, discipline to assertion, and sacrificial service to selfish desire.

SUGGESTED READINGS

Self-Affirmation

Barth, Karl. *The Humanity of God.* Atlanta: John Knox, 1960.

Berne, Eric. *Principles of Group Treatment.* New York: Grove, 1966. A pioneer in transactional analysis.

Boisen, Anton T. *The Exploration of the Inner World: A Study of Mental Disorder and Religious Experience.* New York: Harper, 1936. Autobiographical orientation. Affirms religion as vehicle for self-organization.

May, Rollo. *Man's Search for Himself.* New York: W. W. Norton, 1953. A sensitive, cautious statement on finding inner strength.

Rogers, Carl R. *Client-Centered Therapy.* Boston: Houghton-Mifflin, 1951. A standard work for an emphasis that has become an inspiration for therapeutic Christianity.

See also bibliography at end of Chapter 5.

Unitarianism

Allen, Joseph H. *Our Liberal Movement in Theology.* New York: Arno, 1972. Focuses on Unitarianism in New England.

Scholefield, Harry B., ed. *A Pocket Guide to Unitarianism.* Boston: Beacon Press, 1954. Brief statements by seven Unitarian clergymen.

Tapp, Robert B. *Religion among the Unitarian Universalists.* New York: Seminar, 1973. Careful statistical study that is psychologically suggestive.

Wright, Conrad. *Three Prophets of Religious Liberalism.* Boston: Beacon Press, 1961. Text of crucial addresses by Channing, Emerson, and Parker.

Positive Thinking

Meyer, Donald. *The Positive Thinkers.* Garden City NY: Doubleday, 1965.

Peale, Norman V. *A Guide to Confident Living,* Englewood Cliffs NJ: Prentice-Hall, 1948 or *The Power of Positive Thinking,* Englewood Cliffs NJ: Prentice-Hall, 1952. Peale has written extensively, but the same themes are repeated with numerous illustrations.

See also materials on Imagination in Suggested Readings for Chapter 7.

CHAPTER TWELVE

RELIGION OF SPONTANEITY: THE WAY OF MYSTICISM

A Benedictine monk passes through the court of a Kentucky monastery fingering his rosary, seemingly oblivious to the weather and the world. A Tibetan lama churns his miniature prayer wheel and quietly recites his mantra, "Om Mani Padme hum."[1] A Christian devotee in a church centers her attention on a cross over the altar and her consciousness of neighbors diminishes as she recollects an episode from religious history. A Sufi dervish whirls maddeningly to celebrate an experience of rapture in which truth is known. A Hasidic Jew wraps himself in a prayer shawl, as if to shut out the world, while he recites the Shema.

What do these devotees have in common? All belong to a contemplative tradition that cuts across religious systems and intends to deepen personal relationship with the divine. External objects of

---

[1] A mantra is a formula repeated over and over as a method for controlling consciousness. The mantra cited is a familiar one; there is little consensus on its proper translation and meaning.

experience, sometimes bodily functions themselves, are judged to be interruptions of the good life. Religious exercises ranging from mild to strenuous aim to cut through these external distractions to achieve an intimate relationship with the sacred. The highest goal is to overcome the ordinary, routine confinements of daily living and enter into full participation in a life of religious spontaneity.

THE CHARACTER OF RELIGION OF SPONTANEITY

Religion of spontaneity is a life-style that centers in self-transcending experiences. Since its goal is to move beyond the self, which is confined to time and space, the way may appropriately be thought of and understood in broad terms as a way of mysticism. In the most specific sense mysticism has been used as a synonym for ecstasy, a word literally meaning "to stand outside oneself."[2] In this narrow usage mysticism is associated with those extreme emotional states in which persons lose conscious control over their behavior, as in a trance. More broadly, however, the word designates all nonrational and superrational experience and includes a wide range of phenomena in which varying degrees of control are sacrificed. Not only extreme trance states, but also more modest experiences of inspiration and devotion in which sensitivity is heightened are included. Thus, mysticism includes at one extreme the loss of conscious, cognitive control and at the other extreme mild modifications in consciousness. All along the continuum the concern is to escape formalistic and rationalistic functions of personhood that are considered to oppress openness and sensitivity to the genuine life of the spirit.

The goal of the religious way of mysticism is more than escape from debilitating human forms. It further aims to transcend history, culture, and personality to attain unity, if not union, with God, and at least to allow deity to move in close upon the human spirit. Mystics may function in a religious community and come out of the mystical experience with an intense obligation to the community, but the mystical experience itself is intended to separate them from

---

[2]A valuable and comprehensive analysis of ecstasy is Marghanita Laski, *Ecstasy: A Study of Some Secular and Religious Experiences* (Bloomington: Indiana University Press, 1967).

ordinary affairs in order to "experience God on God's level."[3] Experiences of complete separation may be rare and episodic; indeed they may come only once in a lifetime, but for the mystic these are watershed moments, and the most captivating, powerful, and instructive experiences possible for human beings. In them intuition and illumination are brought into focus so that spiritual truth is known through directly apprehending and being apprehended by deity. The experience is nonrational (to be distinguished from irrational), immediate, and vividly real. Persons passing this way feel that they have inwardly transcended their human limitations and taken into themselves the life and character of the divine.

In religion of spontaneity emotion is the significant factor in the relationship with deity. Those who practice mysticism are not merely emotional about their religion, but they conceive emotion as the primary vehicle through which God is known. The Fundamentalist can be extremely emotional in defending an external code, but the ecstatic enthusiast believes that emotion is more dependable than cognition in the discovery of divinity. He presupposes that, to some degree, the divine spirit may make its abode with the human spirit in a relationship that resembles the intimacy that develops between lovers. This attitude is expressed vividly by a Persian Sufi named al-Hallaj: "Betwixt me and Thee there lingers an 'it is I' that torments me. Ah, of Thy grace, take away this 'I' from between us!"[4]

The religious hope implicit here is that the "I" may be taken away in order that the union may be perfected, an idea similar to the "Christ mysticism" expressed by the Christian Paul of Tarsus,[5]

For his sake I have thrown everything away; I consider it all as mere

---

[3]Martin E. Marty, "Religion Development in Historical, Social and Cultural Development," in Strommen, ed., *Research on Religious Development* (New York: Hawthorn, 1971) 44-45. See also J. Danielou, *God and the Ways of Knowing*, Walter Roberts, trans. (Chicago: World, 1957) 215ff.

[4]As quoted in Thomas Arnold and Alfred Guillaume, eds., *The Legacy of Islam* (Oxford: Clarendon Press, 1931) 218.

[5]The phrase should be used with some care. For Paul being "in Christ" meant the affirmation of his personal existence and communion with all others who belong to Christ.

garbage, so that I may gain Christ and be completely united with him. I no longer have a righteousness of my own, the kind that is gained by obeying the Law. I now have the righteousness that is given through faith in Christ, the righteousness that comes from God and is based on faith. All I want is to know Christ and to experience the power of his resurrection, to share in his sufferings, and become like him in his death, in the hope that I myself will be raised from death to life.[6]

Paul does not appear to be as willing as al-Hallaj to sacrifice his personal identity, but both share the goal of subjecting the personal "I" to the interest of the divine. Both are willing to stand outside themselves in order to be "filled by the Spirit."

The religious life-style described here both resembles and differs from religion of authority. Both styles willingly accept God's power over human events, but the two types understand their relationship to providential control quite differently.[7] Religion of authority defines authority as external and devotes its energy to justifying and sustaining an authority assumed to have the *right* to control. The devotee, as it were, aims to keep distance between himself and the authority, objectifying it in creed, code, and liturgy to which is owed unqualified obedience. Goodenough refers to this as "blue-print religion," that which shows a person "how he should act in legalism, believe in orthodoxy, feel according to given artistic conventions, obey in the church."[8]

Religion of spontaneity, on the other hand, aims to move in close upon deity or have deity move in close upon the devotee. The purpose is to become so identified with divinity that divine life itself permeates human life. Religious practices attempt to place the self in a position for this to happen, to eliminate interferences, to "will one thing," and to permit "the Spirit to have its way."

The mystical way is also similar to but different from religion of becoming. They share confidence in the experiential aspects of

---

[6]Philippians 3:8b-11.

[7]Capps, Donald and Walter Capps, *The Religious Personality* (Belmont CA: Wadsworth, 1970) 5.

[8]Goodenough, Edwin R. *The Psycology of Religious Experiences* (New York: Basic Books, 1965) 151.

faith; both are convinced that the holy may be found in moments of inspiration and insight. Yet, the two ways explain peak religious experiences differently. Religion of becoming sees them as the upsurge of inherent qualities, the breakthrough of human virtue. For religion of spontaneity, however, such high moments come only when the self is overcome or bypassed so that authentic reality may intrude upon human experience.

The mood of religion of spontaneity is ambiguous, to say the least. The divine presence that is earnestly desired is also overwhelming and frightening. Nearness breeds fear because the presence of the Almighty heightens awareness of pride, obstinacy, and sin. Thus, those who pursue mysticism often agonize over human frailties that disrupt relationships with deity, and live with suffering as their constant companion.[9] Their estrangement causes them to feel that they have drunk from the cup of divine wrath and have been cut off from the land of the living. Like the prophet Jeremiah, they may even complain with impatience, and perhaps some bitterness, that their sufferings have not been vindicated by the righteous God.

> *Lord, you have deceived me,*
>   *and I was deceived.*
> *You are stronger than I am,*
>   *and you have overpowered me.*
>
> *Curse the day I was born!*
> *Forget the day my mother*
>   *gave me birth!*
> *Curse the man who made my father glad*
>   *when he brought him the news,*
> *"It's a boy! You have a son!"*[10]

But the mood of this religious life-style is also marked by optimism and hope. The agony of suffering is balanced by a sense of

---

[9]Compare William James on "the sick soul," *The Varieties of Religious Experience* (New York: Modern Library, 1902) 125-62; also Rudolph Otto, *The Idea of the Holy* (New York: Oxford University Press, 1923).

[10]Jeremiah 20:7a, 14-15.

purpose in suffering. To suffer is to have the dross burned out so that the holy deity may draw near. Since identification with the divine is the goal of religious life, pain can be endured. The peak of genuine encounter with "the presence" justifies the drudgery. Thus, the sustaining force for religion of spontaneity is anticipation of the high moment in which God's nearness is experienced in a peculiar way. From this ensues a special knowledge of the Almighty and the claim that this makes on human experience.

PSYCHO-THEOLOGICAL INTERPRETATIONS OF MYSTICISM

Two better known classical interpretations of the mystic way come from William James and Evelyn Underhill.[11] Although each sees the phenomenon from slightly differing perspectives, their descriptions overlap considerably and taken together provide a comprehensive view of this extraordinary experience.

In *Varieties* James disclaims any personal enjoyment of mysticism, but he spends an entire chapter to convince his audience that these states are real and of paramount importance for the psychology of religion. According to James, mysticism, like religion itself, defies precise definition but may be marked off from other states of consciousness by four characteristics:[12]

1 *Ineffability.* The mystic is unable to put his experience into words. Mystical states are more "states of feeling than states of intellect." It is as impossible to describe the mystical experience to one who has not had it as to describe a symphony to one who has never heard music.

2 *Noetic quality.* These experiences transmit knowledge of a special sort. "They are states of insight into depths of truth unplumbed by the discursive intellect." They reveal and illuminate, although they remain inarticulate.

---

[11]W. T. Stace, *Mysticism and Philosophy* (Philadelphia: Lippincott, 1960) is not as well known as the writings of James and Underhill and is intuitive in its approach, but nonetheless is an extensive and valuable study.

[12]James, *The Varieties of Religious Experience,* 370-72.

3 *Transiency.* The mystical state is fleeting. It cannot be maintained for long periods of time, rarely over thirty minutes, and often can be only imperfectly reproduced in memory.

4 *Passivity.* In mysticism the participant feels "grasped and held by a superior power." The mystic may fix his attention or do bodily exercises to induce the state, but once the state of consciousness has set in the participant feels carried along beyond any exercise of will.

Evelyn Underhill, a practitioner of mysticism over many years, has written a sizable volume entitled *Mysticism: A Study in the Nature and Development of Man's Spiritual Consciousness.* In the book she wishes to encourage contemplation as the human activity by which a person enhances life, breaks the barrier of personality, "escapes the sense-world, ascends to the apex of his spirit, and enters for a brief period into the more extended life of the All."[13] Underhill marks out several characteristics of this type of experience:[14]

1 Mysticism is "*active and practical,* not passive and theoretical." The mystic disciplines the self in the contemplative way, rather than idly waiting for the experience to occur.

2 Mysticism is *transcendental* and *spiritual,* setting its heart on the "changeless one," not on the visible universe.

3 Mysticism sees *divinity as an object to be loved,* not as an object for exploration.

4 Mysticism aims to achieve the *unitive state,* a definite form of enhanced life in which latent forms of consciousness are released to remake one's character.

5 True mysticism is *never self-seeking.*

Underhill then describes the mystic way as a clearly-marked path by which mysticism progresses toward intensity. The steps in the process are (1) awakening, (2) purification, (3) illumination, (4) the "dark night of the soul," and (5) the unitive state. She thus perceives the experience to involve gradual ascent, not without struggle, by which the full powers of selfhood become realized.

---

[13]Evelyn Underhill, *Mysticism: A Study in the Nature and Development of Man's Spiritual Consciousness* (New York: Meridian, 1955) 74.

[14]Ibid., 81ff.

The Underhill and James models portray religion of spontaneity in dramatic form. They offer devotees disciplines through which they may become open to definite but sporadic religious states in which persons are extremely sensitive to divine presence. These intense moments are "so unusually personal as to defy description in any but the most figurative and cryptic language. It involves the apprehension of a transcendental Presence which radically influences the individual's point of view and way of life."[15] Although such experiences may be limited in number and quite transient, they represent the best that happens in religion and foster values beyond the ordinary and stimulate ongoing commitment to deity known in the high moment. In short, these fleeting moments serve to integrate personhood around an invading spirit.

The mystical emphasis has a cherished history in religion, both in the East and West. Mystics are not always cut from the same pattern; mysticism is not the same in all places and in all ages.[16] But whenever or wherever mysticism appears, its theme is that the deity moves directly upon the human spirit, whose chief end it is to remain open to the unanticipated ways of divine intervention.

Mystics tend to elevate their experience above "ordinary" religion, but mystical features lie at the heart of all religious enterprises that stress the importance of a primary encounter with the divine. For some the meeting may be intensely emotional and private; for others it may be more pedestrian and ordinary. But in either case "the primary element of all religion" is "religious feeling understood as an immediate, spontaneous, connatural response to transcendent reality."[17] The practicing mystic allows that sense to dominate consciousness. "No experience will bring to the individual a vividness of religious certainty equal to that enjoyed by the mystic."[18]

---

[15]Walter H. Clark, *The Psychology of Religion* (New York: Macmillan, 1958) 275.

[16]See Rudolf Otto, *Mysticism: East and West: A Comparative Analysis of the Nature of Mysticism,* Bertha L. Bracey and and Richenda C. Payne, trans. (New York: Macmillan, 1970).

[17]Charles Davis, *Body as Spirit: The Nature of Religious Feeling* (New York: Seabury Press,1976) 34.

[18]Clark, *The Psychology of Religion,* 262.

VARIATIONS ON THE MYSTICISM THEME

How does the life of religious spontaneity come about? The nature of mysticism itself makes it difficult to program without the forms interfering with the experience. The task is to brush aside the visible universe to allow free reign to spirit. Those ordinarily concerned with getting and spending, eating and sleeping, living and dying must in some way surpass these routine concerns to embrace the refreshing inspiration of the ultimate. Hence, various religious traditions are marked by efforts to cultivate the mystical style, as for example the yoga tradition in Hinduism, contemplative prayer in Buddhism, or meditative techniques in several religions. One discipline that cuts across many groups as a vehicle for inducing the mystical state has been asceticism.

Asceticism

Religion of spontaneity may seek its purposes through asceticism, a life-style which assumes that preoccupation with the human body may be a major threat to full expressions of the inward life or maximum invasion of human life by the divine. The key to asceticism is withdrawal. The ascetic hopes that by withdrawal from the demands of the secular world, which includes often those things considered necessary for physical survival, contact may be made with the ultimate and life may become more "spiritual." Withdrawal from these ordinary pursuits of self-interest is perceived in terms of discipline and denial. Human beatitude is not the fulfillment of basic personal needs, but forsaking those needs in the interest of higher values. In this sense asceticism differs from delayed gratification, an attitude that postpones satisfaction because of social demands or because other needs are given priority.[19] Asceticism assumes that needs are deterrents to the genuinely good life and therefore must be forsaken or at least minimized in order to nurture the arrival of full spiritual blessing.

In its milder forms asceticism appears in the traditional teachings of Christianity on self-denial that are typically built upon Jesus's admonition to his disciples, "If anyone wants to come with me,

---

[19]See above, pp. 236-41.

he must forget himself, carry his cross, and follow me."[20] Often the verse is interpreted in its least demanding form as "denying things to oneself" and comes out in moralistic statements that prohibit smoking, drinking, or using cosmetics. This is a kind of poor man's asceticism, socialized and cut down to an easily manageable size for those who prefer the ascetic way in modest doses. At the other extreme asceticism engages in severe bodily mortification as is vividly illustrated in a Philippine Christian cult that celebrates the crucifixion by nailing a volunteer "Christ" to a cross; or the Chinese Buddhist Bodhidharma, who supposedly meditated for nine years with his face to a wall; or the fourteenth century German mystic Suso, who wore a leather girdle with a hundred and fifty sharply filed brass nails pointed toward his flesh. Extreme forms of denial, mortification, and flagellation of the body are practiced in order to escape this-worldliness.[21]

Between these extremes is monastic asceticism, which intends the disciplined control of usual desire in order to "practice the presence of God" but avoids the excesses of irrational self-torture. It takes self-denial more seriously than mere sacrifice of luxury, but does not try to erase the body. Monasticism aims to develop "a systematic method of rational conduct with the purpose of overcoming the *status naturae,* to free man from the power of irrational impulses and his dependence on the world and on nature."[22] Although Roman Catholic medieval monasticism was sometimes marked by excesses, the best in that tradition aimed to bring actions under control as a means to discover the ultimate purposes of life and to act with ethical responsibility. The Roman Catholic theologian Thomas Merton describes the high purposes of monasticism.

> The monk is sanctified by living the monastic life in all its fullness, all its wholeness, . . . one is almost tempted to say, a whole new

---

[20]Matthew 16:24.

[21]Max Weber saw other-worldly asceticism as a chief characteristic of orthodox Hinduism. See his *The Religion of India: The Sociology of Hinduism and Buddhism,* Hans H. Gerth and Don Martindale, trans. (Glencoe IL: Free Press, 1958) 146f.

[22]Max Weber, *The Protestant Ethic and the Spirit of Capitalism,* Talcott Parsons, trans. (New York: Scribner's, 1958) 118-19.

mode of being.

....

In living this life "in the Spirit," one is purified of inordinate passion, becomes humble, pliable, docile to the divine teaching, and eventually perfect in charity.[23]

The most noble features of monastic asceticism may be observed in the winsome St. Francis of Assisi, "a world-figure Christ in a medieval incarnation."[24] An intense religious experience led St. Francis as a young man to turn his back upon earthly possessions (with the encouragement of a father who disinherited him for being too slothful in business) and become "married to Lady Poverty." His entire life was given to plainness, simplicity, and benevolence: following the "the rule of Christ" as he saw it in the New Testament. He worked or begged for food, wore unadorned clothing, and devoted himself to preaching to and caring for the poor, the sick, and the outcast. His concern for persons was matched by a sensitivity to nature so that he reportedly preached to the birds and the beasts.[25] St. Francis was so devoted to poverty and altruism that he on one occasion forbade a novice the ownership of a psalter on the grounds that any possession would threaten his concern for the rule of Christ and eventually risk his saying to an associate, "Bring me my psalter!" Quite contrary to the Hebrew Deuteronomist who praised Yahweh for blessings given as reward for faithfulness or the householder in Jesus' parable who built new and bigger barns to store his bounty or the materialist of any age who identifies personal worth with possessions, St. Francis perceived the difference between what persons *are* and what they *have* and forsook the latter in the interest of the former. By giving up all that he had and assuming the role of a servant, St. Francis enacted asceticism at its best—the vision of overcoming selfish desires for fellowship with the Holy Spirit.[26]

---

[23]Thomas Merton, *Mystics and Zen Masters* (New York: Farrar, Straus and Giroux, 1961) 155.

[24]John B. Noss, *Man's Religions*, 5th ed. (New York: Macmillan, 1974) 473.

[25]Modern depictions of St. Francis typically show him with animals.

[26]Compare Philippians 2:1-11.

Monastic asceticism has psychological parallels in the Protestant tradition. Max Weber sees the same dynamics at work in the Puritan ideals of separation from worldly practices. Contrary to many popular stereotypes, Puritans were not just blue-nosed legalists. The goal of their asceticism was an alert, intelligent life. They, like the Roman Catholic monastics, intended a rational asceticism. Through the destruction of spontaneous, impulsive enjoyment and methodical control over the whole person, Puritans hoped to bring order into the conduct of their adherents.[27] Numerous American Protestant groups share wholly or partially the Puritan attitude.

Consciousness-Expanding Drugs

Recently, attempts have been made to produce self-transcendent consciousness through the use of psychedelic (mind expanding) drugs, including psilocybin, mescaline, and LSD. Such substances have been used for religious purposes over many centuries, and a notable example is the use of mescaline derived from the peyote cactus by a group of American Indians. The experience associated with the ingestion of these drugs dramatically resembles the spontaneous mystical experience. Since the early 1960s, the relationship between the phenomena has been the subject of significant research and considerable reaction.

An elaborate and carefully controlled experiment to examine the claims of similarity between psychedelic drug experience and mysticism has been conducted by Walter Pahnke.[28] First, a nine-category typology of the mystical state was carefully defined from primary reports of mystics and descriptions of scholars who have examined the mystical experience. Then, drug experiences were studied empirically to determine the correlations between the ex-

---

[27]Weber, *The Protestant Ethic and the Spirit of Capitalism*, 119.

[28]Pahnke's original work was reported in his unpublished doctoral dissertation at Harvard in 1963. The experiment is summarized in his article, "Drugs and Mysticism," *International Journal of Parapsychology* 8 (1966): 295-314, which is included in L. B. Brown, ed., *Psychology and Religion* (Baltimore: Penguin, 1973) 301-19. See also his article with William A. Richards, "Implications of LSD and Experimental Mysticism," *Journal of Religion and Health* 5 (1966): 175-208.

periences of the drug users and the nine categories of mystical consciousness. Pahnke employed a double-blind procedure, so that
neither subjects nor experimenters knew which was the control or
experimental group. The drug used with the experimental group
was psilocybin; the control group ingested nicotinic acid, a vitamin
that produces warmth and tingling but no psychedelic effects.

After five hours of earlier preparation and screening, twenty
Christian theological students who had volunteered for the experiment attended a Good Friday religious service. Half the group had
been given the psychedelic drug and half the placebo. Data regarding their reactions were collected during the experiment and
at various times up to six months afterwards and carefully analyzed
according to the nine-category typology of mystical experience. The
analysis demonstrated that "the experimentals as a group achieved
to a statistically significant degree a higher score in each of the nine
categories than did the controls."[29] Subjects who received psilocybin in the supporting setting of a religious service apparently experienced phenomena quite similar to the experience of the mystic.

However, the results were not uniform. What could be said for
the experimentals as a group could not be said for them as individuals. Persons receiving the same doses of psilocybin varied considerably in the intensity and completeness of their response, leading
Pahnke to conclude "that the 'drug effect' is a delicate combination
of psychological set and setting in which the drug itself is the trigger or facilitating agent."[30] For some in the experiment the drug
was a *necessary* but not a *sufficient* condition for the full mystical experience.

The Pahnke experiment, which has become the starting point
for subsequent discussions of this problem, demonstrates that mind-
expanding drugs can produce states quite like mystical experience,
but reactions are not automatic and consistent. Personal and social
factors seem to influence the results. For those steeped in rigidity
and rationality, psychedelic drugs may perform the important
function of releasing feelings, but the faith with which persons en-

---

[29]Pahnke, "Drugs and Mysticism," in Brown, ed., *Psychology and Religion*, 309.
[30]Ibid., 315.

ter the drug experience is likely to be substantially the faith that they bring out of the experience. Walter Clark, who himself has examined this question for over a decade,[31] believes that he has confirmed Pahnke's findings. He suggests as a conservative hypothesis: "In some situations and with some people, and especially when both subject and guide intend it, the psychedelic drugs release very profound religious experience of a mystical nature."[32]

The intricate philosophical and ethical arguments about psychedelic drugs are too complex to be rehearsed here, but two observations seem appropriate to the psychological understanding of the phenomenon. First, as a trigger or inducing agent the use of psychedelic drugs is of the same psychological order as numerous other religious rituals. Paul Pruyser suggests a wide variety of inducing agents used by the religious community to intensify their perceptual acumen: "demanding physical exercises, dietary experiments, regulated breathing, posturing, and dancing, through the ingestion of toxins, through sleep deprivation and exposure to noxious stimuli, through concentrated medications or rhythmic shouting and handclapping."[33] In addition the more ordinary and less dramatic acts of planned worship (standing, sitting, bowing, singing, and meditating) are inducement devices. From the purely functional point of view, no qualitative differences can be made among those measures, including the use of psychedelic drugs. All are the triggers used for a desired religious experience that does not derive its value from the nature of inducement.

But psychedelic drugs are not merely one among several inducement items. These substances enjoy neither social approval nor sacred tradition. Further, evidence regarding the possible harm of the drugs is not clear. H. Newton Malony's remark seems appropriate: "There is a question as to whether religionists can continue

---

[31]See Walter H. Clark, *Chemical Ecstasy: Psychedelic Drugs and Religion* (New York: Sheed and Ward, 1969).

[32]Clark, et al., *Religious Experience: Its Nature and Function in the Human Psyche* (Springfield IL: Charles C. Thomas, 1973) 19.

[33]Paul Pruyser, *A Dynamic Psychology of Religion* (New York: Harper, 1968) 22.

to utilize so controversial a 'trigger.' Are there not more benign means of achieving the same ends?"[34]

Second, indiscriminate use of drugs to induce religious experience risks the promotion of what Huston Smith calls the religion of religious experience, a kind of faith "bent on the acquisition of desired states of experience irrespective of their relation to life's other demands and components."[35] Smith, who is sympathetic with controlled drug experimentation, is suspicious that drugs may induce religious experiences without producing religious lives. If religion cannot survive *without* religious experience, it also cannot endure for long *on* experience alone. Zen Buddhism consequently insists that once the devotee has attained *satori* (enlightenment) he must be driven back into the real world where discipline shapes daily life. Smith concludes, "Chemicals *can* aid the religious life, but only where set within a context of faith (meaning by this the conviction that what they disclose is true) and discipline (meaning diligent exercise of the will in the attempt to work out the implications of the disclosures for the living of life in the everyday, common-sense world)."[36]

Both asceticism and consciousness-expanding drugs are means to an end, and must be tested minimally by the criteria of faith and discipline.

DYNAMICS OF THE MYSTIC WAY

Attempts to account for mysticism as a religious life-style differ considerably on its dynamics. Some are inclined to follow Leuba's evaluation that the mystic way is a type of reaction of persons who are emotionally and sexually deprived.[37] Others are more generous and acknowledge the positive contributions that outstanding

---

[34]In Clark, et al., *Religious Experience*, 88.

[35]Huston Smith, "Do Drugs Have Religious Import?" *The Journal of Philosophy* 61 (1964): 529.

[36]Ibid., 530.

[37]J. H. Leuba, *The Psychology of Religious Mysticism* (New York: Harcourt Brace, 1925). Compare Herbert Moller, "Affective Mysticism in Western Civilization," *Psychoanalytic Review* 52 (1965): 115-30.

mystics have made toward human advancement.[38] Clark notes that Moses came to lead Israel out of bondage after he encountered the Holy in a bush that was burning but not consumed. St. Francis of Assisi deserted wealth and began his unique career following an intense religious awakening. A crucial mystical experience turned Pascal toward religion, and St. Teresa was little more than a hysterical hypochondriac before a mystical vision transformed her into an effective administrator and reformer.[39] Such religious stalwarts as the German Dominican, Meister Eckhart; the famous author of *The Imitation of Christ,* Thomas à Kempis; the Hindu philosopher, Sankara; the founder of Hasidic Judaism, Israel of Moldavia; the founder of the Society of Friends, George Fox; the vigorous advocate of Rinzai Zen, Daisetz T. Suzuki; and countless others may not be dismissed as mere religious eccentrics. The maturity of those who pursue religion of spontaneity is to be judged by the same criteria as are those who follow other religious life-styles, but mystics may not be summarily dismissed as neurotics or psychotics.[40]

Several observations may suggest the psychological dynamics of the mystic way. First, mysticism may be partially understood as the uninhibited affirmation of basic human values. Here it is informative to note mysticism's kinship with Maslow's peak-experiences, which he described as "secularized religious or mystical or transcendent experiences."[41] Mystics could easily use Maslow's list of characteristics of the peak experience to describe their own awakening: perception of the universe as integrated and unified, self-validating, ego-transcending, disorientation in time and space, wonder and awe, and unitive consciousness.[42] Maslow held that

---

[38]See for example Wayne Oates, *The Psychology of Religion* (Waco TX: Word Books, 1973) 118-22.

[39]Walter H. Clark, "Intense Religious Experience," in Strommen, ed., *Research on Religious Development,* 524-25.

[40]See Ralph Hood, Jr., "Psychological Strength and the Report of Intense Religious Experience," *Journal for the Scientific Study of Religion* 13 (1974): 65-71.

[41]Abraham Maslow, *Religions, Values, and Peak-Experiences* (New York: Viking, 1964) 59.

[42]Ibid., 59-68.

these higher experiences were instinctoid, that is, rooted in the basic needs of persons. Transcendent aesthetic, creative, and religious urges are as basic and permanent to personality as sexuality is and they rank higher on the hierarcheal scale of human values. The expression of these superior values comes not through passivity, but by way of intention and discipline. Persons learn to handle their feelings as they might learn to play a musical instrument. Thus, for Maslow mystical experiences were not mysterious at all, but testimony to a disciplined life tapping the higher values inherent in personhood. Underhill would heartily agree.

Second, some facets of mysticism may be accounted for by heightened perception. Wayne Oates emphasizes that the basic difference between the mystic and nonmystic "lies in the capacity to perceive."[43] He likens the mystical experience to empathetic listening in counseling "in which the boundaries between selves as objects are relaxed and selves as subjects begin to flow back and forth into each other with such depth that a Third Presence soon becomes vivid and very real even if names for this Presence are never called."[44] This feature is most attractive to those who advocate the use of psychedelic drugs to induce expanded consciousness.

Third, the language of the mystic is often replete with images of sexuality; the favorite metaphor for relationship to the divine seems to be marriage. The possibility for seeing such language as a thin veneer covering repressed sexuality or as sublimation of unexpressed emotional needs is certainly present. Many mystics may find in their sense of intimacy with the divine kinds of satisfaction that are unfulfilled in their relationships with persons, but the psychologist must guard against making the same kind of literalistic assumptions that the Fundamentalist makes about biblical materials. The ineffable dimension of mysticism makes extensive use of figurative language necessary, and the mystic's claim that sex and marriage images are used as analogies should be taken seriously. This caution notwithstanding, the relationship between the

---

[43]Oates, *The Psychology of Religion*, 119.

[44]Ibid., 120.

intimacy of mysticism and the intimacy of sexuality suggests one way in which the dynamics of mysticism may be understood.[45]

A fourth item that may serve as a model for the psychological interpretation of mysticism is fantasy. Usually fantasy suggests flights of escape into a private world marked by illusion and hallucination. Mystical experiences tend to exalt visions and auditions that are hallucinatory in character, but mysticism does not sanction hallucination as the voice of God. The type of piety that insists upon hallucination being considered religious is as materialistic as "those forms of skepticism which attempt to explain events in purely materialistic terms."[46]

The beatific vision is not hallucination.[47] It is rather a temporary interruption that must be translated into real action in a real world. In this sense the beatific vision is constructive fantasy; "it functions as a temporary detour to reality adaptation."[48] For example, the child with an imaginary playmate indulges fantasy but not hallucination. The experience is an interlude by which the child adjusts to the environment. Can mysticism be compared to a fantasy interlude without implying that it is either childish or unreal? Mysticism, like fantasy, may separate persons from the ordinary routine long enough for life to be seen from a different perspective. The ultimate test comes in whether or not the mystic returns from the freshening experience to mobilize human potential in a real world. In this sense healthy mysticism has inevitable moral consequences.

Fifth, the general psychoanalytic formula of infantile desires for escape and security have been applied to mysticism.[49] Accordingly,

---

[45]Cf. Ralph Wood, Jr., and J. R. Hall, "Gender Differences in the Description of Erotic and Mystical Experiences," *Review of Religious Research* 21 (1980): 195-207.

[46]G. Stephens Spinks, *Psychology and Religion: An Introduction to Contemporary Views* (Boston: Beacon Press, 1963) 159.

[47]See Underhill, *Mysticism,* 226ff.

[48]Pruyser, *A Dynamic Psychology of Religion,* 301.

[49]See for example M. Ostrow and B. A. Scharfstein, *The Need to Believe: The Psychology of Religion* (New York: International Universities, 1954) 115-25.

the mystic's union with God represents the reappearance in new forms of the old infantile wish to return to the succor and security of the mother's breast. This interpretation is given some support by Spangler's comparative study of the backgrounds of twenty-five mystics and twenty-five schizophrenics.[50] He found that both groups tended toward withdrawal and dependency. Such elements undoubtedly exist in individual mystical experiences, but the interpretation suffers from the overgeneralized approach of psychoanalysis to religion and does not take seriously the insistence of many mystics that the high moment of mysticism be translated into positive and responsible social action.

Finally, sociocultural factors must also be considered in understanding mysticism. Belonging to a tradition or sharing in a group that sanctions such behavior obviously provides support and encouragement to what might otherwise be considered eccentric, if not abnormal.

Not one of these factors, nor perhaps all of them together, is comprehensive enough to fathom the recesses of individual mystical experience. As James has said, mystical reality deifies the spoken or printed word, but this in no sense invalidates the deep categories of human life nor makes neurotics of those who attempt to release them.

PENTECOSTALISM:
A CASE STUDY IN CARICATURE

During the twentieth century, an important development for religion of spontaneity has occurred within mainstream Christianity. The movement is the rise of numerous Holiness and Pentecostal denominations. In the early decades of this century Pentecostals represented a kind of frantic fringe of Protestantism in the United States, but more recently, especially since World War II, these groups have grown dramatically, attracted an increasing proportion of middle-class adherents, and generally have become less sus-

---

[50]J. D. Spangler, "Becoming a Mystic: An Analysis of Developmental Factors According to the Murray 'Need-Press' Theory" Ph.D. dissertation, Brown University, 1961, as reported in Walter H. Clark, "Intense Religious Experience," in Merton P. Strommen, ed. *Research on Religious Development*, 524.

pect by Protestant officialdóm. Charismatic groups within conventional churches that have adopted some of the spirit-oriented ideas of Pentecostalism have generated additional sympathy for the movement. Pentecostalism and its spin-off influence upon other denominations portray boldly the religion of spontaneity.

The Pentecostal Movement

Pentecostals seem to agree that the Pentecostal experience is not a recent innovation and that in one form or another has been present throughout Christian history. As a modern movement it has roots in the Wesley tradition as expressed in the red-hot Methodism promoted by George Whitefield. Its incubator was what some perceived as the theological stagnation and moral lethargy of post-Civil War American religion. Protesting against religious inertia and cold formalism, "the complacent, prosperity-ridden coldly formalistic Church and its members,"[51] a group of "Holiness" folk set out to discover a way of separation and perfection by which a depraved and doomed soul could find a more "spiritual" religion.

Pentecostalism is a daughter of the Holiness movement of the late nineteenth century. It burst forth on the American scene around the activities of Charles Parham, an unlettered preacher who operated Bethel Bible College in Topeka, Kansas. In 1901 after extended prayer and Bible study, the few students at Bethel testified that they had experienced "baptism of the Holy Spirit" and been granted the gift of speaking in "other tongues." The enthusiasm and missionary vigor of Parham's early student converts, although not initially successful, after several years caused Kansas, Missouri, and Texas to become Pentecostal strongholds. From that tri-state base the movement fanned out across the United States and, with the assistance of the Yale-trained evangelist R. A. Torrey, to Europe as well. Adherents who looked for a fresh touch from God were convinced that they had received the touch by being filled with the Spirit and proclaimed their confidence with an enthusiasm rarely equaled in church history.

During the first decade of the Pentecostal revival, these believers continued to think of themselves as Methodists, Baptists, or Lu-

---

[51]John T. Nichol, *Pentecostalism* (New York: Harper, 1966) 26.

therans, and as different only in their emphasis upon the need for the blessing of the Holy Spirit. By the teens and twenties, however, new denominations such as the Pentecostal Holiness Church, the Church of God, and Assemblies of God had come to be identified by their Pentecostal emphases and become bulwarks of the movement. In recent years the movement has again broken out of its denominational bounds in "Neo-Pentecostalism," a phrase generally designating groups within the conventional denominations that have returned to the informal life of the Spirit, particularly to tongue-speaking. Thus, Neo-Pentecostalism does not belong to mainstream Pentecostalism, but represents groups from within established denominations, both Protestant and Roman Catholic, that since the mid-fifties have adapted the Pentecostal emphasis upon tongue-speaking and other "gifts of the Spirit." Both Pentecostalism and Neo-Pentecostalism are held together by the firm conviction that all Christians are called to the full life of the Spirit and thus represent religion of.spontaneity in bold forms.

The Holiness-Pentecostal movement has a simple and straightforward message: "The only problem in the world is sin. The only way to overcome sin is through an encounter with God and its resulting special experience, thus arousing the will to perfect sanctification or a life free from sin, both of which assure one of being among the saved in the golden age to come, for which one only need wait in patient holiness."[52]

Sanctification, or the complete cleansing of the believer from indwelling sin and its pollution, is an important belief in this religious life-style. The discipline of the Pentecostal Holiness Church includes negative sanctions against the use of tobacco and intoxicants in any form, filthiness of speech, foolish talking, gossip, jesting, immodest or extravagant dress, and doing pleasure on Sunday. The Pentecostal perception of these moral proscriptions differs, however, from the ethical stance of religion of authority. The moral regulations are not means to the good life but measures of the Spirit's presence. Violation of the prohibitions is a sure sign of the departure of the Spirit and demands a return to the disciplines of

---

[52]Joseph R. Washington, *Black Sects and Cults* (Garden City NY: Doubleday, 1973) 60-61.

prayer, meditation, and worship. In Pentecostalism the "Spirit-filled" church is a powerful agent for assuring the presence of the Holy Spirit in its members, and ethical behavior, which is defined quite specifically, is an external manifestation of the Spirit's presence. But an even more significant demonstration is tongue-speaking.

Glossolalia

The most startling feature of Pentecostalism has been glossolalia,[53] or "speaking with other tongues." The worshiper, usually under the impress of intense emotional excitement, utters a series of disconnected, unstructured "syllables." Although the utterances exhibit vocalization patterns that can be measured, they are non-communicative as language.[54] The tongue-speaker uses ordinary vowel and consonant sounds, but strings them together haphazardly. Speed, volume, and inflection may leave the impression of sentences, but decoding and translating are impossible.[55]

In Pentecostalism glossolalia is an expected and highly desirable experience available to all believers, the capstone of a progressively intense relation with God. Salvation is perceived to come in three stages: regeneration, sanctification, and baptism with the Holy Spirit. The final stage comes to the sanctified believer (fully cleansed from sin) when the Holy Spirit comes down, takes up residence within a person, and generates a blessed state of unimagined ecstasy. The believer is unable to describe what happens except by analogy, but the necessary sign and ultimate assurance that he has been baptized with the Holy Spirit is glossolalia. This is the superlative gift of the Spirit. The "other tongue" is more the language of the Spirit than the words of the practitioner. A Pen-

---

[53]The technical term is formed from two common Greek words, *glossa* (tongue) and *lalein* (to speak).

[54]Compare Felicitas D. Goodman, *Speaking in Tongues: A Cross Cultural Study* (Chicago: University of Chicago Press, 1972) 121-25.

[55]Charles Parham mistakenly interpreted tongue-speaking as the gift of foreign language and so advised his students to cease their study of biblical languages and envisioned the possibility of missionaries no longer needing to learn the native language.

tecostal describes his experience of glossolalia as a "manifestation of the mind of the Spirit of God employing human speech organs. When man is speaking with tongues, his mind, intellect, understanding are quiescent. It is the faculty of God that is active. Man's will, certainly, is active, and his spirit, and his speech organs; but the mind that is operating is the mind of God through the Holy Spirit."[56]

The Pentecostal is convinced that tongue-speaking is justified by biblical teachings. Special emphasis is placed on the day of Pentecost as reported in Acts 2. The outpouring of the Holy Spirit is believed to be, as Peter's speech in the chapter suggests, the fulfillment of a prophecy in Hebrew Scriptures.

> *Afterward I will pour out my*
> *spirit on everyone;*
> *Your sons and daughters will*
> *proclaim my message*
> *and your young men will see visions.*[57]

Further, the outpouring of the Spirit with accompanying glossolalia remains a relevant, recurring phenomenon consistent with the promise, "But when the Holy Spirit comes upon you, you will be filled with power."[58] Armed with what is interpreted as biblical support, the Pentecostal cements self in a religious community where glossolalia "is the single most powerful cohesive factor."[59]

The unusual character of glossolalia has attracted the attention of the scholarly world, and an extensive bibliography has developed around the attempt to understand the experience as a psychological-religious phenomenon.[60] Interpretations have varied from the straightforward affirmation of glossolalia as a supernatural manifestation of the Holy Spirit to be understood with no psy-

---

[56]Cited in Nichol, *Pentecostalism*, 11-12.

[57]Joel 2:28.

[58]Acts 1:8.

[59]Goodman, *Speaking in Tongues*, 88.

[60]An extensive bibliography may be found in John P. Kildahl, *The Psychology of Speaking in Tongues* (New York: Harper, 1972) 87-106.

chological rubrics, to the curt dismissal of tongue-speaking as psychoticism or severe neuroticism.

Attempts to assess the dynamics of glossolalia must take into account several interrelated features. (1) Tongue-speaking depends upon openness of personality and may, therefore, resemble other experiences that expand one's consciousness of psychic reality. (2) The bulk of those engaged in the Neo-Pentecostal movement seem to share a deep need for personal security and emotional expression.[61] (3) Glossolalia bears some semblance to children's language and consequently raises a whole series of questions regarding repression and relation to authority.[62] (4) What happens to people induced to speak in tongues is similar to the process of hypnotism;[63] both entail high levels of confidence in significant leaders. (5) Glossolalia fails to meet the linguistic requirements of human language and may represent severe dissociative behavior.[64] Whether or not individuals who speak in tongues are judged to be healthy or unhealthy, the behavior is no ordinary, everyday occurrence. As the birthmark of Pentecostalism, glossolalia sets the movement apart as an illustration in caricature of a spontaneous religious life-style. No forms, not even those of daily speech, can contain religion of spontaneity. The deity's work is perceived in unanticipated moments of divine intervention to which, according to the Pentecostalist, the believer must be forever open.

SUGGESTED READINGS

Mysticism

Bridges, Hal. *American Mysticism from William James to Zen.* New York: Harper, 1970.

Ellwood, Robert S., Jr. *Mysticism and Religion.* Englewood Cliffs NJ: Prentice-Hall, 1980.

---

[61]See James N. Lapsley and John H. Simpson, "Speaking in Tongues: pt. 1," *Pastoral Psychology* 14 (May 1964): 48-55.

[62]See Wayne E. Oates, "A Socio-Psychological Study of Glossolalia," in Frank Stagg, et al., *Glossolalia: Tongue Speaking in Biblical, Historical, and Psychological Perspectives* (Nashville: Abingdon, 1967) 76f.

[63]Kildahl, *The Psychology of Speaking in Tongues,* 37-38.

[64]Goodman, *Speaking in Tongues,* 124-25.

Otto, Rudolf. *Mysticism: East and West: A Comparative Analysis of the Nature of Mysticism.* Bertha L. Bracey and Richenda C. Payne, trs. New York: Macmillan, 1970. Old but valuable analysis.

Stace, W. T. *Mysticism and Philosophy.* Philadelphia: Lippincott, 1960.

Suzuki, Daisetz T. *Mysticism: Christian and Buddhist.* New York: Harper, 1957. Comparison of Meister Eckhart with Zen and Shin.

Underhill, Evelyn. *Mysticism.* New York: Meridian, 1955. A classic on the topic.

Psychedelic Drugs

Braden, William. *The Private Sea: LSD and the Search for God.* New York: Quadrangle, 1967. Easy, journalistic reading.

Clark, Walter H. *Chemical Ecstasy: Psychedelic Drugs and Religion.* New York: Sheed and Ward, 1969. Sympathetic treatment and valuable annotated bibliography.

Pahnke, Walter N. "Drugs and Mysticism," *International Journal of Parapsychology* 8 (1966): 295-314.

Smith, Huston. "Do Drugs Have Religious Import?" *The Journal of Philosophy* 61 (1964): 517-30.

Slotkin, James S. *The Peyote Religion.* New York: Free Press, 1956.

Zachner, R.C. *Mysticism: Sacred and Profane.* New York: Oxford University Press, 1961.

Pentecostalism

Abell, Troy D. *Better Felt Than Said: The Holiness-Pentecostal Experience in Southern Appalachia.* Waco TX: Markham, 1982.

Anderson, Robert M. *Vision of the Disinherited: The Making of American Pentecostalism.* New York: Oxford University Press, 1979.

Nichol, John T. *Pentecostalism.* New York: Harper, 1966. Historical survey.

Synon, Vinson. *The Holiness-Pentecostal Movement in the United States.* Grand Rapids MI: Eerdmans, 1971. Traces ideological and behavioral roots to Wesley.

Wood, William W. *Culture and Personality Aspects of the Pentecostal Holiness Religion.* Hawthorne NY: Mouton, 1965. Psychological comparison of Pentecostals and non-Pentecostals using Rorschach records.

Glossolalia

Goodman, Felicitas D. *Speaking in Tongues: a Cross-Cultural Study of Glossolalia.* Chicago: University of Chicago Press, 1972.

Hine, V. H. "Pentecostal Glossolalia: Toward a Functional Interpretation," *Journal for the Scientific Study of Religion* 8 (1969): 211-26.

Kildahl, John P. *The Psychology of Speaking in Tongues.* New York: McGraw-Hill, 1964

Lovekin, Adams, and H. Newton Malony. "Religious Glossolalia: A Longitudinal Study of Personality Changes," *Journal for the Scientific Study of Religion* 17 (1977): 383-93.

Runyon, Theodore, ed. *What the Spirit Is Saying to the Churches.* New York: Hawthorn, 1975. Excellent interpretative article.

Sherrill, John L. *They Speak with Other Tongues.* New York: Harper, 1972. Sympathetic to the practice.

Stagg, Frank, E. Glenn Hinson, and Wayne E. Oates. *Glossolalia: Tongue Speaking in Biblical, Historical, and Psychological Perspectives.* Nashville: Abingdon, 1967.

Williams, Cyril G. *Tongues of the Spirit: A Study of Pentecostal Glossolalia and Related Phenomena.* Cardiff: University of Wales Press, 1981.

CHAPTER THIRTEEN

TOWARD
A MATURE RELIGION

Persons develop patterns for expressing their religious commitments according to their unique lives. They are influenced both by personal needs and by religious systems to which they have been exposed. These individual life-styles may conform to one of the stereotypical patterns that have been described or combine features from them in endless variety. Which belief-behavior system holds maximum promise for maintaining sanity and health, aiding the full function of persons as human beings? Conversely, what kind of religious experience fosters limited vision and circumscribes human potentiality, or even encourages madness?

Religions of authority, becoming, and spontaneity do not automatically fall on one side of the health-disease ledger. Each is to be evaluated by how it serves individuals. Does religious participation enhance or deter maturation? To speak to that question it is necessary both to define maturity and to establish criteria by which the individual and his religion may be psychologically evaluated.

MATURITY: AN ILLUSIVE ISSUE

Throughout its modern history, psychology has shown a concern for the concept of maturity. Valuable insights into the healthy function of persons have emerged from this concern, but the descriptions of maturity are not at all precise nor uniformly agreed upon among psychologists. Early pioneers sometimes speak with a certainty that is foreign to the contemporary psychologist who appreciates the complexities of human behavior and is reluctant to offer absolutes.[1] Nonetheless, psychological descriptions of maturity have moved beyond the "absence of symptoms" stage and incorporate several criteria that seem consistently present among those concerned with this issue, especially psychotherapists. Among these criteria are (1) an accurate perception of reality, (2) the capacity to relate positively and intimately to other people, (3) an understanding and acceptance of oneself, (4) an integration and balance of psychic processes, and (5) the actualizing of one's potentiality.

These are ideal characteristics—more goals toward which persons move than ends that they attain. They give maturity an idealistic ring and an illusive quality. The mature person, like other items of perfection, is more easily described on paper than observed in real life. Who has seen a fully mature person? Typically ideal achievement is not expected in all categories, and judgments about maturity are likely to be made according to reasonableness. Persons are inclined to sacrifice accomplishment in one area of their development as the price for growth in other areas, such as the musician who narrows the range of close relationships with other people to develop his full capacities through long hours of practice. The laboratory scientist may forsake routine procedures or the artist may intentionally distort reality in the search for more refined or metaphorical descriptions of things. The observer does not become alarmed at such distortions as long as they are under conscious control and directed toward worthy ends. Maturity is judged not on achieving a one hundred percent mark in all dimensions of per-

---

[1]Orlo Strunk, Jr., *Mature Religion* (Nashville: Abingdon, 1965) 8.

sonal growth, but by adding up the score in a number of areas and arriving at a reasonable sum.

The illusive character of maturity means that evaluation is a matter of subjective discrimination and thence reflects as much the assumptions of the observer as the status of the observed. In situations of extreme emotional upheaval the assessment of immaturity or illness is usually clear, although specific cultures seem to tolerate exceptionally intense variations. Appalachian mountain life will absorb quite bizarre behavior on grounds of rugged individualism. Persons who in other areas might end up in a hospital are accepted and supported by the culture itself. Usually, however, society is intolerant toward persons whose distortion of reality, conflict with their neighbors, or impulsive behavior threatens the social order.

Often the religious community will support eccentric behavior as generously as any social group. The separation between saints and mad men is not always clear. Similarities between religion and mental illness sometimes make them easily confused in popular thinking. As James's *Varieties* and other sources have pointed out, the imaginative, creative religious experience is occasionally marked by an intensity and highly metaphorical imagery that resembles illness. Many who have been judged by their contemporaries to be insane, or at least unusually fanatical, were only later accepted as saints. The eccentric prophet Ezekiel, who reported strange visions of creatures, wheels, and dry bones, in a less tolerant climate would have met men in white jackets long before completing his mission.[2] Jesus' family attempted to take him home because people were saying, "He's gone mad!"[3] The Roman official shouted at the apostle, "You are mad, Paul! Your great learning is driving you mad!"[4] The religious institution sometimes executes those who challenge the establishment, but often it tolerates considerable diversity because the ideas and insights of eccentrics may be beyond their time and circumstances.

---

[2]Ezekiel 10, 37.

[3]Mark 3:21.

[4]Acts 26:24.

Hence, religious maturity and social acceptance do not always coincide. An intensely religious person "may choose the living out of a high ethic, or the nurturing of spiritual experience at the expense of some of the values of mental health."[5] The saint may feel compelled to act according to principle rather than conform to maturity norms. To avoid stilling the prophetic voice the religious establishment will often tolerate considerable variation, even enduring attempts of the very pious to justify their eccentric, private behavior in the name of "high ethic" or "superior value." Organizations, like individuals, need disruptive experience to stimulate growth. At this point the religious institution needs a superior confidence in the ability of history to separate the true from the false prophet and vindicate insights that are genuinely corrective. The mature religious organization entertains with patience even radical ideas, feelings, and behavior because, perchance, additional revelation may be contained in them.

The ticklish maturity issue is often compounded in discussions of religion, because theological adequacy and psychological maturity do not always coincide. Theological norms that are determined by the adequacy of concepts to define the nature of deity and divine-human relationships do not necessarily correlate with psychological norms having to do with the function of theological ideas and forms in the life of individuals or groups. An inadequate theological concept may serve as an adequate focus around which a personality may be unified, as when an authoritarian God is the object of unquestioning devotion. Likewise, a valid theological idea may foster immaturity, as when a mother uses God's love to exploit and manipulate her children. The crucial issue for the psychology of religion is not one of weighing the relative theological merit of religion of authority, becoming, or spontaneity; that task is left to theology. Psychology is concerned with the function of each religious life-style in personal and group survival. The concern may be formulated in one of two ways: (1) Is religion itself a mark of maturity or immaturity? (2) What characterizes a mature, as compared to an immature, religion?

---

[5]Joseph Havens, ed., *Psychology and Religion: A Contemporary Dialogue* (New York: Van Nostrand, 1968) 104.

MATURE PERSONS AND RELIGION

The question of religious maturity may be centered around whether or not religion itself signifies illness or health. Sigmund Freud, of course, believed that religion was consistently immature in that it preserved childish resolutions to early conflicts. To him, speaking of religious maturity was double-talk, a contradiction of terms. To be mature, persons must learn to survive without religion as surely as they learn to live without a mother's breast or the protection of family environment. Although it represents a socially acceptable mode for regulating infantile wishes, religion always remains the cosmic dramatization of dynamics that are rooted in early parent-child relationships. Maturity means putting away childish things, including religion. On the other hand, Freud's dissident colleague Jung identified religion with health. For him religion places persons in touch with the collective experience of the race and, thus, is an authentic device by which human beings reach for values beyond themselves. The opposing views of Freud and Jung bring the question into bold relief: Does religion preserve infantilism or cultivate growth?[6]

Religion and Personal Adjustment

Numerous empirical studies have explored the role that religion plays in personal adjustment and have produced an impressive body of data on the correlation of certain kinds of religious experience with indicators of physical and mental health.[7] The religious factors used most regularly in these studies are frequency of church attendance and denominational affiliation, both items that can be easily identified and quantified. This research provides important information about religion's role in specific adjustment situations, such as offering support and companionship for the elderly, but the evidence is nonconclusive in regard to whether or not religion supports or disrupts health. Church attenders have

---

[6]See above, pp. 74-6, 79-81.

[7]A large block of these studies is summarized in Michael Argyle and Benjamin Beit-Hallahmi, *The Social Psychology of Religion* (Boston: Routledge and Kegan Paul, 1975) 124-51. The discussion here draws heavily upon their summary.

lower rates of chronic bronchitis and fatal one-car accidents, but religious students report themselves to be more anxious, to have lower self-esteem, and feel less adequate. Jews are more likely to seek psychiatric help than Roman Catholics or Protestants, but it is unclear whether or not this is accounted for by religious affiliation or other characteristics of the several religious communities. Participation in religious groups enhances support and socialization, but this does not seem to be qualitatively different from that support derived from nonreligious groups. Religious beliefs act as deterrents to impulsive behavior in some individuals and groups, but changes in religious attitudes among young delinquents do not seem to alter their moral behavior. Numerous clinical studies "conclude that neither affiliation nor degree of religious involvement seems related in any significant way to suicide attempts."[8]

An important study done by Wayne Oates and a group of his students examined possible aspects of religion in mental illness and discovered several types of relationships. Using interviews and case records, the group studied sixty-eight persons admitted as patients to a public mental hospital serving the thirty counties of southeastern Kentucky. People of this area belong largely to Appalachia and generally are fiercely religious. The Oates analysis revealed that:

— 51.5 percent of the sample showed no evidence of religious interest or past religious influence,
— 20.5 percent used religious ideas and symbols to "clothe" their illnesses, although little or no religious concerns appeared in their pre-psychotic history,
— 10.3 percent had experienced religion as a precipitating factor in the crisis which brought the person to the hospital, and
— 17.2 percent exhibited long-standing relationships between religion and personality patterns erupting in illness.[9]

The Oates data are impressive, particularly at the point of the large percentage of his sample that exhibited little or incidental religious

[8]Ibid., 145.

[9]Wayne E. Oates, *Religious Factors in Mental Illness* (New York: Association, 1955) 5-9.

involvement in psychotic breakdown, even among those who shared "Bible belt" culture. It might have been expected that the connections would have been more pronounced among those whose background accepted religion as an important part of life, including tolerance of independent and eccentric religious behavior. The Oates study suggests that the relationship between religion and illness is not as dramatic as might be expected.

A more intimate connection between religion and personal adjustment comes from Anton Boisen, a minister who suffered a major personality collapse. In his classic, *The Exploration of the Inner World,* Boisen leads the reader through the wilderness of his own mental disorder and summarizes his subsequent research into the nature of illness itself. For Boisen recovery from illness and religious awakening were the same story. His inner disharmony produced a probing for ultimate loyalties that permitted healing to occur. Boisen generalizes on his experience and observation.

> Religious experience as well as mental disorder may involve severe emotional upheaval, and mental disorder as well as religious experience may represent the operation of the healing forces of nature. The conclusion follows that certain types of mental disorder and certain types of religious experience are alike attempts at reorganization. . . . Where the attempt is successful and some degree of victory is won, it is commonly recognized as religious experience. Where it is unsuccessful or indeterminate, it is commonly spoken of as "insanity."[10]

Care should be taken not to overread Boisen's interpretation of his own experience, but his report represents one testimony as to the positive relationship between religion and health.

Demonology

In a sense the New Testament references to demons and their exorcism represent a biblical comment upon religion's relation to health. In the first century C.E. persons believed that ill health was to be attributed to the indwelling of a malign spirit and healing depended upon exorcism of the demon. Thus in a graphic way the

---

[10]Anton T. Boisen, *The Exploration of the Inner World: A Study of Mental Disorder and Religious Experience* (New York: Harper, 1936) ix.

biblical materials associate illness with the demonic. During the 1970s, archaic ideas of demons and exorcism were revived by popular novels and commercial movies. Both ancient and contemporary interests make it important to place demonology in its proper context.

The sketchy descriptions of disturbed persons found in biblical narratives have sometimes been compared to contemporary diagnostic categories and Jesus' healings to modern psychotherapeutic procedures. Such comparisons should be exercised with great care. Biblical materials are not medical records and diagnosis from a distance is risky at best. Rather, the narratives speak from their own historical and scientific contexts as first century attempts to make sense of disturbing realities.

From this viewpoint demons represent prescientific explanations of illnesses that clearly distort human beneficence. Demons personify those powerful and sinister forces that oppose the good life, thwarting divine purpose for human beings. The forces are so real that they "assume the appearance of individuality."[11] The exorcism movements of the last decade are reminders of the tremendous power of destructive psychic states (personified in biblical materials as demons), but fail to recognize that these are disruptive "splits of personality" or "fragmentary selves."[12] Such are resolved in contemporary forms, not by a magical exorcism ritual, but by serious therapeutic processes. According to T. H. Gaster, demonology from the standpoint of religious psychology "represents an externalization of human experiences. Feelings and sensations, moods and impulses, even physical conditions, which might otherwise be described as obtaining autonomously *within* a man, are portrayed, on this basis, as outer forces working *upon* him."[13]

As prescientific but graphic personifications of psychic states belonging to functional disorders, demonology should be thought

---

[11]Edward Langton, *Essentials of Demonology: A Study of Jewish and Christian Dogma, Its Origins and Development* (London: Epworth, 1945) 145.

[12]Ibid.

[13]T. H. Gaster, "Demon, Demonology," in Buttrick, et al., eds., *The Interpreter's Dictionary of the Bible,* vol. 1 (Nashville: Abingdon, 1962) 818.

of as "an intuitive and ontological approach to human suffering. Psychotherapeutic approaches are more empirical and observational in nature."[14] This view leads Edward Thurneysen to describe "pastoral care as exorcism," not as a magical ritual, but as the announcement of a message that liberates from "the dark reign of evil."[15]

In sum, then, the evidence suggests that religion's relationship to illness and health may be debated either way. Religious and irreligious persons get sick; persons recover from illness with and without the aid of religion. For some individuals religion functions as a defense against growth, a haven for irresponsibility, and a means for feeling superior while blaming others. For the mentally ill it may provide extreme symbols through which severe disturbance is expressed. For others religion serves as a belief-value system around which personality is integrated and contributes to individual well-being. It encourages "the calm and courageous acceptance of a heavy burden of responsibility."[16] What makes the difference? In some measure the answer to this question depends upon the quality of the religion itself and whether or not it meets minimum standards of psychological maturity.

CRITERIA FOR MATURE RELIGION

The presence of religion does not guarantee a well-integrated personality, nor does its absence automatically forbode disintegration and illness. Some relatively mature persons may be uninvolved with official religion. Other mature people do not share in formal religion with the same intensity as some do. Religion, as any other belief-behavior system, will mirror patterns of personality organization and may even be studied as a diagnostic tool.[17] A fragmented, disorganized self could hardly be expected to exhibit a well-

---

[14]Wayne E. Oates, *The Psychology of Religion* (Waco TX: Word Books, 1973) 264.

[15]Eduard Thurneysen, *A Theology of Pastoral Care,* Jack A. Worthington and Thomas Weiser, trans. (Atlanta: John Knox Press, 1962) 315-33.

[16]Boisen, *The Exploration of the Inner World,* 137.

[17]Compare Edgar Draper, et al. "On the Diagnostic Value of Religious Ideation," *Archives of General Psychiatry* 13 (1965): 202-207.

integrated, mature faith. The presence or absence of religion seems a less important indicator of illness or health than that of the way it functions in personality organization.

A mature religious faith is minimally one that encourages, rather than limits, mature personhood. More than three decades ago Gordon Allport suggested that maturity may be measured by a person's ability (1)to extend interests beyond biological impulses to include humane values, (2) to reflect upon personal experience with detachment and insight, and (3) to integrate the self around a unifying philosophy of life.[18] Accordingly, mature religion would foster the unfolding of a mature personhood in expanding human concerns, allow for reflection and insight, and incorporate the corners and recesses of experience into a unified whole. The extensive scope of mature religion in healthy personality organization is reflected in Orlo Strunk's psychological definition of mature religion. The statement is both clear and comprehensive:

> Mature religion is a dynamic organization of cognitive-affective-conative factors possessing certain characteristics of depth and height—including a highly conscious and articulate belief system purged, by critical processes, of childish wishes and intensely suited and comprehensive enough to find meaning in all of life's vicissitudes. Such a belief system, though tentative in spirit, will include a conviction of the existence of an Ideal Power to which the person can sense a friendly continuity—a conviction grounded in authoritative and ineffable experience. The dynamic relationship between this belief system and these experiential events will generate feelings of wonder and awe, a sense of oneness with the All, humility, elation, and freedom; and with great consistency will determine the individual's responsible behavior in all areas of personal and interpersonal relationships, including such spheres as morality, love, work, and so forth.[19]

Strunk's statement is intentionally general and synthetic. He aims to incorporate insights on religious maturity from Freud, Jung, Fromm, James, Allport, and Frankl, as well as his own. The defi-

---

[18]Gordon Allport, *The Individual and His Religion* (New York: Macmillan, 1950) 52-54.

[19]Strunk, *Mature Religion*, 144-45.

nition draws together religious feelings, actions, and beliefs, and emphasizes the necessary impact that mature religion makes upon daily life. It avoids restricting mature religion to a single faith and leaves open the possibility that numerous religious life-styles may exhibit mature characteristics. Minimum standards by which any religious system or private experience may be tested must include several items.

First, *mature religion leaves ample room for growth.* In his classic affirmation of Christian love, the Apostle Paul said, "When I was a child, my speech, thinking were all those of a child; now that I am a man, I have no more use for childish ways."[20] Religious beliefs held in childhood are not false because they have been learned at an early age, but the "speech, feelings, and thinking" associated with them are those of the child. Maturity requires that childish behavior be submitted to critical and reflective judgment and given expanded meanings that are informed and enriched by the ongoing struggle with life's basic issues. Mature religion willingly exposes religious beliefs, feelings, and actions to the growing edge of new data and critical analysis.

Second, *mature religion enhances the ordering of life without blinding persons to residues of the chaotic, demonic, and irrational.* William Rogers sees this combination of order with chaos as a central issue in psychotherapy. He writes, "What is frequently called for in the process of therapy is an atmosphere of safety and freedom in which the client can experience more fully the disordered chaos of his denied experiences and feelings, and can become aware that these threatening experiences can be accepted and dealt with in their chaotic, frightening forms by both the therapist and himself in constructive ways."[21]

Mature religious faith takes seriously both order and chaos. It neither denies the sinister as if deity removes all problems, nor does it indulge the demonic as if human life has no value. Nor does it hang back waiting for utopian perfection. Rather, mature faith rec-

---

[20] I Corinthians 13:11.

[21] William R. Rogers, "Order and Chaos in Psychopathology and Ontology," in Peter Homans, ed., *The Dialogue between Theology and Psychology.* Essays in Divinity Series, ed. Gerald C. Brauer (Chicago: University of Chicago Press, 1968) 259-60.

ognizes the chaotic without lingering over it in preoccupation and moves on with goals and purposes. From the Christian standpoint, the attitude that balances a realistic appraisal of the demonic with a unifying loyalty is close to the heart of repentance. The believer who regards God as one who accepts less than perfect human beings is better able to forgive the self and affirm decisively a commitment to positive ends.

Third, *mature religion encompasses the whole range of human experience.* For the purposes of analysis, our discussion has used numerous categories to analyze religious experience: religion of childhood, youth, and adulthood; religion of cognition, affection, and volition; religion of obedience, affirmation, and mysticism. Such divisions, however, do the wholeness of personhood an injustice. Religious systems often have a way of cutting out a block of human experience and endowing it with holy sanction: reason at the expense of feeling, individualism at the expense of corporate responsibility, happiness at the expense of sacrifice, and other examples. The religiously mature person, even when his personal religion is built of selected blocks, attempts to incorporate the many facets of personality into a comprehensive understanding of life and destiny. Even when parts are not essential to one's own construction, the mature person learns not to despise them in others.

Victor Frankl, a European psychiatrist who spent most of World War II in German concentration camps, concluded that human beings must somehow weave their experience into a fabric of wholeness. Reflecting on his firsthand exposure to suffering, indignity, torture, and death, Frankl became convinced that the key to human existence is the will to meaning.[22] Essential to being human is the discovery of a meaning comprehensive enough to cover both the routine, pleasurable activities of ordinary life and also convulsive tragedy, which sooner or later overtakes every person. Mature religion requires openness to all human realities, the harsh

---

[22]See Frankl's *Man's Search for Meaning: An Introduction to Logotherapy* (Boston: Beacon Press, 1962) which contains autobiographical notations on his concentration camp experience as well as his theoretical formulations on the existential importance of meaning.

as well as pleasant, and the pursuit of meaning that makes ultimate sense of all reality.

Fourth, *mature religion encourages the freedom of the individual without flaunting responsibility.* Psychology has convincingly taught contemporary persons that inalterable conditions circumscribe human freedom. Heredity, social environment, instinctual needs, and conditioning establish boundaries that are crossed only with great psychic difficulty—if at all. The legacy of such instruction has often been the sacrifice of both freedom and responsibility. If I am victim, why bother with commitment and decision? If others are victims, why care?

Human beings are certainly caught in a nexus of social and personal forces from which separation is impossible. Nevertheless, within limits persons can choose freely. In choosing and in taking responsibility for choices, persons express their capacity to be truly human. Mature religion in belief and organization sanctions such free and responsible involvement.

Fifth, *mature religion is certain enough to permit commitment and action without demanding absoluteness.* Gordon Allport states that the mature religious sentiment is necessarily heuristic, that is, "it can act wholeheartedly even without absolute certainty. It can be sure without being cocksure."[23] For those religious styles that stress absoluteness and decry doubt as faith's enemy, this is a hard word because heurism advocates "taking risks in advance of certainties."[24] Heuristic religion acts upon beliefs that are accepted for the time being in full consciousness that new information and insight might demand a revision in beliefs.

The appeal in heuristic religion is not for guarded commitment, but for a leap of faith that accepts the limits of human vision. This stance recognizes that "what we see now is like a dim image in a mirror."[25] No one's perception is clear enough to see the whole truth. A fanatical religion that insists upon absoluteness is in this sense idolatrous because it exalts human conception above the liv-

---

[23]Allport, *The Individual and His Religion,* 72.

[24]Ibid., 73.

[25]I Corinthians 13:12.

ing God, who moves among persons as a shadow. Mature faith neither worships its own formulations about God nor waits until all the facts are in before deciding to act. Rather, heuristic religion builds faith upon the data that are known and remains tentatively open to additional light. Mature commitment does not depend upon how *certain* the believer is, but upon how *central* religion is in self-structure.

Briefly stated, religion may be described as immature when it

— holds to childish ideas and actions uncritically,
— denies the sinister elements of personality,
— shuts off segments of human experience as irrelevant,
— indulges individualism, and
— demands absolute answers.

Conversely, mature faith

— critically examines and reexamines cherished beliefs and practices,
— acknowledges the demonic, but without preoccupation,
— utilizes all personal resources to bring all life's experiences under religious scrutiny,
— affirms personal freedom and responsibility, and
— acts with certainty while seeking new light.

CONCLUSION

Two words that continually come to mind in discussions of maturity are *balance* and *patience*. The disciple who pursues mature faith is like a person on a teeter board trying to keep in complementary balance seemingly contradictory forces: childlike playfulness and adult stability, self-interests and social responsibility, institutional loyalty and personal integrity, and countless others. The twin sister of balance is patience. The illusiveness of "the vital balance" demands infinite patience: patience with oneself in confidence that forgiveness and reclamation can occur, patience toward other religious life-styles because they are acknowledged as the product of psychological preference and not the essence of faith, patience with different belief systems in the conviction that the last word has not been spoken and all truth has not yet been perceived. The practice of patience and the achievement of balance are delicate maneuvers hardly achieved until they slip away. Nonetheless, they are feats of eloquence comprising the singularly human vocation.

SUGGESTED READINGS

Demonology

Langton, Edward. *Essentials of Demonology: A Study of Jewish and Christian Dogma, Its Origin and Development.* London: Epworth. 1945.

McCasland, S. Vernon. *By the Finger of God: Demon Possesion and Exorcism in Early Christianity in the Light of Modern Views of Mental Illness.* New York: Macmillan. 1951.

Ward, Coleen A., and Michael Beaubrun. "Psychodynamics of Demon Possession," *Journal for the Scientific Study of Religion* 19 (1980): 201-207.

Religion and Mental Illness

Boisen, Anton T. *The Exploration of the Inner World: A Study of Mental Disorder and Religious Experience.* New York: Harper. 1936.

Oates, Wayne E. *Religious Factors in Mental Illness.* New York: Association, 1955. Introductory.

Pattison, Mansell, ed. *Clinical Psychiatry and Religion.* Boston: Little, Brown, 1969.

Rokeach, Milton. *Three Christs of Ypsilanti.* New York: Knopf, 1969. Studies three mental hospital inmates.

Mature Religion

Allport, Gordon W. *The Individual and His Religion.* New York: Macmillan, 1950. Especially Chapter 3.

Burke, Joseph F. "Mature Religious Behavior: A Psychological Perspective and Its Implications," *Journal of Religion and Health* 17 (1978): 177-83.

Lapsley, James N. *Salvation and Health.* Philadelphia: Westminster, 1972.

Strunk, Orlo, Jr. *Mature Religion.* Nashville: Abingdon, 1965.

BIBLIOGRAPHY

Abell, Troy D. *Better Felt Than Said: The Holiness-Pentecostal Experience in Southern Appalachia*. Waco TX: Markham, 1982.

Abelson, Robert P. "Computers, Polls, and Public Opinion—Some Puzzles and Paradoxes." *Trans-Action* 5 (1968): 20-27.

_____. "Modes of Resolution of Belief Dilemmas." *Journal of Conflict Resolution* 3 (1959): 343-52.

Ackerknecht, Erwin H. *A Short History of Medicine*. New York: Ronald Press, 1968.

Aden, LeRoy. "Faith and the Developmental Cycle." *Pastoral Psychology* 24 (1976): 215-30.

Adorno, T. W., et al. *The Authoritarian Personality*. New York: Harper, 1950.

Allen, Gay W. *William James: A Biography*. New York: Viking Press, 1967.

Allen, Joseph H. *Our Liberal Movement in Theology*. New York: Arno Press, 1972.

Allen, Robert O., and Bernard Spilka. "Committed and Consensual Religion: A Specificiation of Religion-Prejudice Relationships." *Journal for the Scientific Study of Religion* 6 (1967): 291-306.

Allport, Gordon W. *Becoming: Basic Considerations for a Psychology of Personality*. New Haven: Yale University Press, 1955.

_____. *The Individual and His Religion: A Psychological Interpretation*. New York: Macmillan, 1950.

_____. *The Nature of Prejudice*. Reading MA: Addison-Wesley, 1954.

_____. *Pattern and Growth in Personality*. New York: Holt, Rinehart and Winston, 1961.

_____. *The Person in Psychology: Selected Essays*. Boston: Beacon Press, 1968.

_____. *Personality: A Psychological Interpretation*. New York: Holt, Rinehart and Winston, 1939.

_____. *Personality and Social Encounter*. Boston: Beacon Press, 1960.

_____. "The Religious Context of Prejudice." *Journal for the Scientific Study of Religion* 5 (1965): 447-57.

_____. "What Is a Trait of Personality?" *Journal of Abnormal and Social Psychology* 35 (1941): 368-72.

_____, and J. Michael Ross. "Personal Religious Orientation and Prejudice." *Journal of Personality and Social Psychology* 5 (1967): 432-43.

_____, James M. Gillespie, and Jacqueline Young. "The Religion of the Post-War College Student." *The Journal of Psychology* 25 (1948): 3-33.

Anderson, Barry F. *Cognitive Psychology.* New York: Academic Press, 1975.

Anderson, Robert M. *Vision of the Disinherited: The Making of American Pentecostalism.* New York: Oxford University Press, 1979.

Appelbee, Arthur N. *The Child's Concept of Story: Ages Two to Seventeen.* Chicago: University of Chicago Press, 1978.

Argyle, Michael A. *Religious Behavior.* Boston: Routledge and Kegan Paul, 1958.

_____, and Benjamin Beit-Hallahmi. *The Social Psychology of Religion.* Boston: Routledge and Kegan Paul, 1975.

Arnold, Thomas, and Alfred Guillaume, eds. *The Legacy of Islam.* Oxford: Clarendon Press, 1931.

Asch, Solomon E. "Effects of Group Pressure upon the Modification and Distortion of Judgment." In *Groups, Leadership, and Men.* Harold S. Guetzkow, ed. New York: Russell and Russell, 1963.

_____. *Social Psychology.* Englewood Cliffs NJ: Prentice-Hall, 1952.

Ashby, W. Ross. *An Introduction to Cybernetics.* New York: John Wiley, 1958.

Auden, W. H. *The Dyer's Hand.* New York: Random House, 1962.

Babcock, C. R. *Lévi-Strauss: Structuralism and Sociological Theory.* London: Hutchinson, 1975.

Bailey, Kenneth K. *Southern White Protestantism in the Twentieth Century.* New York: Harper, 1964.

Bainbridge, William S., and Rodney Stark. "The 'Consciousness Reformation' Reconsidered." *Journal for the Scientific Study of Religion* 20 (1981): 1-16.

Banton, Michael, ed. *Anthropological Approaches to the Study of Religion.* New York: Praeger, 1966.

Barber, T. X., et al., eds. *Biofeedback and Self-Control (1970): An Aldine Annual on the Regulation of Bodily Processes and Consciousness.* Chicago: Aldine-Atherton, 1971.

Barbour, Ian G. *Issues in Science and Religion.* Englewood Cliffs NJ: Prentice-Hall, 1966.

_____. *Myths, Models, and Paradigms: A Comparative Study in Science and Religion.* New York: Harper, 1974.

_____, ed. *Science and Religion: New Perspectives on the Dialogue.* New York: Harper, 1968.

Barfield, Owen. "Matter, Imagination, and Spirit." *Journal of the American Academy of Religion* 42 (1974): 621-29.

Barr, James. *Fundamentalism.* Philadelphia: Westminster, 1978.

Barth, Karl. *Church Dogmatics.* Vols. 1 and 2. G. T. Thompson and Harold Knight, trans. New York: Scribner's, 1956.

_____. *Evangelical Theology: An Introduction*. Grover Foley, trans. New York: Holt, Rinehart and Winston, 1963.

_____. *The Humanity of God*. Atlanta: John Knox, 1960.

Barton, Allen H. "Selected Problems in the Study of Religious Development." In *Research on Religious Development*. Merton P. Strommen, ed. New York: Hawthorn, 1971.

Batson, C. Daniel. "Experimentation in Psychology of Religion: An Impossible Dream." *Journal for the Scientific Study of Religion* 16 (1977): 412-18.

_____. "Experimentation in Psychology of Religion: Living with or in a Dream." *Journal for the Scientific Study of Religion* 18 (1979): 90-93.

Batson, C. Daniel, and W. Larry Ventis. *The Religious Experience: A Social-Psychological Perspective*. New York: Oxford University Press, 1982.

Beck, Cline M., Brian S. Crittendon, and Edmund V. Sullivan, eds. *Moral Education: Interdisciplinary Approaches*. Toronto: University of Toronto Press, 1971.

Beit-Hallahmi, Benjamin, ed. *Research in Religious Behavior: Selected Readings*. Monterey CA: Brooks/Cole, 1973.

_____. "Psychology of Religion, 1880-1930: The Rise and Fall of a Psychological Movement." *The Journal of the History of the Behavioral Sciences* 10 (1974): 84-90.

Belgum, David. *Guilt: Where Psychology and Religion Meet*. Minneapolis: Augsburg, 1969.

Bellah, Robert N. "Christianity and Symbolic Realism." *Journal for the Scientific Study of Religion* 9 (1970): 89-96.

_____. "Civil Religion in America." *Daedalus* 96 (1967): 1-21.

_____. "Religion in the University: Changing Consciousness, Changing Structures," in *Religion in the Undergraduate Curriculum*. Claude Welch, ed. Washington DC: Association of American Colleges, 1972.

_____. "Religious Evolution." *American Sociological Review* 29 (1964): 358-74.

Bem, Daryl. *Beliefs, Attitudes, and Human Affairs*. Monterey CA: Brooks/Cole, 1970.

Bender, I. E. "Changes in Religious Interest: A Retest of 15 Years." *Journal of Abnormal and Social Psychology* 57 (1958): 41-46.

Benson, Purnell H. *Religion in Contemporary Culture: A Study of Religion through Social Science*. New York: Harper, 1960.

Berdyaev, Nicholas. *Solitude and Society*. London: Centenary, 1938.

Berger, Peter L. *The Sacred Canopy: Elements of a Sociological Theory of Religion*. Garden City NY: Doubleday, 1967.

_____. "Some Second Thoughts on Substantive versus Functional Definitions of Religion." *Journal for the Scientific Study of Religion* 13 (1974): 125-33.

Berne, Eric. *Principles of Group Treatment*. New York: Grove Press, 1966.

Bertocci, Peter A. "Psychological Interpretations of Religious Experience." In *Research on Religious Development*. Merton P. Strommen, ed. New York: Hawthorn, 1971.

_____. "Review of A. Maslow, *Religions, Values, and Peak-Experiences*." *Contemporary Psychology* 10 (1965): 449-51.

Bettelheim, Bruno. *Freud and Man's Soul*. New York: Knopf, 1983.

_____. "Individual and Mass Behavior in Extreme Situations." *Journal of Abnormal and Social Psychology* 38 (1943): 417-52.

Bier, William S., ed. *Conscience: Its Freedom and Limitations.* New York: Fordham University Press, 1971.

Binkley, Luther J. "What Characterizes Religious Language?" *Journal for the Scientific Study of Religion* 1 (1962): 18-21.

Birch, Charles. "What Does God Do in the World?" *Union Seminary Quarterly Review* 30 (1975): 76-84.

Bock, David C., and Neil C. Warren. "Religious Belief as a Factor in Obedience to Destructive Commands." *Review of Religious Research* 13 (1972): 185-91.

Boisen, Anton T. *The Exploration of the Inner World: A Study of Mental Disorder and Religious Experience.* New York: Harper, 1936.

_____. *Religion in Crisis and Custom: A Sociological and Psychological Study.* New York: Harper, 1955.

Bonthius, Robert H. *Christian Paths to Self-Acceptance.* New York: King's Crown Press, 1948.

Booth, Howard J. *Edwin Dilles Starbuck: Pioneer in the Psychology of Religion.* Washington: University Press of America, 1981.

_____. "Pioneering Literature in the Psychology of Religion: A Reminder." Unpublished paper delivered to a colloquium on psychology and religion, University of Lancaster, Lancaster, England, January, 1976.

Braden, William. *The Private Sea: LSD and the Search for God.* New York: Quadrangle, 1967.

Braginsky, Benjamin M, and Dorothea D. Braginsky. *Mainstream Psychology: A Critique.* New York: Holt, Rinehart and Winston, 1974.

Bregman, Lucy. "Fantasy: The Experiences and the Interpreter." *Journal of the American Academy of Religion* 43 (1975): 723-40.

Brehm, Jack W. *A Theory of Psychological Reactance.* New York: Academic, 1966.

Bretall, Robert, ed. *A Kierkegaard Anthology.* Princeton: Princeton University Press, 1951.

Bridges, Hal. *American Mysticism from William James to Zen.* New York: Harper, 1970.

Brill, A. A., trans. and ed. *The Basic Writings of Sigmund Freud.* New York: Random House, 1938.

Bronfenbrenner, Urie. "Freudian Theories of Identification and Their Derivatives." *Child Development* 31 (1960): 15-40.

Brooks, Henry C. "Analytic Psychology and the Image of God." *Andover Newton Quarterly,* n.s. 6 (1965): 35-55.

Brown, L. B., ed. *Psychology and Religion.* Baltimore: Penguin Books, 1973.

Browning, Don S. *Generative Man: Psychoanalytic Perspectives.* Philadelphia: Westminster, 1973.

_____. *Pluralism and Personality: William James and Some Contemporary Cultures of Psychology.* Lewisburg PA: Bucknell University Press, 1980.

_____. "William James's Philosophy of Mysticism." *Journal of Religion* 59 (1979): 56-70.

Brunner, H. Emil. *Revelation and Reason: The Christian Doctrine of Faith and Knowledge*. Olive Wyon, trans. Philadelphia: Westminster, 1946.

Bryant, Robert H. *The Bible's Authority Today*. Minneapolis: Augsburg, 1968.

Bryson, Lymon, Louis Funkelstein, and R. M. MacIver, eds. *Conflicts of Power in Modern Culture*. New York: Harper, 1947.

Buber, Martin. *I and Thou*. 2d ed. Ronald G. Smith, trans. New York: Scribner's, 1958.

Bufford, Rodger K. "God and Behavior Mod: Some Thoughts Concerning the Relationships between Biblical Principles and Behavior Modification." *Journal of Psychology and Theology* 5 (1977): 13-22.

Bugental, J. F. T., ed. *Challenges of Humanistic Psychology*. New York: McGraw-Hill, 1967.

Buhler, Charlotte. "Humanistic Psychology as an Educational Program." *American Psychologist* 24 (1969): 736-42.

Bultmann, Rudolf. *Theology of the New Testament*. Vol. 1. New York: Scribner's, 1951.

Burke, Joseph F. "Mature Religious Behavior: A Psychological Perspective and Its Implications." *Journal of Religion and Health* 17 (1978): 117-83.

Bushnell, Horace. *Christian Nurture*. Rev. ed. New Haven: Yale University Press, 1916.

Buttrick, George A., et al., eds. *The Interpreter's Dictionary of the Bible*. Vols. 1-4. Nashville: Abingdon, 1962.

Byrne, Joseph F. *The Psychology of Religion*. New York: Free Press, 1984.

Campbell, Dennis M. *Authority and the Renewal of American Theology*. New York: United Church Press, 1976.

Cannon, Walter B. *Bodily Changes in Pain, Hunger, Fear, and Rage*. New York: Appleton, 1922.

_____. *The Wisdom of the Body*. New York: W. W. Norton, 1932.

Capps, Donald. "Orestes Bronson: The Psychology of Religious Affiliation." *Journal for the Scientific Study of Religion* 7 (1968): 197-209.

_____, and Walter H. Capps. *The Religious Personality*. Belmont CA: Wadsworth, 1970.

_____, and M. Gerald Bradford, eds. *Encounter with Erikson: Historical Interpretation and Religious Biography*. Chico CA: Scholars Press, 1977.

Carpenter, Finley. *The Skinner Primer: Behind Freedom and Dignity*. New York: Free Press, 1974.

Carr, H. A., and F. A. Kingsbury. "The Concept of Trait." *Psychological Review* 45 (1938): 497-524.

Chesterton, G. K. *St. Francis of Assisi*. Garden City NY: Doubleday, 1957.

Childs, Brevard S. *Memory and Tradition in Israel*. Studies in Biblical Theology No. 37. Napier IL: Alec R. Allenson, 1962.

Clark, Elmer T. *The Psychology of Religious Awakening*. New York: Macmillan, 1929.

Clark, Walter H. *Chemical Ecstasy: Psychedelic Drugs and Religion*. New York: Sheed and Ward, 1969.

_____. "How Do Social Scientists Define Religion?" *Journal of Social Psychology* 47 (1958): 143-47.

_____. *The Psychology of Religion: An Introduction to Religious Experience and Behavior.* New York: Macmillan, 1958.

_____, H. Newton Malony, James Daane, and Alan R. Tippett. *Religious Experience: Its Nature and Function in the Human Psyche.* Springfield IL: Charles C. Thomas, 1973.

Clarke, Colin C. *Romantic Paradox: An Essay on the Poetry of Wordsworth.* London: Routledge and Kegan Paul, 1962.

Clebsch, William A. *From Sacred to Profane America: The Role of Religion in American History.* New York: Harper, 1968.

Clinebell, Howard J., Jr., and Charlotte H. Clinebell. *The Intimate Marriage.* New York: Harper, 1970.

Coates, Thomas J. "Personality Correlates of Religious Commitment: A Further Verification." *Journal of Social Psychology* 89 (1973): 159-60.

Cobb, John. *A Christian Natural Theology.* Philadelphia: Westminster, 1965.

Coe, George A. *The Psychology of Religion.* Chicago: University of Chicago Press, 1916.

Cohen, Morris R., and Ernest Nagel. *An Introduction to Logic and Scientific Method.* New York: Harcourt, Brace, and World, 1934.

Cohn, Werner. "Is Religion Universal? Problems of Definition." *Journal for the Scientific Study of Religion* 2 (1962): 25-32.

Cole, Stewart G. *The History of Fundamentalism.* Hampden CT: Archon Books, 1963.

Cox, David. *Jung and St. Paul: A Study of the Doctrine of Justification by Faith and Its Relation to the Concept of Individuation.* New York: Association, 1959.

Cox, Harvey. *The Feast of Fools.* New York: Harper, 1969.

_____. *The Secular City.* New York: Macmillan, 1965.

Cragg, Gerald R. *Freedom and Authority: A Study of English Thought in the Early Seventeenth Century.* Philadelphia: Westminster, 1975.

Crapps, Robert W. "Religion of the Plain Folk in the Southern United States: A Teaching Design." *Perspectives in Religious Studies* 4 (1977): 37-53.

_____, Edgar V. McKnight, and David A. Smith. *Introduction to the New Testament.* New York: Ronald, 1969.

Crites, Stephen. "The Narrative Quality of Experience." *Journal of the American Academy of Religion* 34 (1971): 291-311.

Crowder, Robert G. *Principles of Learning and Memory.* New York: Halsted, 1976.

Cutler, Donald, ed. *The Religious Situation.* Boston: Beacon Press, 1968.

Danielou, Jean. *God and the Ways of Knowing.* Walter Roberts, trans. New York: World, 1957.

Darwin, Charles. *Origin of Species by Means of Natural Selection.* Chicago: Encyclopaedia Britannica, 1955.

Davis, Charles. *Body as Spirit: The Nature of Religious Feeling.* New York: Seabury Press, 1976.

Davis, Henry. *Moral and Pastoral Theology.* 4th ed. New York: Sheed and Ward, 1943.

DeFord, Frank. "Religion in Sport." *Sports Illustrated* 44 (19 April 1976): 88ff.; (26 April 1976): 55ff.; (3 May 1976): 42ff.

Descartes, René. *Discourse on the Method of Rightly Conducting the Reason and Seeking Truth in the Sciences.* John Veitch, trans. La Salle IL: Open Court, 1899.

Dittes, James E. "Secular Religion: Dilemma of Churches and Researchers." *Review of Religious Research* 10 (1969): 65-81.

_____. "Two Issues in Measuring Religion," in *Research on Religious Development.* Merton P. Strommen, ed. New York: Hawthorn, 1971.

Doty, Robert W. "The Brain," in *Issues in Physiological Psychology.* Francis Leukel, ed. St. Louis: C. V. Mosby, 1974.

_____. "Philosophy and the Brain," in *Issues in Physiological Psychology.* Francis Leukel, ed. St. Louis: C. V. Mosby, 1974.

Dudley, R. L. "Alienation from Religion in Adolescents from Fundamentalist Religious Homes." *Journal for the Scientific Study of Religion* 17 (1978): 389-99.

Dunbar, H. Flanders. *Mind and Body: Psychosomatic Medicine.* New York: Random House, 1947.

Dupre, Louis. "Alienation and Redemption through Time and Memory: An Essay on Religious Time Consciousness." *Journal of the American Academy of Religion* 43 (1975): 671-80.

Durkheim, Emile. *The Elementary Form of the Religious Life.* J. W. Swain, trans. New York: Free Press, 1965.

Duska, Ronald, and Mariellen Whelan. *Moral Development: A Guide to Piaget and Kohlberg.* New York: Paulist, 1975.

Ebeling, Gerhard. *The Nature of Faith.* Ronald G. Smith, trans. Philadelphia: Fortress, 1961.

Eckardt, A. Roy, ed. *The Theologian at Work: A Common Search for Understanding.* New York: Harper, 1968.

Edwards, Jonathan. *Religious Affections.* John E. Smith, ed. New Haven: Yale University Press, 1959.

_____. "A Treatise Concerning Religious Affections," in *Jonathan Edwards: Representative Selections.* Clarence H. Faust and Thomas H. Johnson, eds. New York: Hill and Wang, 1962.

_____. *A Treatise Concerning Religious Affections.* Worcester MA: Isaiah Thomas, 1808.

Eissler, Ruth S., et al., eds. *The Psychoanalytic Study of the Child.* Vol. 15. New York: International Universities Press, 1968.

Eliade, Mircea. *Patterns in Comparative Religion.* Rosemary Sheed, trans. New York: Sheed and Ward, 1958.

_____. *The Sacred and the Profane: The Nature of Religion.* Willard R. Trask, trans. New York: Harper, 1961.

Eliade, Mircea, and Joseph Kitagawa, eds. *The History of Religions: Essays in Methodology.* Chicago: University of Chicago Press, 1959.

Elkind, David. *Children and Adolescents: Interpretative Essays on Jean Piaget.* New York: Oxford University Press, 1950.

_____. "The Origins of Religion in the Child." *Review of Religious Research* 12 (1970): 35-42.

Elkind, David, and Sally Elkind. "Varieties of Religious Experience in Young Adolescents." *Journal for the Scientific Study of Religion* 2 (1962): 102-12.

Ellul, Jacques. *The Ethics of Freedom*. Geoffrey W. Bromiley, trans. and ed. Grand Rapids MI: Eerdmans, 1976.

Ellwood, Robert S., Jr. *Mysticism and Religion*. Englewood Cliffs NJ: Prentice-Hall, 1980.

_____. *Religious and Spiritual Groups in Modern America*. Englewood Cliffs NJ: Prentice-Hall, 1973.

Englesman, Joan C. *The Feminine Dimension of the Divine*. Philadelphia: Westminster, 1979.

Erikson, Erik H. *Childhood and Society*. Rev. ed. New York: W. W. Norton, 1963.

_____. *Dimensions of a New Identity*. New York: W. W. Norton, 1974.

_____. *Gandhi's Truth*. New York: W. W. Norton, 1969.

_____. *Identity and the Life Cycle: Psychological Issues*. New York: International Universities Press, 1959.

_____. *Insight and Responsibility*. New York: W. W. Norton, 1964.

_____. *The Life Cycle Completed: A Review*. New York: W. W. Norton, 1982.

_____. *Life History and the Historical Moment*. New York: W. W. Norton, 1975.

_____. *Toys and Reasons: Stages in the Ritualization of Experience*. New York: W. W. Norton, 1977.

_____. *Young Man Luther*. New York: W. W. Norton, 1958.

_____. *Youth: Change and Challenge*. New York: Basic Books, 1963.

_____, ed. *The Challenge of Youth*. Garden City NY: Doubleday, 1965.

Estes, Weldon L. "The Curricular Status of Religion in Land-Grant Colleges and Universities." Ph.D. diss., University of Tennessee, 1963. *Dissertation Abstracts* 26 (1965): 206.

Evans, C. R., and A. D. J. Robertson. *Cybernetics*. Baltimore: University Park Press, 1968.

Evans, Richard I. *B. F. Skinner: The Man and His Ideas*. New York: Dutton, 1968.

_____. *Dialogue with Erich Fromm*. New York: Harper, 1966.

_____. *Dialogue with Erik Erikson*. New York: Harper, 1967.

Faber, Heije. *Psychology of Religion*. Philadelphia: Westminster, 1975.

Fairchild, Roy W. "Delayed Gratification: A Psychological and Religious Analysis." In *Research on Religious Development*. Merton P. Strommen, ed. New York: Hawthorn, 1971.

Farber, Leslie H. *The Ways of the Will: Essays toward a Psychology and Psychopathology of Will*. New York: Basic Books, 1966.

Faust, Clarence H., and Thomas H. Johnson, eds. *Jonathan Edwards: Representative Selections*. Rev. ed. New York: Hill and Wang, 1962.

Fechner, Gustav T. *Elements of Psychophysics*. Helmut E. Adler, trans. New York: Holt, Rinehart and Winston, 1966.

Feinberg, Charles L., ed. *The Fundamentals for Today*. Grand Rapids MI: Kregel Publications, 1961.

Feldman, Kenneth A. "Change and Stability of Religious Orientation during College, Part 1: Freshman-Senior Comparison." *Review of Religious Research* 11 (1969): 40-60.

_____. "Change and Stability of Religious Orientation during College, Part 2: Social-Cultural Correlates." *Review of Religous Research* 12 (1970): 103-108.

Ferm, Vergilius, ed. *Classics of Protestantism*. New York: Philosophical Library, 1959.

Ferré, Frederick. "The Definition of Religion." *Journal of the American Academy of Religion* 38 (1970): 3-16.

Festinger, Leon. *Conflict, Decision, and Dissonance*. Stanford CA: Stanford University Press, 1964.

_____, Henry W. Reicken, and Stanley Schachter. *When Prophecy Fails*. New York: Harper, 1956.

_____. *A Theory of Cognitive Dissonance*. Stanford CA: Stanford University Press, 1957.

_____, and James M. Carlsmith. "Cognitive Consequences of Forced Compliance." *Journal of Abnormal and Social Psychology* 58 (1959): 203-10.

Flacks, Richard, ed. *Conformity, Resistance, and Self-Determination*. Boston: Little, Brown, 1973.

Flakoll, David A. "A History of Method in the Psychology of Religion (1900-1960)." *Journal of Psychology and Theology* 4 (1976): 51-62.

Flanders, Henry J., Robert W. Crapps, and David A. Smith. *People of the Covenant: An Introduction to the Old Testament*. 2nd ed. New York: Wiley, 1973.

Fletcher, Joseph. *The Ethics of Genetic Control*. Garden City NY: Doubleday, 1974.

_____. *Situation Ethics: The New Morality*. Philadelphia: Westminster, 1966.

Flynn, Eileen P. *Human Fertilization in Vitro: A Catholic Moral Perspective*. Washington DC: University Press of America, 1984.

Forsyth, P. T. *The Principle of Authority in Relation to Certainty, Sensitivity and Society*. London: Independent Press, 1952.

Fowler, James W. *Stages of Faith: The Psychology of Human Development and the Quest for Meaning*. New York: Harper, 1981.

_____. *Becoming Adult, Becoming Christian*. New York: Harper and Row, 1984.

_____. "Faith Development Theory and Aims of Religious Socialization." In *Emerging Issues in Religious Education*. G. Durka and J. Smith, eds. New York: Paulist, 1976.

_____. "Stages in Faith: The Structural-Developmental Approach." In *Values and Moral Education*. T. C. Hennessey, ed. New York: Paulist, 1976.

_____. "Toward a Developmental Perspective on Faith." *Religious Education* 69 (March-April, 1974): 207-19.

_____, and Sam Keen. *Life Maps: Conversations on the Journey of Faith*. J. Berryman, ed. Waco TX: Word, 1978.

Foxfire, 7 (1973)

Frankl, Victor E. *Man's Search for Meaning: An Introduction to Logotherapy*. Ilse Lasch, trans. Boston: Beacon Press, 1962.

_____. *The Unconscious God: Psychotherapy and Theology*. New York: Simon and Schuster, 1975.

Franklin, R. L. *Freewill and Determinism: A Study of Rival Conceptions of Man*. Atlantic Highlands NJ: Humanities Press, 1968.

Frazer, James G. *The Golden Bough.* New York: Macmillan, 1922.

Freud, Sigmund. *Civilization and Its Discontents.* James Strachey, ed. New York: W. W. Norton, 1962.

_____. *Collected Papers.* Vols. 1-3. Joan Riviere, trans. London: Hogarth, 1948-1950.

_____. *The Ego and the Id.* 4th ed. Joan Riviere, trans. London: Hogarth, 1947.

_____. *The Future of an Illusion.* W. D. Robson-Scott, trans. and James Strachey, ed. Garden City NY: Doubleday, 1964.

_____. *A General Introduction to Psychoanalysis.* Joan Riviere, trans. New York: Perma Giants, 1948.

_____. *Leonardo da Vinci and a Memory of His Childhood.* Alan Tyson, trans. New York: W. W. Norton, 1964.

_____. *Moses and Monotheism.* Katherine Jones, trans. New York: Vintage, 1955.

_____. *New Introductory Lectures.* W. J. H. Sprott, trans. New York: W. W. Norton, 1933.

_____. *Totem and Taboo.* In *The Basic Writings of Sigmund Freud.* A. A. Brill, trans. and ed. New York: Random House, 1938.

Fromm, Erich. *The Anatomy of Human Destructiveness.* New York: Holt, Rinehart and Winston, 1973.

_____. *The Art of Loving.* New York: Harper, 1956.

_____. *The Dogma of Christ and Other Essays on Religion, Psychology, and Culture.* New York: Holt, Rinehart and Winston, 1963.

_____. *Escape from Freedom.* New York: Holt, Rinehart and Winston, 1941.

_____. *Man for Himself.* New York: Holt, Rinehart and Winston, 1947.

_____. *Psychoanalysis and Religion.* New Haven: Yale University Press, 1950.

_____. *The Sane Society.* New York: Holt, Rinehart and Winston, 1955.

_____. *You Shall Be as Gods: A Radical Interpretation of the Old Testament and Its Traditions.* New York: Holt, Rinehart and Winston, 1966.

Furness, Norman F. *The Fundamentalist Controversy, 1918-1931.* New Haven: Yale University Press, 1954.

Gargan, E. T. "Radical Catholics of the Right," *Social Order* 11 (1961): 409-19.

Gasper, Louis. *The Fundamentalist Movement.* Hawthorne NY: Mouton and Company, 1963.

Gay, Volney P. *Reading Freud: Psychology, Neurosis, and Religion.* Chico CA: Scholars Press, 1983.

Gesell, Arnold, Francis Ilg, and Louise Ames. *The Child from Five to Ten.* New York: Harper, 1946.

_____. *The First Five Years of Life: The Pre-School Years.* New York: Harper, 1940.

_____. *Youth: The Years from Ten to Sixteen.* New York: Harper, 1956.

Gilkey, Langdon B. *Naming the Whirlwind: The Renewal of God-Language.* Indianapolis: Bobbs-Merrill, 1969.

_____. *Religion and the Scientific Future: Reflections on Myth, Science, and Theology.* New York: Harper, 1970.

Gill, Merton M., and Margaret Brenman. *Hypnosis and Related States: Psychoanalytic Studies in Regression.* New York: International Universities Press, 1959.

Gilligan, Carol. *In a Different Voice: Psychological Theory and Women's Development.* Cambridge: Harvard University Press, 1982.

Glasser, John W. "Conscience and Superego," in *Psyche and Spirit: Readings in Psychology and Religion.* John J. Heaney, ed. New York: Paulist, 1973.

Glasser, William. *Reality Therapy.* New York: Harper, 1965.

Gleason, John J., Jr. *Growing up to God: Eight Steps in Religious Development.* Nashville: Abingdon, 1975.

Glen, J. Stanley. *Erich Fromm: A Protestant Critique.* Philadelphia: Westminster, 1966.

Glock, Charles Y. *Survey Research in the Social Sciences.* New York: Russell Sage Foundation, 1967.

_____, ed. *Religion in Sociological Perspectives: Essays in the Empirical Study of Religion.* Belmont CA: Wadsworth, 1973.

_____, and Robert N. Bellah, eds. *The New Religious Consciousness.* Berkeley: University of California Press, 1976.

Goble, Frank G. *The Third Force: The Psychology of Abraham Maslow.* New York: Grossman, 1970.

Godin, André, ed. *Child and Adult before God.* Chicago: Loyola University Press, 1965.

_____, ed. *From Cry to Word: Contributions toward a Psychology of Prayer.* Brussels: Lumen Vitae Press, 1968.

_____, ed. *From Religious Experience to a Religious Attitude.* Chicago: Loyola University Press, 1965.

_____, ed. *Research in Religious Psychology.* Brussels: Lumen Vitae Press, 1957.

Goldbrunner, Josef. *Holiness Is Wholeness.* Stanley Goodman, trans. New York: Pantheon, 1955.

Goldenson, Robert M. *The Encyclopedia of Human Behavior.* Vols. 1-3. Garden City NY: Doubleday, 1970.

Goldman, Ronald. *Religious Thinking from Childhood to Adolescence.* New York: Seabury Press, 1964.

Goodenough, Edwin R. *The Psychology of Religious Experiences.* New York: Basic Books, 1965.

Goodman, Felicitas D. *Speaking in Tongues: A Cross-Cultural Study of Glossolalia.* Chicago: University of Chicago Press, 1972.

Goody, Jack. "Religion and Ritual: The Definitional Problem." *British Journal of Sociology* 12 (1961): 142-64.

Gore, Rick. "The Awesome World within a Cell." *National Geographic* 150 (1976): 350-95.

Gorlow, Leon, and Harold E. Schroeder. "Motives for Participating in the Religious Experience." *Journal for the Scientific Study of Religion* 7 (1968): 241-51.

Gorsuch, Richard L. "Practicality and Ethics of Experimental Research When Studying Religion." *Journal for the Scientific Study of Religion* 21 (1982): 370-72.

Graebner, O. E. *Child Concepts of God.* Chicago: Lutheran Education Association, 1960.

Green, Harold P. "Genetic Technology: Law and Policy for the Brave New World." *Indiana Law Journal* 48 (1973): 559-80.

Grinker, Roy R., and John P. Spiegel. *War Neuroses.* New York: Blakiston, 1945.

Groch, Judith. *The Right to Create.* Boston: Little, Brown, 1969.

Gross, Martin L. *The Psychological Society.* New York: Random House, 1978.

Guetzkow, Harold S., ed. *Groups, Leadership, and Men.* New York: Russell and Russell, 1963.

Hall, Calvin, S. *A Primer of Freudian Psychology.* Cleveland: World, 1954.

_____, and Vernon J. Nordby. *A Primer of Jungian Psychology.* New York: Taplinger, 1973.

Hall, G. Stanley. *Adolescence.* Vols. 1-2. New York: Appleton, 1904.

Hamilton, Kenneth. *The Promise of Kierkegaard.* Philadelphia: Lippincott, 1969.

Hammond, Guyton. *Man in Estrangement.* Nashville: Vanderbilt University Press, 1965.

Hammond, Philip E., and Benton Johnson, eds. *American Mosaics: Social Patterns of Religion in the United States.* New York: Random House, 1970.

Hampshire, Stuart. *Freedom of the Individual.* New York: Harper, 1969.

Hanna, Charles B. *The Face of the Deep: The Religious Ideas of C. G. Jung.* Philadelphia: Westminster, 1967.

Häring, Bernhard. *Ethics of Manipulation: Issues in Medicine, Behavior Control and Genetics.* New York: Seabury Press, 1975.

Harman, Harry H. *Modern Factor Analysis.* 2nd ed. Chicago: University of Chicago Press, 1960.

Harms, Ernest. "The Development of Religious Experience in Children." *American Journal of Sociology* 50 (1944): 112-22.

Havens, Joseph, ed. *Psychology and Religion: A Contemporary Dialogue.* New York: Van Nostrand, 1968.

Healey, F. G., ed. *What Theologians Do.* Grand Rapids MI: Eerdmans, 1970.

Heaney, John J., ed. *Psyche and Spirit: Readings in Psychology and Religion.* New York: Paulist, 1973.

Heidegger, Martin. *Being and Time.* John Macquarrie and Edward Robinson, trans. New York: Harper, 1962.

Heilbut, Tony. *The Gospel Sound: Good News and Bad Times.* Garden City NY: Doubleday, 1975.

Helmholtz, Hermann L. *Treatise on Physiological Optics.* James P. C. Southall, ed. New York: Dover, 1962.

Herberg, Will. *Protestant-Catholic-Jew.* Garden City NY: Doubleday, 1960.

Herbert, A. Gabriel. *Fundamentalism and the Church.* Philadelphia: Westminster, 1957.

Hill, Samuel. *Religion and the Solid South.* Nashville: Abingdon, 1972.

Hiltner, Seward. *Preface to Pastoral Theology.* Nashville: Abingdon, 1958.

_____. "The Psychological Understanding of Religion." *Crozier Quarterly* 24 (1947): 3-36.

Hine, V. H. "Pentecostal Glossolalia: Toward A Functional Interpretation." *Journal for the Scientific Study of Religion* 8 (1969): 211-26.

Hodges, Daniel L. "Breaking a Scientific Taboo: Putting Assumptions about the Supernatural into Scientific Theories of Religion." *Journal for the Scientific Study of Religion* 13 (1974): 393-408.

Hoffman, Martin L., and Lois W. Hoffman, eds. *Review of Child Development Research.* Vol. 1. New York: Russell Sage Foundation, 1964.

_____. "Childrearing Practices and Moral Development: Generalizations from Empirical Research." *Child Development* 34 (1963): 205-318.

_____. "Development of Internal Moral Standards in Children." *Research on Religious Development.* Merton P. Strommen, ed. New York: Hawthorn, 1971.

Holm, N. G. "Mysticism and Intense Experiences." *Journal for the Scientific Study of Religion* 21 (1982): 268-76.

Homans, Peter. *Theology after Freud.* Indianapolis: Bobbs-Merrill, 1970.

_____. *Jung in Context: Modernity and the Making of a Psychology.* Chicago: University of Chicago Press, 1979.

_____, ed. *The Dialogue between Theology and Psychology.* Essays in Divinity series, Vol. 3. Gerald C. Brauer, ed. Chicago: University of Chicago Press, 1968.

_____. "Psychology and Hermeneutics: Jung's Contribution." *Zygon* 4 (1969): 333-55.

_____. "Toward a Psychology of Religion." In *The Dialogue between Theology and Psychology.* Gerald C. Brauer, ed. Chicago: University of Chicago Press, 1968.

_____. "Transcendence, Distance, Fantasy: The Protestant Era in Psychological Perspective." *Journal of Religion* 49 (1969): 205-27.

Hood, Ralph W., Jr. "Religious Orientation and the Experience of Transcendence." *Journal for the Scientific Study of Religion* 12 (1973): 441-48.

_____. "Psychological Strength and the Report of Intense Religious Experience." *Journal for the Scientific Study of Religion* 13 (1974): 65-71.

_____. "Eliciting Mystical States of Consciousness with Semistructured Nature Experiences." *Journal for the Scientific Study of Religion* 16 (1977): 155-63.

Horney, Karen. *New Ways in Psychoanalysis.* New York: W. W. Norton, 1939.

Hosinski, T. E. "Science, Religion, and the Self-Understanding of Man." *Religion in Life* 42 (1973): 179-93.

Howe, Reuel L. *The Creative Years.* New York: Seabury Press, 1959.

Howie, John. "Is Effort of Will a Basis for Moral Freedom?" *Religious Studies* 8 (1972): 345-49.

Hudock, George A. "Gene Therapy and Genetic Engineering." *Indiana Law Journal* 48 (1973): 533-58.

Hunter, Archibald M. *A Pattern for Life.* Philadelphia: Westminster, 1953.

Husserl, Edmund. *Ideas: General Introduction to Pure Phenomenology.* New York: Collier, 1967.

Hutch, R. A. "The Personal Ritual of Glossolalia." *Journal for the Scientific Study of Religion* 19 (1980): 255-66.

Huxley, Aldous. *Brave New World.* New York: Harper, 1969.

Irwin, Francis W. *Intentional Behavior and Motivation: A Cognitive Theory*. Philadelphia: Lippincott, 1971.

Jacobi, Jolandi. *The Psychology of C. G. Jung*. New Haven: Yale University Press, 1968.

James, William. *Essays in Pragmatism*. Albury Castell, ed. New York: Hafner, 1948.

_____. *The Principles of Psychology*. Vols. 1-2. New York: Holt, Rinehart and Winston, 1890.

_____. *The Varieties of Religious Experience: A Study in Human Nature*. New York: Modern Library, 1902.

_____. *The Will to Believe and Other Essays in Popular Philosophy*. New York: Dover, 1956.

Jenkins, Daniel T. *Tradition, Freedom, and the Spirit*. Philadelphia: Westminster, 1951.

Johnson, Aubrey R. *The Vitality of the Individual in the Thought of Ancient Israel*. Cardiff: University of Wales Press, 1949.

Johnson, Roger A., et al. *Critical Issues in Modern Religion*. Englewood Cliffs NJ: Prentice-Hall, 1973.

Jonas, Hans. "Technology and Responsibility: Reflections on the New Tasks of Ethics." *Social Research* 40 (1973): 31-54.

Jones, E. Stanley. *Is the Kingdom of God Realism?* New York: Abingdon-Cokesbury, 1940.

Jones, Ernest. *The Life and Work of Sigmund Freud*. Vols. 1-3. New York: Basic Books, 1953-1957.

Jones, Harbin B. "The Effects of Sensual Drugs on Behavior: Clues to the Function of the Brain." In *Advances in Psychology*. Grant Newton and Austin H. Riesen, eds. Vol. 11. New York: John Wiley, 1974.

Jung, Carl G. *Answer to Job*. R. F. C. Hull, trans. Princeton: Princeton University Press, 1973.

_____. *Contributions to Analytic Psychology*. H. G. Baynes and C. F. Baynes, trans. London: Routledge and Kegan Paul, 1928.

_____. *Mandala Symbolism*. R. F. C. Hull, trans. Princeton: Princeton University Press, 1972.

_____. *Memories, Dreams, Reflections*. Aniela Jeffs, ed., Richard Winston and Clara Winston, trans. New York: Pantheon Books, 1963.

_____. *Modern Man in Search of a Soul*. W. S. Dell and C. F. Baynes, trans. London: K. Paul, Trench, Trubner, 1933.

_____. *Psychology and Religion*. New Haven: Yale University Press, 1938.

Katz, Solomon. "Toward a New Science of Humanity." *Zygon* 10 (1975): 12-13.

Kaplan, Justin D., ed. *Dialogues of Plato*. New York: Washington Square Press, 1951.

Kaufman, Gordon D. *The Context of Decision: A Theological Analysis*. Nashville: Abingdon, 1961.

_____. *An Essay on Theological Method*. Chico CA: Scholars Press, 1975.

Keen, Sam. *Apology for Wonder*. New York: Harper, 1969.

_____. *To a Dancing God*. New York: Harper, 1970.

Kellenberger, J. "Mysticism and Drugs." *Religious Studies* 14 (1978): 175-91.

Kelley, Dean M. *Why Conservative Churches Are Growing: A Study in Sociology of Religion.* New York: Harper & Row, 1972. Reprinted with a new preface for the ROSE 11 edition (Macon GA: Mercer University Press, 1986).

Kelsey, Morton T. *Tongue-Speaking: An Experiment in Spiritual Experience.* Garden City NY: Doubleday, 1961.

_____. *Companions on the Inner Way: The Art of Spiritual Guidance.* Los Angeles: Crossroads, 1983.

Kieffer, George H. *Bioethics: A Textbook of Issues.* Reading MA: Addison-Wesley, 1979.

Kierkegaard, Søren. *Concluding Unscientific Postscript.* In *A Kierkegaard Anthology.* Robert Bretall, ed. Princeton: Princeton University Press, 1951.

_____. *Purity of Heart Is to Will One Thing.* Douglas V. Steere, trans. New York: Harper, 1956.

_____. *Stages on Life's Way.* Walter Lowrie, trans. Princeton: Princeton University Press, 1940.

Kildahl, John P. *The Psychology of Speaking in Tongues.* New York: Harper, 1972.

Kirscht, John P., and Ronald C. Dillehay. *Dimensions of Authoritarianism: A Review of Research and Theory.* Lexington: University of Kentucky Press, 1967.

Klineberg, Göte. "Perception-like Images in the Religious Experience of the Child." In *Child and Adult before God.* André Godin, ed. Chicago: Loyola University Press, 1965.

_____. "A Study of the Religious Experience in Children from Nine to Thirteen Years of Age." *Religious Education* 54 (1959): 211-16.

Klinger, Eric. *Structure and Functions of Fantasy.* New York: Wiley-Interscience, 1971.

Kluckhohn, Florence R., and F. L. Strodtbeck. *Variations in Value-Orientations.* New York: Harper, 1961.

Knight, James A. *Conscience and Guilt.* New York: Appleton-Century-Crofts, 1969.

Koffka, Kurt. *Principles of Gestalt Psychology.* New York: Harcourt Brace, 1935.

Kohlberg, Lawrence. *The Philosophy of Moral Development: Moral States and the Idea of Justice—Essays in Moral Development.* New York: Harper & Row, 1981.

_____. "A Cognitive-Developmental Approach to Moral Education." *The Humanist* 32 (1972): 13-16.

_____. "Early Education: A Cognitive-Developmental Approach." *Child Development* 39 (1968): 1013-62.

_____. "Moral Education in the Schools: A Developmental View." *School Review* 74 (1966): 1-30.

_____. "Development of Moral Character and Moral Ideology." In *Review of Child Development Research.* Vol. 1 Martin L. Hoffman and Lois W. Hoffman, eds. New York: Russell Sage Foundation, 1964.

_____. "Stages of Moral Development as a Basis for Moral Education." In *Moral Education: Interdisciplinary Approaches.* Clive M. Beck, Brian S. Crittendon, and Edmund V. Sullivan, eds. Toronto: University of Toronto Press, 1971.

_____, and Carol Gilligan. "The Adolescent as a Philosopher: The Discovery of the Self in a Preconventional World." *Daedalus* 100 (1971): 1051-86.

_____ , and Rochelle Mayer. "Development as the Aim of Education." *Harvard Educational Review* 42 (1972): 449-96.

_____ , and E. Turiel, eds. *Recent Research in Moral Development.* New York: Holt, Rinehart and Winston, 1973.

Kotesky, Ronald L. "An Integration of Statistics and Christianity." *Journal of Psychology and Theology* 3 (1975): 195-201.

Kroner, Richard. *The Religious Function of Imagination.* New Haven: Yale University Press, 1941.

Kubler-Ross, Elizabeth. *On Death and Dying.* New York: Macmillan, 1970.

Kuhn, Thomas S. *The Structure of Scientific Revolutions.* 2nd ed. Chicago: University of Chicago Press, 1970.

Küng, Hans. *Freud and the Problem of God.* Edward Quinn, trans. New Haven: Yale University Press, 1979.

La Barre, Weston. *They Shall Take up Serpents: Psychology of the Southern Snake-Handling Cult.* New York: Schocken, 1969.

Lacey, Oliver L. *Statistical Methods in Experimentation.* New York: Macmillan, 1953.

Lande, Nathaniel, and Afton Slade. *Stages: Understanding How You Make Moral Decisions.* New York: Harper and Row, 1979.

Langton, Edward. *Essentials of Demonology: A Study of Jewish and Christian Dogma, Its Origins and Development.* London: Epworth, 1945.

Lapsley, James N. *Salvation and Health.* Philadelphia: Westminster, 1972.

_____ , and John H. Simpson. "Speaking in Tongues: Token of Group Acceptance and Divine Approval." *Pastoral Psychology* 14 (May 1964): 48-55.

Lashley, Karl S. *Brain Mechanisms and Intelligence.* Chicago: University of Chicago Press, 1929.

Laski, Marghanita. *Ecstasy: A Study of Some Secular and Religious Experiences.* Bloomington: Indiana University Press, 1967.

Laughlin, Charles, Jr., and Eugene d'Aquili. *Biogenetic Structuralism.* New York: Columbia University Press, 1974.

_____ . "The Biopsychological Determinants of Religious Ritual Behavior." *Zygon* 10 (1975): 32-58.

Lecky, Prescott. *Self-Consistency: A Theory of Personality.* Fort Myers Beach FL: Island Press, 1945.

Lee, Robert, and Martin Marty, eds. *Religion and Social Conflict.* New York: Oxford University Press, 1964.

Lee, Roy S. *Freud and Christianity.* London: James Clarke and Co., 1948.

Leeper, Robert W. "A Motivational Theory of Emotion to Replace 'Emotion as Disorganized Response'." *Psychological Review* 55 (1948): 5-21.

Lemert, Charles C. "Defining Non-Church Religion." *Review of Religious Research* 16 (1975): 186-97.

Lenski, Gerhard. *The Religious Factor: A Sociological Study of Religion's Impact on Politics, Economics, and Family Life.* Garden City NY: Doubleday, 1961.

Leuba, James H. *A Psychological Study of Religion.* New York: Macmillan, 1912.

_____ . *The Psychology of Religious Mysticism.* New York: Harcourt Brace, 1925.

Leukel, Francis, ed. *Issues in Physiological Psychology*. St. Louis: C. V. Mosby, 1974.

Levinson, Daniel J. *The Seasons of a Man's Life*. New York: Knopf, 1978.

Levinson, Henry S. *Science, Metaphysics, and the Chance of Salvation: An Interpretation of the Thought of William James*. Chico CA: Scholars Press, 1978.

Lewin, Kurt. *Field Theory in Social Science*. New York: Harper, 1951.

_____. *A Dynamic Theory of Personality*. Donald K. Adams and Karl E. Zener, trans. New York: McGraw-Hill, 1935.

Lewis, Helen B. *Freud and Modern Psychology: The Emotional Basis of Mental Illness*. New York: Plenum, 1981.

Lickona, Thomas, ed. *Moral Development and Behavior: Theory, Research and Social Issues*. New York: Holt, Rinehart and Winston, 1976.

Lifton, Robert J. *History and Human Survival*. New York: Random House, 1970.

_____. *Home from the War*. New York: Simon and Schuster, 1973.

_____. *The Life of the Self*. New York: Simon and Schuster, 1976.

Linschoten, Hans. *On the Way toward a Phenomenology Psychology: The Psychology of William James*. Pittsburgh: University of Pittsburgh Press, 1968.

Lipset, S.M. "Religion and Politics in the American Past and Present." In *Religion and Social Conflict*. Robert Lee and Martin Marty, eds. New York: Oxford University Press, 1964.

Loevinger, Jane. *Ego Development*. San Francisco: Jossey-Bass, 1976.

London, Perry, Robert E. Schulman, and Michael S. Black. "Religion, Guilt, and Ethical Standards." *Journal of Social Psychology* 63 (1964): 145-59.

Loomba, R. M. "The Religious Development of Children." *Psychological Abstracts* 345 (1944): 35.

Lovekin, Adams, and H. Newton Malony. "Religious Glossolalia: A Longitudinal Study of Personality Changes." *Journal for the Scientific Study of Religion* 17 (1977): 383-93.

Luckmann, Thomas. *The Invisible Religion: The Problem of Religion in Modern Society*. New York: Macmillan, 1967.

McCann, R. V. "Developmental Factors in the Growth of a Mature Faith." *Religious Education* 50 (1955): 147-55.

McCasland, S. Vernon. *By the Finger of God: Demon Possession and Exorcism in Early Christianity in the Light of Modern Views of Mental Illness*. New York: Macmillan, 1951.

McDougall, William. *An Introduction to Social Psychology*. 16th ed. Boston: J. W. Luce, 1923.

_____. *Outline of Abnormal Psychology*. New York: Scribner's, 1926.

MacGregor, Geddes. *Introduction to Religious Philosophy*. Boston: Houghton Mifflin, 1959.

McKellar, Peter. *Imagination and Thinking: A Psychological Analysis*. New York: Basic Books, 1957.

McKenzie, John G. *Guilt: Its Meaning and Significance*. London: Allen & Unwin, 1962.

McKenzie, John L. *Authority in the Church*. New York: Sheed and Ward, 1966.

MacLeod, R. B. "Phenomenology: A Challenge to Experimental Psychology." In *Behaviorism and Phenomenology*. T. W. Mann, ed. Chicago: University of Chicago Press, 1964.

Magee, John B. *Religion and Modern Man: A Study of the Religious Meaning of Being Human*. New York: Harper, 1967.

Malinowski, Brownislaw. *Magic, Science and Religion*. Garden City NY: Doubleday, 1955.

Mann, T. W., ed. *Behaviorism and Phenomenology*. Chicago: University of Chicago Press, 1964.

Manschreck, Clyde L., ed. *Erosion of Authority*. Nashville: Abingdon, 1971.

Marsden, George M. *Fundamentalism and American Culture: The Shaping of Twentieth-Century Evangelicalism, 1870-1925*. New York: Oxford University Press, 1980.

Marty, Martin E. *A Nation of Behavers*. Chicago: University of Chicago Press, 1976.

_____. *The New Shape of American Religion*. New York: Harper, 1959.

_____. "Religious Development in Historical, Social, and Cultural Context." In *Research on Religious Development*. Merton P. Strommen, ed. New York: Hawthorn, 1971.

Maslow, Abraham H. *The Farther Reaches of Human Nature*. New York: Viking, 1971.

_____. *Motivation and Personality*. 2nd. ed. New York: Harper, 1970.

_____. *Religions, Values, and Peak-Experiences*. New York: Viking, 1964.

_____. *Toward a Psychology of Being*. 2nd. ed. New York: Van Nostrand Reinhold, 1968.

_____. "Eupsychia: The Good Society." *Journal of Humanistic Psychology* 1 (1961): 1-11.

Maves, Paul B. "Religious Development in Adulthood." In *Research on Religious Development*. Merton P. Strommen, ed. New York: Hawthorn, 1971.

May, Rollo. *The Courage to Create*. New York: W. W. Norton, 1975.

_____. *Love and Will*. New York: W. W. Norton, 1969.

_____. *Man's Search for Himself*. New York: W. W. Norton, 1953.

Mead, Frank S. *Handbook of Denominations in the United States*. 6th ed. Nashville: Abingdon, 1975.

Meadow, Mary Jo, and Richard D. Kahoe. *Psychology of Religion: Religion in Individual Lives*. New York: Harper & Row, 1984.

Meiland, Jack W. *The Nature of Intention*. New York: Methuen, 1970.

Mellert, Robert. *What is Process Theology?* New York: Paulist, 1975.

Menninger, Karl. *Whatever Became of Sin?* New York: Hawthorn, 1973.

Merton, Thomas. *Mystics and Zen Masters*. New York: Farrar, Straus and Giroux, 1961.

Meyer, Donald. *The Positive Thinkers: A Study of the American Quest for Health, Wealth, and Personal Power from Mary Baker Eddy to Norman Vincent Peale*. Garden City NY: Doubleday, 1965.

Meyer, George W., ed. *Selected Poems: William Wordsworth*. Arlington Heights IL: AHM Publishing Corporation, 1950.

Milgram, Stanley. *Obedience to Authority: An Experimental View.* New York: Harper, 1969.

Miller, David L. *Gods and Games: Toward a Theology of Play.* New York: Harper, 1972.

Miller, James G. "Toward a General Theory for the Behavioral Sciences." *American Psychologist* 10 (1955): 513-31.

Milner, Peter M. *Physiological Psychology.* New York: Holt, Rinehart and Winston, 1970.

Mischel, Walter, and John Grusec. "Waiting for Rewards and Punishments: Effects of Time and Probability on Choice." *Journal of Personality and Social Psychology* 5 (1967): 24-31.

Moberg, David O. "Theological Position and Institutional Characteristics of Protestant Congregations: An Exploratory Study." *Journal for the Scientific Study of Religion* 9 (1970): 53-58.

_____. "Religiosity in Old Age." *The Gerontologist* 5 (1965): 78-87.

Moller, Herbert. "Affective Mysticism in Western Civilization." *Psychoanalytic Review* 52 (1965): 115-30.

Moore, LeRoy, Jr. "From Profane to Sacred America." *Journal of the American Academy of Religion* 39 (1971): 321-38.

Moore, Robert L. *John Wesley and Authority: A Psychological Perspective.* Chico CA: Scholars Press, 1979.

Mowrer, O. Hobart, ed. *Morality and Mental Health.* Chicago: Rand McNally, 1964.

_____. *The Crisis in Psychology and Religion.* New York: Van Nostrand, 1962.

Müller, F. Max, ed. *The Sacred Books of the East.* Oxford: Clarendon Press, 1879-84.

Murphy, Gardner. "Psychology in the Year 2000." *American Psychologist* 24 (1969): 523-31.

Nagel, Ernest, and Morris R. Cohen. *An Introduction to Logic and Scientific Method.* New York: Harcourt, Brace and World, 1934.

_____. *The Structure of Science.* New York: Harcourt, Brace and World, 1961.

Narramore, Bruce. "Perspectives on the Integration of Psychology and Theology." *Journal of Psychology and Theology* 1 (1973): 3-18.

Neale, Robert E. *In Praise of Play.* New York: Harper, 1972.

Nelson, C. Ellis, ed. *Conscience: Theological and Psychological Perspectives.* New York: Newman, 1973.

Newbigin, Leslie. *The Household of God.* London: S.C.M. Press, 1958.

Noss, John B. *Man's Religions.* 5th ed. New York: Macmillan, 1974.

Nichol, John T. *Pentecostalism.* New York: Harper, 1966.

Nygren, Anders. *Meaning and Method: Prolegomena to a Scientific Philosophy of Religion and a Scientific Theology.* Philip S. Watson, trans. Philadelphia: Fortress, 1972.

Nye, Robert D. *Three Psychologies: Perspectives from Freud, Skinner, and Rogers.* 2nd ed. Monterey CA: Brooks/Cole, 1981.

Oates, Wayne E. *The Psychology of Religion.* Waco TX: Word Books, 1973.

_____. *Religious Factors in Mental Illness.* New York: Association, 1955.

Ogden, Schubert M. "The Authority of Scripture for Theology." *Interpretation* 30 (1976): 242-61.

_____. "Sources of Religious Authority in Liberal Protestantism." *Journal of the American Academy of Religion* 44 (1976): 403-16.

Orbach, Harold L. "Aging and Religion: A Study of Church Attendance in the Detroit Metropolitan Area." *Geriatrics* 16 (1961): 535-40.

Orum, Anthony M. "Religion and the Rise of the Radical White: The Case of Southern Wallace Support in 1968." *Social Science Quarterly* 51 (1970): 674-88.

Ostrow, M., and B. A. Scharfstein. *The Need to Believe: The Psychology of Religion.* New York: International Universities Press, 1954.

Otto, Rudolf. *The Idea of the Holy.* John W. Harvey, trans. New York: Oxford University Press, 1926.

_____. *Mysticism: East and West: A Comparative Analysis of the Nature of Mysticism.* Bertha L. Bracey and Richenda C. Payne, trans. New York: Macmillan, 1970.

Outler, Albert C. *Psychotherapy and the Christian Message.* New York: Harper, 1954.

Pahnke, Walter N. "Drugs and Mysticism." *International Journal of Parapsychology* 8 (1966): 295-314.

_____, and William A. Richards. "Implications of LSD and Experimental Mysticism." *Journal of Religion and Health* 5 (1966): 175-208.

Paloutzian, Raymond F. *Invitation to the Psychology of Religion.* Glenview IL: Scott, Foresman, 1983.

Pascal, Blaise. *Pensées.* Intro. by T. S. Eliot. New York: E. P. Dutton, 1958.

Pask, Gordon. *An Approach to Cybernetics.* London: Hutchinson, 1961.

Pattison, E. Mansell, ed. *Clinical Psychiatry and Religion.* Boston: Little, Brown, 1969.

Pavlov, Ivan P. *Conditional Reflexes.* F. C. Aurep, trans. Oxford: Clarendon Press, 1927.

Peale, Norman V. *A Guide to Confident Living.* Englewood Cliffs NJ: Prentice-Hall, 1948.

_____. *The Power of Positive Thinking.* Englewood Cliffs NJ: Prentice-Hall, 1952.

Perry, Ralph B. *The Thought and Character of William James.* Vols. 1-2. Boston: Little, Brown, 1935.

Pfister, Oscar. *Christianity and Fear.* New York: Macmillan, 1948.

_____. *Psychoanalysis and Faith: The Letters of Sigmund Freud and Oscar Pfister.* Heinrich Menz and Ernst L. Freud, eds., and Eric Mosbacher, trans. New York: Basic Books, 1964.

Piaget, Jean. *The Grasp of Consciousness: Action and Concept in the Young Child.* Susan Wedgewood, trans. Cambridge: Harvard University Press, 1976.

_____. *The Language and Thought of the Child.* New York: Harcourt Brace, 1932.

_____. *The Moral Judgment of the Child.* London: Kegan Paul, Trench, Trubner, 1931.

_____. *On the Development of Memory and Intention.* Eleanor Duckworth, trans. Worcester MA: Clark University Press, 1968.

_____, and Barbel Inhelder. *The Psychology of the Child.* Helen Weaver, trans. New York: Basic Books, 1969.

Pierce, C. A. *Conscience in the New Testament.* London: S.C.M. Press, 1955.

Polanyi, Michael. *The Tacit Dimension.* Garden City NY: Doubleday, 1966.

Pressey, Sidney L., and Raymond G. Kuhlen. *Psychological Development through the Life Span.* New York: Harper, 1957.

Prince, George M. "Creativity, Self, and Power." In *Perspective in Creativity.* Irving A. Taylor and J. W. Getzels, eds. New York: Aldine, 1975.

Pruyser, Paul W. *A Dynamic Psychology of Religion.* New York: Harper, 1968.

_____. "Anxiety, Guilt, and Shame in the Atonement." *Theology Today* 21 (1964): 15-33.

_____. "Lessons from Art Theory for the Psychology of Religion." *Journal for the Scientific Study of Religion* 15 (1976): 1-14.

_____. "Psychological View of Religion in the 1970s." *Pastoral Psychology* 23 (1972): 21-38.

Pugh, George E. "Human Values, Free Will, and the Conscious Mind." *Zygon* 11 (1976): 2-24.

Rahner, Hugo. *Man at Play.* Brian Battershaw and Edward Quinn, trans. New York: Herder and Herder, 1972.

Rank, Otto. *The Trauma of Birth.* London: Routledge and Kegan Paul, 1929.

_____. *Will Therapy and Truth and Reality.* New York: Knopf, 1950.

Reid, A. C. *Elements of Psychology.* Englewood Cliffs NJ: Prentice-Hall, 1938.

Reik, Theodor. *Dogma and Compulsion: Psychoanalytic Studies of Religion and Myths.* New York: International University Press, 1951.

Restle, Frank, Richard M. Shiffrin, N. John Castelhan, Harold R. Lindman, and David B. Pisoni, eds. *Cognitive Theory.* Vol. 1. Hillsdale NJ: Laurence Erlbaum Associates, 1975.

Rhodes, Arnold B., ed. *The Church Faces the Isms.* Nashville: Abingdon, 1958.

Richardson, J. T. "Psychological Interpretations of Glossolalia: A Reexamination of Research." *Journal for the Scientific Study of Religion* 12 (1973): 99-207.

Richey, Russell E., and Donald G. Jones, eds. *American Civil Religion.* New York: Harper, 1974.

Ricouer, Paul. *Freud and Philosophy: An Essay on Interpretation.* New Haven: Yale University Press, 1970.

_____. *The Symbolism of Evil.* Emerson Buchanan, trans. New York: Harper, 1967.

_____. "Reaction to Freud." In *Psyche and Spirit.* John J. Heaney, ed. New York: Paulist, 1973.

Riesman, David. "Where Is the College Generation Headed?" *Atlantic* 207 (1961): 39-45.

Rizzuto, Ana-Maria. *The Birth of the Living God: A Psychoanalytic Study.* Chicago: University of Chicago Press, 1979.

Roazen, Paul. *Freud and His Followers.* New York: Knopf, 1975.

Roberts, David E. *Psychotherapy and a Christian View of Man.* New York: Scribner's, 1950.

Robinson, Daniel N. *The Enlightened Machine: An Analytic Introduction to Neuropsychology.* Encino CA: Dickenson, 1973.

Robinson, John A. T. *Honest to God.* Philadelphia: Westminster, 1963.

Rogers, Carl R. *Client-Centered Therapy: Its Current Practice, Implications, and Theory.* Boston: Houghton Mifflin, 1951.

Rokeach, Milton. *Three Christs of Ypsilanti.* New York: Knopf, 1969.

_____. *The Open and Closed Mind: Investigations into the Nature of Belief Systems and Personality Systems.* New York: Basic Books, 1960.

_____. "Value Systems in Religion." *Review of Religious Research* 11 (1969): 3-23.

Rose, Arnold. "Alienation and Participation: A Comparison of Group Leaders and the Mass." *American Sociological Review* 27 (1962): 834-38.

Rowland, G. Thomas, and J. Carson McGuire. *The Mind of Man: Some Views and a Theory of Cognitive Development.* Englewood Cliffs NJ: Prentice-Hall, 1971.

Rowley, H. H. *The Servant of the Lord and Other Essays on the Old Testament.* London: Lutterworth, 1952.

Royce, Josiah. *The Philosophy of Loyalty.* New York: Macmillan, 1909.

Runyon, Theodore, ed. *What the Spirit is Saying to the Churches.* New York: Hawthorn, 1975.

Sadler, William A., Jr. *Existence and Love: A New Approach to Existential Phenomenology.* New York: Scribner's, 1969.

_____, ed. *Personality and Religion: The Role of Religion in Personality Development.* New York: Harper, 1970.

Sampson, Edward E. "Student Activism and the Decade of Protest." *Journal of Social Issues* 23 (1967): 1-33.

Sandeen, Ernest R. *The Roots of Fundamentalism: British and American Millenarianism, 1800-1930.* Chicago: University of Chicago Press, 1970.

Sandler, Joseph. "On the Concept of Superego." In *Psychoanalytic Study of the Child.* Vol. 15. Ruth S. Eissler et al., eds. New York: International Universities Press, 1960.

Sargant, William. *The Battle for the Mind.* London: Heinemann, 1967.

_____. *The Mind Possessed: A Physiology of Possession, Mysticism, and Faith Healing.* London: Heinemann, 1973.

Schachter, Stanley. *The Psychology of Affiliation: Experimental Studies of the Sources of Gregariousness.* Stanford CA: Stanford University Press, 1959.

Schaer, Hans. *Religion and the Cure of Souls in Jung's Psychology.* R. F. C. Hull, trans. New York: Pantheon Books, 1950.

Schilling, Harold K. *The New Consciousness in Science and Religion.* New York: United Church Press, 1973.

Schleiermacher, Friedrich. *On Religion: Speeches to Its Cultured Despisers.* John Oman, trans. New York: Harper, 1958.

_____. *The Christian Faith.* H. R. Mackintosh and J. S. Stewart, trans. and eds. Edinburgh: T. & T. Clark, 1928.

Scholefield, Harry B., ed. *A Pocket Guide to Unitarianism.* Boston: Beacon Press, 1954.

Schroeder, W. Widick. "Cognitive Structures and Religious Research." *Review of Religious Research* 3 (1961): 72-81.

Schutz, William E. *Joy: Expanding Human Awareness*. New York: Grove, 1967.

Scobie, Geoffrey E. W. *Psychology of Religion*. New York: John Wiley, 1975.

Scott, William A., ed. *Sources of Protestant Theology*. New York: Bruce, 1971.

Scudder, Delton L., ed. *Organized Religion and the Older Adult*. Institute of Gerontology Series. Vol. 8. Gainesville: University of Florida Press, 1958.

Sears, R. R. "The Growth of Conscience." In *Personality Development in Children*. Vol. 1. Iscoe Stevenson and H. Stevenson, eds. Austin: University of Texas Press, 1960.

Sheehy, Gail. *Passages: Predictable Crises in Adult Life*. New York: Dutton, 1976.

Sherrill, John L. *They Speak with Other Tongues*. New York: McGraw-Hill, 1964.

Sherrill, Lewis J. *The Gift of Power*. New York: Macmillan, 1950.

──────────. *Guilt and Redemption*. Atlanta: John Knox, 1945.

──────────. *The Struggle of the Soul*. New York: Macmillan, 1951.

Shinn, Roger. "Genetic Decisions: A Case Study in Ethical Method." *Soundings* 52 (1969): 299-310.

Siegman, A. W. "An Empirical Investigation of the Psychoanalytic Theory of Religious Behavior." *Journal for the Scientific Study of Religion* 1 (1961): 74-78.

Simmons, Paul D. *Birth and Death: Bioethical Decision-Making*. Philadelphia: Westminster, 1983.

Simonson, Harold P. "Jonathan Edwards and the Imagination." *Andover Newton Quarterly* 16 (1975): 109-18.

Sinsheimer, Robert L. "Genetic Engineering: The Modification of Man." In *Issues in Physiological Psychology*. Francis Leukel, ed. St. Louis: C. V. Mosby, 1974.

Skinner, B. F. *About Behaviorism*. New York: Knopf, 1974.

──────────. *Beyond Freedom and Dignity*. New York: Bantam Books, 1971.

──────────. *Science and Human Behavior*. New York: Macmillan, 1953.

──────────. *Walden Two*. New York: Macmillan, 1948.

Slotkin, James S. *The Peyote Religion*. New York: Free Press, 1956.

Smart, Ninian. *The Phenomenon of Religion*. New York: Herder and Herder, 1973.

──────────. "Scientific Studies of Religion." In *What Theologians Do*. F. G. Healey, ed. Grand Rapids MI: Eerdmans, 1970.

Smith, Huston. "Do Drugs Have Religious Import?" *The Journal of Philosophy* 61 (1964): 517-30.

Smith, Wilfred C. *Meaning and End of Religion*. New York: Macmillan, 1962.

Solomon, Philip, et al., eds. *Sensory Deprivation*. Cambridge: Harvard University Press, 1961.

Sommerfield, Richard. "Conceptions of the Ultimate and the Social Organization of Religious Bodies." *Journal for the Scientific Study of Religion* 7 (1968): 178-96.

Southard, Samuel. *Religious Inquiry: An Introduction to the Why and How*. Nashville: Abingdon, 1976.

Spilka, Bernard. "The Current State of the Psychology of Religion." *Bulletin of the Council on the Study of Religion* 9 (October 1978): 96-99.

──────────, Ralph W. Hood, Jr., and Richard L. Gorsuch. *The Psychology of Religion: An Empirical Approach*. Englewood Cliffs NJ: Prentice-Hall, 1985.

Spinks, G. Stephens. *Psychology and Religion: An Introduction to Contemporary Views.* Boston: Beacon Press, 1963.

Sprague, James M., and Alan N. Epstein, eds. *Progress in Psychology and Physiological Psychology.* Vol. 6. New York: Academic Press, 1976.

Stace, W. T. *Mysticism and Philosophy.* Philadelphia: Lippincott, 1960.

Stacey, W. David. *The Pauline View of Man.* New York: Macmillan, 1956.

Stagg, Frank, E. Glenn Hinson, and Wayne E. Oates. *Glossolalia: Tongue Speaking in Biblical, Historical, and Psychological Perspectives.* Nashville: Abingdon, 1967.

Starbuck, Edwin D. *The Psychology of Religion.* New York: Scribner's, 1899.

_____. "Some Aspects of Religious Growth." *American Journal of Psychology* 8 (1897): 70-124.

_____. "A Study of Conversion." *American Journal of Psychology* 8 (1897): 268-308.

Stark, Rodney. "Age and Faith: A Changing Outlook on an Old Process." In *Research in Religious Behavior.* Benjamin Beit-Hallahmi, ed. Monterey CA: Brooks/Cole, 1973.

_____. "A Taxonomy of Religious Experience." *Journal for the Scientific Study of Religion* 5 (1965): 97-116.

_____, and Charles Y. Glock. *American Piety: The Nature of Religious Commitment.* Berkeley: University of California Press, 1968.

_____, and Charles Y. Glock. *Christian Belief and Anti-Semitism.* New York: Harper, 1966.

_____, and Charles Y. Glock. *Religion and Society in Tension.* Rochester NY: Ward, 1965.

Stewart, Charles W. *Adolescent Religion: A Developmental Study of the Religion of Youth.* Nashville: Abingdon, 1967.

Streng, F. J. "Studying Religion: Possibilities and Limitations of Different Definitions." *Journal of the American Academy of Religion* 40 (1972): 219-37.

Strommen, Merton P., ed. *Research on Religious Development.* New York: Hawthorn, 1971.

Strunk, Orlo, Jr. *Mature Religion.* Nashville: Abingdon, 1965.

_____. *Religion: A Psychological Interpretation.* Nashville: Abingdon, 1962.

_____, ed. *Readings in the Psychology of Religion.* Nashville: Abingdon, 1959.

_____. "Humanistic Religious Psychology: A New Chapter in the Psychology of Religion." *The Journal of Pastoral Care* 24 (1970): 90-97.

_____. "The Present Status of the Psychology of Religion." *The Journal of Bible and Religion* 25 (1957): 287-92.

_____. "The Psychology of Religion: An Historical and Contemporary Survey." *Psychological Newsletter* 9 (1958): 181-99.

Sullivan, Harry S. *The Interpersonal Theory of Psychiatry.* New York: W. W. Norton, 1953.

Suzuki, Daisetz T. *Mysticism: Christian and Buddhist.* New York: Harper, 1957.

Sweiker, William F. "Religion as a Superordinate Meaning System and Socio-Psychological Integration." *Journal for the Scientific Study of Religion* 8 (1969): 300-307.

Synon, Vinson. *The Holiness-Pentecostal Movement in the United States.* Grand Rapids MI: Eerdmans, 1971.

Tapp, Robert B. *Religion among the Unitarian Universalists: Converts in the Stepfather's House.* New York: Seminar Press, 1973.

Tavard, George H. *The Pilgrim Church.* New York: Herder and Herder, 1967.

Taylor, Irving A., and J. W. Getzels, eds. *Perspectives in Creativity.* New York: Aldine, 1975.

Te Selle, Sallie M. "Parable, Metaphor, and Theology." *Journal of American Academy of Religion* 42 (1974): 630-45.

Teilhard de Chardin, Pierre. *Science and Christ.* Rene Hague, trans. New York: Harper, 1968.

Thurneyson, Eduard. *A Theology of Pastoral Care.* Jack A. Worthington and Thomas Wieser, trans. Atlanta: John Knox, 1962.

Tillich, Paul. *The Courage to Be.* New Haven: Yale University Press, 1952.

_____. *Dynamics of Faith.* New York: Harper, 1957.

_____. *On the Boundary: An Autobiographical Sketch.* New York: Scribner's, 1966.

_____. *The Protestant Era.* Chicago: University of Chicago Press, 1948.

_____. *Systematic Theology.* Vols. 1, 3. Chicago: University of Chicago Press, 1951.

_____. *The Religious Situation.* H. Richard Niebuhr, trans. New York: Meridian, 1956.

Tisdale, John R., ed. *Growing Edges in the Psychology of Religion.* Chicago: Nelson-Hall, 1980.

Toland, John. *Christianity Not Mysterious.* Reprint of 1st ed. London, 1696. New York: Garland, 1978.

Tournier, Paul. *Guilt and Grace: A Psychological Study.* Arthur W. Heathcote, trans. New York: Harper, 1962.

_____. *Learn to Grow Old.* Edwin Hudson, trans. New York: Harper, 1972.

_____. *The Meaning of Persons.* Edwin Hudson, trans. New York: Harper, 1957.

_____. *The Whole Person in a Broken World.* John Doberstein and Helen Doberstein, trans. New York: Harper, 1964.

Tremmel, W. C. *Religion: What Is It?* New York: Holt, Rinehart and Winston, 1976.

Troeltsch, Ernst. *The Social Teaching of the Christian Churches.* Vols. 1-2. Olive Wyon, trans. New York: Harper, 1960.

Trueblood, Elton D. *Philosophy of Religion.* New York: Harper, 1957.

Underhill, Evelyn. *Mysticism: A Study in the Nature and Development of Man's Spiritual Consciousness.* New York: Meridian, 1955.

Uris, Leon. *Exodus.* Garden City NY: Doubleday, 1958.

van der Leeuw, Gerardus. *Religion in Essence and Manifestation.* London: Allen and Unwin, 1938.

van Herik, Judith. *Freud on Femininity and Faith.* Berkeley: University of California Press, 1982.

van Kaam, Adrian. *Religion and Personality.* Garden City NY: Doubleday, 1968.

Visser't Hooft, W. A. "Responsible University in a Responsible Society." *Ecumenical Review* 23 (1971): 252-66.

Wach, Joachim. *Sociology of Religion.* Chicago: University of Chicago Press, 1944.

Wallace, Anthony F. C. *Culture and Personality.* 2nd ed. New York: Random House, 1970.

——————. *Religion: An Anthropological View.* New York: Random House, 1966.

Ward, Coleen A., and Michael Beaubrun. "Psychodynamics of Demon Possession." *Journal for the Scientific Study of Religion* 19 (1980): 201-207.

Warlick, Harold G., Jr. *Liberation from Guilt.* Nashville: Broadman, 1976.

Warnock, Mary. *Imagination.* Berkeley: University of California Press, 1976.

Warren, Neil C. "Empirical Studies in the Psychology of Religion: An Assessment of the Period 1960-1970." *Journal of Psychology and Theology* 4 (1976): 63-68.

Washington, Joseph R. *Black Sects and Cults.* Garden City NY: Doubleday, 1973.

Watts, Alan W. *Psychotherapy: East and West.* New York: Pantheon, 1961.

Weaver, Robert F. "Beyond Supermouse: Changing Life's Genetic Blueprint." *National Geographic* 166 (1984): 818-47.

Weber, Max. *The Protestant Ethic and the Spirit of Capitalism.* Talcott Parsons, trans. New York: Scribner's, 1958.

——————. *The Religion of India: The Sociology of Hinduism and Buddhism.* Hans H. Gerth and Don Martindale, trans. and eds. Glencoe IL: Free Press, 1958.

Weigert, Andrew J. "Functional, Substantive, Political: A Comment on Berger's 'Second Thoughts on Defining Religion'." *Journal for the Scientific Study of Religion* 13 (1974): 483-86.

Weiner, Irving, ed. *Clinical Methods in Psychology.* New York: Wiley, 1976.

Weiner, Norbert. *God and Golem, Inc.* Boston: MIT Press, 1964.

Weiss, Edward, and O. Spurgeon English. *Psychosomatic Medicine: The Clinical Application of Psychopathology to General Medical Problems.* Philadelphia: Sanders, 1949.

Welch, Claude. *Religion in the Undergraduate Curriculum.* Washington DC: Association of American Colleges, 1972.

Welch, David, George A. Tate, and Fred Richards, eds. *Humanistic Psychology: A Source Book.* Buffalo NY: Prometheus, 1978.

Whale, John S. *Christian Doctrine.* Cambridge: Cambridge University Press, 1941.

Wheelis, Allen. "Will and Psychoanalysis." *Journal of the American Psychoanalytic Association* 4 (1956): 285-303.

White, Victor. *God and the Unconscious.* Chicago: Regnery, 1953.

Whitehead, Alfred N. *Religion in the Making.* New York: Macmillan, 1926.

Wicklund, Robert A. *Freedom and Reactance.* New York: Wiley, 1974.

Wiebe, Don. "Explanation and Theological Method." *Zygon* 11 (1976): 35-49.

Wilder, Amos N. *Theopoetic: Theology and the Religious Imagination.* Philadelphia: Fortress, 1976.

——————. "Theology and Theopoetic: Part 1: What Forms Will a Theopoetic Take Today?" *Christian Century* 90 (1973): 593-96.

_____. "Theology and Theopoetic: Part 2: Renewal of the Imagination." *Christian Century* 90 (1973): 1195-98.

_____. "Theology and Theopoetic: Part 3: Ecstasy, Imagination, and Insight." *Christian Century* 91 (1974): 428-29.

Williams, Cyril G. *Tongues of the Spirit: A Study of Pentecostal Glossolalia and Related Phenomena.* Cardiff: University of Wales Press, 1981.

Williams, J. Paul. "The Nature of Religion." *Journal for the Scientific Study of Religion* 2 (1962): 3-14.

Williams, Preston N., ed. *Ethical Issues in Biology and Medicine.* Cambridge MA: Schenkman, 1973.

Wilson, Colin. *New Pathways in Psychology: Maslow and the Post-Freudian Revolution.* New York: Taplinger, 1972.

Wilson, W. C. "Extrinsic Religious Values and Prejudice." *Journal of Abnormal and Social Psychology* 60 (1960): 286-88.

Wolf, William J. *The Almost Chosen People: A Study of the Religion of Abraham Lincoln.* Garden City NY: Doubleday, 1959.

Wollheim, Richard, and James Hopkins, eds. *Philosophical Essays on Freud.* New York: Cambridge University Press, 1982.

Wood, William W. *Culture and Personality Aspects of the Pentecostal Holiness Religion.* Hawthorne NY: Mouton, 1965.

Wratchford, Eugene P. *Brain Research and Personhood: A Philosophical Theological Inquiry.* Washington DC: University Press of America, 1979.

Wright, Conrad. *Three Prophets of Religious Liberalism: Channing-Emerson-Parker.* Boston: Beacon Press, 1961.

Yale, John, ed. *What Vedanta Means to Me: A Symposium.* Garden City NY: Doubleday, 1960.

Yinger, J. Milton. *Religion in the Struggle for Power.* Durham NC: Duke University Press, 1946.

_____. *Religion, Society, and the Individual: An Introduction to the Sociology of Religion.* New York: Macmillan, 1957.

_____. *Sociology Looks at Religion.* New York: Macmillan, 1963.

_____. *The Scientific Study of Religion.* New York: Macmillan, 1970.

Zachner, R. C. *Mysticism: Sacred and Profane.* New York: Oxford University Press, 1961.

Zilboorg, Gregory. *Psychoanalysis and Religion.* New York: Farrar, Straus and Giroux, 1962.

Zimbardo, Philip, E. B. Ebbesen, and C. Maslach. *Influencing Attitudes and Changing Behavior.* 2nd ed. Reading MA: Addison-Wesley, 1977.

Zuck, John. "Religion and Fantasy." *Religious Education* 70 (1975): 585-604.

INDEX